Images of
SOCIETY

Readings That Inspire and Inform Sociology

THIRD EDITION

Images of
SOCIETY

Readings That Inspire and Inform Sociology

THIRD EDITION

JERRY P. WHITE
University of Western Ontario

MICHAEL CARROLL
Wilfrid Laurier University

NELSON / **E D U C A T I O N**

NELSON / EDUCATION

Images of Society, Third Edition
by Jerry P. White and Michael Carroll

Vice President, Editorial Higher Education:
Anne Williams

Acquisitions Editor:
Maya Castle

Marketing Manager:
Terry Fedorkiw

Developmental Editor:
Toni Chahley

Permissions Coordinator:
Strand Acquisitions Inc.: Jennie Peddlesden

Senior Content Production Manager:
Imoinda Romain

Production Service:
Cenveo Publisher Services

Copy Editor:
Erin Moore

Proofreader:
Jitendra Kumar Das

Indexer:
Claudia Self

Production Coordinator:
Ferial Suleman

Design Director:
Ken Phipps

Managing Designer:
Franca Amore

Interior and Cover Design:
Cathy Mayer

Cover Image:
© Hedda Gjerpen/iStockphoto.com

Compositor:
Cenveo Publisher Services

Printer:
R.R. Donnelley

Library and Archives Canada Cataloguing in Publication

Images of society: readings that inspire and inform society / Jerry P. White, Michael Carroll. —3rd ed.

Includes bibliographical references and index.
ISBN 978-0-17-651416-7

1. Sociology—Textbooks. I. White, Jerry P. (Jerry Patrick), 1951–
II. Carroll, Michael P., 1944–

HM586.I46 2012
301   C2012-903328-6

ISBN-13: 978-0-17-651416-7
ISBN-10: 0-17-651416-3

Contents

Preface

THE GOALS OF THIS SOCIOLOGY READER

When we first began this project, we set ourselves several goals. Because we have both taught Introductory Sociology for many years (and have read or reviewed a great many readers), our first goal was to avoid what we saw to be as some of the weaknesses associated with readers, while preserving the strengths. We wanted a book that was accessible and current, less expensive to buy, and engaging to excite readers.

To achieve these goals we restricted the number of readings while still offering choice, and editing out material that could safely be deleted without damaging the core argument in that particular reading. Unlike many readers that might contain far more readings or longer readings, we have been very careful about how many to include. Longer books often have more material than can be used in a term; this book has been designed on the assumption that instructors can use a majority of the selections if they wish. Students will find that the readings are to the point, and that they avoid redundant discussions, repetition, and overlap between chapters.

Another critical decision we made concerned the selection of the particular readings to be included. This is not as simple a process as it might appear. It is our view that editors too often select readings based primarily on how appealing those readings are going to be with instructors. While this is not surprising given that instructors are the ones who decide if a text is adopted, it often leads (in our view) to the inclusion of readings that students cannot relate to or that belong more in an advanced course, rather than an introductory course. We wanted to include selections that students taking Introductory Sociology would find interesting and accessible. We sought readings that students would want to read. As a result, although this book contains a number of "classic" articles that might be encountered in some sociology readers, it also contains many other articles that you will find both interesting and unique to this book.

Finally, we had a third goal that was paramount: to convey to you the passion to understand the world, in all its complexity, that fuels the sociological enterprise. We want to open up the distinctive ways of thinking that sociologists bring to bear on what they study. This meant looking for articles that (for the most part) went beyond simple description in order to generate insight into the world in which we all live. Paraphrasing Peter Berger "You can't be a sociologist and not want to open every door in front of you to see what's behind it." We want to engender in you that same feeling and to equip you with what C. Wright Mills calls the "sociological imagination" so that when you go through those doors you can understand what you encounter.

CHANGES TO THIS EDITION

We believe that instructors who use the book and students who study it are best equipped to judge what works and what does not. We have held focus groups of students and surveyed professors on their likes and concerns with previous editions. This has led to some important changes in this edition. Based on feedback from students and professors, we have dropped a number of chapters that were either too difficult or had become less relevant for sociology students today. This has allowed the book to take on more than a dozen new readings. These new readings are, for the most part, much more "today" and "current" while being great sources for learning sociology. We have introduced new areas such as education and Indigenous peoples while keeping the articles that had rave reviews from users. We also have several articles written expressly for the book such as Wolfgang Lehmann's work on universities, Laura Murphy on sexual assault, and Sharon Roberts on the social construction of beauty. Overall, the book offers the same wide variety as the first two editions but with the following timely additions:

- Chapter 1: What Should Students Understand after Taking Introduction to Sociology? by Caroline Hodges Persell, Kathryn M. Pfeiffer, and Ali Syed
- Chapter 5: Ethical Issues in Disaster Research: Lessons from Hurricane Katrina, by Carrie Y. Barron Ausbrooks, Edith J. Barrett, and Maria Martinez-Cosio
- Chapter 7: Sterilizing the "Feeble-Minded": Eugenics in Alberta, Canada, 1929–1972, by Jana Grekul, Harvey Krahn, and Dave Odynak
- Chapter 9: Cultural Aspects of Disability, by Juliene G. Lipson and Judith G. Rogers
- Chapter 10: Why Do People Get Tattoos? by Miliann Kang and Katherine Jones
- Chapter 14: 2006 Census: Families, Marital Status, Households and Dwelling Characteristics, by Statistics Canada
- Chapter 19: Sexual Assault in Canada: Gendered Expectations, Myths, and Resistances, by Laura Murphy
- Chapter 20: Pornography and Violence: A New Look at the Research, by Mary Anne Layden
- Chapter 24: Revisiting the Stanford Prison Experiment: A Lesson in the Power of Situation, by Philip G. Zimbardo
- Chapter 25: Online Communication and Negative Social Ties, by Gustavo S. Mesch and Ilan Talmud
- Chapter 26: Religion: The Comeback, by Reginald Bibby
- Chapter 27: Islamophobia: A New Racism? by Vic Satzewich
- Chapter 28: The Disneyization of Society, by Alan Bryman
- Chapter 31: A New Barrier: Extra-Credential Inflation, Wolfgang Lehmann
- Chapter 32: The Gender Income Gap and the Role of Education, by Donna Bobbitt-Zeher
- Chapter 33: Why Do Skilled Immigrants Struggle in the Labour Market? A Field Experiment with Six Thousand Résumés, by Philip Oreopoulos
- Chapter 34: Aboriginal People, Resilience and the Residential School Legacy, by Madeleine Dion Stout and Gregory Kipling
- Chapter 35: Stolen Sisters, Second Class Citizens, Poor Health: The Legacy of Colonization in Canada, by Wendee Kubik, Carrie Bourassa, and Mary Hampton
- Chapter 39: Be Thin: Contradictions Within the Social Construction of Beauty and Happiness, by Sharon E. Roberts
- Chapter 40: A Tale of Two Technologies: HPV Vaccination, Male Circumcision, and Sexual Health, by Laura M. Carpenter and Monica J. Casper

We have included hard-hitting pieces about who has privilege, the forced sterilization of Canadians deemed to be "defective," and cyber bullying. Aboriginal peoples' issues and the research concerning Aboriginal well-being is of great importance, and new additions to the book explore this issue, examining where problems come from and why we must work together to find solutions.

THE ORGANIZATION OF THE BOOK

The readings are grouped together into sections that map the way most sociology texts are arranged. This organization should facilitate coordinating these readings with whatever textbook you will be using. Please note that the articles are written in the original language, just as their authors presented them. In the case of some selections, then, especially those published several decades ago, the language is at times not "politically correct." In some articles the only pronoun used is "he," which reflects the gender bias of the time in which they were written. Although we still believe that the core argument being made in such articles is insightful, we do not suggest that these problematic elements should be overlooked.

LEARNING AND STUDY AIDS: HELPING STUDENTS AND INSTRUCTORS GET THE MOST OUT OF THE READINGS

Each article has a brief prologue that gives you an idea of the main points contained in the work. New to this edition, we have added evocative questions after the introduction that set the stage for what you will read. We suggest that before reading the article, you read this opening paragraph and the questions below it. The questions are aimed to help you focus your thoughts on some main points being made by the author(s). Thinking through the answers to these guiding questions will enable both students and instructors to engage critically with the readings, and are intended to facilitate discussions that may follow.

Also new to this edition are critical thinking questions, found at the end of each chapter, which are intended to guide a discussion of the reading, or help students write notes on the main lessons to be drawn from the chapter. In this way the articles can be used to broaden your understanding, or they may be used to promote class and tutorial discussion.

Finally, and very importantly, we also feel that the learning and study aids are very easily used by instructors or graduate teaching assistants to make points and engage students in discussion.

ACKNOWLEDGEMENTS

We want to thank all those who have contributed so much to this project, including the team at Nelson Education Ltd.: Maya Castle, Acquisitions Editor, Toni Chahley, Developmental Editor, and Erin Moore, Copy Editor. And thanks also to the over 300 students, graduate teaching assistants, professors, and instructors who have given us the feedback we needed to make this an effective teaching tool.

We would also like to thank the following reviewers, whose feedback helped shape this new edition:
Sharon Roberts, University of Waterloo
Stephen Svenson, University of Waterloo
Darcie Olijnek, Vancouver Community College

We want to give a very special thanks to Laura Murphy who has worked on many aspects of the book. She has helped with the collecting of student and instructor opinions, made suggestions on articles, and helped with the educational aids for the chapters.
Enjoy.

MICHAEL P. CARROLL
Wilfrid Laurier University

JERRY P. WHITE
University of Western Ontario

CUSTOM PUBLISHING OPTIONS

It's your course; why compromise? Nelson Education is making it easier than ever to customize this sociology textbook to create a highly personalized and convenient course resource for your students. Learn how custom publishing with Nelson Education can help you teach your course, your way, by visiting **www.nelsoncustom.com**.

FOSTERING CONVERSATIONS ABOUT TEACHING SOCIOLOGY IN CANADA

We invite you to join *Fostering Conversations about Teaching Sociology in Canada*, a virtual community site built by sociology educators for sociology educators. A dynamic, continually-evolving blog that houses dozens of self-reflexive pieces about various aspects of teaching—including student engagement, assessment, course preparation, and teaching with technology—*Fostering Conversations* is an educator's toolkit and a virtual home for sharing teaching ideas, practices, and complexities. Housing contributions by educators from across the country, including universities and colleges large and small, *Fostering Conversations* provides a framework for cross-institutional conversations about the craft of teaching in the twenty-first century. Join the conversation today! Visit **http://community .cengage.com/Site/fosteringconversations**.

PART 1

Chapter 1

What Should Students Understand after Taking Introduction to Sociology?

CAROLINE HODGES PERSELL, KATHRYN M. PFEIFFER, AND ALI SYED

When taking an introductory course, it may be difficult to determine what you can expect to actually learn over the duration of the term. It may also be daunting to take an introductory course in sociology, so having a good idea of what you can look forward to and being able to delineate between sociology and other disciplines can be a big help. With this in mind, these three authors decided to conduct a survey focused on compiling a list of what should be taught in sociology. Altogether, 124 leading professors in the field of sociology in the United States all who had taught an introductory course within the previous two years, were asked to identify what one or two principles were the most important for students to learn in an introductory course. Nine main themes were compiled and are outlined below. Here are some questions to think about before and during the reading of this chapter:

1. What are some of the expectations you have of taking Introduction to Sociology?
2. How do you understand the social world in which you live in?

WHAT DO LEADERS THINK STUDENTS SHOULD UNDERSTAND AFTER TAKING INTRODUCTION TO SOCIOLOGY?

1) *The "social" part of sociology or learning to think sociologically.* This was by far the most frequently mentioned principle that leaders wanted students to understand after taking an introductory course, and they articulated four dimensions. First, was that students understand the importance of getting beyond the individual when trying to understand and explain the social world. One of the leaders wanted students to understand "the existence of social factors [because] most students come in assuming psychological explanations." A second desired students to grasp "that things matter that are above the level of the individual and intra-psychic processes." A third emphasized "the reality of the social. I think our culture is very individualistic, and students have a very individualistic world view. Society is real; it matters."

Second, various responses elaborated on the meaning of the "social." "It isn't just individuals. There are groups and institutions. . . .

Source: Source: Persell, Caroline Hodges, Kathryn M. Pfeiffer and Ali Syed. "What Should Students Understand After Taking Introduction to Sociology?" *Teaching Sociology, Vol. 35, No. 4 (Oct. 2007), pp. 305-309.* Reproduced with Permission of the American Sociological Association.

[I] expect a new and broader perspective on the world . . . that goes beyond the individual." Another noted, "Societies can be studied from the point of view of social architecture [structure]. Societies can be better understood if we know the architecture and framework of that society. The introductory course should try to enhance that understanding." Others mentioned social structure, culture, groups, organizations, institutions, demography, social processes, social forces, norms and the normative foundation of society as key components of the social world to which students should be exposed.

Third, the most frequently stressed idea within this theme was that macro-level factors and individuals are interconnected. One interviewee said, "I want my students to be able to see beyond themselves and think about the groups they belong to and how these groups can have an effect on individual characters. The individual is always in constant interaction with the [social] environment. There is agency but there are [also] constraints." Similarly, another stressed that it was important for students to understand "that they live in a social world in which they are constrained by a variety of social forces but in which they [also] have individual ability to carve out direction for themselves. While pushed by forces, they can adapt. . . . Relatedly, we live in a very fast-changing world. It is important to understand what those changes are and chart one's course and direction in relation to those changes."

Another said, "[I want students to get] a general understanding of the sociological **paradigm** that human behaviors are impacted by societal structures." Another stressed, "It is very important to link personal lives with macro-level factors; for example, if someone is suffering from mental distress, what does that have to do with unemployment?" Another added how the normative foundation of society shapes people's actions. "Essentially, society is created by people acting in accordance with all kinds of unstated rules and understandings." One other summed up this goal, "I would like [students] to understand what a distinctively sociological under-

standing of different types of social phenomena would be. . . . So, [they should] understand that divorce rates in the United States are not simply a function of couples breaking apart, but also reflect larger social forces—changes in gender norms, roles, changes in law, changes in the political system, changes in the labor market. . . . In other words, [students should understand] the multiple ways in which social forces impact particular kinds of social outcomes."

Another noted that "This is related to Mills' conception of the relationship between biography and social structure. In terms of one's biography, students should calculate their trajectory, where they have been, where they are now, and where they are going, in relation to the trajectory of the social structure—where it has been, where it is now, and where it is going. . . . In current theoretical parlance, this is a matter of linking micro and macro levels, or the relationship between agency and structure."

Finally, some hoped students would push their understanding of the social even deeper, to "be able to see behind the surface appearance [of social phenomena] in the way that we as sociologists typically try to do in our work." Another put it this way: "Understanding the sociological lens, or the sociological imagination [involves realizing that] what often appears natural isn't. There are often paradoxes in social life. For example, inequality comes from abundance, not scarcity. Deviance serves as a social bond." Thus these leaders stressed the importance of looking beyond the obvious to uncover seemingly incongruous relationships.

They also thought that it was critically important for undergraduates to understand that their own lives, not just other people's lives, are affected by various social factors. This is a threshold principle of sociology, but one that is difficult for highly individualized, often middle class, college students to understand and accept.

2) *The scientific nature of sociology.* The scientific aspect of sociology was the second most frequently mentioned element that leaders wanted students to get from an introductory sociology course. As one said, "Thinking about the social requires self-conscious attention to methods. How do we know what we do? If they read something in the paper, I want them to ask, 'How do they know that?' When we want to draw a conclusion, on what basis do we do that?" Another noted, "Society as an **empirical** object has properties. I like to think about it as comparable to physics in some ways, in the sense that it's an empirical object that has mechanisms and whose properties can be studied, So, it's basically a question of changing their relationship to society, to learn to think about it differently, to try to approach it as an object of knowledge, as opposed to just something to live in." Similarly, another said it was important for students to learn that "sociology is a science, and how to distinguish sciences from other ways of thinking about the world, and why certain things that they clearly understand as science, such as chemistry and biology, are science. And why sociology, ideally, is also a science and how it fits into the other sciences." Reflected another, "We can actually explain things people take for granted . . . and the reason we are able to do that is because sociology is scientific and systematic and other forms of social commentary are not, such as journalism." A number emphasized that they wanted students to understand that sociology is not "just people giving their opinions." Instead, "Sociologists systematically collect and analyze data. The field has rigor. There is value to calling in a sociologist to understand a social phenomena."

In addition to stressing systematic data collection and analysis, respondents noted the importance of students learning something about social science reasoning, or as one put it, "what it means to make a 'sociological argument.'" Another commented, "[I want students to understand] the logic by which sociologists make arguments and the relationships between theory and data and assessing evidence." A few leaders explicitly stressed causality: "I want them to understand causal relationships and the logic of social science. How to argue and present a case, not just by doing it more loudly and often

but by presenting evidence." Another noted, "It is important for students to understand the puzzle-solving aspects of sociology, to understand how we approach the scientific study of social life. I want them to learn that sociology has a methodological way of analyzing the world that is useful in all kinds of situations. They tend to reason from a single example, 'my grandmother . . .' rather than considering all possible causal mechanisms that could be operating in a situation. I want them to be able to think through a problem and how they might be able to answer it. What would you need to know to answer a particular question? I want them to be able to identify that."

In sum, leaders wanted students to appreciate the scientific or systematic nature of data collection and analysis used in sociological research, rather than seeing sociology as simply a bundle of different opinions. They wanted students to grasp the importance of marshalling evidence to support an argument. Some refined this further to emphasize an understanding of causal relationships. One respondent hoped students would gain some awareness of "the potential, possibilities, and limitations of research as a form of inquiry."

3) Complex and critical thinking. Nearly a third of the respondents identified complex and critical thinking as important. As one elaborated, "By critical thinking I mean the ability to not necessarily accept beliefs or ideas just because they were raised to think a certain way, or even because the professor says it in class. Instead, I hope they will ask, what are the important questions to ask? Should the question be a different one from the one being raised here? How do we use evidence to think about this question? How do we get new evidence?" Another said, "I want them to see that issues are not black and white, but that there are nuances, depth to issues . . . not just good/bad." For some, skepticism was central to critical thinking. For example, one said, "I want [students] to take a critical stance toward science and political life." Another mentioned, "[I want students to] be able to read reports in the news more skeptically and critically." Still another explained, "[I want students to take away] the idea that sciences are fallible."

Five others stressed skills in their discussions of critical thinking, such as "general high-level skills including writing, thinking, and speaking," and "how to communicate clearly, especially in writing." One noted, "I think analytical thinking is really hard to teach . . . but if you never teach it, you never give the people who want to think that way the opportunity to do so."

For many respondents, the understanding that there are multiple perspectives on any given question or issue was key to their conception of critical thinking. Complex and critical thinking involves approaching social issues and problems with a nuanced view that takes multiple perspectives into account and raises new questions. Sources of knowledge, such as the sciences and news media are to be treated with some degree of skepticism. Several leaders believed that it is key for students to develop certain skills in the introductory course that facilitate complex and critical thinking, including critical reading, writing, and speaking skills, as well as analytical thinking.

4) *The centrality of inequality.* Eight respondents stressed the importance of having students understand more about social stratification and inequality. In the words of one respondent, it is "really important to integrate issues of stratification in a way that clearly ties into the theme of social structures, that ties to issues of equal opportunity and also a person's location in a social [structure]." Another expressed it thus, "The way in which opportunities are enhanced or constrained by previous life experiences—in families, schools, neighborhoods, based on race, gender, social class [or] where you grew up—these past situations reverberate across the entire life course. There are processes that begin early in life and create unequal outcomes throughout one's life. In a nutshell, I want [students] to understand the sources of social inequalities." Others mentioned the importance of students understanding that "inequality is all about power" or what someone else called "constructions of power."

5) *A sense of sociology as a field.* Eight respondents also indicated that they hoped the introductory course would help students understand something about sociology as a field, as well as to prepare them to major in it. As one said, "I try to prepare students for the major, so when they take upper division course they have heard of Weber, social structure, and some other important things. I try to introduce them to the discipline as a discipline, so they can see the profession as a social entity, with departments, journals, positions, etc." As one interviewee put it, such an introduction includes "some sense of the history of the discipline, and how and why sociologists prioritize some questions and think certain questions are important." One leader emphasized the importance of "understanding that there are theoretical underpinnings" to sociology, and several discussed the importance of teaching the main theoretical traditions in sociology, including symbolic interactionism, structural functionalism, and conflict theory. One emphasized the importance of discussing commonalities among the three major theoretical paradigms in sociology, as well as differences. Another aimed for "an understanding of the way that the discipline is organized in subdivisions and that there is an overlap in those sub-disciplines with other disciplines."

6) *The social construction of ideas.* At least two respondents directly, and three others implicitly, stressed the importance of the social construction of ideas, in gender and race, for example. As one noted, "The things we take for granted as natural are really socially constructed, e.g., human nature. But ideas about human nature differ wildly in different societies. [Take] the example of love and marriage. To us it seems natural that they go together. But, just feeling it is natural doesn't make it so. The feeling is real, but we can explain where that feeling comes from and why it might be different in other societies. Our sense of time is another example of this, as are categories or ideas about race, gender. They differ across societies. I teach this through cross-cultural and historical contrasts.

Gender, for example, seems very natural, even genetic, but gender structure varies by culture and society," while another emphasized race as a social construction.

7) *The difference between sociology and other social sciences.* Four respondents wanted students to recognize the differences between sociology and other social sciences, for example, to "understand 'the sociological perspective' and how it differs from the approaches taken in other fields" or to "understand the ways that sociology interfaces with other disciplines." As one said, "I cover the institutions of society because that makes clear the links to other social sciences and gives a whole view [of the] breadth of sociology and the things we study." Another indicated the desire "to engage multidisciplinary arguments, to bring in economics, anthropology, as well as sociology . . . [to help students] see the distinctiveness of sociology but also . . . be able to read the media from a broad social science perspective."

8) *The importance of trying to improve the world.* Four respondents indicated that it was important that students use their understanding of sociology to relate to the world and even improve it. One of the interviewees said, "I want [students] to be able to use some of what they've learned in sociology. . . in the way they approach problems, read the newspaper, and apply it to their everyday lives." Another hoped students would "get some appreciation of the work sociologists are doing trying to change or improve the nature of society. . . . Sociology has applications that are possible from our knowledge. "It has importance for the world." Still others emphasized activism, as in the case of one who hoped students would be able to "link the basic sociological concepts and theories with social activism or 'public sociology' and bring in the principles of humanity, equality, the humanitarian spirit." Another hoped to enable students "to position themselves in their larger society, [including] their responsibilities to the larger society" and wished to impart "an ethical perspective on many social issues."

9) *The importance of social institutions in society.* Three respondents specifically discussed the salience of key social institutions in society. One respondent summarized this sentiment when he expressed the desire for students to gain "a general understanding of the important institutions in society; that would include everything from the family to the economy to the polity to . . . health care, the important institutional sectors that sociologists—of course, the bulk of the sociology work force—actually devote all their time to studying."

In addition to these nine general themes, there were some substantive areas that one or two respondents hoped would be included in introductory sociology. One area was demography, or "the importance of thinking about population composition for understanding social change . . . for example, the age structure of a society." A second said, "I would like [students] to have a foundation in organizations and population and in social psychology." Someone else noted, "There are a couple of areas in the field of sociology that I think are being ignored, [specifically] community sociology and social networks. The study of new technologies is completely absent in sociology at the introductory level." Another acknowledged that the central themes could be woven into whatever topics were taught: "These themes (group membership and the importance of careful methods) . . . go through the review of topics . . . in an intro course."

Critical Thinking Questions

1. After reading this article, has your impression of sociology changed?
2. What distinguishes sociology from other disciplines, such as psychology or the natural sciences?

Chapter 2
The Sociological Imagination

C. WRIGHT MILLS

Mills' goal in this article, a classic in sociology, is to convey a sense of what is distinctive about the way sociologists think and train their students to think. He calls attention to the fact that the "Sociological Imagination" must take into account not only how society operates at a given point in time (referred to as *milieux*) but also how societies have been affected by the massive changes that have taken place over the past century or so (referred to as *history*). He also notes that an individual's place within a society (referred to as *biography*) lends itself to understanding the whole picture. Many scholars and academics differ on their understanding of the "Sociological Imagination." However, most would agree that, in order to fully understand a society, one must look at social structures such as institutions (i.e., government, education), as well as the individual's ability to make his or her own decisions within his or her social framework (often referred to as autonomy or agency). Try to keep this in mind as you read this article.

1. How does Mills describe the "Sociological Imagination"? And how does the "Sociological Imagination" impact our understanding of the social world?
2. What is the difference between "troubles" and "issues"? How does one inform the other?

THE PROMISE

Nowadays men often feel that their private lives are a series of traps. They sense that within their everyday worlds, they cannot overcome their troubles, and in this feeling, they are often quite correct: What ordinary men are directly aware of and what they try to do are bounded by the private orbits in which they live; their visions and their powers are limited to the close-up scenes of job, family, neighborhood; in other **milieux**, they move vicariously and remain spectators. And the more aware they become, however vaguely, of ambitions and of threats which transcend their immediate locales, the more trapped they seem to feel.

Underlying this sense of being trapped are seemingly impersonal changes in the very structure of continent-wide societies. The facts of contemporary history are also facts about the success and the failure of individual men and women. When a society is industrialized, a peasant becomes a worker; a feudal lord is liquidated or becomes a businessman. When classes rise or fall, a man is employed or unemployed; when the rate of investment goes up or down, a man takes new heart or goes broke. Neither the life of an individual nor the history of a society can be understood without understanding both.

Source: THE SOCIOLOGICAL IMAGINATION by Wright Mills (2000) 2842w from "The Promise" pp.3–11 © Oxford University Press, Inc. By permission of Oxford University Press, Inc.

Yet men do not usually define the troubles they endure in terms of historical change and institutional contradiction. Seldom aware of the intricate connection between the patterns of their own lives and the course of world history, ordinary men do not usually know what this connection means for the kinds of men they are becoming and for the kinds of history-making in which they might take part. They do not possess the quality of mind essential to grasp the interplay of man and society, of biography and history, of self and world.

Surely it is no wonder. In what period have so many men been so totally exposed at so fast a pace to such earthquakes of change? That Americans have not known such catastrophic changes as have the men and women of other societies is due to historical facts that are now quickly becoming 'merely history.' The history that now affects every man is world history. Within this scene and this period, in the course of a single generation, one sixth of mankind is transformed from all that is feudal and backward into all that is modern, advanced, and fearful. Political colonies are freed; new and less visible forms of imperialism installed. Revolutions occur; men feel the intimate grip of new kinds of authority. Totalitarian societies rise, and are smashed to bits—or succeed fabulously. Everywhere in the underdeveloped world, ancient ways of life are broken up and vague expectations become urgent demands. Everywhere in the overdeveloped world, the means of authority and of violence become total in scope and bureaucratic in form.

The very shaping of history now outpaces the ability of men to orient themselves in accordance with cherished values. And which values? Even when they do not panic, men often sense that older ways of feeling and thinking have collapsed and that newer beginnings are ambiguous to the point of moral stasis. Is it any wonder that ordinary men feel they cannot cope with the larger worlds with which they are so suddenly confronted? That they cannot understand the meaning of their epoch for their own lives?

That—in defense of selfhood—they become morally insensible, trying to remain altogether private men? Is it any wonder that they come to be possessed by a sense of the trap?

It is not only information that they need—in this Age of Fact, information often dominates their attention and overwhelms their capacities to assimilate it. It is not only the skills of reason that they need—although their struggles to acquire these often exhaust their limited moral energy.

What they need, and what they feel they need, is a quality of mind that will help them to use information and to develop reason in order to achieve lucid summations of what is going on in the world and of what may be happening within themselves. It is this quality, I am going to contend, that journalists and scholars, artists and publics, scientists and editors are coming to expect of what may be called the sociological imagination.

1

The sociological imagination enables its possessor to understand the larger historical scene in terms of its meaning for the inner life and the external career of a variety of individuals. It enables him to take into account how individuals, in the welter of their daily experience, often become falsely conscious of their social positions. Within that welter, the framework of modern society is sought, and within that framework the psychologies of a variety of men and women are formulated. By such means the personal uneasiness of individuals is focused upon explicit troubles and the indifference of publics is transformed into involvement with public issues.

The first fruit of this imagination—and the first lesson of the social science that embodies it—is the idea that the individual can understand his own experience and gauge his own fate only by locating himself within his period, that he can know his own chances in life only by becoming aware of those of all individuals in his circumstances. In many ways it is a terrible lesson; in many ways a magnificent one. We do not know the limits of man's capacities for supreme effort or willing degradation, for agony or glee, for pleasurable brutality or the sweetness of reason. But in our time we have come to know that the limits of 'human nature' are frighteningly broad. We have come to know that every individual lives, from one generation to the next, in some society; that he lives out a biography, and that he lives it out within some historical sequence. By the fact of his living he contributes, however minutely, to the shaping of this society and to the course of its history, even as he is made by society and by its historical push and shove.

The sociological imagination enables us to grasp history and biography and the relations between the two within society. That is its task and its promise. To recognize this task and this promise is the mark of the classic social analyst. It is characteristic of Herbert Spencer—turgid, polysyllabic, comprehensive; of E. A. Ross—graceful, muckraking, upright; of Auguste Comte and Emile Durkheim; of the intricate and subtle Karl Mannheim. It is the quality of all that is intellectually excellent in Karl Marx; it is the clue to Thorstein Veblen's brilliant and ironic insight, to Joseph Schumpeter's many-sided constructions of reality; it is the basis of the psychological sweep of W. E. H. Lecky no less than of the profundity and clarity of Max Weber. And it is the signal of what is best in contemporary studies of man and society.

No social study that does not come back to the problems of biography, of history and of their intersections within a society has completed its intellectual journey. Whatever the specific problems of the classic social analysts, however limited or however broad the features of social reality they have examined, those who have been imaginatively aware of the promise of their work have consistently asked three sorts of questions:

1. What is the structure of this particular society as a whole? What are its essential components, and how are they related to one another? How does it differ from other varieties of social order? Within it, what is the meaning of any particular feature for its continuance and for its change?

2. Where does this society stand in human history? What are the mechanics by which it is changing? What is its place within and its meaning for the development of humanity as a whole? How does any particular feature we are examining affect, and how is it affected by, the historical period in which it moves? And this period—what are its essential features? How does it differ from other periods? What are its characteristic ways of history-making?

3. What varieties of men and women now prevail in this society and in this period? And what varieties are coming to prevail? In what ways are they selected and formed, liberated and repressed, made sensitive and blunted? What kinds of 'human nature' are revealed in the conduct and character we observe in this society in this period? And what is the meaning for 'human nature' of each and every feature of the society we are examining?

Whether the point of interest is a great power state or a minor literary mood, a family, a prison, a creed—these are the kinds of questions the best social analysts have asked. They are the intellectual pivots of classic studies of man in society—and they are the questions inevitably raised by any mind possessing the sociological imagination. For that imagination is the capacity to shift from one perspective to another—from the political to the psychological; from examination of a single family to comparative assessment of the national budgets of the world; from the theological school to the military establishment; from considerations of an oil industry to studies of contemporary poetry. It is the capacity to range from the most impersonal and remote transformations to the most intimate features of the human self—and to see the relations between the two. Back of its use there is always the urge to know the social and historical meaning of the individual in the society and in the period in which he has his quality and his being.

That, in brief, is why it is by means of the sociological imagination that men now hope to grasp what is going on in the world, and to understand what is happening in themselves as minute points of the intersections of biography and history within society. In large part, contemporary man's self-conscious view of himself as at least an outsider, if not a permanent stranger, rests upon an absorbed realization of social relativity and of the transformative power of history. The sociological imagination is the most fruitful form of this self-consciousness. By its use men whose mentalities have swept only a series of limited orbits often come to feel as if suddenly awakened in a house with which they had only supposed themselves to be familiar. Correctly or incorrectly, they often come to feel that they can now provide themselves with adequate summations, cohesive assessments, comprehensive orientations. Older decisions that once appeared sound now seem to them products of a mind unaccountably dense. Their capacity for astonishment is made lively again. They acquire a new way of thinking, they experience a transvaluation of values: in a word, by their reflection and by their sensibility, they realize the cultural meaning of the social sciences.

2

Perhaps the most fruitful distinction with which the sociological imagination works is between 'the personal troubles of milieu' and 'the public issues of **social structure**.' This distinction is an essential tool of the sociological imagination and a feature of all classic work in social science.

Troubles occur within the character of the individual and within the range of his immediate relations with others; they have to do with his self and with those limited areas of social life of which he is directly and personally aware. Accordingly, the statement and the resolution of troubles properly lie within the individual as a biographical entity and within the scope of his immediate milieu—the social setting that is directly open to his personal experience and to some extent his willful activity. A trouble is a private matter: values cherished by an individual are felt by him to be threatened.

Issues have to do with matters that transcend these local environments of the individual and the range of his inner life. They have to do with the organization of many such milieux into the institutions of an historical society as a whole, with the ways in which various milieux overlap and interpenetrate to form the larger structure of social and historical life. An issue is a public matter: some value cherished by publics is felt to be threatened. Often there is a debate about what that value really is and about what it is that really threatens it. This debate is often without focus if only because it is the very nature of an issue, unlike even widespread trouble, that it cannot very well be defined in terms of the immediate and everyday environments of ordinary men. An issue, in fact, often involves a crisis in institutional arrangements, and often too it involves what Marxists call 'contradictions' or 'antagonisms.'

In these terms, consider unemployment. When, in a city of 100,000, only one man is unemployed, that is his personal trouble, and for its relief we properly look to the character of the man, his skills, and his immediate opportunities. But when in a nation of 50 million employees, 15 million men are unemployed, that is an issue, and we may not hope to find its solution within the range of opportunities open to any one individual. The very structure of opportunities has collapsed. Both the correct statement of the problem and the range of possible solutions require us to consider the economic and political institutions of the society, and not merely the personal situation and character of a scatter of individuals.

Consider war. The personal problem of war, when it occurs, may be how to survive it or how to die in it with honor; how to make money out of it; how to climb into the higher safety of the military apparatus; or how to contribute to the war's termination. In short, according to one's values, to find a set of milieux and within it to survive the war or make one's death in it meaningful. But the structural issues of war have to do with its causes; with what types of men it throws up into command; with its effects upon economic and political, family and religious institutions, with the unorganized irresponsibility of a world of nation-states.

Consider marriage. Inside a marriage a man and a woman may experience personal troubles, but when the divorce rate during the first four years of marriage is 250 out of every 1,000 attempts, this is an indication of a structural issue having to do with the institutions of marriage and the family and other institutions that bear upon them.

Or consider the metropolis—the horrible, beautiful, ugly, magnificent sprawl of the great city. For many upper-class people, the personal solution to 'the problem of the city' is to have an apartment with private garage under it in the heart of the city, and forty miles out, a house on a hundred acres of private land. In these two controlled environments—with a small staff at each end and a private helicopter connection—most people could solve many of the problems of personal milieux caused by the facts of the city. But all this, however splendid, does not solve the public issues that the structural fact of the city poses. What should be done with this wonderful monstrosity? Break it all up into scattered units, combining residence and work? Refurbish it as it stands? Or, after evacuation, dynamite it and build new cities according to new plans in new places?

In so far as an economy is so arranged that slumps occur, the problem of unemployment becomes incapable of personal solution. In so far as war is inherent in the nation-state system and in the uneven industrialization of the world, the ordinary individual in his restricted milieu will be powerless—with or without psychiatric aid—to solve the troubles this system or lack of system imposes upon him. In so far as the family as an institution turns women into darling little slaves and men into their chief providers and unweaned dependents, the problem of a satisfactory marriage remains incapable of purely private solution. In so far as the overdeveloped megalopolis and the overdeveloped automobile are built-in features of the overdeveloped society, the issues of urban living will not be solved by personal ingenuity and private wealth.

What we experience in various and specific milieux, I have noted, is often caused by structural changes. Accordingly, to understand the changes of many personal milieux we are required to look beyond them. And the number and variety of such structural changes increase as the institutions within which we live become more embracing and more intricately connected with one another. To be aware of the idea of social structure and to use it with sensibility is to be capable of tracing such linkages among a great variety of milieux. To be able to do that is to possess the sociological imagination.

Critical Thinking Questions

1. What do you think Mills means by our "private lives are a series of traps"?
2. "Neither the life of an individual nor the history of society can be understood without understanding both." What is the implication of this statement? Provide an example.

Chapter 3

The Nature of Attitude Surveys (from "The American Soldier—An Expository Review")

PAUL F. LAZARSFELD

Sociologists, as you will soon come to discover, use a wide variety of **methodologies** to conduct social research. Since the end of World War II, an increasing number of sociologists have come to rely on the "attitude survey" to gather data about the societies in which they live. In this brief selection, Paul Lazarsfeld first identifies the limitations of the "attitude survey," then discusses some of the ways in which attitude surveys can provide us with quite unexpected insights.

1. What are the key differences between social science and natural science? What is the importance of these differences when doing social research?
2. What is "obviousness"? How do sociologists use notions of "obviousness"? Why do you suppose this is important?

The limitations of survey methods are obvious. They do not use experimental techniques; they rely primarily on what people say, and rarely include objective observations; they deal with aggregates of individuals rather than with integrated communities; they are restricted to contemporary problems—history can be studied only by the use of documents remaining from earlier periods.

In spite of these limitations survey methods provide one of the foundations upon which social science is being built. The finding of regularities is the beginning of any science, and surveys can make an important contribution in this respect. For it is necessary that we know what people usually do under many and different circumstances if we are to develop theories explaining their behavior. Furthermore, before we can devise an experiment we must know what problems are worthwhile; which should be investigated in greater detail. Here again surveys can be of service.

Finding regularities and determining criteria of significance are concerns the social sciences have in common with the natural sciences. But there are crucial differences between the two fields of inquiry. The world of social events is much less "visible" than the realm of nature. That bodies fall to the ground, that things are hot or cold, that iron becomes rusty, are all immediately obvious. It is much more difficult to realize that ideas of right and wrong vary in different cultures; that customs may serve a different function from the one which the people practising them believe they are serving; that the same person may show marked contrasts in his behavior as a member of a family and as a member of an occupational group. The mere description of human behavior, of its variation from group to group and of its

---

Source: Lazarsfeld, Paul F., "The American Soldier—An Expository Review," *Public Opinion Quarterly*, 1949, Vol. 13, No. 3, pp. 378–380, by permission of Oxford University Press.

changes in different situations, is a vast and difficult undertaking. It is this task of describing, sifting and ferreting out interrelationships which surveys perform for us. And yet this very function often leads to serious misunderstandings. For it is hard to find a form of human behavior that has not already been observed somewhere. Consequently, if a study reports a prevailing regularity, many readers respond to it by thinking "of course that is the way things are." Thus, from time to time, the argument is advanced that surveys only put into complicated form observations which are already obvious to everyone.

Understanding the origin of this point of view is of importance far beyond the limits of the present discussion. The reader may be helped in recognizing this attitude if he looks over a few statements which are typical of many survey findings and carefully observes his own reaction. A short list of these, with brief interpretive comments, will be given here in order to bring into sharper focus probable reactions of many readers.

Better educated men showed more psychoneurotic symptoms than those with less education. (The mental instability of the intellectual as compared to the more impassive psychology of the-man-in-the-street has often been commented on.)

Men from rural backgrounds were usually in better spirits during their Army life than soldiers from city backgrounds. (After all, they are more accustomed to hardships.)

Southern soldiers were better able to stand the climate in the hot South Sea Islands than Northern soldiers (of course, Southerners are more accustomed to hot weather).

White privates were more eager to become non-coms than Negroes. (The lack of ambition among Negroes is almost proverbial.)

Southern Negroes preferred Southern to Northern white officers. (Isn't it well known that Southern whites have a more fatherly attitude toward their "darkies"?)

As long as the fighting continued, men were more eager to be returned to the States than they were after the German surrender. (You cannot blame people for not wanting to be killed.)

We have in these examples a sample list of the simplest type of interrelationships which provide the "bricks" from which our empirical social science is being built. But why, since they are so obvious, is so much money and energy given to establish such findings? Would it not be wiser to take them for granted and proceed directly to a more sophisticated type of analysis? This might be so except for one interesting point about the list. *Every one of these statements is the direct opposite of what actually was found.* Poorly educated soldiers were more neurotic than those with high education; Southerners showed no greater ability than Northerners to adjust to a tropical climate; Negroes were more eager for promotion than whites; and so on.

If we had mentioned the actual results of the investigation first, the reader would have labelled these "obvious" also. Obviously something is wrong with the entire argument of "**obviousness**." It should really be turned on its head. Since every kind of human reaction is conceivable, it is of great importance to know which reactions actually occur most frequently and under what conditions; only then will a more advanced social science develop.

Critical Thinking Questions

1. What are the limitations of survey methods? Given these limitations, should we completely discard the use of surveys? Why or why not?
2. Using your "sociological lens" choose and critique one example of "obviousness" that you have come across in your daily life.

Chapter 4

The Study Design for a Survey of American Sexual Behaviour

PART 2

EDWARD O. LAUMANN, JOHN H. GAGNON,
ROBERT T. MICHAEL, AND STUART MICHAELS

Sexual intercourse in our society is generally thought to be something that is private and intimate. Therefore, you might expect that it would be difficult to get people to participate in a study designed to investigate their sexual behaviour and beliefs. It turns out, however, that this is not the case. As sociologists, we know that there are ways of designing surveys (in general) that elicit trust and cooperation on the part of respondents—and if these are built into a survey of sexual habits, as this selection demonstrates, people will cooperate. This selection is valuable, most of all because it provides a clear and concise overview of how to go about designing a good survey, no matter what it is that you are investigating. Students may be interested to know that in 2010 the National Survey of Sexual Health and Behavior was conducted through the University of Chicago. This survey focused on safe sex practices, male and female pleasure, as well as sexual patterns among youth. For more information, please access http://www.nationalsexstudy.indiana.edu/.

1. How did the researchers conduct their research on such a sensitive topic? Did they deal with issues that arose appropriately? Could their methods have been improved at all?

Most people with whom we talked when we first broached the idea of a national survey of sexual behavior were skeptical that it could be done. Scientists and laypeople alike had similar reactions: "Nobody will agree to participate in such a study." "Nobody will answer questions like these, and, even if they do, they won't tell the truth." "People don't know enough about sexual practices as they relate to disease transmission or even to pleasure or physical and emotional satisfaction to be able to answer questions accurately." It would be dishonest to say that we did not share these and other concerns. But our experiences over the past seven years, rooted in extensive pilot work, focus-group discussions, and the fielding of the survey itself, resolved these doubts, fully vindicating our growing conviction that a national survey could be conducted according to high standards of scientific rigor and replicability. . . .

When we began working on the design of the survey in 1988, the only comprehensive American study of sexuality based on a large cross section of the population was the famous two-volume Kinsey Report published almost forty years before; but Kinsey's sampling design, essentially volunteer and purposive in character, failed to meet even the most elementary requirements for drawing a truly representative sample of the population at large.

The society in which we live treats sex and everything related to sex in a most ambiguous and ambivalent fashion. Sex is at once highly fascinating, attractive, and, for many at certain stages in their lives, preoccupying, but it can also be frightening, disturbing, or guilt inducing. For many, sex is considered to be an extremely private matter, to be discussed only with one's closest friends or intimates, if at all. And, certainly for most if not all of us, there are elements of our sexual lives never acknowledged to others, reserved for our own personal fantasies and self-contemplation. It is thus surprising that the proposal to study sex scientifically, or any other way for that matter, elicits confounding and confusing reactions.

The fact remains that, until quite recently, scientific research on sexuality has been taboo and therefore to be avoided or at best marginalized. While there is a visible tradition of (in)famous sex research, what is, in fact, most striking is how little prior research exists on sexuality in the general population. "Normal sex" was somehow off limits, perhaps because it was considered too ordinary, trivial, and self-evident to deserve attention. To be fair, then, we cannot blame the public and the politicians entirely for the lack of sustained work on sexuality at large—it also reflects the prejudices and understandings of researchers about what are "interesting" scientific questions. There has simply been a dearth of mainstream scientific thinking and speculation about sexual issues.

While we entered relatively uncharted waters in choosing the sexual content to be included in our survey, we found that we faced many of the same problems that any major survey research enterprise confronts. We discovered that the techniques that work in other domains work just as well when studying sexuality. For example, most of the problems involved in securing the participation of respondents in a survey are the same whether one is conducting a general purpose survey of political opinions, a study of labor force participation, or one of sexual behavior. Respondents must be convinced that the research has a legitimate purpose, that it is not some attempt to trick them into buying something, that their confidentiality will be protected, etc.

In order to understand the results of our survey, the National Health and Social Life Survey (NHSLS), one must understand how these results were generated. To construct a questionnaire and field a large-scale survey, many research design decisions must be made. To understand the decisions made, one needs to understand the multiple purposes that underlie this research project. Research design is never just a theoretical exercise. It is a set of practical solutions to a multitude of problems and considerations that are chosen under the constraints of limited resources of money, time, and prior knowledge.

SAMPLE DESIGN

The sample design for the NHSLS is the most straightforward element of our **methodology** because nothing about **probability sampling** is specific to or changes in a survey of sexual behavior.

Probability sampling, that is, sampling where every member of a clearly specified population has a known probability of selection—what lay commentators often somewhat inaccurately call random sampling—is the sine qua non of modern survey research. There is no other scientifically acceptable way to construct a representative sample and thereby to be able to generalize from the actual sample on which data are collected to the population that that sample is designed to represent. Probability sampling as practiced in survey research is a highly developed practical application of statistical theory to the problem of selecting a sample. Not only does this type of sampling avoid the problems of bias introduced by the researcher or by subject self-selection bias that come from more casual techniques, but it also allows one to quantify the variability in the estimates derived from the sample. . . .

SAMPLE SIZE

How large should the sample be? There is real confusion about the importance of sample size. In general, for the case of a probability sample, the bigger the sample, the higher the precision of its estimates. This precision is usually measured in terms of the amount of **sampling error** accruing to the statistics calculated from the sample.

The most common version of this is the statement that estimated proportions (e.g., the proportion of likely voters planning to vote for a particular candidate) in national political polls are estimated as being within ± 2 or 3 percent of the overall population figure. The amount of this discrepancy is inversely related to the size of the sample: the larger the sample, the smaller the likely error in the estimates. This is not, however, a simple linear relation. Instead, in general, as the sample size increases, the precision of the estimates derived from the sample increases by the square root of the sample size. For example, if we quadruple the sample size, we improve the estimate only by a factor of two. That is, if the original sample has a sampling error of ± 10 percent, then the quadrupled sample size will have an error of ± 5 percent.

In order to determine how large a sample size for a given study should be, one must first decide how precise the estimates to be derived need to be. To illustrate this reasoning process, let us take one of the simplest and most commonly used statistics in survey research, the proportion. Many of the most important results reported in this book are proportions. For example, what proportion of the population had more than five sex partners in the last year? What proportion engaged in anal intercourse? With condoms? Estimates based on our sample will differ from the true proportion in the population because of

sampling error (i.e., the random fluctuations in our estimates that are due to the fact that they are based on samples rather than on complete enumerations or censuses). If one drew repeated samples using the same methodology, each would produce a slightly different estimate. If one looks at the distribution of these *estimates*, it turns out that they will be normally distributed (i.e., will follow the famous bell-shaped curve known as the Gaussian or normal distribution) and centered around the true proportion in the population. The larger the sample size, the tighter the distribution of estimates will be.

We began with an area probability sample, which is a sample of households, that is, of addresses, not names. Rather than approach a household by knocking on the door without advance warning, we followed standard practice of sending an advance letter, hand addressed by the interviewer, about a week before the interviewer expected to visit the address. In this case, the letter was signed by the principal investigator, Robert Michael, who was identified as the dean of the Irving B. Harris Graduate School of Public Policy Studies of the University of Chicago. The letter briefly explained the purpose of the survey as helping "doctors, teachers, and counselors better understand and prevent the spread of diseases like AIDS and better understand the nature and extent of harmful and of healthy sexual behavior in our country." The intent was to convince the potential respondent that this was a legitimate scientific study addressing personal and potentially sensitive topics for a socially useful purpose.

Gaining respondents' cooperation requires mastery of a broad spectrum of techniques that successful interviewers develop with experience, guidance from the research team, and careful field supervision. This project required extensive training before entering the field. While interviewers are generally trained to be neutral toward topics covered in the interview, this was especially important when discussing sex, a topic that seems particularly likely to elicit emotionally freighted sensitivities both in the respondents and in the interviewers. Interviewers needed to be fully persuaded about the legitimacy and importance of the research. Toward this end, almost a full day of training was devoted to presentations and discussions with the principal investigators in addition to the extensive advance study materials to read and comprehend. Sample answers to frequently asked questions by skeptical respondents and brainstorming about strategies to convert reluctant respondents were part of the training exercises.

MODE OF ADMINISTRATION: FACE-TO-FACE, TELEPHONE, OR SELF-ADMINISTERED

Perhaps the most fundamental design decision, one that distinguishes this study from many others, concerned how the interview itself was to be conducted. In survey research, this is usually called the *mode* of interviewing or of questionnaire administration. We chose face-to-face interviewing, the most costly mode, as the primary vehicle for data collection in the NHSLS.

We decided to use face-to-face interviewing as our primary mode of administration of the NHSLS for two principal reasons: it was most likely to yield a substantially higher response rate for a more inclusive cross section of the population at large, and it would permit more complex and detailed questions to be asked.

Recruiting and Training Interviewers

We firmly believed that it was very important to recruit and train interviewers for this study very carefully. In particular, we worried that interviewers who were in any way uncomfortable with the topic of sexuality would not do a good job and would adversely affect the quality of the interview. We thus took special steps in recruiting interviewers to make it clear what the survey was about, even showing them especially sensitive sample questions.

The Questionnaire

The questionnaire itself is probably the most important element of the study design. It determines the content and quality of the information gathered for analysis. Unlike issues related to sample design, the construction of a questionnaire is driven less by technical precepts and more by the concepts and ideas motivating the research.

The problem that we faced in writing the questionnaire was figuring out how best to ask people about their sex lives. There are two issues here that should be highlighted. One is conceptual, having to do with how to define sex, and the second has to do with the level or kind of language to be used in the interview.

There are a number of activities that commonly serve as markers for sex and the status of sex partner, especially intercourse and orgasm. While we certainly wanted to include these events and their extent in given relationships and events, we also felt that using them to define and ask about sexual activity might exclude transactions or partners that should be included. Since the common meaning and uses of the term *intercourse* involve the idea of the intromission of a penis, intercourse in that sense as a defining act would at the very least exclude a sexual relationship between two women. There are also many events that we would call sexual that may not involve orgasm on the part of either or both partners.

For these reasons, in the key section of the questionnaire where we ask respondents to enumerate their sex partners in the past twelve months, we use the following definition of sex: "Here, by 'sex' or 'sexual activity,' we mean any mutually voluntary activity with another person that involves genital contact and sexual excitement or arousal, that is, feeling really turned on, even if intercourse or orgasm did not occur." This definition serves to elicit a broader list of partners and events than some more common definitions. In the description of the sexual relationship, the specific content in terms of sexual techniques and outcomes such as orgasm are collected. This definition also excluded forced sex. This was dealt with separately in a later section of the questionnaire. This was done to protect respondents from emotional upset earlier in the questionnaire and also because forced sex seems to define a partially separate domain.

Another major issue is what sort of language is appropriate in asking questions about sex. It seemed obvious that one should avoid highly technical language because it is unlikely to be understood by many people. One tempting alternative is to use **colloquial language** and even slang since that is the only language that some people ever use in discussing sexual matters.

Slang and other forms of colloquial speech, however, are likely to be problematic in several ways. First, the use of slang can produce a tone in the interview that is counterproductive because it downplays the distinctiveness of the interviewing situation itself. An essential goal in survey interviewing, especially on sensitive topics like sex, is to create a neutral, nonjudgmental, and confiding atmosphere and to maintain a certain professional distance.

The second major shortcoming of slang is that it is highly variable across class and education levels, ages, regions, and other social groupings. It changes meanings rapidly and is often imprecise.

Masturbation was generally felt to be the most sensitive topic of any we discussed, making both respondents and interviewers the most uncomfortable. We thus adopted a form to be filled out by the respondents themselves in an effort to increase the accuracy of the report of the practice. The forms were administered in such a way that the interviewer did not see the answers. On completion, the form was put immediately into an envelope, which was then sealed before it was returned to the interviewer.

Issues of respondent confidentiality are at the very heart of survey research. The willingness of respondents to report their view and experiences fully and honestly depends on the rationale offered for why the study is important and on the assurance that the information provided will be treated as confidential. We offered respondents a strong rationale for the study, our interviewers made great efforts to conduct the interview in a manner that protected respondents' privacy, and we went to great lengths to honor the assurances that the information would be treated confidentially.

PART 2

Critical Thinking Questions

1. What is the importance of conducting research with a representative sample?
2. What is the best method of interviewing participants when conducting social research: face-to-face, by telephone, or with self-administered surveys (either handwritten or online)? Why?

Chapter 5

Ethical Issues in Disaster Research: Lessons from Hurricane Katrina

CARRIE Y. BARRON AUSBROOKS, EDITH J. BARRETT, AND MARIA MARTINEZ-COSIO

Sociological research is often conducted in the midst of social upheaval and/or addresses topics that are of a sensitive nature. As such, research participants may be vulnerable due to their social status or context. This is particularly obvious when doing research at the time of a disaster, such as in the wake of Hurricane Katrina in 2005 (the most costly and one of the most deadly hurricanes in U.S. history). While social research is important, it is imperative that we consider whether the benefits of research, while important, are worth the cost to the research respondents. This is a dilemma that many social researchers often face and is highlighted in the following article.

1. What challenges and concerns face researchers when investigating vulnerable populations?
2. What role do ethics play when conducting social research, and what impacts might they have?

INTRODUCTION

During August 2005, in perhaps the single largest unexpected migration since the Civil War, nearly half a million people left sections of Louisiana and Mississippi as a result of Hurricane Katrina. According to some estimates, nearly 50,000 school-aged children were relocated to Texas cities, and by December 2005, almost 4,000 student evacuees were enrolled in schools in the Dallas-Fort Worth area (Texas Education Agency 2005). For scholars interested in the effects of disasters on the social and emotional well-being of individuals, especially of children, the mass exodus following Hurricane Katrina

presented a rare opportunity. Our research project sought to understand how schools react to the influx of children fleeing the disaster, most of whom had lost nearly all of their possessions and whose families were stressed nearly to their limits. We found ourselves also struggling to conduct research with the assistance of over-stretched public institutions. In this article, we outline some of the ethical challenges we faced and how we sought to overcome them.

Disasters are a part of human life. Research can provide useful information on how to prevent disaster and, just as importantly, how to deal with disaster once it happens. Research

Source: With kind permission from Springer Science+Business Media: Ausbrooks, Carrie Y. Barron, Edith J. Barrett, and Maria Martinez-Cosio. "Ethical Issues in Disaster Research: Lessons from Hurricane Katrina." *Population Research & Policy Review* 28 (2009): 93–106.

has already greatly increased society's knowledge about the human impact of disasters and has "helped shape public policy, public education, and service delivery following disasters and terrorist attacks" (Kilpatrick 2004: 362). Yet such research forces social scientists to weigh the ethics of intruding on individuals' privacy and interfering with the business of institutions against the value of obtaining timely data.

CHALLENGES OF WORKING WITH DISASTER SURVIVORS

Every social science discipline has its own professional codes of ethics, and federal regulations address issues that are common to all types of human subject research (e.g., protection of subjects' welfare, the right to privacy, informed consent, and prevention from deception and the abuse of vulnerable populations). Out of the atrocities reported during the 1947 Nuremberg War Trials, came a set of ten internationally accepted rules for the use of human subjects. The Nuremberg Code, as it came to be known, included requirements for voluntary informed consent of research subjects, rules about weighing risks against benefits, and freedoms allowing subjects to terminate their participation at any time (Merriam 1998; Elliott and Stern 1997). Five years later, the U.S. Secretary of Defense recognized these principles in issuing a directive, which mirrored the Nuremberg Code and provided that the full and voluntary consent of subjects would be a requirement of human experimentation for the Department of Defense.

Of course, the declaration by the U.S. Secretary of Defense hardly put a stop to all abuses of human subjects. U.S. history is rife with examples of problems. The most notorious is no doubt the Tuskegee Syphilis study, in which 399 black men with syphilis were lead to believe they were being treated when, in fact, the goal was to study the progress of the disease. Subjects were never given the option to withdraw from the study, even after a highly effective treatment became widely used. Other egregious examples

led the U.S. Department of Health and Human Services to call for new guidelines. Today, ethical treatment of human subjects is informed by the Belmont Report (The National Commission 1979), which established three ethical principles and guidelines for the protection of human subjects in non-biomedical research: respect for persons, beneficence, and justice. The Belmont Report also includes protections for vulnerable populations, such as pregnant women, handicapped or mentally disabled persons, prisoners, and children (Stalcup 2004). Despite international and federal regulations governing human subject research, no specific code of ethical standards exists for conducting **disaster research** (Black 2003).

Informed Consent with Disaster Victims

Individuals must be given the opportunity to decide what will and will not happen to them, and they must be allowed to withdraw from a study at any time without repercussions. Consent must be voluntary and not coerced. Populations that would typically be vulnerable to coercion—children, prisoners, pregnant women, mentally disabled persons, economically or educationally disadvantaged individuals—are entitled to added protection, as are other groups that might be considered vulnerable in particular situations (e.g., terminally ill patients, active-duty military personnel, or persons in a subordinate position to the researcher conducting the protocol) (Stern and Lomax 1997).

Some believe that disaster victims/survivors also tend to be in a particularly vulnerable position. They need services, and hence they could be easily manipulated. Therefore, special protections should be included in disaster research protocols, as would be done in any other research protocol that intends to enroll incapacitated subjects. Proximity to the trauma increases the psychological impact, and therefore, at a minimum, individuals who would require special protection are individuals who are injured during the disaster, the family members of those who are injured, individuals who escaped the disaster, direct observers, first responders, rescue workers, recovery personnel, and others directly affected by the event (Fleischman and Wood 2002).

In our study of teenage survivors of Hurricane Katrina, we were dealing with a traditionally vulnerable group—children—in a situation that potentially made them even more vulnerable—new students in an unfamiliar state, neighborhood, and school. We created multiple layers of protections for the youth. First, we sought permission from the appropriate departments in school districts' central administration. Then before any child was allowed to participate in our study (which involved completing a detailed survey on their psychosocial, emotional, and educational well-being), we demanded parental permission and student consent. The informed consent forms were written at a 6th grade level to maximize the likelihood that they would be understood by parents and students (who were in grades 7 through 12).

In our study, not only did we have to rely on parents' willingness to allow their children to participate, we also had to depend on the children to return the signed form to the designated school personnel. This process reduced our sample size. Nonetheless, because of the multiple stages of our informed consent process, we can feel confident that the students and their parents intentionally chose to participate. While anyone doing school-based research would face similar informed consent issues, our experiences were unique in that parents were not always available. The transience of displaced disaster survivors places a distinctive twist on obtaining informed consent.

Subject Confidentiality

Subject privacy and confidentiality are important in all types of research, but in disaster research perhaps even more so because of the vulnerable position of the survivors.

Schools that receive funding from the U.S. Department of Education are subject to the provisions of the Protection of Pupil Rights Act [PPRA—20 U.S.C. §1232 (h)(b)], which protects the privacy of students' education records. The act mandates that no student can be required to participate in a survey, analysis or evaluation that reveals certain types of information (e.g., political beliefs, psychological problems, sexual behaviors, illegal behavior, etc.) without the prior consent of the student or his/her parents. Both FERPA and PPRA are designed to protect the privacy of minor students, and because of these laws, we first sought school district approval, then parents' approval, and finally student approval before beginning any data collection.

Generally, schools must have written permission from the parent or eligible student in order to release any information from a student's education record. Schools do not need consent to disclose "directory" information, such as students' names, addresses, telephone numbers, dates and places of birth, honors and awards, and dates of attendance, unless the parent or student who is at least 18 years of age has requested that "directory" information not be disclosed.

Although schools are allowed to release this information, in our experience, they are extremely reluctant to do so. No school district or individual school involved in our study gave us direct access to the addresses of relocated Katrina students. Instead, we were required to work through the schools to make contact with the parents and obtain their permission for participation. To do this, school counselors identified the relocated students and gave them a parental informed consent form to deliver to their parents. Students who brought back signed permission were allowed to participate. However, because we could not speak directly with the students, we could not emphasize the relevance of the study. Nor could we pursue follow-up efforts. The process was arduous, no doubt left a number of children and their parents unidentified, and resulted in a sample heavily weighted toward accessible parents and students.

Subject Compensation

The practice of paying subjects for their participation in research has been in place for over 100 years and has included both monetary and non-monetary compensation (e.g., meals, transportation). Payment to subjects can have a positive impact on the research project. Payment facilitates timely recruitment of the appropriate number and type of research subjects. It may increase the response rate, and it may especially encourage participation by hard-to-reach subjects and underrepresented groups. Reimbursement for subjects' expenses reduces any financial sacrifice in terms of time and inconvenience (Grady 2005). On the other hand, paying parents for the participation of their children may impair their ability to make a decision in the best interest of their child (Wendler et al. 2002). When children are subjects in a study, Wendler et al. (2002) argue that they, rather than their parents, should receive the compensation.

Regardless of the rationale for paying research subjects, it does raise ethical concerns. The major ethical concern regarding payments to participants is that it may be perceived as coercive. It may also lead potential subjects to misrepresent themselves in order to be considered for the research project. When offered money, the decision-making ability of impoverished individuals may be impaired. Monetary payments may be more attractive to individuals with low socioeconomic status thus resulting in a disproportionate research burden on this population and skewing the subject pool so that the generalization of the data is confounded. On the other hand, offering no money or a very small amount of money to the economically disadvantaged can potentially skew the subject pool away from them and "contravene principles of distributive justice, especially for research perceived as beneficial to participants" (Grady 2005: 1685).

In our study, we provided $20 store gift cards to the student and parent respondents as a means of showing our appreciation for their assistance during such a difficult time for them. The type of gift card and the amount selected was our way of assisting them in obtaining necessities that may have been lost to Hurricane Katrina. Students were compensated for returning the survey at 6 months and again at 12 months, thus theoretically earning $60 for their participation in our study. Parents were compensated at baseline and again if they returned the 6- or 12-month follow-up survey; parents could be paid a total of $40. Given the confusion in the lives of so many disaster survivors, some compensation seems warranted.

CHALLENGES OF WORKING WITH STRESSED INSTITUTIONS

In our research, schools were the gatekeepers to our access to the subjects (students as well as teachers and principals). Without the active participation of the schools and school districts, our research would have been impossible. Schools in particular have an obligation to maintain the privacy of their students. However, when one of the responsibilities of researchers is to collect such data in order to provide evidence that informs policy and practice, the inability to obtain it presents a challenge, which in turn impacts the researchers' abilities to meet their responsibilities.

Using Texas Education Agency data, we identified 156 independent school districts in the Dallas-Fort Worth region, and from that list, we chose to approach eight of the large urban independent school districts. In the end, only four districts agreed to participate in the project.

To simplify the process, district staff helped us identify schools that had the greatest number of Katrina students, and the research team limited its efforts only to those schools. Nonetheless, even once inside the schools, there were numerous logistical hurdles. Working with already busy counselors meant that our project got limited attention, and yet, without direct access to the students, we were forced to rely on their assistance. Ultimately, our sample size

PART 3

was smaller than anticipated (only 120 students, when we had hoped for a starting sample of at least 400), and though we had Katrina students from 28 different schools, no single school had more than 15 students represented. Had we been given the addresses of the students, we could have approached them individually and likely achieved a much larger sample. One school district, not even considering the timeliness of our research, denied us access stating the district policy that:

Due the fact that our District received so many requests to do surveys over the years, we made the decision not to allow surveys unless they were mandated by the state government or the federal government.

As reticent as schools and other local agencies may be to participate in social science research under normal conditions, the added burden of dealing with the disaster makes their involvement even less likely. Yet, local agencies are often the access points for finding disaster survivors. Such was the case in our study. We needed school participation in order to find the students, and because our study investigated the role of schools in helping students, we also needed their active participation as research subjects. Shortly after Hurricane Katrina, though, public schools in the targeted area were overwhelmed just dealing with the needs of the new students. Their energies were focused on serving the students' academic needs and not necessarily on advancing social science knowledge. Our solution was to offer findings from our work that would be directly useful to the schools in their future planning. We promised the schools information about the needs of students and about the practices used by schools in the area. Some schools agreed to participate because of the perceived value of the findings. Other schools chose not to participate. Sadly, without the participation of reluctant institutions, some disaster research simply cannot take place. That it took so long to gain access to the students through the schools was typical for post-disaster research.

CHALLENGES OF MEETING THE REQUIREMENTS OF GOOD SOCIAL SCIENCE

Conducting methodologically sound disaster research is critical for the value of the findings. Over the years, codes of ethics published by professional organizations have stressed the importance of informed consent, safeguarding subjects' privacy, assuring confidentiality and/or anonymity, avoiding deception, and preventing harm to subjects arising from the research as critical ethical issues. While it is important to ensure that the rights of research subjects are protected, it is also important that a regulatory environment be established that does not impede critical research. Making ethical decisions regarding disaster research should include careful consideration of its potential benefits, as well as whether risks to participants are balanced by the benefits of the study. Thus, we must also consider the ethics of not conducting research when research is needed to answer important questions (Kilpatrick 2004).

Researchers have certain obligations to subjects. They must ensure that studies are designed to minimize harms and risks to subjects and that the researchers themselves do not intentionally inflict harm. Researchers must also protect the welfare, and promote the well-being of the research subjects. Subjects must be provided the opportunity to make voluntary and noncoerced decisions about participation, and participation cannot be overly burdensome to specific individuals or populations. In disaster research, sensitivity to the victims of the event is important, as the possibility exists that re-traumatizing may occur during participation in research (Fleischman and Wood 2002).

The primary role of researchers is to collect data. Researchers are neither judges nor therapists. Neither are they made of stone and devoid of emotional response to human issues, including great suffering and pain that may unfold during research activities. It is important that the researchers are able to refer participants to appropriate resources when problems arise during the research study (Merriam 1998). Researchers must also remember that they are guests in the private space of research subjects, who are, therefore, entitled to respect and protection from harm during the course of the research. In our project, we made contact with local social service agencies and were prepared to make referrals if asked.

Researchers often spend a great deal of time with the research subjects, becoming quite close to them in the process. When the study ends and researchers leave the study site, the subjects, particularly those in primitive or war-torn areas, may be left confused. As a result, good intentions may be lost if one or both parties fails to recognize the value of those intentions or the needs of the other party (Tomaselli et al. 2005).

CONCLUSION

The nature of catastrophic events renders research in their aftermath uniquely challenging. Yet, studies of their effects are critical to decision making and policy development in preparation for future crises. For investigators conducting disaster research, the ethical considerations for the timely collection of valid data become even more complex as the level of chaos, stress, and uncertainty among survivors and the institutional actors who must address their needs increases. The differing perspectives of researchers, policy makers and local agencies further increase the contextual complexity. In addition, subjects are in a particularly vulnerable situation. The research protocol must be designed and implemented quickly to capture the moment, and researchers often find themselves at the mercy of overstressed gate-keeping institutions. These issues may create conditions for breaches of ethics to occur.

Despite the ethical and logistical hurdles, researchers have a responsibility to conduct significant research and to widely disseminate the knowledge from their investigations so it

may be applied. Throughout this article, we have described some of the ethical issues associated with conducting disaster research. It is not an exhaustive list. Sustained quality disaster research will provide a broader knowledge base to extend the parameters of current ethics regulations toward the development of a universal ethical standard.

REFERENCES

Black, R. (2003). Ethical codes in humanitarian emergencies: From practice to research? *Disasters,* 27(2), 95–108.

Elliott, D., & Stern, J. E. (Eds.). (1997). *Research ethics: A reader.* Hanover, NH: University Press of New England.

Fleischman, A. R. & Wood, E. B. (September 2002). Ethical issues in research involving victims of terror. *Journal of Urban Health: Bulletin of the New York Academy of Medicine,* 79(3).

Grady, C. (July 2005). Payment of clinical research subjects. *The Journal of Clinical Investigation,* 115(7), 1681–1687. Retrieved December 19, 2006, from http://www.jci.org/cgi/reprint/115/7/1681.

Kilpatrick, D. G. (2004). The ethics of disaster research: A special section. *Journal of Traumatic Stress,* 17(5), 361–362.

Merriam, S. B. (1998). *Qualitative research and case study applications in education.* San Francisco, CA: Jossey-Bass.

Protection of Human Subjects, 45 CFR 46 (2005). Retrieved December 8, 2006, from http://www.nihtraining.com/ohsrsite/guidelines/45cfr46.html.

Stalcup, C. M. (2004). Reviewing the review boards: Why institutional review board liability does not make good business sense. *Washington University Law Quarterly,* 82, Wash. U.L.Q. 1593. Retrieved November 28, 2006, from http://law.wustl.edu/WULQ/82-4/index.html.

Stern, J. E., & Lomax, K. (1997). Human experimentation. In D. Elliott & J. E. Stern (Eds.), *Research ethics: A reader* (pp. 286–295). Hanover, NH: University Press of New England.

Texas Education Agency. (2005). Hurricane-related information. Retrieved 01/14/07 from http://www.tea.state.tx.us/hcane/. [See also http://www.tea.state.tx.us/press/hurricanegrant.pdf, accessed 1/14/07; http://www.tea.state.tx.us/hcane/KatEvaMap.pdf, accessed 1/14/07.]

PART 3

Tomaselli, K., McLennan-Dodd, V., & Shepperson, A. (2005). Research to do, results to sell: Enabling subjects and researchers. *Society in Transition, 36*(1), 24–27.

Wendler, D., Rackoff, J. E., Emanual, E. J., & Grady, C. (2002). The ethics of paying for children's participation in research. *The Journal of Pediatrics, 141*(2), 166–171.

Critical Thinking Questions

1. Are there other methods that the researchers could have employed to improve their project?
2. Do you think that disaster research is necessary? Why or why not?

Chapter 6
The Tuskegee Syphilis Experiment

CAROL A. HEINTZELMAN

It's useful to begin thinking about the "Tuskegee Syphilis Experiment," the study described here, by taking note of something mentioned at the end of this article: A substantial number of black Americans continue to mistrust the public health system and have fears of vaccinations. Why would people in the 21st century develop a fear like this? The answer lies in recognizing that something like the Tuskegee Syphilis Experiment could happen. Here was a U.S. government-sponsored study that sought to determine the effects of syphilis by following poor black men infected with the disease, over several decades. In order to ensure they saw the true impacts of syphilis they made certain that these men did not receive treatments (such as penicillin) that were available. How are we to explain how something like this came to be? Racist attitudes are certainly part of the answer, although some other processes must also be at work.

"The United States government did something that was wrong—deeply, profoundly, morally wrong. It was an outrage to our commitment to integrity and equality for all our citizens ... clearly racist."
—President Clinton's apology for the Tuskegee Syphilis Experiment to the eight remaining survivors, May 16, 1997

1. What factors led to this experiment taking place and persisting?
2. Do you think this experiment would have been carried out in the same way if non-African Americans had been participants? Why or why not?

The Tuskegee Study of Untreated Syphilis in the African American Male is the longest non-therapeutic experiment on human beings in medical history, as noted by Arthur L. Caplan (1992). Begun in 1932 by the United States Public Health Service (USPHS), the study was purportedly designed to determine the natural course of untreated latent syphilis in some 400 African American men in Tuskegee, Macon County, Alabama. The research subjects, all of whom had syphilis when they were enrolled in the study—contrary to the "urban myth" that holds "black men in Alabama were injected with the virus that causes syphilis" (Walker, 1992)—were matched against 200 uninfected subjects who served as a control group.

The subjects were recruited with misleading promises of "special free treatment," which were actually spinal taps done without anesthesia to study the neurological effects of syphilis, and they were enrolled without their informed consent.

The subjects received heavy metals therapy, standard treatment in 1932, but were denied antibiotic therapy when it became clear in the 1940s that penicillin was a safe and effective treatment for the disease. When penicillin became widely available by the early 1950s as the preferred treatment for syphilis, this therapy was again withheld. On several occasions, the USPHS actually sought to prevent treatment.

The first published report of the study appeared in 1936, with subsequent papers issued every four to six years until the early 1970s. In 1969, a committee at the federally operated Center for Disease Control decided the study should continue. Only in 1972, when accounts of the study first appeared in the national press, did the Department of Health, Education and Welfare (HEW) halt the experiment.

At that time, 74 of the test subjects were still alive; at least 28, but perhaps more than 100, had died directly from advanced syphilis. An investigatory panel appointed by HEW in August 1972 found the study "ethically unjustified" and argued that penicillin should have been provided to the men. As a result, the National Research Act, passed in 1974, mandated that all federally funded proposed research with human subjects be approved by an institutional review board (IRB). By 1992, final payments of approximately $40,000 were made to survivors under an agreement settling the class action lawsuit brought on behalf of the Tuskegee Study subjects. President Clinton publicly apologized on behalf of the federal government to the handful of study survivors in April 1997.

Several major ethical issues involving human research subjects need to be studied further. The first major ethical issue to be considered is informed consent, which refers to telling potential research participants about all aspects of the research that might reasonably influence their decision to participate. A major unresolved concern is exactly how far researchers' obligations extend to research subjects. Another concern has to do with the possibility that a person might feel pressured to agree or might not understand precisely what he or she is agreeing to. The investigators took advantage of a deprived socioeconomic situation in which the participants had experienced low levels of care. The contacts were with doctors and nurses who were seen as authority figures.

The USPHS practiced deception in recruiting subjects for the study. It was never explained to the subjects that the survey was designed to detect syphilis. The term "bad blood," which was a local colloquialism for everything from anemia to leukemia, was used by the doctors and never defined for the subjects. Subjects were never told they had syphilis, the course of the disease, or treatment. The treatment presented consisted of spinal taps, which were described as "spinal shots" (Heintzelman, 1995).

The second major ethical issue is the withholding of treatment for research purposes. This is the gravest charge against the study. Patient welfare was consistently overlooked, although there have been multiple attempts to justify why penicillin treatment was withheld. Some physicians felt that repair of existing damage would be minimal, and others felt that the damage that could result from reactions to the penicillin therapy, including fever, angina, and ruptured blood vessels, would outweigh its benefits. At the time of the Tuskegee Study, no data was available on the efficiency of penicillin treatment in late syphilis, and short- and long-term toxic effects of drugs had not been well documented. In short, when the study was evaluated periodically, researchers judged that the benefits of nontreatment outweighed the benefits of treatment. Moreover, the subjects were never given a choice about continuing in the study once penicillin had become available; in fact, they were prevented from getting treatment.

The decision was made based on several factors, including the quiescent state of the disease, assumptions about the participants, and fear related to the danger of lethal reactions if the men were to receive penicillin. So treatment was not offered, and even when the experiment ended in 1972, the remaining funds could not be used for treatment, according to USPHS grant guidelines (Heintzelman, 1996).

Several other ethical issues surrounded the study. First, Alabama had passed a law in 1927 that required the reporting and treatment of several venereal diseases, including syphilis, by medical personnel. The USPHS ignored the state law, choosing to disregard the impact of untreated syphilis on wives of the married men who were subjects.

Second, accurate records were not kept. The number of subjects who died from syphilis was never known. The number of survivors was estimated to be between 76 and 111, and the number of dying was estimated between 28 and 101.

Third, beliefs within the medical profession about the nature of African Americans, sexual behavior, and disease clouded the study. As a result, the health of an entire community was jeopardized by leaving a communicable disease untreated.

Fourth, although no comprehensive report was ever published, the study was reported in medical journals for nearly 40 years without protest from anyone in the medical community. The investigating doctors never questioned the morality of the study. Also, HEW had no mechanism for periodic reassessment of the ethics and scientific values of the studies being conducted.

The Tuskegee Syphilis Study forced the nation to rethink and redefine practices involving human experimentation, especially those involving minority populations. As a consequence, HEW established a National Human Investigation Board, and legislation was passed requiring the establishment of Institutional Review Boards (IRBs).

A class action suit filed in the 1970s on behalf of the survivors resulted in no new law and avoided the issue of government responsibility for injury in such an experiment. Each survivor received a settlement of approximately $40,000.

The most enduring legacy of the Tuskegee Syphilis Study is its repercussions in the African American community, which have implications in light of the AIDS epidemic. The study laid the foundations for African Americans' continued distrust of the medical establishment, especially public health programs and a fear of vaccinations. It reinforced views about the medical establishment and the federal government, as well as disregard for African American lives. Although community outreach efforts have done much to combat the misconceptions, there seems to be evidence that African Americans did not seek treatment for AIDS in the early 1980s because of distrust of health care providers regarding the diagnosis, prognosis, and treatment of AIDS.

James H. Jones, an historian and specialist in bioethical issues, wrote in *Bad Blood: The Tuskegee Syphilis Experiment* (1993) the following:

> As a symbol of racism and medical malfeasance, the Tuskegee Study may never move the nation to action, but it can change the way Americans view illness. Hidden within the anger and anguish of those who decry the experiment is a plea for government authorities and medical officials to hear the fears of people whose faith has been damaged, to deal with their concerns directly, and to acknowledge the link between public health and community trust. Government Authorities and medical officials must strive to cleanse medicine of social infection by eliminating any type of racial or moral stereotypes of people or their illnesses. They must seek to build a health system that will make adequate health care available to all Americans. Anything less will leave some groups at risk, as it did the subjects of the Tuskegee Study (p. 241).

REFERENCES

Caplan, A. L. (1992). Twenty years after: The legacy of the Tuskegee syphilis study—When evil intrudes. *Hastings Center Report, 22,* 29–32.

Heintzelman, C. A. (1995, March). Ethical issues in social work research: The Tuskegee syphilis study, 41st Annual Program Meeting, Council on Social Work Education, San Diego, California.

Heintzelman, C. A. (1996). Human subjects and informed consent: The legacy of the Tuskegee syphilis study. *Scholars,* 6 (1), 23–30.

Jones, J. H. (1993). *Bad blood: The Tuskegee syphilis experiment.* New York: The Free Press.

Monette, D. R., Sullivan, T. J., & DeJong, C. R. (2002). *Applied social research: Tool for the human services* (5th ed.). New York: Harcourt.

Walker, A. (1992). *Possessing the secret of joy.* London: Vantage Press.

Critical Thinking Questions

1. How did this experiment end? How was it justified?
2. What is required in a study with human participants? Was this the case with the Tuskegee Syphilis Experiment?
3. What lessons can be drawn from this example when thinking about social research and the ethics of doing research? Think about informed consent; physical and mental distress; and the issue of not providing treatment when you know it could help the patient.
4. Do you think this study could ever be done ethically?
5. What further lessons can we learn as sociologists regarding the importance of understanding and questioning commonsense notions from this article?

Chapter 7

Sterilizing the "Feeble-Minded": Eugenics in Alberta, Canada, 1929–1972

JANA GREKUL, HARVEY KRAHN, AND DAVE ODYNAK

PART 3

Many Canadians know little about the Eugenics Movement in Alberta, where the *Sexual Sterilization Act* of 1928–1972 encouraged surgical sterilization of those labelled "**feeble-minded**" or "mentally defective." Often those who were targeted as "feeble" or "defective" were from more socially vulnerable groups, such as newcomer immigrants, women, Indigenous peoples, and youth. The Sexual Sterilization Act was put into place to prevent such "undesirables" from passing along their "defective" genes to future generations. Further, mental institutions were used to house "feeble-minded" individuals, some for long periods of time, and others until they were surgically sterilized. To begin to understand why this movement began, and persisted for such a long period of time, it is helpful to employ Mills' tools of biography, history, and milieux (described in Chapter 2) when reading through this chapter.

1. How did the Eugenics Movement in Alberta gain momentum and stay within favour for such a long time?
2. Why do you suppose many Canadians may have little to no knowledge about the Canadian Eugenics Movement?

ABSTRACT

Between 1929 and 1972, the Alberta Eugenics Board recommended that 4739 residents of the province be sterilized. However, only 60% of these individuals, 2834 in total, were ultimately sterilized since the legislation under which the Eugenics Board operated required patient consent to be obtained unless the individual recommended for sterilization was diagnosed as "mentally defective." Women, teenagers and young adults, and Aboriginals were particularly targeted by the Alberta Eugenics Board.

INTRODUCTION

In Alberta, Canada, between 1929 and 1972, over 2800 people were sterilized under the authority of the province's *Sexual Sterilization Act*. The creation of the *Alberta Eugenics Board* to coordinate the sterilization program reflected the widespread popularity of **eugenics** beliefs at the time.

Legislation authorizing involuntary sterilization was enacted by governments on both sides of the Atlantic, including many state governments in the USA. In Canada, Alberta and British Columbia were the only two provinces

Source: Grekul, Jana. "Sterilizing the 'Feeble-minded': Eugenics in Alberta, Canada, 1929-1972." *Canadian Review of Sociology* 45.3 (2008): 247-266. Reprinted with permission of John Wiley & Sons.

with such legislation. However, despite similar size populations, about ten times as many people were sterilized in Alberta as in British Columbia.

In its more benign forms, the eugenics ideology and social movement promoted healthy living and "social purity" (McLaren 1990; Paul 1995). In its more draconian form, the movement sought ways to ensure that the more "fit" members of society had children while "undesirable elements" were bred out of the population. In most countries where eugenics beliefs were enshrined in legislation, efforts were made to limit reproduction among "unfit" groups through public education, institutionalization and, sometimes, forced sterilization. In Nazi Germany, eugenics beliefs wrapped in the flag of national socialism led to the forced sterilization of thousands (Proctor 1988), but also to death camps for Jews and other undesirable groups and to the "Lebensborn" program in which young German women with classic Nordic features were encouraged to mate with members of Hitler's elite SS troops.

North American social engineers did not go this far but in many jurisdictions, including Alberta, they did initiate involuntary sterilization programs. The origins and activities of the Alberta Eugenics Board have been previously described (Christian 1974; Chapman 1977; McLaren 1990; Cairney 1996; Caulfield and Robertson, 1996; Park and Radford 1998) but several critical questions about the activities of the Alberta Eugenics Board remain unanswered.

First, why were only 60% of the patients passed for sterilization eventually sterilized, given the immense power invested in the Board? Second, how aggressively did the Alberta Eugenics Board pursue its sterilization mission, compared to similar organizations elsewhere in North America? Third, why did the Board continue to sterilize Albertans long after other US and Canadian jurisdictions had abandoned the practice?

THE EUGENICS MOVEMENT IN EUROPE AND NORTH AMERICA

The popularity of eugenics beliefs in the latter part of the 19th century can be traced, in large part, to the faith and hope invested by politicians and social elites in a vision of "progress" and in the power of science to achieve this vision (Ladd-Taylor 1997; McLaren 1990; Paul 1995; Rafter 1992; Reilly 1991). Underneath such "progressive" goals lay solidly-entrenched patterns of structured social inequality and equally pervasive racist and sexist attitudes and beliefs. Informed by social philosophers like Herbert Spencer who had coined the term "survival of the fittest," the accepted thinking was that, over time, as with Darwin's evolution of species, society would evolve into a more advanced form.

In Britain in 1883, Sir Francis Galton introduced the term "eugenics" to describe how, by intervening in human hereditary processes, social reformers could improve the race. In America, informed by several widely-discussed family histories that claimed to show that the "unfit" were reproducing at a faster rate than more advanced segments of society, social planners called for an aggressive government response to combat the problem.

Eugenics ideas quickly made their way into Canada. The western provinces, especially British Columbia and Alberta, provided a particularly receptive and hospitable climate for the eugenics movement.

The *Sexual Sterilization Act* was passed in 1928. Brought in by the UFA (United Farmers of Alberta), it remained in place under the subsequent Social Credit governments of William Aberhart and Ernest Manning. The Act allowed for the sterilization of inmates of mental health institutions if it could be shown that *"the patient might safely be discharged if the danger of the procreation with its attendant risk of multiplication of evil by transmission of the disability to progeny were eliminated."*

A four-person Eugenics Board was created to determine if sterilization was appropriate for each case considered. Board members had to unanimously agree before sterilization was authorized. In addition, the patient had to give her/his consent, unless they were mentally incapable. If so, the consent of a next of kin had to be obtained.

The Eugenics Board began its work in 1929. They concluded that "sterilization is the only rational procedure" for dealing with mental defectives who are "unduly prolific both within and without marriage" and who are "prone to pass on to posterity their own defects and to bring into the world children double handicapped by both heritage and early environment" (Baragar et al. 1935: 907).

From the outset, obtaining the consent of patients recommended for sterilization, or of their next of kin, had proved to be very difficult. In 1937, the government moved to amend the Sexual Sterilization Act to address this consent problem. Under the new rules, if individuals were deemed to be "mentally defective," their consent was no longer required before sterilization could take place. A second critical component of the 1937 amendment broadened the reasons for sterilization to include cases where it was believed that "the exercise of the power of procreation by any such psychotic person involves the risk of mental injury, either to such person or to his progeny." With this legislative change, sterilization could now also be recommended to preserve the mental well-being of individuals "incapable of intelligent parenthood" as well as to avoid children being raised in stressful family environments by unstable parents. In 1942 a second amendment to the Act broadened the category of mental patients who could be sterilized to include individuals with syphilis, epilepsy (if there was evidence of mental deterioration), and Huntington's Chorea. In such cases, however, consent of the patient was still required.

Alberta's *Sexual Sterilization Act* remained in force, and the Eugenics Board continued its operations, until 1972. Little more was heard about the activities of the Board until the mid-1990s when Leilani Muir, a woman who had been sterilized as a teenager, successfully sued the Alberta government and won a settlement.

Other victims of the Eugenics Board started similar legal actions. In 1998, Ralph Klein's Conservative government tried to avoid potentially huge settlements by invoking the "notwithstanding" clause in the Canadian Constitution. A huge public outcry resulted, and the government backed down. An impartial panel was set up to settle cases out of court using a standardized payment formula. Several hundred victims accepted settlements but close to 300 did not, choosing instead to engage the services of several Edmonton legal firms. These firms contracted with the Population Research Laboratory at the University of Alberta to systematically analyze all of the available records of the Eugenics Board (information made available by the defendant, the Alberta Government).

In 1999, the plaintiffs settled out of court with the Alberta government. Because of the confidential information it contains, the report has not been made public. Some of the findings reported in this paper are extracted from the electronic database, but in such a way that confidential (individual-level) information is not compromised.

EUGENICS BOARD COMPOSITION AND PRACTICES

The *Sexual Sterilization Act* required that the Eugenics Board have four members, including the Chair. Two members were supposed to be physicians. Most were professionals (medical doctors, psychiatrists, social workers).

Most patients were "presented" to the Board by a representative of the institution in which they were resident, usually a medical doctor/psychiatrist. Alberta Hospital (Ponoka) was the main "feeder" institution, presenting 60% of all the cases ever considered by the Board. The Provincial Training School (PTS) in Red

PART 3

Deer presented 21% of all cases, while Alberta Hospital (Oliver) in Edmonton presented 14%. Deerhome, another smaller training school in Red Deer, presented 4%.

Board members would interview presented patients, relying on the presentation summary sheets prepared in advance for additional information. If patients were unable to attend the meeting, the Board might visit them on their ward to observe and ask questions. Final decisions about sterilization were usually made at the same meeting, although sometimes decisions were deferred until additional information was available. On average, the Board discussed 13 cases per meeting. This translates into, at best, about 13 minutes of Board discussion for each sterilization recommendation.

EUGENICS BOARD DECISIONS

Our calculations reveal that, between 1929 and 1972, the Eugenics Board considered a total of 4785 cases. For 60 of these cases, the Board deferred its decision because it wanted to see additional information or because it was uncertain whether the case fell within its mandate. In time, 14 of these 60 "deferrals" were re-considered and passed for sterilization. Thus, over a 44-year period, the Alberta Eugenics Board "passed" (recommended sterilization) 99% of the cases brought before it, and deferred a decision on the rest. *It never said "no."*

Nevertheless, about 40% of the patients "passed" by the Board were never sterilized. Furthermore, for many of those sterilized, the operation took place long after the Board's decision. The explanation for these detours or delays in what otherwise was a highly efficient system lies in the need to obtain the consent of patients and/or next of kin. A patient could withhold consent, or a parent or spouse might be reluctant to provide consent, potentially delaying the operation indefinitely. The 1937 amendment to the Sexual Sterilization Act was meant to deal with such roadblocks by allowing sterilization without consent, if the patient was "mentally defective." But by the 1950s and 1960s, many fewer "patient consent" decisions were being made. Why did it take a decade before the Eugenics Board took advantage of the loosened consent rules in the 1937 amendment?

By the 1950s the Board had begun to see many more patients from the Provincial Training School (PTS) in Red Deer (and, to a lesser extent, Deerhome), and fewer from the provincial mental hospitals (Ponoka and Oliver). The training schools handled children and youth who were typically diagnosed as "mentally defective" when presented to the Eugenics Board. In contrast, only one-third of the adults presented by Alberta Hospital (Ponoka), the most active of the "feeder" institutions, had a "mentally defective" diagnosis. Thus, it was only when PTS became the primary presenting institution that the advantages of the 1937 legislative amendment were exploited.

To an extent, the growing involvement of these training schools in the provincial sterilization program in the 1950s and 1960s simply reflected the growth of the Alberta training school population. In 1931, PTS accounted for only 11% of the 1701 inhabitants of the four "feeder" institutions (Deerhome did not open until the late 1950s). By 1961, 37% of the 4178 patients in the four institutions were residents of PTS or Deerhome.

Returning to the issue of "consent," because patients presented at PTS (and Deerhome) were almost always diagnosed as "mentally defective," their consent (or that of their next of kin) was not required. The Board could simply record *"passed clear"* on its documents and recommend sterilization. Thus, patient consent was required for only 1% of all cases "presented and passed" at PTS, compared to 59% of the cases "presented and passed" at Alberta Hospital (Ponoka). Since the Eugenics Board had given the institutions the option not to discuss the operation with a patient (or her/his family), in some cases such discussion probably never took place.

Almost all (89%) individuals "presented and passed" *without* any consent requirements attached to the decision were ultimately sterilized (91% of women and 86% of men). In stark contrast, sterilization took place in only 15% of the cases where "patient consent" alone *was* a requirement (21% of women and 9% of men). If the consent of both the patient and some other person was required, the probability of sterilization was between 40% and 60%, depending on the conditions.

GROUPS TARGETED BY THE ALBERTA EUGENICS BOARD

Gender

After a slow start, the Board's activity peaked between 1934 and 1939. A second peak occurred in the late 1950s when, because of its rapid expansion, PTS became a primary "feeder" institution. With a few exceptions (particularly in the 1930s), more women than men appeared in front of the Board. Over the decades, 2203 men (46%) and 2582 women (54%) were presented.

According to Census data, 55% of the Alberta population was male in 1931. The gender distribution of the Alberta population slowly shifted in the following decades (54% male in 1941, 52% in 1951 and 1961, 51% in 1971), but women never outnumbered men. Consequently, the larger number of women presented to the Board does not mirror the gender distribution in the provincial population.

Annual Public Health Reports show that the proportion of female residents in the two provincial mental hospitals and PTS varied between 31% and 42% from 1931 to 1970. Hence, gender-biased decisions (to present an individual to the Board) within these institutions, rather than a larger proportion of female residents, accounted for the more frequent presentation of women to the Eugenics Board. Not only were women more likely to be presented to the Board but, once presented, they were also more likely to be sterilized.

Sixty-four percent of all women ever presented were sterilized, compared to 54% of all men presented. This gender imbalance existed even though, as noted above, women presented to the Board were less likely to be diagnosed as mentally defective and, consequently, somewhat more likely to have a consent requirement attached to their sterilization decision. It appears that, following a Board decision, medical and social work professionals in the province's mental health system were considerably more effective at convincing (or coercing) women into accepting sterilization.

This two-stage gender bias (more likely to be presented, and more likely to be sterilized, once presented) meant that 58% of the 2834 individuals eventually sterilized were women (N = 1651). In most years, more women than men were sterilized.

Age

Using birth date information from our "1 in 5" database, we estimate that 12% of all cases ever presented to the Eugenics Board involved children (under 15 years old). Another 27% were teenagers age 15 to 19, and 17% were young adults age 20 to 24. The remainder (44%) were 25 and older. Census data for the period 1921 to 1971 reveal that children (under 15) accounted for 29% to 36% of the total provincial population during this era. Thus, children were underrepresented among patients presented to the Board. Older Albertans (40 and older) were also under-represented, making up only 5% of the presentations but between 22% and 31% of the total population.

Teenagers represented less than 10% of the provincial population, but constituted 27% of the cases presented to the Board. Young adults also accounted for less than 10% of the population, but 17% of all cases presented. As we have already observed, the Provincial Training School (PTS) in Red Deer was responsible for presenting most of these young people. In virtually all these cases, patient consent was not

PART 3

required. Consequently, 38% of all Albertans sterilized were teenagers.

Race and Ethnicity

Information in the "1 in 5" database allowed us to categorize individuals presented to the Board as: "Canadian" (11%); Anglo-Saxon (31%); French (6%); West European (18%); East European (19%); Aboriginal (6%); and Other/Not known (9%). Census reports from the era did not use a "Canadian" category so we combined this group with Anglo-Saxons. This large group was under-represented among patients presented, until the 1960s. For example, in the 1930s, Anglo-Saxon/Canadian patients made up 43% of the individuals presented, while the 1936 Census showed 52% of Albertans with Anglo-Saxon origins. Individuals of Western European origin (e.g., German, Norwegian, Italian) were also under-represented, accounting for 18% of presentations but 21% to 28% of the provincial population during the years the Board was operating.

In contrast, Eastern Europeans (e.g., Ukrainian, Polish, Russian) were marginally over-represented (19% of cases presented, but never more than 17% of the population). Most noticeably overrepresented were Aboriginals (identified as "Indian," "Metis," "halfbreed," "treaty" and "Eskimo"). While the province's Aboriginal population hovered between 2% and 3% of the total over the decades in question, Aboriginals made up 6% of all cases presented.

We estimate that 55% of all patients presented, and the same proportion of Anglo-Saxon/Canadian patients, were diagnosed as "mentally defective." Both Western and Eastern European patients were less likely to receive such diagnoses (46% and 44%, respectively), but 77% of Aboriginal patients did. As a result, patient consent was required in only 17% of the Aboriginal cases, compared to 49% of Eastern European cases, 44% of Western European cases, and 38% of Anglo-Saxon/Canadian patients. As a result, 74% of all Aboriginals presented to the Board were eventually sterilized (compared to 60%

of all patients presented). In contrast, because patient consent was so often required, less than half (47%) of both Eastern and Western European patients were eventually sterilized.

Why So Long?

The unique political history and culture of this western Canadian province provides part of the answer. Both the United Farmers of Alberta and the Social Credit regime that followed the UFA were (at least in their early years) radical populist parties that capitalized on widespread anti-Eastern (Canada) sentiments and traded on a strong "we'll show you we can do it on our own" image (Finkel 1989: 22). Albertans were rugged and strong-minded, and willing to experiment with new political, economic (i.e., Social Credit), and social ideas.

Charismatic leadership was also part of the explanation. The eugenics campaign in Alberta was promoted by highly influential middle-class social reformers such as Judge Emily Murphy and Nellie McClung and, during the first decades of Social Credit rule, by highly popular political leaders. In fact, the province exhibited an unusual degree of overlap between political and religious elites. William Aberhart, leader of the Social Credit Party and Premier, was a fundamentalist religious leader who maintained a loyal following via an extremely popular weekly religious radio program (Finkel 1989). His successor, Ernest Manning, also continued this tradition with his Sunday morning "Back to the Bible Hour" radio broadcast. With political and religious leadership intertwined, it was unlikely that active opposition to government social programs, including involuntary sterilization, would emerge in the province.

Equally important was the relative weakness of the Roman Catholic Church in Alberta, a province with a more prominent Protestant presence than, for example, Ontario (Dowbiggin 1997: 187), Manitoba, and, particularly, Quebec. Alberta politicians were not particularly beholden to the Catholic church hierarchy which was strongly opposed to any form of birth control including sterilization.

In Alberta, with the blessing of an authoritarian provincial government that relied heavily on experts and took little notice of public criticism, and in the absence of strong opposition from the Catholic church, this medical empire-building included a highly efficient sterilization bureaucracy that linked the Eugenics Board with a series of compliant "feeder" institutions. One of these institutions in particular—the Provincial Training School (PTS) in Red Deer—kept this bureaucratic machine running until the early 1970s.

While the eugenics movement had been discredited, both morally and scientifically, by mid-20th century, in Alberta public criticism was muted, if it existed at all. To some extent, this silence simply reflected the absence of criticism of the Social Credit government in general. However, the oil boom that began in 1947 also meant that most Albertans were prospering and, consequently, disinclined to criticize the government. Furthermore, many residents of the province were recent arrivals and probably knew little, if anything, about the provincial mental health system, including the Eugenics Board.

Prosperity and economic growth, and an almost non-existent opposition, allowed the Social Credit government to maintain power for an unusually long time. The eugenics bureaucracy that its experts had constructed continued to operate, quietly and efficiently within the larger and growing mental health system. Secure in their power and in their beliefs, and receiving little attention, let alone criticism, the doctors, psychiatrists, and social workers on the Eugenics Board and in the "feeder" institutions (especially PTS) continued sterilizing Albertans until, finally, in 1972, a change in government put an end to the system and the practice.

REFERENCES

Baragar, C. A., Geo. A. Davidson, W. J. McAlister and D. L. McCullough. 1935. "Sexual Sterilization: Four Years Experience in Alberta." *American Journal of Psychiatry.* Vol. 91(2): 897–923.

Cairney, Richard. 1996. "'Democracy Was Never Intended for Degenerates': Alberta's Flirtation with Eugenics Comes Back to Haunt It." *Canadian Medical Association Journal.* September 15, 155 (6).

Caulfield, Timothy and Gerald Robertson. 1996. "Eugenic Policies in Alberta: From the Systematic to the Systemic?" *Alberta Law Review.* Vol. XXXV, No. 1. 59–79.

Chapman, Terry. 1977. "The early eugenics movement in Western Canada." *Alberta History.* 25: 9–12.

Christian, Timothy J. 1974. *The Mentally Ill and Human Rights in Alberta: A Study of the Alberta Sexual Sterilization Act.* Edmonton, Alberta: Faculty of Law, University of Alberta. Unpublished research report.

Dowbiggin, Ian Robert. 1997. *Keeping America Sane: Psychiatry and Eugenics in the United States and Canada, 1880–1940.* Ithaca and London: Cornell University Press.

Ladd-Taylor, Molly. 1997. "Saving Babies and Sterilizing Mothers: Eugenics and Welfare Politics in the Interwar United States." *Social Politics.* Spring. 136–153.

Larson, Edward J. 1995. *Sex, Race, and Science: Eugenics in the Deep South.* Baltimore: Johns Hopkins University Press.

McLaren, Angus. 1990. *Our Own Master Race: Eugenics in Canada, 1885–1945.* Toronto: McClelland & Stewart Inc.

Muir v. Her Majesty the Queen. 1995. Trial Exhibits.

Park, Deborah C. and John P. Radford. 1998. "From the Case Files: Reconstructing a history of involuntary sterilization." *Disability and Society.* Vol. 13, No. 3 317–342.

Paul, Diane B. 1995. *Controlling Human Heredity: 1865 to the Present.* New Jersey: Humanities Press International, Inc.

Proctor, R. 1988. *Racial Hygiene: Medicine Under the Nazis.* Cambridge, MA: Harvard University Press.

Radford, John P. 1994. "Response and Rejoinder: Eugenics and the Asylum." *Journal of Historical Sociology.* Vol. 7 No. 4 December. 462–473.

Rafter, Nicole Hahn. 1992. "Claims-Making and Socio-Cultural Context in the First U.S. Eugenics Campaign." *Social Problems.* 39: 17–34.

Reilly, Philip. 1991. *The Surgical Solution: A History of Involuntary Sterilization In the United States.* Baltimore and London. The Johns Hopkins University Press.

Critical Thinking Questions

1. How does the Eugenics Movement compare and contrast with the Tuskegee Syphilis Experiment (Chapter 6)? Specifically, what are the similarities and differences between the two, and what lessons can be learned overall?

2. Reproductive and genetics technologies, such as prenatal screening, are commonplace and often inform selective abortions. Many disability activists refer to selective abortion as a modern form of eugenics. Do you agree or disagree?

Chapter 8

Body Ritual among the Nacirema

HORACE MINER

This particular selection is widely reprinted in sociology readers, but it is one for which a prologue would only spoil the fun. Let us say only that one of the things Miner wanted to do was
to demonstrate that much of what strikes us as "exotic" in anthropological accounts of other
cultures might appear quite differently to the people involved.

1. Why did the author take the time to describe the Nacirema in such great detail?

PART 4

The anthropologist has become so familiar with the diversity of ways in which different people behave in similar situations that he is not apt to be surprised by even the most exotic customs. In fact, if all of the logically possible combinations of behavior have not been found somewhere in the world, he is apt to suspect that they must be present in some yet undescribed tribe. In this light, the magical beliefs and practices of the Nacirema present such unusual aspects that it seems desirable to describe them as an example of the extremes to which human behavior can go.

The Nacirema are a North American group living in the territory between the Canadian Cree, the Yaqui and Tarahumare of Mexico, and the Carib and Arawak of the Antilles. Little is known of their origin, although tradition states that they came from the east. According to Nacirema mythology, their nation was originated by a culture hero, Notgnihsaw, who is otherwise known for two great feats of strength—the throwing of a piece of wampum across the river Pa-To-Mac and chopping down of a cherry tree in which the Spirit of Truth resided.

While much of the people's time is devoted to economic pursuits, a large part of the fruits of these labors and a considerable portion of the day are spent in ritual activity. The focus of this activity is the human body, the appearance and health of which loom as a dominant concern in the ethos of the people. While such a concern is certainly not unusual, its ceremonial aspects and associated philosophy are unique.

The fundamental belief underlying the whole system appears to be that the human body is ugly and that its natural tendency is to debility and disease. Incarcerated in such a body, man's only hope is to avert these characteristics through the use of ritual and ceremony. Every household has one or more shrines devoted to this purpose. The more powerful individuals in the society have several shrines in their houses and, in fact, the opulence of a house is often referred to in terms of the number of such ritual centers it possesses. Most houses are of wattle and daub construction, but the shrine rooms of the more wealthy are walled with stone. Poorer families imitate the rich by applying pottery plaques to their shrine walls.

Source: Miner, Horace. "Body Ritual among Nacirema." *American Anthropologist* 58/3, (June 1956): 503–507. By permission of Blackwell Publishing, a company of John Wiley & Sons, Inc.

While each family has at least one such shrine, the rituals associated with it are not family ceremonies but are private and secret. The rites are normally only discussed with children, and then only during the period when they are being initiated into these mysteries. I was able, however, to establish sufficient rapport with the natives to examine these shrines and to have the rituals described to me.

The focal point of the shrine is a box or chest which is built into the wall. In this chest are kept the many charms and magical potions without which no native believes he could live. These preparations are secured from a variety of specialized practitioners. The most powerful of these are the medicine men, whose assistance must be rewarded with substantial gifts. However, the medicine men do not provide the curative potions for their clients, but decide what the ingredients should be and then write them down in an ancient and secret language. This writing is understood only by the medicine men and by the herbalists who, for another gift, provide the required charm.

The charm is not disposed of after it has served its purpose, but is placed in the charm-box of the household shrine. As these magical materials are specific for certain ills, and the real or imagined maladies of the people are many, the charm-box is usually full to overflowing. The magical packets are so numerous that people forget what their purposes were and fear to use them again. While the natives are very vague on this point, we can only assume that the idea in retaining all the old magical materials is that their presence in the charm-box, before which the body rituals are conducted, will in some way protect the worshiper.

Beneath the charm-box is a small font. Each day every member of the family, in succession, enters the shrine room, bows his head before the charm-box, mingles different sorts of holy water in the font, and proceeds with a brief rite of ablution. The holy waters are secured from the Water Temple of the community, where the priests conduct elaborate ceremonies to make the liquid ritually pure.

In the hierarchy of magical practitioners, and below the medicine men in prestige, are specialists whose designation is best translated as "holy-mouth-men." The Nacirema have an almost pathological horror of and fascination with the mouth, the condition of which is believed to have a supernatural influence on all social relationships. Were it not for the rituals of the mouth, they believe that their teeth would fall out, their gums bleed, their jaws shrink, their friends desert them, and their lovers reject them. They also believe that a strong relationship exists between oral and moral characteristics. For example, there is a ritual ablution of the mouth for children which is supposed to improve their moral fiber.

The daily body ritual performed by everyone includes a mouth-rite. Despite the fact that these people are so punctilious about care of the mouth, this rite involves a practice which strikes the uninitiated stranger as revolting. It was reported to me that the ritual consists of inserting a small bundle of hog hairs into the mouth, along with certain magical powders, and then moving the bundle in a highly formalized series of gestures.

In addition to the private mouth-rite, the people seek out a holy-mouth-man once or twice a year. These practitioners have an impressive set of paraphernalia, consisting of a variety of augers, awls, probes, and prods. The use of these items in the exorcism of the evils of the mouth involves almost unbelievable ritual torture of the client. The holy-mouth-man opens the client's mouth and, using the above mentioned tools, enlarges any holes which decay may have created in the teeth. Magical materials are put into these holes. If there are no naturally occurring holes in the teeth, large sections of one or more teeth are gouged out so that the supernatural substance can be applied. In the client's view, the purpose of these ministrations is to arrest decay and to draw friends. The extremely sacred and traditional character of the rite is evident in the fact that the natives return to the holy-mouth-men year after year, despite the fact that their teeth continue to decay.

It is to be hoped that, when a thorough study of the Nacirema is made, there will be careful inquiry into the personality structure of these people. One has but to watch the gleam in the eye of a holy-mouth-man, as he jabs an awl into an exposed nerve, to suspect that a certain amount of sadism is involved. If this can be established, a very interesting pattern emerges, for most of the population shows definite masochistic tendencies. It was to these that Professor Linton referred in discussing a distinctive part of the daily body ritual which is performed only by men. This part of the rite includes scraping and lacerating the surface of the face with a sharp instrument. Special women's rites are performed only four times during each lunar month, but what they lack in frequency is made up in barbarity. As part of this ceremony, women bake their heads in small ovens for about an hour. The theoretically interesting point is that what seems to be a preponderantly masochistic people have developed sadistic specialists.

The medicine men have an imposing temple, or *latipso*, in every community of any size. The more elaborate ceremonies required to treat very sick patients can only be performed at this temple. These ceremonies involve not only the thaumaturge but a permanent group of vestal maidens who move sedately about the temple chambers in distinctive costume and headdress.

The *latipso* ceremonies are so harsh that it is phenomenal that a fair proportion of the really sick natives who enter the temple ever recover. Small children whose indoctrination is still incomplete have been known to resist attempts to take them to the temple because "that is where you go to die." Despite this fact, sick adults are not only willing but eager to undergo the protracted ritual purification, if they can afford to do so. No matter how ill the supplicant or how grave the emergency, the guardians of many temples will not admit a client if he cannot give a rich gift to the custodian. Even after one has gained and survived the ceremonies, the guardians will not permit the neophyte to leave until he makes still another gift.

The supplicant entering the temple is first stripped of all his or her clothes. In everyday life the Nacirema avoids exposure of his body and its natural functions. Bathing and excretory acts are performed only in the secrecy of the household shrine, where they are ritualized as part of the body-rites. Psychological shock results from the fact that body secrecy is suddenly lost upon entry into the *latipso*. A man, whose own wife has never seen him in an excretory act, suddenly finds himself naked and assisted by a vestal maiden while he performs his natural functions into a sacred vessel. This sort of ceremonial treatment is necessitated by the fact that the excreta are used by a diviner to ascertain the course and nature of the client's sickness. Female clients, on the other hand, find their naked bodies are subjected to the scrutiny, manipulation and prodding of the medicine men.

Few supplicants in the temple are well enough to do anything but lie on their hard beds. The daily ceremonies, like the rites of the holy-mouth-men, involve discomfort and torture. With ritual precision, the vestals awaken their miserable charges each dawn and roll them about on their beds of pain while performing ablutions, in the formal movements of which the maidens are highly trained. At other times they insert magic wands in the supplicant's mouth or force him to eat substances which are supposed to be healing. From time to time the medicine men come to their clients and jab magically treated needles into their flesh. The fact that these temple ceremonies may not cure, and may even kill the neophyte, in no way decreases the people's faith in the medicine men.

There remains one other kind of practitioner, known as a "listener." This witchdoctor has the power to exorcise the devils that lodge in the heads of people who have been bewitched.

The Nacirema believe that parents bewitch their own children. Mothers are particularly suspected of putting a curse on children while teaching them the secret body rituals. The counter-magic of the witchdoctor is unusual in its lack of ritual. The patient simply tells the "listener" all his troubles and fears, beginning with the earliest difficulties he can remember. The memory displayed by the Nacirema in these exorcism sessions is truly remarkable. It is not uncommon for the patient to bemoan the rejection he felt upon being weaned as a babe, and a few individuals even see their troubles going back to the traumatic effects of their own birth.

In conclusion, mention must be made of certain practices which have their base in native esthetics but which depend upon the pervasive aversion to the natural body and its functions. There are ritual fasts to make fat people thin and ceremonial feasts to make thin people fat. Still other rites are used to make women's breasts larger if they are small, and smaller if they are large. General dissatisfaction with breast shape is symbolized in the fact that the ideal form is virtually outside the range of human variation. A few women afflicted with almost inhuman hypermammary development are so idolized that they make a handsome living by simply going from village to village and permitting the natives to stare at them for a fee.

Our review of the ritual life of the Nacirema has certainly shown them to be a magic-ridden people. It is hard to understand how they have managed to exist so long under the burdens which they have imposed upon themselves. But even such exotic customs as these take on real meaning when they are viewed with the insight provided by Malinowski when he wrote (1948:70):

> Looking from far and above, from our high places of safety in the developed civilization, it is easy to see all the crudity and irrelevance of magic. But without its power and guidance early man could not have mastered his practical difficulties as he has done, nor could man have advanced to the higher stages of civilization.

REFERENCES

Linton, Ralph. 1936. *The Study of Man.* New York, D. Appleton-Century Co.

Malinowski, Bronislaw. 1948. *Magic, Science, and Religion.* Glencoe, The Free Press.

Critical Thinking Questions

1. As sociologists, what lessons can we take away from this article?
2. Does this article influence how you would report your research findings? Or how you will read other research findings?

Chapter 9

Cultural Aspects of Disability

JULIENE G. LIPSON AND JUDITH G. ROGERS[1]

Whether we as Westerners are looking at people's behaviours and activities in other countries or right here, we very seldom take the time to understand whether their culture impacts their practices. This article explores the cultural and social issues related to disability. The two authors are social scientists with disabilities of their own, and they set out to try and understand the different subcultures surrounding disability and to explain to the reader how to understand them as well. They argue that non-disabled people don't see how the disabled can create many different subcultures and that this is not so different from newcomers to Western countries who have very definite shared cultural understandings.

1. What is a subculture, and why are the authors claiming people with disabilities have experiences that create them?

PART 4

People with disabilities are a minority group by virtue of restricted access to education, full employment, and other resources as people with disabilities are not simply disabled; they are disabled within a specific culture that determines the meaning of their experiences. In other words, if the environment were adapted to the varying capacities of all persons, definitions of disability would be very different than those to which we are accustomed. However, "to date almost all research on disabled men and women seems to assume the irrelevance of gender, race, ethnicity, sexual orientation, or social class. Having a disability presumably eclipses these dimensions of social experience" (Fine & Asch, 1988, p. 3).

Ingstad and Whyte (1995) stated that the concept of disability itself must be viewed in cultural context. Some cultures recognize blind people, lame people, and "slow" people but do not lump them together in a general category of disability.

The concepts of disability, handicap, and rehabilitation were generated in Europe and North America, which prize autonomy and do not prize dependence. Group-oriented cultures that value interdependence over independence may simply take for granted that people with disabilities are helped by family or community members and not stigmatized by their dependence. Based on cultural relativism, which assumes that phenomena must be understood within their relevant cultural contexts, the disadvantage posed by a disability depends on the capacities seen as most important in a particular cultural context.

Variations in type, severity, and age of onset of disabilities make it difficult to talk about a culture of disability. Disabilities are inherited, congenital, and/or acquired, and they contribute to an enormous range of life experiences in sociocultural and economic contexts. Within each type of disability—developmental, psychiatric, or physical—as well as within each condition, there is also a range of experiences. For example, the identity and experiences of a person who acquired a physical disability as an adult are very different from those of someone who was born with her disability and did not experience a radical change in her body and identity.

A source of variation is the subculture into which an individual is socialized. Many people with congenital or early onset disabilities are cut off from mainstream society so that they are not primarily socialized within the mainstream culture.

Deaf culture is a strong subculture in which people share language, perspectives, mores, and behaviors, many of them since infancy or early childhood.

Within any single condition, there is a range of severity that shapes both the person's life and others' responses to him. Another source of variation is the stability or changeability of the condition, such as spinal cord injury versus a disabling chronic illness such as multiple sclerosis. People with unstable conditions experience remissions, exacerbations, and different rates of decline. Individuals also vary in whether their friends/reference groups are disabled or not and whether they identify with the pan-disability subculture or a specific disability.

Despite these caveats, it is useful to describe some subculture issues as well as the social context in which disability is experienced, such as stigma and marginalization.

SUBCULTURAL ISSUES

The complex societies of North America are composed of subcultures in which cultural rules are learned and transmitted, providing a template for personal and social interaction. Individuals who share a subculture usually share a locality, language, values, and patterns of interactions that distinguish them from other equally distinctive culture groups. Such subcultures share to a lesser or greater extent the values and lifestyle of the dominant society but also maintain their own distinctive mores and lifestyle.

Maintenance of these differences may be by choice—for example, an immigrant group's efforts to maintain a mother tongue or cuisine—or imposed on the group—for example, lack of power or money that excludes a group from participating in the mainstream.

[T]he Harris Poll ("Economic Life and Disability," 1999) found that people with disabilities were some 2 1/2 times less likely than those without disabilities to be employed. "One third (34%) of adults with disabilities live in a household with a poverty-level annual income."

Although there are a number of disability subcultures, the commonalities shared by people with disabilities are poverty and marginalization by the dominant society. Longmore (1987) noted that historical research shows that across social settings and disabilities, people with disabilities have been subjected to a common experience of social oppression.

Maintaining a subculture is dependent on such factors as communication, a sufficient number of people with similar experiences, community, social and physical structures, and visibility versus invisibility. In our electronic age, communication can be developed and maintained in the absence of frequent interactions or face-to-face or telephone communication.

For the most part, however, visibility and face-to-face interaction facilitate both a subculture and the individual's feeling part of it. People who live in urban areas in which many people with disabilities are visible and active have a vastly different experience than those who live in rural areas or small towns where few people with disabilities are visible.

The existence and strength of disability subcultures are influenced by community, social, organizational, and environmental structures that support people with disabilities. For example, in Berkeley, where the independent living movement originated, vigorous political action over many years and excellent agencies facilitate mainstream participation of many people with disabilities.

Structures also include organizations that focus on a specific disability or disease such as United Cerebral Palsy or the Multiple Sclerosis Association. Such organizations support research, are based on the medical model, and may or may not include support groups. Independent support groups are formed by people with the same or similar disability. Sharing similar experiences may be critical for maintaining a subculture. Support groups and organizations are particularly effective in socializing someone who is newly disabled, helping the person adjust his or her identity to better match the current condition and learn to cope with it.

Another structure is the physical environment. Some cities with a strong independent living movement made substantial progress in making public buildings accessible Some buildings and even the occasional conference are designated fragrance free. Selected street corners have curb cuts for wheelchairs, and traffic signals chirp or blink in addition to simply going from red to green. Motorized wheelchairs and scooters on the street demonstrate the visibility of people with disabilities in these cities.

Disability subcultures are also shaped by whether the disability is visible or invisible. "The Distribution of Disability" (1999) pointed out that "it is a common perception that the so-called "visible disabilities," like wheelchair use and visual disabilities, dominate the demographics of disability [but] . . . the "invisible disabilities" are far more prominent. It appears to us that people with visible disabilities are accorded more empathy and privileges than those with invisible disabilities, especially in cities with strong independent living movements. However, they also experience more open prejudice. The range of responses to people with visible disabilities is much wider than to those with invisible disabilities.

They may elicit either negative or empathic responses only when they reveal their disabilities through some symbol such as a piece of equipment. Another example is one of Lipson's (2000) environmentally ill interviewees:

> When I go outside, I use a mask and oxygen, occasionally I use a wheelchair. People respond differently to these things. The mask scares them, they think I have something contagious, they stay away. People relate to people in a wheelchair in a friendly way. With oxygen, it's more like "You poor thing, you're sick." I'd rather be scary than pitied. . . . Sometimes I say something, many times I just don't have the energy to bother.

However, people with visible disabilities who experience daily open prejudice often feel that having a hidden disability engenders privileges. In a sense, it may be similar to ethnic minority peoples' perceptions of the situations of those in a different group. For example, some African Americans, who are visible, have difficulty understanding the impact of anti-Semitism because most Jews are White. However, in a community that values ethnic diversity, it may be easier to be part of a racial/ethnic minority than it is to be disabled—the general public is not sensitized to the social dilemmas of people with disabilities.

[A] colleague described an incident in which she and her middle-aged friend who has a cardiac disability parked in a handicapped zone. They were getting ready to put up the blue placard when an elderly woman began shouting at them for parking there. Some of Lipson's interviewees avoid wearing a mask even when it would be helpful because they do not want to be seen as weird or crazy; others wear it to signal that they are not safe in situations in which people are wearing fragrances or are smoking.

Finally, there is the issue of language. Language reflects personal and societal attitudes and also categorizes people in a way that may lead to stereotyping. An example is an agency's radio commercial soliciting donations of old cars to help 'the blind' to be more independent. Some people with disabilities resent being

PART 4

so categorized and dislike being disregarded as individuals. An example is the objection to being called a disabled person rather than a person with a disability because the first phrase implies that the disability is the entire person. However, identity is an individual matter.

Another language example occurred in a San Francisco Health Department hearing in which a disability advocate objected strongly to a social worker's use of the phrase wheel chair bound; she said, "We are not bound to our wheel chairs!" Many people with disabilities reject politically correct euphemisms usually coined by nondisabled people—handi-capable, differently-abled, and physically challenged are seen as trivializing and demeaning. On the other hand, in the early days of the independent living movement, some people with disabilities used such insider terms as crip or gimp to symbolize their identity and solidarity, similar to the use of queer among some gays and lesbians. Others, however, found such terms highly offensive. The issue, however, is that dissatisfaction with politically correct language mirrors what happens in the broader society. If one is marginalized and does not feel accepted, there are few satisfying words to describe what one is.

TYPES OF DISABILITY STRUCTURES

Two general types of disability subcultures are pan-disability activist groups and those based on a specific type of disability such as a disabling chronic disease or a specific type of injury (e.g., cerebral palsy). Disability activists, who are often associated with independent living centers, are a very strong pan-disability subculture. Historically, the independent living movement developed in opposition to organizations that focus on particular disabilities or diseases because they are based on the medical model. Examples of norms and values distinct from those in mainstream society are strong advocacy for equal access to buildings, jobs, and education;

resistance to being pitied, defined, or controlled by medical/rehabilitation professionals and the public; and embracing disability as a normal and acceptable way of being. The public message that it is fine to be disabled; you should be happy that you are disabled is demonstrated in the unacceptability of sharing one's own dissatisfaction or depression with the general public or with other disabled people. People within this subculture do not accept Christopher Reeves as a spokesperson because of his assertion that he wants to walk again; they see this as ludicrous and explain that he has not adjusted to his disability.

A current initiative developed in this subculture is "Not Dead Yet." Advocates are vociferously opposed to Dr. Jack Kevorkian's activities, asserting that most people he has helped to die are disabled and depressed. Depression is viewed as posing an attitudinal barrier. It is seen as an illustration of ethnocentrism among able-bodied people who essentially cannot see beyond their own fears: "You poor dear, you can't do anything, I wouldn't want to live that way. If I were you, I'd want to kill myself." This initiative points out that the public cannot imagine that people have accommodated to their disabilities. They do not recognize that by nature, human beings are able to accommodate to numerous difficulties and tragedies.

DISABILITY IN SOCIAL CONTEXT

Many of the problems experienced by people with disabilities are the overlay of stigma and bias from nondisabled people; in some cases, such attitudinal barriers create more problems than the disabilities themselves. People with disabilities constitute a marginalized minority group socially, economically, occupationally, and educationally. For example, a comment that it is 'outrageous' for a well-known gourmet restaurant to be asked to build a ramp was made to one of the authors. The argument is 'you folks are too expensive,' and the implication is that 'you should just settle for second best.' There is little recognition that the choice to make a private establishment more accessible can benefit everyone.

Public discourse and policy discussions on various issues can also imply bias and inspire fear in people with disabilities. An example is the period during which the U.S. Congress was discussing welfare reform, with some representatives advocating cutting off funds to 'welfare moms who have too many babies.' Some people with disabilities felt threatened although they were not targeted for welfare reform because they identified with women on public assistance and interpreted this rhetoric to mean that certain kinds of people should not be parents, a reminder of the eugenics movement.

We heard other examples in our study of pregnancy and disability such as women being confronted by complete strangers in public places. Caitlin told a typical story:

> Like I get on the bus, pull my chair back, with the baby on the front of me, and a lady says 'Are you okay? That's your baby? Oh my God! How could you?' I ask, 'Do you have kids?' "Yeah, three." "Well, how did you have a baby?" The bus driver is laughing. She said, "Well, how do you take care of it?" "Well, how do you take care of yours?" "Well, I can do it, I'm ablebodied." I say, "I can do it too, I'm disabled.

This bias makes it more difficult to engage in regular life activities, for example, we interviewed women who wanted to be parents despite such bias. Michelle "wanted to have a child so I could be part of the flow of history." Arlene said, "having a baby made me less handicapped because I was able to fulfill one of the female roles in society and I was really rewarded for it." Heather was "proving [that she] was as independent and self-reliant as anyone." Faith "loved being associated with the nondisabled population," adding that the shared concerns of parenthood offered a basis for friendship with nondisabled people.

However, the social pressures on disabled parents can be enormous. One aspect is increased scrutiny by health and social service providers. One woman informed us that:

> My biggest fear is CPS [Child Protective Services]. They can come at any time, and if my next door neighbor sees something out of the normal, if it doesn't look right how I carry her. . . . We have people from three different agencies helping us, a lot of eyes, so we have to be real careful about things.

Finally, just as there is no one disability subculture, attitudes of nondisabled people also vary considerably. It may be that marginalized groups who face discrimination hold fewer or different biases. For example, Rogers' van broke down in a poverty-stricken urban neighborhood. Homeless people in the area did not hesitate to ask her for spare change, perhaps because her motorized wheelchair symbolized having sufficient economic resources.

CONCLUSIONS

We believe that conceptions of culturally competent care must be broadened to include disability. People with disabilities are a marginalized group that face considerable bias and attitudinal barriers both in the general public and from health care providers. Because of this, disability activists often express hostility toward the health care system, especially because health care providers attempt to medicalize every aspect of the situations of people with disabilities. Health care providers rarely recognize the social nature of and lack of effort to remedy the environment that is at the basis of many problems experienced by people with disabilities.

We believe that culturally competent care must include efforts to work with people with disabilities from their own point of view. This is the same as attempting to understand the culture and values of patients from cultural backgrounds different from our own.

NOTE

1. Many of our examples involve pregnancy/birth/
parenting with a disability. Lipson first began
studying disability in 1996 when she joined Rogers
in the study of physically disabled women's experiences of health care during pregnancy, birth,
and the postpartum period. She had little previously knowledge of disability, but she developed
multiple chemical sensitivity in 1997 and began
ethnographic research on this condition. Rogers
sustained a birth injury and grew up with mild
cerebral palsy. She is an occupational therapist at
Through the Looking Glass, the National Resource
Center for Parents with Disabilities. After birthing
her two children, she began the interviews that led
to her book on pregnancy and birth among women
with physical disabilities. She is currently writing
the second edition.

REFERENCES

Davis, L. (1997). Introduction. In L. Davis (Ed.), *The
disability studies reader* (pp. 1–6). New York:
Routledge.

The distribution of disability. (1999). Disability agenda:
A quarterly publication of the National Organization
on Disability [On-line], 3(4). Available: http://www.
nod.org/attitudes.html#snapshot.

Economic life and disability. (1999). Disability agenda:
A quarterly publication of the National Organization
on Disability [On-line], 2(3). Available: http://www.
nod.org/agendaarchive.html.

Fine, M., & Asch, A. (Eds.). (1988). *Women with disabilities. Essays in psychology, culture and politics.*
Philadelphia: Temple University Press.

Ingstad, B., & Whyte, S. R. (1995). *Disability and culture.*
Berkeley, CA: University of California Press.

Kinder, D. C. (1996). The Americans with Disabilities
Act: A brief overview [On-line]. Available: http://
janweb.icdi.wvu.edu/kinder/overview.htm.

Kirshbaum, M. (1999). Message from the director
(Through the Looking Glass fundraising news-
letter). Berkeley, CA: Author.

Lipson, J. (1999). Cross-cultural nursing: The cultural
perspective. *Journal of Transcultural Nursing,*
10, 6.

Lipson, J. (2000). Self-care and symptom management in multiple chemical sensitivity sufferers.
Manuscript submitted for publication.

Lipson, J., & Rogers, J. (2000). Pregnancy, birth and
disability: Women's health care experiences.
Health Care for Women International, 21, 11–26.

Longmore, P. (1987). Elizabeth Bouvia: Assisted suicide
and social prejudice. *Issues in Law and Medicine,*
3, 141–168.

Meleis, A. I., Isenberg, M., Koerner, J., & Stern, P.
(1995). *Diversity, marginalization, and culturally-
competent health care: Issues in knowledge
development.* Washington, DC: American Academy
of Nursing. Downloaded from tcn.sagepub.com at
Univ of Western Ontario on December 26, 2011.

National Organization on Disability/Louis Harris and
Associates. (1998).

NOD/Harris 1998 survey of Americans with disabilities
[On-line]. Available: http://www.nod.org.

Olkin, R. (1999). *What psychotherapists should know
about disability.* New York: Guilford.

Rogers, J., & Matsumura, M. (1991). *Mother to be: A
guide to pregnancy and birth for women with disabilities.* New York: Demos Publications.

Treloar, L. (1999). People with disabilities—the same
but different: Implications for health care practice.
Journal of Transcultural Nursing, 10, 358–364.

Critical Thinking Questions

1. Why is living with disability the same as having a minority culture?
2. Is it reasonable to claim that there are many subcultures for people with disabilities?
3. What are the similarities/parallels between visible minorities and people with disabilities from a sociological perspective? What are the differences?
4. Why do some people with visible or evident disabilities say that those with non-visible disabilities experience a very different life than they do?
5. What does it mean to be culturally considerate to disabled people?
6. How has the article changed your views about disability?

Chapter 10
Why Do People Get Tattoos?

MILIANN KANG AND KATHERINE JONES

What is particularly interesting about tattooing from a sociological point of view is that, in a reasonably short amount of time, tattooing has transformed from being highly **taboo** to being more socially acceptable. Of course, while the level of acceptance differs from person to person, particularly depending on gender, age, ethnicity, and class, tattoos have become increasingly mainstream. This article will highlight how different groups of individuals have reappropriated tattoos and why they have done so.

1. How have the perceptions of tattooing changed over time?
2. Are tattoos still taboo?

PART 4

As increasingly diverse groups of people get tattoos, popular perceptions are often out of synch with the individual meanings behind them.

Who gets tattoos, and why? A self-described "24-year-old, insecure female who isn't a perfect, thin, beautiful supermodel" writes in the *Body Modification* e-zine that her Pegasus tattoo has helped her overcome hatred of her body. "It is rearing up on its hind legs with its wings spread like it's about to take off, much like the way I want to break free of my self doubt and start loving me for me." The same e-zine carries an account of an operations manager at a Borders Books and Café who says about hiring tattooed employees, "We look for it. It makes things more interesting and more fun." While these individuals give varied and multilayered meanings to their own and other's tattoos, their personal assertions are sometimes at odds with the pervasive popular interpretations of tattoos as signs of rebellion or faddishness.

The growing number of enthusiasts exhibit a broad array of tattooing practices, from a discreet flower on the hip to full body and facial tattoos. According to a 2003 survey by Scripps Howard News Service and Ohio State University, 15 percent of the U.S. adult population has tat-toos, and the figure rises to 28 percent for adults younger than 25. In addition, 88 percent of those interviewed said they know at least one person who has a tattoo. According to *U.S. News and World Report*, tattooing was the sixth fastest-growing retail business in 1997. What accounts for the rising popularity and visibility of tattoos?

Most tattooed people see their tattoos as unique aspects of themselves, but sociologists who study tattooing focus on group patterns and overall trends. They examine the influence of media and consumer culture and the influence of gender, sexuality, race, and class on "body politics." While no single explanation accounts for the increasing popularity of tattoos, researchers find that people use tattoos to express who they are, what they have lived through, and how they see themselves in relation to others and to their social worlds. Studies also find that people cannot fully control the meaning of their own tattooed bodies; the social contexts in which they live shape the responses to and interpretations of their tattoos by others.

Paul Sweetman writes, "The popular image of the tattooee as young, male and working-class is now increasingly outdated, as more and more men and women, of various age-groups and socio-economic backgrounds, choose to enter the tattoo studio." In trying to understand these new tattooees, we focus on three groups—youth, women, and members of tattoo subcultures. We then discuss whether tattoos actually satisfy the aims of those who get them.

TATTOOED YOUTH

Tattooing is especially popular among teenagers and college students. At a stage when young people are seeking to assert their independence, tattoos may provide a way to ground a sense of self in a seemingly changing and insecure world.

Myrna Armstrong and her collaborators have examined the prevalence of tattooing (as well as body piercing) among today's teenagers. Through the results of two surveys, one based on 642 high school students in Texas and one based on a national sample of 1,762 students, they conclude that most tattooed adolescents, contrary to stereotypes, are high-achieving students and rarely report gang affiliations.

Since the 1980s, tattooing has won a following among teenagers and college students, who have altered the reputation of tattooed people from that of criminals and laborers to that of artists and free thinkers. Whereas many cities, including New York, once banned tattoo parlors, they have become ubiquitous in most college towns. Numerous Hollywood celebrities, musicians, and models have visible tattoos, including Angelina Jolie, Lucy Liu, Janet Jackson, Johnny Depp, and Nick Carter—inspiring many youth to emulate their pop idols by becoming tattooed. This has resulted in what Michael Atkinson calls the "supermarket era" of tattooing, marked by easy availability and consumer choice.

Despite this aura of mass consumption, Atkinson finds that tattoos and the tattooing experience give young people feelings of greater control and authority over their own lives. Christine, for example, explains her tattoos as an effort to reclaim her body from the pressures of school, peers, and parents. "I want everyone to know that I'm sick of being told what to do and how to look." Tattoos can become a symbolic battleground between adolescents asserting autonomy over their own bodies and authority figures trying to enforce standard codes of appearance.

Adolescents may also use tattoos as a way to signify and solidify group memberships as they move between schools and communities. Susan's tattoo enforces her ties to childhood friends. "We grew up in [town] together, and these flowers [pointing to tattoo] were painted all over the gym in our elementary school. . . . I love knowing my girls and I will always be together like that." Another young woman, Renee, describes to Atkinson how several women from her residence hall floor decided together to get tattoos of their university logo. While these individuals believe that tattoos can provide some semblance of belonging and security in a changing world, these promises of permanence often fall short in the face of real personal transitions and shifting social norms.

As these young people illustrate, tattoos are a powerful means by which a generation can assert independence and commemorate important events, ranging from going away to college to living alone for the first time to getting married. In marking these rites of passage, young people give tattoos multiple and at times contradictory meanings. Whatever the particular statements that young people are making with their tattoos, the act of getting a tattoo increasingly serves as a vehicle to mark adulthood.

TATTOOING WOMEN

Women's interest in tattooing has also been increasing in the United States since the 1960s.

Today almost half of tattooed people are women, according to various sources. A 2003 Harris poll found that 15 percent of women and 16 percent of men have tattoos. (The same poll found that 31 percent of gays, lesbians, and bisexuals had at least one tattoo.)

Tattooing offers many women control over their own bodies. Some have used the tattoo to challenge the limited roles of wife and mother and to explore other ways to define themselves. Around the turn of the last century, aristocratic women in England, France, and the United States, including Winston Churchill's mother and members of the Vanderbilt family, sported tattoos. Margo DeMello asserts that many Victorian women were drawn to tattoos as a way of demonstrating that they were "less likely to accept the idea of the quiet, pale, and bounded female body." In addition, she says, "tattoos have long been a sign of that resistance within the working class."

Perceptions of tattooed women as sexually promiscuous and lower-class have a long history. Albert Parry describes a rape case in late-1920s Boston in which the prosecutor, upon realizing that the young woman he was defending had a tattoo, requested that the case be dropped.

While men and women both get tattoos, men are more likely to use tattoos to reinforce traditional notions of masculinity, whereas women often both defy and reproduce conventional standards of femininity. In interviews with Atkinson, Caroline states, "Women nowadays believe that whatever men can do women can do better, and that includes tattooing." Zeta explains that tattoos provide a concrete way of challenging traditional gender norms: "I could talk and talk and talk about wearing grungy clothes and not dyeing my hair to look like a Barbie doll, and no one would care since all of that is superficial." While Zeta believes the permanence of a tattoo demonstrates a deep and tangible commitment to alternative gender definitions, other women use tattoos to conform to mainstream standards of femininity.

As tattoos become more common, they are less able to express subversive definitions of women and their bodies. Atkinson argues that many of the young women he interviewed used their tattoos to enforce rather than challenge traditional femininity. Their tattoos were placed in either easily hidden or sexualized areas of the body such as the shoulder, hip, or lower back. The images were also traditionally feminine, such as animals, flowers, and hearts. DeMello argues that while feminist scholars have rushed to embrace tattooing's liberatory potential for women, "People aren't interested in the women who get men's names on them, or who get what their men want on them because it's sexy and feminine rather than 'empowering.'"

Women have pioneered the use of tattoos to reclaim their bodies from traumatic experiences, including disease and abuse. Recently, women recovering from breast cancer have sought tattoos, both to create a new aesthetic for mastectomy scars and to express the devastating effects of the disease. Tattoo artist Sasha Merritt, recognizing the importance of tattooing in the healing process for women who have mastectomy scars, advertises a special rate for breast cancer survivors at the Women's Cancer Resource Center in Oakland, California. Andree Connors, a California writer with a rose tattoo over her mastectomy scar, told *Ms. Magazine* in 1992, "This is an invisible epidemic: everyone looks 'normal' because they're wearing prostheses. So the message does not get across to the world that we are being killed off by breast cancer."

Marking their bodies with tattoos helps women to feel they are reclaiming lost or violated parts of themselves—an especially important process for women healing from abuse or trauma. In an interview with Atkinson, Marion describes her participation in a sexual abuse survivor's group in which ten of the women had gotten tattoos: "Each of us has taken a turn writing a story about our tattoo and what it means. We present them at group meetings and go over how tattooing helps women feel in control of our bodies."

PART 4

Women may use tattooing to reclaim their bodies not only from violence or illness, but from more everyday experiences of feeling unattractive, weak, or different—like the young woman with the Pegasus tattoo. While some critics regard tattooing as another form of self-mutilation, and this indeed may be true in some cases, the self-described experiences of most tattooees seem to contradict this interpretation. Whereas most people who engage in cutting are ashamed of and attempt to hide their scars, most tattooees regard their tattoos as sources of pride and works of art, even those who hesitate to display them in public.

For many women, tattooing is a complex practice that involves both conformity and resistance to the expectation that their bodies be attractive to men. While historically many women have sought tattoos as a way to transgress gender norms, contemporary women increasingly seek tattoos as conventional markers of feminine beauty. In both cases, women have used tattoos as vehicles to create a sense of community with other women around shared experiences, even including abuse or disease.

TATTOO SUBCULTURES

Some individuals may not identify themselves as modern primitives yet still consider themselves part of a tattoo community. Often referred to as "tattoo enthusiasts," they not only have lots of tattoos but also share a commitment to associating with others who have tattoos and to a lifestyle in which tattoos are central. According to DeMello, activities such as reading tattoo publications, attending tattoo conventions, and participating in Internet chat rooms give members of a tattoo subculture a "sense that they have found people who are like them and who are not like everyone else."

This sense of shared values is especially true for those who use tattooing to criticize the consumer values of capitalist society. Ironically, while some individuals invoke tattooing as a critique of consumer society, tattoos have themselves become a popular commodity. While tattoo enthusiasts argue that tattoos are an expression of freedom and control over the body, their tattooing practices are highly sensitive to shifting social trends. And while many hard-core and neo-primitive people are regarded as marginalized and even freakish by mainstream society, they are part of established groups with their own codes of belief and norms of behavior.

LIMITATIONS

The message that a person intends to communicate through a tattoo is not always the message received by others. The complex motivations of people who get tattoos are filtered through historical and cultural lenses that often impose unintended and unwanted meanings on their tattooed bodies. A person's choice of imagery, location of the tattoo, and whether or not to cover it are all influenced by that person's social context. Despite their increasing popularity, tattoos still carry stigma and can provoke discrimination. The University of California at Los Angeles conducted a "Business Attire Survey" in 1999 which revealed that 90 percent of campus recruiters looked negatively on tattoos. Despite evidence to the contrary, teenagers with tattoos are more likely to be perceived as gang members, drug users, dropouts, and troublemakers. A study by Armstrong and McConnell shows that medical professionals still often attribute tattoos to gang affiliation. Racial and ethnic minorities are especially likely to have their tattoos perceived as marks of gang membership or criminal behavior. Defense attorneys often advise their clients that visible tattoos can have a negative influence on middle-class (and white) jurors and judges.

Young people may find it necessary to cover their tattoos not only when looking for work but also on the job. Thus, while they may desire the tattoo as a mark of individuality, rebellion, or creative expression, some tattooees have difficulty reconciling their own intentions with negative social perceptions of their tattoos.

Doug explains to Atkinson that his swastika tattoos were his way to reclaim the ancient symbol from its connections with Nazism. But he covers them because he is afraid they will be misunderstood, marking him as a white supremacist. The historical symbolism and common cultural understanding attached to this design overshadow Doug's intended message.

In addition, tattoos in and of themselves do little to change social conditions and may contribute to the very conditions they seek to challenge. The tattoo speaks to the ongoing, complex need for humans to express themselves through the appearance of their bodies. The tattooed body serves as a canvas to record the struggles between conformity and resistance, power and victimization, individualism and group membership. These struggles motivate both radical and mundane forms of tattooing. The popularity of tattoos attests to their power as vehicles for self-expression, commemoration, community building, and social commentary. At the same time, the tattoo's messages are limited by misinterpretation and the stigma that still attaches to tattooed people.

REFERENCES

Michael Atkinson. *Tattooed: The Sociogenesis of a Body Art* (Toronto University Press, 2003).

Christine Braunberger. "Revolting Bodies: The Monster Beauty of Tattooed Women." *NWSA Journal* 12 (2000): 1–23.

Margo DeMello. *Bodies of Inscription: A Cultural History of the Modern Tattoo Community* (Duke University Press, 2000).

Mary Kosut. "Tattoo Narratives: The Intersection of the Body, Self-Identity and Society." *Visual Sociology* 15 (2000): 79–100.

Margot Mifflin. *Bodies of Subversion: A Secret History of Women and Tattoos.* 2nd ed. (Power House Books, 2001).

PART 4

Critical Thinking Questions

1. Do you think tattooing one's body is a form of deviance or conformity? Why?
2. The social perception of tattoos has changed radically over the past few decades. How do you think tattoos will be interpreted in the future?

Chapter 11

The Civilizing of Genie

MAYA PINES

Cases of children who were deprived of social interaction while they were young have long fascinated sociologists. Some investigators believe that by examining how such children develop in later life, one can assess the relative importance of "nurture" versus "nature" in the socialization process. Others want to determine if there is some "critical period" in child development during which, say, language must be learned if it is to be learned effectively. Both themes are apparent in this selection. This case, however, raises other issues as well. Research on "Genie" was brought to a halt by a lawsuit (filed by Genie's mother), which alleged that investigators had made Genie endure "unreasonable and outrageous testing" for purposes other than treatment. In a 1993 letter to *The New York Times,* Dr. Rigler (the lead scientist working with Genie) wrote that the case never came to trial as it was dismissed. Despite this, Genie's therapy was eventually terminated, and she regressed back to her former state. In the end, Genie became a ward of the court and endured a long succession of foster parents before finally being admitted to a state mental health institution. As you read through this selection, determine for yourself if the researchers seem more interested in helping Genie "get better" or in using Genie as "data."

1. Do you think the work done with Genie was ethical—particularly as she ended up regressing to her former state after the discontinuation of treatment?

Only a few cases are recorded of human beings who have grown up without any real contact with other humans. So rare is the phenomenon that when a 12-year-old "wild boy" was found in the forest of Aveyron in 18th-century France, the government ordered him brought to Paris to be examined by doctors in an institution for deaf-mutes. There he came under the care of the physician Jean Itard, who also acted as the boy's tutor. Itard left detailed records of his experience, which was later dramatized in the 1970 movie *The Wild Child.* Although the boy was not deaf, and despite Itard's work, the child never learned to speak.

In 1970, a wild child was found in California: a girl of 13 who had been isolated in a small room and had not been spoken to by her parents since infancy. "Genie," as she was later dubbed to protect her privacy by the **psycholinguists** who tested her, could not stand erect. At the time, she was unable to speak; she could only whimper.

The case came to light when Genie's 50-year-old mother ran away from her 70-year-old husband after a violent quarrel and took the child along. The mother was partially blind and applied for public assistance. The social worker in the welfare office took one look at Genie

Source: Maya Pines. "The Civilizing of Genie." *Psychology Today,* September 1981. Reprinted by permission of the author.

and called her supervisor, who called the police. Genie was sent to the Los Angeles Children's Hospital for tests. Charges of willful abuse were filed against both her parents, according to the *Los Angeles Times*. On the day he was due to appear in court, however, Genie's father shot himself to death. He left a note in which he wrote, "The world will never understand."

The discovery of Genie aroused intense curiosity among psychologists, linguists, neurologists, and others who study brain development. They were eager to know what Genie's mental level was at the time she was found and whether she would be capable of developing her faculties. "It's a terribly important case," says Harlan Lane, a psycholinguist at Northeastern University who wrote *The Wild Boy of Aveyron*. "Since our morality doesn't allow us to conduct deprivation experiments with human beings, these unfortunate people are all we have to go on."

Genie is now 24 years old. Through years of rehabilitation and special training, she has been observed and repeatedly tested. Hundreds of videotapes record her progress. She has been the subject of several journal articles and a book. Since the book was published in 1977, additional studies have brought into focus some of the issues raised by Genie's case. Far from settling any scientific controversies, she has provided fresh ammunition for arguments on both sides of a major issue: is there a "critical period" in a child's development during which, if **language acquisition** is not stimulated or encouraged, it may be impaired later on or not emerge at all?

She has inspired a California researcher who worked with her, Susan Curtiss, to develop a controversial hypothesis about how language learning affects the two hemispheres of the brain. Genie has also stirred up debate about the relationship between language and other mental abilities. As a result, new research is now in progress on the surprising language ability of some mentally retarded children.

As described in Curtiss's book, *Genie: A Psycholinguistic Study of a Modern-Day "Wild Child"* (Academic Press), Genie is living proof of human resilience. It is surprising that she survived at all. Her father apparently hated children and tried to strangle Genie's mother while she was pregnant with her first child. According to Curtiss's book, when an earlier baby girl was born, he put the child in the garage because he couldn't stand her crying; the baby died of pneumonia at two-and-a-half months. A second child, a boy, died two days after birth, allegedly from choking on his own mucus. A third child was rescued and cared for by his grandmother when he was three years old and is still alive. Genie, the fourth child, was denied such help, however, because shortly after she was born, her grandmother was hit by a truck and killed.

From the age of 20 months, when her family moved into her grandmother's house, until she was 13 and a half, Genie lived in nearly total isolation. Curtiss's book, and newspaper reports, describe Genie's life at the time: naked and restrained by a harness that her father had fashioned, she was left to sit on her potty seat day after day. She could move only her hands and feet. She had nothing to do. At night, when she was not forgotten, she was put into a sort of straitjacket and caged in a crib that had wire-mesh sides and an overhead cover. She was often hungry.

If she made any noise, her father beat her. "He never spoke to her," wrote Curtiss. "He made barking sounds [and] he growled at her. . . . Her mother was terrified of him—and besides, she was too blind to take much care of Genie. The task fell largely on Genie's brother, who, following his father's instructions, did not speak to Genie either. He fed her hurriedly and in silence, mostly milk and baby foods. There was little for Genie to listen to. Her mother and brother spoke in low voices for fear of her father.

When Genie arrived in Children's Hospital in November 1970, she was a pitiful, malformed, incontinent, unsocialized, and severely malnourished creature. Although she was beginning to show signs of pubescence, she weighed

PART 5

only 59 pounds. She could not straighten her arms or legs. She did not know how to chew. She salivated a great deal and spent much of her time spitting. And she was eerily silent.

Various physicians, psychologists, and therapists were brought in to examine her during those first months. Shortly after Genie was admitted as a patient, she was given the Vineland Social Maturity Scale and the Pre-school Attainment Record, on which she scored as low as normal one-year-olds. At first, she seemed to recognize only her own name and the word *sorry*. After a while, she began to say two phrases that she used as if they were single words, in a ritualized way: *stopit* and *nomore*.

Psychologists at the hospital did not really know how much she understood. Nor did they know how to evaluate whatever language she had: to what degree did it deviate from the standard pattern? They eventually asked Victoria A. Fromkin, a UCLA psycholinguist, to study Genie's language abilities. Fromkin brought along a graduate student, Susan Curtiss (now an assistant professor of linguistics at UCLA), who became so fascinated by Genie that she devoted much of the next seven years of her life to researching the girl's linguistic development.

Working with Genie was not an easy task. Although she had learned to walk with a jerky motion and became more or less toilet trained during her first seven months at Children's Hospital, Genie still had many disconcerting habits. She salivated and spat constantly, so much so that her body and clothing were filled with spit and "reeked of a foul odor," as Curtiss recounts. When excited or agitated, she urinated, leaving her companion to deal with the results. And she masturbated excessively.

Nevertheless, Genie was decidedly human, and her delight at discovering the world—as well as her obvious progress—made the struggle worthwhile. When Curtiss started working with Genie, she began by simply spending time with her or taking her to visit places, in order to establish a relationship. She took Genie to the supermarket, where Genie walked around the store and examined the meats and the plastic containers with some curiosity. Every house seemed exciting to Genie, who had spent so much of her life cooped up in one room; on walks she would often go up to the front doors of houses, hoping that someone would open the door and let her in.

During her first seven months of freedom, Genie had learned to recognize many new words—probably hundreds by the time Curtiss started investigating her knowledge of language systematically in June 1971. And she had begun to speak. On a visit with Curtiss to the home of one of the therapists, Genie eagerly explored every room, then picked up a decorator pillow; when asked what it was, she replied "pillow." Asked if she wanted to see the family cat, Genie replied, "No. No. Cat," and shook her head vehemently. Most of the time, however, she said nothing.

At first Genie spoke only in one-word utterances, as toddlers do when they start to talk. Then in July of 1971, she began to string two words together on her own, not just while imitating what somebody else had said. She said "big teeth," "little marble," "two hand." A little later she produced some verbs: "Curtiss come," "Want milk." In November of the same year she progressed to occasional three-word strings: "small two cup," "white clear box."

Unlike normal children, however, Genie never asked questions, despite many efforts to train her to do so. Nor did she understand much grammar. And her speech development was abnormally slow. A few weeks after normal children reach the two-word stage, their speech generally develops so rapidly and explosively that it is difficult to keep track of or describe. No such explosion occurred for Genie. Four years after she began to put words together, her speech remained, for the most part, like a somewhat garbled telegram.

While Genie did not speak in a fully developed, normal way, she acquired some language after she was discovered. That contradicted one aspect of the theory that says language can be learned only during a critical period between two years of age and puberty.

On the other hand, Genie failed to learn the kind of grammatical principles that, according to Noam Chomsky, distinguish the language of human beings from that of animals. For example, she could not grasp the difference between various pronouns, or between active and passive verbs. In that sense, she appeared to suffer from having passed the critical period.

Her language deficiencies could not be attributed to a lack of teachers. Though at first it did not seem possible that she could ever attend any school, within a few months of her arrival at Children's Hospital she began going to nursery classes for normal children. She soon transferred to a special elementary school for handicapped children. Next, she spent several years in a city high school for the mentally retarded. Outside school, a speech therapist worked with her consistently for many years. Meanwhile, one of the therapists and his wife took Genie into their own home to live with their two teenage sons, a teenage daughter, a dog, and a cat. They tried to teach Genie to trace with her fingers the shape of sandpaper letters, to recognize words or work with Play-Doh, as well as deal with the demands of family life. She apparently had no trouble writing her name, and drew a number of pictures based on experiences she had had.

Nor did Genie's deficiencies appear to be inborn. Although many details of her early history are unclear, and Genie's mother has given contradictory accounts of them, Genie seems to have been a normal baby. She suffered from an Rh blood incompatibility, but received an exchange transfusion one day after birth. During her first year of life, before she was isolated from the rest of her family, she may have been on the road to language, since her mother reported that she heard Genie saying words right after she was locked up.

The gift of language has always been viewed as distinctively human, or even as proof of the existence of the soul. Its source has mystified human beings for millennia. In the 13th century, Frederick II, Emperor of the Holy Roman Empire, decided to perform an experiment to find out what kind of speech children would develop if left to their own devices in their early years; he wondered whether it would be Hebrew, Greek, Latin, or the language of their parents. He selected a few newborns and decreed that no one speak to them. The babies were suckled and bathed as usual, but songs and lullabies were strictly forbidden. Frederick II never got his answer, however, for the children all died. The experiment was never repeated.

In the early 19th century, Itard tried desperately to teach Victor, the wild boy of Aveyron, to speak. He began when Victor was about 12 years old—around the time of puberty, as with Genie. However, Victor never spoke more than a few single words, perhaps because of an injury to his throat, where he had a scar.

Chomsky believes that human beings are born with a unique competence for language, built into their brains. But he adds that the innate mechanisms that underlie this competence must be activated by exposure to language at the proper time, which Chomsky speculates must occur before puberty.

Among human beings, four-week-old babies can recognize the difference between some 40 consonants that are used in human languages, as shown by how their sucking and heartbeats change when different consonant sounds are presented by audiotape. That ability seems to be innate, since babies respond to many more consonants than are used in their parents' language—English, for example, has only 24 consonant sounds, yet babies of English-speaking parents react to the consonants present in Japanese. Babies lose that ability as they grow up. By the age of six, when children enter school, their ability to hear the difference between sounds to which they have not been exposed in their own

PART 5

language is severely reduced. Feature detectors responsible for recognizing about a dozen consonant sounds have so far been inferred to exist in the human brain. They need to be triggered by the environment, however; if not, they appear to atrophy.

Had something similar happened to Genie's brain? Curtiss raised that possibility when she reported that Genie, unlike 99 percent of right-handed people, seemed to use the right hemisphere of her brain for language. Since the left hemisphere is predisposed for language in right-handed people, that could account for some of the strange features of Genie's language development.

On tests of "dichotic listening," for example, which involve presenting different sounds to both ears simultaneously and asking the subject to react to them, "Genie's left ear outperformed her right ear on every occasion," Curtiss reports in her book. (Sound from the left ear is linked to the right hemisphere; from the right ear, to the left hemisphere.) Furthermore, "the degree of ear advantage is abnormal: Genie's left ear performed at 100 percent accuracy, while the right ear performed at a level below chance." That indicated Genie was using her right hemisphere as consistently as do people in whom, because of damage or surgery, only the right hemisphere is functioning.

When Genie's brain-wave patterns were examined at the UCLA Brain Research Institute—first as she listened to different sentences, then as she looked at pictures of faces—the data suggested that Genie used her right hemisphere for both language and nonlanguage functions. Genie also proved to be particularly good at tasks involving the right hemisphere, such as recognizing faces. On the Mooney Faces Test, which requires the subject to distinguish real from "false" faces in which features are misplaced and to point out several features on each face, Genie's performance was "the highest reported in the literature for either child or adult," according to Curtiss.

From the very beginning, Genie's vocabulary revealed an extraordinary attention to the visual world, which is the special province of the right hemisphere—to color, shape, and size. All of her first two-word phrases were about static objects. While normal children usually start talking about people and actions or about the relations between people and objects, Genie spoke primarily about the attributes of things: "black shoe," "lot bread."

While summarizing the numerous tests made on Genie until 1979, Curtiss noted that Genie's performance had increased consistently over the years. For example, on the Leiter International Performance Scale, which was developed for use with deaf children and does not require verbal instructions, she had an IQ of 38 in 1971, an IQ of 53 in 1972, an IQ of 65 in 1974, and an IQ of 74 in 1977. However, she had made much less progress on tasks governed primarily by the left hemisphere. Even at the age of 20, she still performed at a three-year-old level on tests of auditory memory (a left-hemisphere task); she scored at a 6- to 12-year-old level on tests of visual memory (which tap both hemispheres), and at an adult level on tests of Gestalt perception (a right-hemisphere task).

The theory of language learning recently offered by Curtiss is an attempt to explain Genie's dependence on her right hemisphere. Possibly, Curtiss wrote in a paper on cognitive linguistics published by UCLA, the acquisition of language is what triggers the normal pattern of hemispheric specialization. Therefore, if language is not acquired at the appropriate time, "the cortical tissue normally committed for language and related abilities may functionally atrophy," Curtiss wrote. That would mean that there are critical periods for the development of the left hemisphere. If such development fails, later learning may be limited to the right hemisphere.

Obviously Genie has many problems besides her lack of syntax or her dependence on the right hemisphere of her brain. During her most formative years—her entire childhood—she was malnourished, abused, unloved, bereft of any toys or companionship. Naturally, she is strange in many ways. Yet her language deficits remain particularly striking since she often found means of explaining what was important to her. She used gestures if necessary (starting in 1974, she received regular lessons in American Sign Language to complement her spoken language). Once she wanted an egg-shaped container that held panty hose that was made of chrome-colored plastic. She signaled her desire by making the shape of an egg with her hands, and then pointing to many other things with a chromium finish. In her book, Curtiss describes how Genie occasionally used her limited language to remember her past and to tell about details of her confinement. "Father hit arm. Big wood. Genie cry," she said once. Another time, when Curtiss took her into the city to browse through shops, Genie said, "Genie happy."

In 1978, Genie's mother became her legal guardian. During all the years of Genie's rehabilitation, her mother had also received help. An eye operation restored her sight, and a social worker tried to improve her behavior toward Genie. Genie's mother had never been held legally responsible for the child's inhuman treatment. Charges of child abuse were dismissed in 1970, when her lawyer argued that she "was, herself, a victim of the same psychotic individual"—her husband. There was "nothing to show purposeful or willful cruelty," he said.

Nevertheless, for many years the court assigned a guardian for Genie. Shortly after Genie's mother was named guardian, she astounded the therapists and researchers who had worked with Genie by filing a suit against Curtiss and the Children's Hospital among others—on behalf of herself and her daughter—in which she charged that they had disclosed private and confidential information concerning Genie and her mother for "prestige and profit" and had subjected Genie to "unreasonable and outrageous" testing, not for treatment, but to exploit Genie for personal

and economic benefits. According to the *Los Angeles Times*, the lawyer who represents Genie's mother estimated that the actual damages could total $500,000.

The case has not yet come to court, but in the two years since it was filed, Genie has been completely cut off from the professionals at Children's Hospital and UCLA. Since she is too old to be in a foster home, she apparently is living in a board-and-care home for adults who cannot live alone. The *Los Angeles Times* reported that as of 1979 her mother was working as a domestic servant. All research on Genie's language and intellectual development has come to a halt. However, the research Genie stimulated goes on. Much of it concerns the relationship between linguistic ability and cognitive development, a subject to which Genie has made a significant contribution.

Apart from Chomsky and his followers, who believe that fundamental language ability is innate and unrelated to intelligence, most psychologists assume that the development of language is tied to—and emerges from—the development of nonverbal intelligence, as described by Piaget. However, Genie's obvious nonverbal intelligence—her use of tools, her drawings, her knowledge of causality, her mental maps of space—did not lead her to an equivalent competence in the grammar normal children acquire by the age of five.

Puzzled by the discrepancy between Genie's **cognitive abilities** and her language deficits, Curtiss and Fromkin wondered whether they could find people with the opposite pattern—who have normal language ability despite cognitive deficits.

That would be further evidence of the independence of language from certain aspects of cognition.

In recent months, they have found several such persons among the mentally retarded, as well as among victims of Turner's syndrome, a chromosomal defect that produces short stature, cardiac problems, infertility, and specific

PART 5

learning difficulties in females. With help from the National Science Foundation (which had also funded some of Curtiss's research on Genie), Fromkin and Curtiss have identified and started working with some children and adolescents who combine normal grammatical ability with serious defects in logical reasoning, sequential ability, or other areas of thinking.

"You can't explain their unimpaired syntax on the basis of their impaired cognitive development," says Curtiss, who is greatly excited by this new developmental profile. She points out that in the youngsters studied, the purely grammatical aspect of language—which reflects Chomsky's language universals—seems to be isolated from the semantic aspect of language, which is more tied to cognition. "Language no longer looks like a uniform package," she declares. "This is the first experimental data on the subject." Thus the ordeal of an abused child may help us understand some of the most puzzling but important aspects of our humanity.

Critical Thinking Questions

1. Did the researchers make assumptions about language and mental ability?
2. Were Genie's challenges due to "nature" or "nurture"?
3. Do you think Genie's language was limited, or do you think the way people (specialists and researchers) perceived her language/communication skills was limited?

Chapter 12

The Concept of "Stages" in Piaget's Theory

ROLF E. MUUSS

PART 5

Once upon a time, children were seen to be little more than imperfect adults. Under this view, socialization was the process by which, bit by bit, children came to acquire the beliefs and values typical of the adults in their culture. A revolution in the study of socialization occurred in the early 20th century, when a number of theorists—notably Sigmund Freud, George Herbert Mead, and Jean Piaget—began to claim that socialization proceeds in separate and discrete stages. The general idea is that while different individuals might proceed through these stages at different rates, all individuals have to pass through the earlier stages to reach the later ones. These different theorists, however, had quite different ideas about what stages were central to the development of young children. In retrospect, Piaget's theory of "stages"—reviewed in this selection—has likely influenced the empirical study of childhood socialization more than any other. When reading this article, consider the more recent cases of social isolation emerging involving young girls being imprisoned for long periods of time. The escapes of these young persons from their captors (e.g., Jaycee Dugard, Elizabeth Smart, Sabine Dardenne, Natascha Kampusch, Elisabeth Fritzl) raises the question about whether Piaget's concepts would be helpful for their reintegration back into society, or whether alternatives might be needed.

1. What are the key similarities and differences across Piaget's four stages?

For Piaget, developmental stages simply mean that a sequential progression in the cognitive structures, which underly problem-solving operations, takes place. Thus, stages emerge in an orderly, invariant sequential pattern, and no stage can be skipped. The earlier stages provide essential building material that the individual integrates and transforms in the process of moving to the next higher level. Significant is that the problem-solving skills that characterize a given stage are qualitatively distinguishable from those found in stages that precede as well as those that succeed it, e.g., elementary school children can solve the same problem when presented in concrete terms that high school students can solve when presented abstractly. And it is this qualitative change that elevates Piaget's theory from simply a description of age-related changes in reasoning to a stage theory. For example, adolescents deal with learning tasks and with their world in substantially different, more abstract, ways than elementary school children because their cognitive structure is different. The appeal of Piaget's stages is that they identify a comprehensive system of different features in the developmental progression of reasoning ability. Furthermore, the developmental progression identified by Piaget

Source: Muuss, Rolf E. *Theories of Adolescence, 6th Edition.* New York: McGraw-Hill, 1996. Reprinted by permission of the author.

is characteristic of most individuals found in a broadly defined age range. The idea of a "stage" does not negate the well-known fact of the existence of intra-individual, interindividual, and intercultural differences; however, it does mean that a given stage-defining operation follows the same sequence in all individuals. In other words, each higher level stage integrates and builds upon the accomplishments and the underlying structure of the preceding stage.

The speed with which an individual progresses through these stages depends upon intellectual ability, educational experiences, cultural and social context, as well as other factors. However, the sequential progression through the stages itself is not a function of these factors, but is invariant. Children who possess low intelligence, come from preindustrial cultures or from dysfunctional families, or have limited educational experiences may progress at a slower rate and may not reach the final stages. The age levels suggested for these stages are not norms, but allow for considerable variations, and therefore, should be treated as approximations.

The landmarks of Piaget's stage-dependent theory, based on major qualitative advances in cognitive structure, are: sensorimotor, preoperational, concrete operational, and formal operational stages. Originally, the theory focused on infancy and childhood but was later expanded to include adolescence. The stage-dependent theory is the core of Piaget's initial systematic theory of development, and is by far the most widely known and most often discussed part of his theory.

THE SENSORIMOTOR STAGE

The *sensorimotor stage of development* (from birth to age 2) is subdivided into six developmental phases. The first phase (birth to 1 month), the *reflex phase*, consists primarily of exercising inborn reflexes such as the sucking reflex, which, as it becomes modified to meet the demands of different situations, becomes the sucking schema. During the second phase (1 to 4 months), which Piaget calls the phase of *primary circular reactions*, reflexes are slowly replaced by voluntary movements. Children may tirelessly practice an emerging schema, such as grasping, since they are motivated by "function pleasure"—a concept quite different from the behavioristic notion of "drive reduction" or "reinforcement." In the third phase (4 to 8 months), that of *secondary circular reactions*, infants begin to pursue objects and events unrelated to themselves—for example, following slow movements of an attractive toy. Or, if an infant learns through trial and error to grasp a cord and make a bell jingle, he or she may repeat such behavior. That such an action can be repeated is evidence of the beginning of intentionality and even an incipient form of goal-directed behavior. The fourth phase (8 to 12 months), that of *coordination of secondary schemata*, is characterized by the emergence of an understanding of means-ends relationships. The child reaches for a box in order to obtain the toy that is inside. When the child begins to search for a toy hidden under a blanket, the concept of **"object permanence"** is beginning to emerge.

During the fifth phase (12 to 18 months), *tertiary circular reactions*, the concept of "object permanence" becomes more stable. The child will search for and find the object even though in the process of hiding it, it may have been moved through a series of displacements. The last of the six phases (18 to 24 months) is that of *internalization of sensorimotor schemata*. The child begins to use foresight and symbolic representation in solving sensorimotor problems. For the first time, the child may investigate whether a hole is big enough before attempting to push an object through it, thus giving evidence that the strictly sensorimotor approach to problem solving is being replaced by thought. The progression from the primarily sensorimotor approach to life to the beginning use of thought is the qualitative difference between this and the preoperational stage.

THE PREOPERATIONAL STAGE

The second period of development (2 to 7 years), called the *preoperational stage*, is a transition period from the predominantly egocentric and sensorimotor stage of early childhood to rudimentary forms of social behavior and the beginning of conceptual thought. Children learn new concepts on the basis of direct, first-hand perceptual experiences—that is, they are still at the mercy of what they see and hear. Reality is what they perceive; other alternatives are not available to them. When a chocolate bar is broken into pieces, they think there is more chocolate, because the pieces look like more candy than the solid bar.

Preoperational children are too dependent on sensory impressions and they do not yet comprehend the *principle of conservation:* a given quantity remains the same, even though the way that quantity has been arranged has changed. One commonly used illustration is the pouring of water from a low but wide glass into a tall but narrow glass in full view of children. Even though they actually observe the water being poured, preoperational children think there is more water in the tall glass because it looks like more. They do not think in terms of a hierarchy of classes and supraclasses. A child may maintain, "We are not in Baltimore; we are in Maryland," without comprehending that one can be included in the other.

The judgments of preoperational children are still intuitive and subjective, but they are beginning to deal with more complex issues. Preoperational children manipulate objects, tools, and toys effectively, express thoughts, and ask questions. Nevertheless, accurate judgment and thought is limited by several factors:

1. Basically, children are still heavily dependent on sensory experiences.
2. They cannot consider two or more dimensions at the same time, rather, they focus on one aspect and consequently neglect to consider the other. A corollary is their directional thinking, also referred to as one-way mapping or one-way functioning, which interferes with mental reversibility.
3. They cannot rearrange or reorganize information in their minds.
4. They are quite limited in their ability to take the point of view of another person.

THE CONCRETE OPERATIONAL STAGE

At approximately age 7 or 8, a major qualitative shift in children's conceptual development takes place. They are now beginning to perform *concrete logical operations* in their mind. This period (from 7 or 8 to approximately puberty) is referred to as the *operational stage in logical thinking*.

During the operational stage, using concrete content, the child learns to master basic logical operations. "Concrete" in this context does not mean that the child can deal only with tangible objects, but that any problem has to be tied to reality. The major limitation evident in the thinking at this level is the child's inability to think abstractly about a problem. Since concrete operations can be performed mentally, overt trial and error becomes unnecessary. For the first time, the child begins to think in accordance with a model of logical reasoning. The important elements of concrete logical operations are:

1. *The logic of classes*, which is based on an understanding of whether or not an object belongs or does not belong in a given class. This enables children to solve problems of classification. They become concerned with the relationship between the parts and the whole. Understanding and classifying parts that belong together help children to gain a better understanding of the whole, the supraclass. Their ability to hold several pieces of information in mind and to reverse their thinking enables them to understand hierarchy of classes and supraclasses.

2. *The logic of relations*, which makes it possible to order and organize several objects in relationship to one another, according to specific criteria. In a test situation, the child is asked to order a series of objects, such as dolls or sticks, according to their size. Such an "operation of serialization" is similar to the classification of a hierarchy, since it involves some understanding of the structure of the whole: "There is no class without classification; there is no systematic relation without serialization" (Piaget, 1962: 126). The logic of relations receives elaboration when the child is asked to set two series of objects into correspondence with one another. For example, matching a series of dolls of increasing size with a corresponding set of hats or sticks. Possessing the "logic of relations," the operational child is able to organize objects according to their size, height, or weight as long as objects are presented concretely. Not until adolescence can such operations be performed abstractly.

3. *The principle of conservation*, to which Piaget attached great importance, is probably the most extensively researched cognitive operation. Realizing that changing a clay ball into a sausage or flattening it out into a pancake does not change its mass, weight, or volume, the operational child now begins to develop an understanding of the principle of conservation.

At the same time that the concrete operations emerge, the child's language, which until approximately age 7 had been predominantly egocentric, has become primarily **sociocentric.**

Sociocentric language implies a genuine effort to understand other people and to communicate thoughts objectively. Research does not substantiate the dramatic transformation from egocentric to sociocentric speech as neatly as the shift from preoperational to operational thought suggests, but research does support the more general idea that, with the beginning of schooling and with increasing age, the proportion of egocentric speech decreases and that of sociocentric speech increases.

The change from egocentric to sociocentric thought is not only reflected in children's language, but permeates their thought processes as well. Sociocentric children can place themselves in the situation of other persons and take those persons' points of view.

Piaget identifies the properties of concrete operations and applies the term *elementary groupings*, or *group-like structures*, to the different ways in which a child's thought process can manipulate classes and relations. Since Piaget postulates a direct relationship between logic and a child's cognitive processes, the concepts he introduces are conveyed in terms of logic and mathematics. An important set of four concrete group-like structures, follows:

Combinativity. Two or more classes can be combined into one larger, more comprehensive class. For example, all men and all women equal all adults. Logical relationships, such as A is larger than B and B is larger than C; therefore, A is larger than C, can be comprehended. The ability to understand classes and to combine subclasses into supraclasses is essential to assemble or disassemble a hierarchy of classifications.

Reversibility. Every operation is reversible. Every operation has an opposite operation that reverses it. Supraclasses can be taken apart so that the effect of combining subclasses is reversed: All adults except all women equals all men. The child's ability to reverse thought processes is an important indicator of cognitive development.

Associativity. Children whose operations have become associative can reach a goal in various ways. They can make detours in thought, but in such a fashion that the results obtained by these different routes remain the same. For example, $(3 + 6) + 4 = 13$, and $6 + (3 + 4) = 13$.

Identity or nullifiability. An operation that is combined with its opposite becomes nullified. Illustrations of nullifiability in mathematics are: give 3 and take 3 away results in null, or 5 times X divided by 5 equals X. If I drive one mile west and one mile east, I am where I started; my actions are nullified.

Primary groupings make combinativity, reversibility, and associativity in thought possible and thus aid a child in achieving a structural equilibrium that is considerably more mobile and flexible than the thought process of a preoperational child. Thus, the approach to problem solving is no longer intuitive or impulsive but rational and logical. However, reasoning is not yet integrated into a single total system of interrelated prepositions.

THE FORMAL OPERATIONS STAGE

The final stage of cognitive development of Piaget's theory is the *stage of formal operations*, which typically emerges during adolescence. Piaget's formal operations include, among others, the use of propositional thinking, combinatorial analysis, proportional reasoning, probabilistic reasoning, correlational reasoning, and abstract reasoning. The concept *formal* implies that what matters is form and logic rather than content. With the progression through these stages, mental operations become increasingly more abstract, more complex, more logical, and the boundaries of the mental structures become more permeable and thus, provide thought process with greater flexibility.

Adolescents not only think beyond the present but analytically reflect about their own thinking. Piaget calls this type of reasoning "second-degree thinking"; it involves operations that produce "thinking about thinking," "statements about statements," or more significantly, "operations on operations." Such operations allow a set of all possible combinations to emerge, which then make possible the construction of new knowledge out of previously acquired knowledge by way of propositional thinking. Thus, the interrelationship of actual observation, learning and vicarious learning, and the layering upon layering of knowledge eventually makes hypothetical reasoning possible and allows the construction of theories.

In their thoughts, adolescents can leave the real objective world behind and enter the world of ideas. They now can control events in their minds through logic deductions of possibilities and consequences. Even the directions of thought processes change. Preadolescents begin thinking about reality by attempting to extend thoughts toward possibility. Adolescents who have mastered formal operations begin by thinking of all logical possibilities and then considering them in a systematic fashion; reality becomes secondary to possibility because adolescents reduce reality to a subset of possibility. To emphasize this point further, one could say that, in operation thinking, reality is the foreground and possibility remains in the background. In formal operational thinking, this relationship is reversed—possibility has become the foreground and reality has become simply one of the many possibilities.

REFERENCE

Piaget, J. Three Lectures. *Bulletin of the Menninger Clinic*, 1962, 26, 120–145.

PART 5

Critical Thinking Questions

1. Recently there have been cases where young girls, imprisoned by captors for prolonged periods of time, have escaped. In some cases, these girls even have children with their captors. What do you suppose the consequences of those experiences may be, according to Piaget?
2. Could Piaget's stages inform Genie's experience (in Chapter 11)? If so, how?

Chapter 13

Columbus and the Making of Historical Myth

BARBARA RANSBY

It is a story that most of us learned in school: A brave Christopher Columbus defied conventional wisdom and the dangers of the Atlantic Ocean to discover the New World. In this selection, Barbara Ransby compares the story of Columbus that appears in history textbooks with the historical record and argues that, by virtue of what these textbooks emphasize and what they omit, they shape not only our view of the past but also our view of the present.

1. Can history be objective? Does it matter who writes it?
2. How does Ransby interpret the commonly held and popular understanding of Christopher Columbus?

As the world approaches the quincentennial commemoration of Christopher Columbus's accidental 'discovery' of America, we are reminded that history is, in large part, a battleground upon which scholars and activists fight to define the lens through which we will view the past. There is also a struggle to define which historical actors will be immortalised as heroes and heroines and which events will be emblazoned into our collective memory as turning-points and historical landmarks. How the story of Christopher Columbus should be told is at the centre of one such intellectual battle. The manufactured, but widely accepted, myth of Columbus as the brave and noble visionary who set sail on an unknown course and discovered a whole new world belies the real legacy of Columbus: a bloody legacy of rape, pillage and plunder. But, it is a myth which is quite consistent with how most of US history is recounted by mainstream historians—as great deeds by great white men which resulted in great things for all humankind. More specifically, it is a myth which celebrates imperial conquest, **male supremacy** and the triumph of military might as necessary components of progress and civilisation.

An examination of the Columbus myth illustrates how elites are able to justify their exploits under the guise of 'necessary evil'. Moreover, a survey of the treatment of Columbus in North American children's textbooks is a further indication of exactly how historical myths are made, and when and where the seeds of the dominant culture are planted. To assess how most Americans are introduced to the story of Columbus in grade school, I examined thirty social studies textbooks published between 1966 and 1990 by major US publishers. Many of the newer texts are currently used in public schools throughout the US, the rest were the intellectual baby food of the current generation of college students.

In the overwhelming majority of writings about Columbus, particularly in children's books, there is a simplistic celebration of Columbus as a 'great discoverer [whose] courage opened a new

Source: Ransby, Barbara. "Columbus and the Making of Historical Myth." *Race & Class* 33 (January/March 1992), 79–86. Reprinted with permission of the Insitute of Race Relations.

world to Europeans', with little or no critical commentary.[1] In the majority of more 'enlightened' texts, however, there is an uncomfortable reconciliation of Columbus, the avaricious, slave-trading pirate, with Columbus, the brave and venturesome Italian mariner who paved the way for the expansion of western civilisation. Implicitly, of course, a new way could not be paved without the removal of obtrusive roadblocks to progress. Those roadblocks included millions of indigenous people who had lived on the lands Columbus supposedly discovered some 25,000 years before his expedition arrived. They were people who had names, cultures, belief systems and a history. They lived in harmony with an entire eco-system which was harshly disrupted with the arrival of European invaders in the 1490s. But elementary schoolchildren are told very little about the Taino and Carib peoples, and even less about the bloody conquest of their civilisations by the European colonisers we now celebrate as national icons. It is a conflict with which mainstream historians are quite uneasy because it does not fit neatly into the panoramic sweep of progress which is how many of them opt to characterise North American history. Many of these writers are much more comfortable quoting selectively from Columbus's journal about how he admired the gentleness and generosity of the 'Indians', carefully omitting his conclusion that their kind and calm demeanour would make them easier to exploit and enslave.

Most children's textbooks also fail to mention that Columbus actually introduced the slave trade to the Americas. When he was unsuccessful in his desperate search for gold and other natural riches in the islands of the Caribbean, he began sending human cargo back to Spain instead. Hundreds of Taino and Carib Indians were torn from their homes and families and shipped to Europe to be sold as servants and slaves in the decades after Columbus's arrival. Social studies texts, for the most part, omit, gloss over or reconstruct this ignominious episode in early American history. One text euphemistically describes the six Tainos Columbus forcibly took back to Spain on his first return trip as his 'guests.'[2] Another text, which admits that the colonisers killed thousands of Indians, still describes the system of coerced labour set up by Columbus in the following terms: 'Columbus tried to make use of the Indians by requiring them to bring him gold and to work for his colonies.'[3] This passage seems to suggest that the native people were idle and unproductive before Columbus's arrival and required his assistance in finding 'useful' and productive work.

Ultimately, the popular myths surrounding Columbus serve as subtle, and sometimes not so subtle, justifications for both male supremacy and **white supremacy**.

Schoolchildren are taught, through omissions, euphemisms and outright distortions, that conquest is a heroic, masculine enterprise worthy of emulation, and that, when the casualties of such conquests are uncivilised people of colour, they are expendable. Three hundred and fifty years after Columbus's initial invasion of the Caribbean, US president Andrew Jackson, himself engaged in a campaign to finish off the process of Native American genocide begun by Columbus, summed up the necessity of the early conquest in these words: 'What good man would prefer a country covered with forests and ranged by a few thousand savages to our extensive republic, studded with cities, towns, and prosperous farms . . . filled with the blessings of liberty, civilisation, and religion?'[4] According to historian Ron Takaki, during the nineteenth century, the ruling elite of the US concluded that 'white violence was a necessary partial evil for the realisation of a general good—the extension of white civilisation and the transformation of the wilderness into an agrarian society.'[5]

Most Americans know, in some vague sense, the grim fate that befell the native populations of the Caribbean islands after Columbus's advent. Within fifty years of the arrival of the European

PART 5

invaders, a population of over 300,000 native people was wholly decimated, with not one member surviving by 1540.[6] This was due in part to disease and displacement, but much of it was due to outright brutality and savagery on the part of the invaders, who waged genocidal wars against those they perceived as obstructions to progress. Women were raped, the environment was ravaged and, eventually, most of what had existed before was destroyed. The land was cleared for the building of a new world. Columbus initially described the so-called Indians he met as 'gentle souls', but when they refused to acquiesce passively to his plans for their subjugation, he was relentless in his brutality against them. Columbus biographer Kirkpatrick Sale describes a scene near the colony of Isabela in 1495:

> to subdue the recalcitrant natives and tame the countryside . . . the soldiers mowed down dozens with point blank volleys, loosed the dogs to rip open limbs and bellies, chased fleeing Indians into the bush to skewer them on sword and pike, and 'with God's aid soon gained a complete victory, killing many Indians and capturing others who were also killed'. Of the valley that was Paradise they made a desert, and called it peace.[7]

Moreover, what happened in the Caribbean islands in the 1490s and early 1500s was only a dress rehearsal for what was to transpire on the North American mainland some 300 years later.

Even though most Americans do not know, or choose not to know, all the gory details of the Columbian conquest, there is a general awareness among most that genocide did occur and that a people was annihilated. Authors of children's texts about Columbus, as hard as they try to evade the brutal truth, are often forced to admit that 'the Indians were treated unfairly', and 'many Indians died'. Yet, both in popular myth and in written texts, authors have attempted to reconcile the good and the bad in the Columbian legacy, minimising the latter and highlighting the former. 'He had his faults, but . . .'

is the sentiment echoed throughout many of the writings about him.

The reticence of scholars to dethrone Columbus, despite the admitted atrocities he committed, is reflected in the following quote by the Columbian researcher and Pulitzer prize winner, John Noble Wilford:

> We do know he was an inept governor of the Spanish settlements in the Caribbean and had a bloodied hand in the brutalisation of the native people and in the start of the slave trade. But we are left wondering if he is to be admired and praised, condemned—or perhaps pitied as a tragic figure.[8]

Despite his admission that Columbus murdered and enslaved Indian people, Wilford is still uncertain whether such behaviour really warrants condemnation. He speculates that perhaps the significance of such actions is outweighed by Columbus's own personal tragedies. Similarly, other texts mention Columbus's reprehensible deeds, but describe them in such dispassionate terms that they seem almost benign. One 1990 textbook casually refers to the genocidal conquest of the native peoples in this way: 'Though they had a keen interest in the peoples of the Caribbean, Columbus and his crews were never able to live peacefully among them.'[9] The author seems perplexed by the fact that the enslavement of native people and the theft of their land was any cause for tension between them and the European invaders. He is also reluctant to assign blame for the mysterious conflict, as indicated by his ambiguous and neutral choice of words. What such erroneous formulations effectively do is reduce the crimes against native people to footnotes in a larger, implicitly more important, text. The main story is about the greatness of western civilisation, the march of progress, the triumph of civilisation over savagery, Christianity over heathenism, and the imposition of order upon the chaos of the wilderness. This is a fundamentally racist formulation, consistent with the ways in which the subjugation and massacre of people of colour have been rationalised both by scholars and by ruling elites for generations. In fact, the rationalisation offered by the apologists for Native American genocide sounds frighteningly similar to the justification for the recent Gulf war. The murder of thousands of Iraqi civilians was described as an unfortunate but necessary action, taken in order to abate the greater evil of unchecked barbarism.

While the Columbian myth is both an American and a European one, it has a special significance in the context of US history and folklore. Even though Columbus was a European, and his first voyage predated the American revolution by nearly 300 years, he is revered by many as the first American hero. The nation's capital is named in his honour, as are several US cities, streets, parks and schools, including one of the country's oldest and most prestigious universities. His birthday is a federal holiday and the US government intends to spend millions of dollars in 1992 to commemorate the quincentenary of his initial transatlantic voyage. The legacy of Columbus has become an integral part of the annals of North American history because it fits so neatly into a larger scenario which celebrates the so-called pioneer spirit as that which has propelled the US to its current greatness. And, after all, Columbus was the first pioneer, followed by the Pilgrims, the cowboys, and US troops guarding the new frontiers of democracy around the globe today. Columbus was one among many great white explorers who courageously ventured into the darkness of the unknown, only to find a wilderness crying out to be tamed. The wilderness included both the land and its people. When the newly formed US began the process of constructing a national identity and culture, the memory of Christopher Columbus was resurrected as a symbol of the virtues of rugged individualism, stoic determination and a ruthless pioneer spirit which the young republic sought to instil in its citizens. It is no coincidence then that in 1692, the bicentennial of Columbus's fateful voyage, there were

no great celebrations in the American colonies. But 100 years later, in the immediate wake of the American revolution, Columbus was lauded in commemorative festivities throughout the newly independent nation.[10]

It is also significant, and not all surprising, that the blatantly racist and sexist nature of the Columbian conquest has in no way diminished the great discoverer's status as an enduring and celebrated American hero. While most children's books essentially ignore the issue of gender and minimise the issue of race in re-telling the story of Columbus, both race and sex are integral features of the conquest of the Caribbean islands. The racist nature of the conquest is readily apparent. Repeatedly, in the descriptions of the world Columbus 'discovered', the native population is referred to as part of the natural landscape, nearly, indistinguishable from the other wild creatures who inhabited the islands. The following passage is typical: '[Columbus] returned to Spain taking with him a few of the curious copper-skinned natives, some birds, and some fish which he found.'[11] No distinction is made by this writer between Columbus's human and non-human souvenirs. Children reading such a passage could easily be left with the impression that the significance of those copper-skinned human beings was no greater than that of the captured fish or birds.

Initially, the native people were described by Columbus as generous and docile creatures. Later, when they got a taste of what their European visitors had in store for them and began to resist colonisation and 'progress', Columbus increasingly characterised them as 'cannibalistic savages' who had to be beaten into submission or extinction.[12] Columbus's animosity towards the native people was not the result of some innate aversion to people of colour or any xenophobic aversion to difference, as indicated by his initially favourable description of them. Rather, deeming them 'racially', socially and culturally inferior served as a convenient rationale for confiscating their land, usurping their labour and, eventually,

PART 5

annihilating them as a people. In fact, it was not their dark skin which Columbus alleged was an indicator of their inferiority, but their culture, their way of life and that fact that they did not embrace Christianity. After all, the Moors and Jews had just been expelled from Spain for the same reasons by Columbus's benefactor, Queen Isabella. So, as early as the fifteenth century, the notion of an inferior 'breed' of men and women served as reason for their exploitation and subjugation.

Columbus's legacy is not only that of racism and imperialism, but of sexual conquest as well. According to Kirkpatrick Sale, 'the women of America were as much a part of the bounty due the conquering Europeans as the other resources in which it luxuriated.'[13] Native American women, like their African and African-American counterparts centuries later, were victims of sexual terrorism as a part of the larger scenario of conquest and colonisation. An Italian sailor, who was a part of Columbus's entourage when he invaded Santa Cruz island, described in his journal a scene that was probably typical:

> I captured a very beautiful Carib woman whom the Lord Admiral [Columbus] gave me, and with whom, having taken her into my cabin, she being naked according to their custom, I conceived desire to take pleasure [rape her]. I wanted to put my desire into execution but she did not want it and treated me with her finger nails in such a manner that I wished I had never begun ... I took a rope and thrashed her well, for which she raised such unheard of screams that you would not have believed your ears.[14]

The rape of Indian women was not uncommon, but seems to have been systematic and routine. Another member of Columbus's crew described the situation in the colony of La Navidad in 1493: 'Bad feelings arose and broke out into warfare because of the licentious conduct of our men towards the Indian women.'[15]

Moreover, the story of Columbus's voyage is, above all, characterized as an adventure story in which men, more specifically European men, are the principal, if not the sole, cognisant actors. It is recounted as a romantic tale of fearless seamen who set out to explore the far reaches of the earth, only to stumble upon a treasure greater than they could have imagined, a new world. It was couched as a distinctly male adventure, a biased but favourable characterisation which ignores and minimises the very real experiences of the native women who were some of the chief victims of the conquest and colonisation.

Schoolchildren in the US are encouraged to view Columbus as a great hero, the Admiral of the Ocean Sea. Most of them learn the familiar rhyme: 'In 1492, Columbus sailed the ocean blue', which firmly implants the legendary figure in their memories. They are even encouraged to learn from, and emulate, his example. One popular text urges teachers to highlight Columbus's virtues so that children see the benefits of patience and courage. And, since most public schools in western nations socialise children not to be critical thinkers, but to be good citizens, hard workers and, if need be, loyal soldiers, the myth of Columbus serves those purposes well. Moreover, openly to acknowledge the brutal and unsavoury origins of European influence in the western hemisphere would mean confronting the bloody traditions spawned from those beginnings. Therefore, Columbus's image has been scrubbed clean and sanitised by many generations of American historians so that he can now be offered up as a sterling example of the glorious era of discovery. His weaknesses, mistakes and horrid transgressions are all excused in the name of progress. The construction of the heroic myth and legend surrounding Columbus also belies the notion that the writing of history is an objective enterprise. And it further underscores the contention that history is ultimately written by the victors, and by those with the power and resources to publish, distribute and thus validate the version of history which best serves the interests of the status quo.

So, in 1992, it is a quite ignoble band of pioneers, with Columbus at the helm, that Americans will celebrate so lavishly on the occasion of the quincentenary. There will be travelling museum exhibitions, elaborate parades and commemorative ceremonies. In Puerto Rico, there will be a flotilla of ships bearing the names of the original three ships sailed by Columbus in 1492 and a re-enactment of the invasion, euphemistically referred to as the landing. And the government of the Dominican Republic is organising as 'archaeological reconstruction' of one of Columbus's unsuccessful Caribbean colonies established in 1494.[16] But, just as native people fought to defend their culture and their lives against imperialist hegemony five centuries ago, today progressive historians, activists and the political descendants of those first American freedom-fighters are struggling to resist yet another insult upon the memory of those who died. American Indian Movement leader Russel Means once compared the legacy of Columbus to the legacy of Hitler. Native Americans and their allies throughout the Americas are determined that such a legacy not be celebrated without visible, vocal and militant opposition. Counter-demonstrations, days of mourning for the victims of genocide and de-commemoration ceremonies are planned throughout the year by groups ranging from the Women of All Red Nations to a multicultural group of educator-activists, called REPOhistory. An intercontinental run for peace and dignity is also planned which will include participants from north, central and south America. One set of runners will begin in Argentina, another in Alaska and the tour will culminate in a ceremony and rally in Mexico City. The general purpose is to link the native communities throughout the hemisphere and to celebrate a common history of resistance and survival—in spite of Columbus. These are but a few of the many efforts underway to reclaim, inch by inch, the confiscated territory which is our history.

NOTES

1. Allen Y. King, I. Dennis and F. Potter, *The United States and the Other Americas* (New York, 1978), p. 47. Other sources used for this article include R.C. Brown and H.J. Bass, One Flag, *One Nation* (Morristown, N.J., 1985); Christopher Columbus, *Journal of First Voyage* (New York, 1924); D.T. Gerace (ed), *Columbus and His World: proceedings of the first San Salvador conference* (Ft. Lauderdale, Fl., 1987); H.F. Graff, *America: the glorious republic* (Boston, 1986); H.F. Graff and P. Bohannan, *The Call of Freedom: the grand experiment* (New York, 1978); L.S. Kenworthy, *One Nation: the United States* (Lexington, 1972); S.E. Morison, *Admiral of the Sea* (Boston, 1942); P.E. Taviani, *Christopher Columbus: the grand design* (London, 1985).
2. George Shaftel, *Decisions in United States History* (Lexington, Mass., 1972), p. 19.
3. D. Buggey et al, *America, America* (Glenview, Il., 1977), p. 65.
4. Quoted in Ronald T. Takaki, *Iron Cages: race and culture in nineteenth century America* (Seattle, 1979), p. 103.
5. Ibid.
6. Buggey, op. cit., p. 65.
7. Kirkpatrick Sale, *The Conquest of Paradise: Christopher Columbus and the Columbian legacy* (New York, 1990), p. 154.
8. J.N. Wilford, 'Discovering Columbus', in *New York Times Magazine* (11 August 1991).
9. Clarence L. Ver Steeg, *The American Spirit: a history of the American people* (Englewood, N.J., 1990), p. 262.
10. Wilford, op. cit.
11. Heller and Potter, *One Nation Indivisible* (Columbus, Ohio, 1966), p. 8.
12. G. Shaftel, *Decisions in United States History* (Lexington, Mass., 1972).
13. Sale, op. cit., p. 141.
14. Ibid., p. 140.
15. Ibid., p. 139.
16. Ibid., p. 143.

PART 5

Critical Thinking Questions

1. What does Ransby argue the "sanitized story of Columbus" teaches elementary school students? What are the consequences of this?

2. How does the myth of Christopher Columbus compare with his real legacy? How does this myth fit in with most of U.S. history? Canadian history?

3. What purpose(s) does the myth of Columbus serve? And to whom? What do you think is the significance of the continuance of this myth?

4. Why might some students who read this article feel threatened with the idea of rejecting the story of Columbus?

Chapter 14

2006 Census: Families, Marital Status, Households and Dwelling Characteristics

STATISTICS CANADA

Many students can become overwhelmed when looking at statistical data. It can be helpful to instead focus upon the overall trends and differences captured in the data, rather than getting bogged down by the hard numbers. This chapter gives you the raw material to understand the reality of families and marriage trends in Canada through the statistical snapshot (data captured at one point in time) provided.

1. What does the 2006 Census tell us about the changing Canadian family?
2. What family types have declined? What family types have increased?

Wednesday, September 12, 2007

Statistics Canada today releases a "family portrait" of Canadians using the third set of data from the 2006 **Census.**

This release examines developments in families, marital status, households and living arrangements in Canada between 2001 and 2006, and how children fit into these evolving family structures.

In addition, it provides information on the number of same-sex couples, both those living in a common-law union and, for the first time, those who are married.

In total, the census **enumerated** 8,896,840 census families in 2006, up 6.3% from 2001.

The census enumerated 6,105,910 married-couple families, an increase of only 3.5% from

2001. In contrast, the number of common-law-couple families surged 18.9% to 1,376,865, while the number of lone-parent families increased 7.8% to 1,414,060.

Consequently, married-couple families accounted for 68.6% of all census families in 2006, down from 70.5% five years earlier. The proportion of common-law-couple families rose from 13.8% to 15.5%, while the share of lone-parent families increased slightly from 15.7% to 15.9%.

Two decades ago, common-law-couple families accounted for only 7.2% of all census families. Married-couple families represented 80.2%, and lone-parent families, 12.7%.

In Quebec, where the prevalence of common-law-couple families has been one of the defining family patterns for years, the number of common-law-couple families increased 20.3% between 2001 and 2006 to 611,855.

Source: Adapted From Statistics Canada, "2006 Census: Families, Marital Status, Households and Dwelling Characteristics", *The Daily*, Catalogue 11-001, Wednesday, September 12, 2007. http://www.statcan.gc.ca/daily-quotidien/070912/tdq070912-eng.htm (October, 2011)

They accounted for 44.4% of the national total. Close to one-quarter (23.4%) of all common-law-couple families in Canada lived in the two census metropolitan areas of Montréal and Québec.

Among lone-parent families, growth between 2001 and 2006 was most rapid for families headed by men. Their number increased 14.6%, more than twice the rate of growth of 6.3% among those headed by women.

SAME-SEX MARRIED COUPLES COUNTED FOR THE FIRST TIME

The number of same-sex couples surged 32.6% between 2001 and 2006, five times the pace of opposite-sex couples (+5.9%).

For the first time, the census counted same-sex married couples, reflecting the legalization of same-sex marriages for all of Canada as of July 2005. In total, the census enumerated 45,345 same-sex couples, of which 7,465, or 16.5%, were married couples.

Half of all same-sex couples in Canada lived in the three largest census metropolitan areas, Montréal, Toronto and Vancouver, in 2006. Toronto accounted for 21.2% of all same-sex couples, Montréal, 18.4% and Vancouver, 10.3%.

In 2006, same-sex couples represented 0.6% of all couples in Canada. This is comparable to data from New Zealand (0.7%) and Australia (0.6%).

Over half (53.7%) of same-sex married spouses were men in 2006, compared with 46.3% who were women. Proportions were similar among same-sex common-law partners in both 2006 and 2001.

About 9.0% of persons in same-sex couples had children aged 24 years and under living in the home in 2006. This was more common for females (16.3%) than for males (2.9%) in same-sex couples.

HOUSEHOLDS: LARGE INCREASE IN ONE-PERSON HOUSEHOLDS

Since 2001, there has been a large increase in one-person households.

During this time, the number of one-person households increased 11.8%, more than twice as fast as the 5.3% increase for the total population in private households. At the same time, the number of households consisting of couples without children aged 24 years and under increased 11.2% since 2001.

The households with the slowest growth between 2001 and 2006 were those comprised of couples and children aged 24 years and under; these households edged up only 0.4%.

Between 2001 and 2006, the number of private households increased 7.6%, while the population in private households rose 5.3%.

The census counted more than three times as many one-person households as households with five or more persons in 2006. Of the 12,437,470 private households, 26.8% were one-person households, while 8.7% were households of five or more persons.

MORE YOUNG ADULTS LIVING WITH THEIR PARENTS

Over the last two decades, one of the trends for young adults has been their growing tendency to remain in, or return to, the parental home. This upward trend has continued over the past five years.

In 2006, 43.5% of the 4 million young adults aged 20 to 29 lived in the parental home, up from 41.1% in 2001. Twenty years ago, 32.1% of young adults lived with their parents.

Among individuals aged 20 to 24, 60.3% were in the parental home in 2006, up from 49.3% in 1986. Among those aged 25 to 29, 26.0% were in the parental home in 2006, up from 15.6% two decades earlier.

Saskatchewan (31.8%) and Alberta (31.7%) had the lowest proportions of young adults aged 20 to 29 living in the parental home in 2006. Among the other provinces, Newfoundland and Labrador (52.2%) and Ontario (51.5%) had the highest.

Among the census metropolitan areas, Toronto had the highest proportion of young adults who lived in their parents' home in 2006. Nearly 6 in 10 (57.9%) young adults aged 20 to 29 lived with their parents in Toronto, well above the national average (43.5%).

UNMARRIED PEOPLE OUTNUMBER LEGALLY MARRIED PEOPLE FOR THE FIRST TIME

For the first time, the census enumerated more unmarried people aged 15 and over than legally married people.

In 2006, more than one-half (51.5%) of the adult population were unmarried, that is, never married, divorced, separated or widowed, compared with 49.9% five years earlier. Conversely, only 48.5% of persons aged 15 and over were legally married in 2006, down from 50.1% in 2001.

Twenty years earlier, 38.6% of the population aged 15 and over were unmarried, while 61.4% were married.

PART 6

Critical Thinking Question

1. Why do you suppose the "traditional family" (two parents, plus children) is still the social ideal, despite the growth of other types of families?

Chapter 15

Experimental Family Organization: An Historico-Cultural Report on the Oneida Community

WILLIAM M. KEPHART

Ours is a culture in which (1) the relationship between husband and wife is supposed to be characterized by emotional intimacy and (2) parents are supposed to love their children as "special treasures." The fact that this is not always true does not change the fact that they are cultural ideals. This, however, has not always been the case in Western societies. Indeed, many commentators have noted that these two characteristics of family life did not emerge as cultural ideals in Western societies until after the 18th century. What is "family life" like in a society where monogamy and emotional intimacy between sexual partners is discouraged and where "special attachments" between individual parents and their children are discouraged? This selection presents some evidence that bears on that question by describing the Oneida Community. We might note that in the decades since this article was first published, some new materials on the Oneida Community have come to light that answer some of the questions that Kephart was not able to answer (see, for example, Spencer Klaw, *Without Sin: The Life and Death of the Oneida Community*, Penguin Books, 1993).

1. What were some of the factors that led to social cohesion among the Oneida?

By way of background, it should be mentioned that the Community was founded in 1848 on the old Indian lands along the Oneida Creek in central New York State. John Humphrey Noyes, founder and long-time leader of the group, was a graduate of Yale Theological Seminary, although his theological views and Perfectionist philosophy had proved too heretical for the people of Putney, Vermont, where he had been preaching. Noyes' theology revolved around **spiritual equality** which, as he interpreted it, included both the economic and sexual spheres. In the Kingdom of God, all persons were to love and to share equally—a so-called Bible communism. Noyes gained some adherents, and in Putney the little group of Perfectionists actually started to practice what they preached. Predictably, however, there was little future for the group in an area that had been close to the heart of Puritanism, and Noyes and his followers were eventually run out of town.

Reassembling at Oneida, New York, they constructed a large Community Mansion House, and by expanding their efforts were able to increase the size of the group to several hundred members. And for many decades the

Source: Kephart, William M. "Experimental family organization: an historico-cultural report on the Oneida Community." *Marriage and Family Living* (August 1963): 261–271. Copyright © 1963 John Wiley and Sons. Reproduced with permission of Blackwell Publishing Ltd.

Oneida Community sustained one of the most unusual social experiments the world has ever seen. Economic communism, **group marriage**, scientific breeding, sexual equality—it couldn't happen here, but it did!

Indeed, the Community flourished until around 1880, after which a business enterprise (Oneida, Ltd.) was set up and the stock apportioned among the members. It is hoped that the following remarks will shed some light on this very remarkable historico-cultural episode, one which—for some reason—has been neglected by both historians and sociologists.

SOCIAL ORGANIZATION AND FAMILY FUNCTIONS

What was there, in the elements of social organization, which successfully held the Community together in the face of both internal problems and external pressures? To begin with, much of the communality of action derived from the fact that the entire membership was housed under one roof. The original communal home was built in 1849, but because of the increase in members it was replaced in 1862 by a spacious brick building known as the Mansion House. In subsequent years, wings were added as needed. The building still stands, in its entirety; in fact, during my visit to Oneida, I stayed at the Mansion House and can attest to the fact that it is a striking architectural form, internally as well as externally. Noyes helped both in the planning and in the actual construction, and while sociologists might question the extent to which physical structure influences social organization, the Mansion House would seem to be a case in point.

Although each adult had a small room of his own, the building was designed to encourage a feeling of togetherness, hence the inclusion of a communal dining hall, recreation rooms, library, concert hall, outdoor picnic area, etc. It was in the Big Hall of the Mansion House that John Humphrey Noyes gave most of his widely-quoted home talks. It was here that musical concerts, dramas, readings, dances, and other forms of socializing were held. Community members were interested in the arts, and were able to organize such activities as symphony concerts, glee club recitals, and Shakespearian plays, even though practically all the talent was home grown. Occasionally, outside artists were invited, but on a day-to-day basis the Community was more or less a closed group, with members seldom straying very far from home base. What might be called their reference behavior related entirely to the group. The outside community was, figuratively and literally, "outside," and was always referred to as the The World.

And, of course, it was the Mansion House itself which served as the structural base for practically all Community activity. Insofar as the Perfectionists were concerned, the totality of their existence lay within the walls of the Mansion House. The building was designed to encompass and facilitate this totality pattern, and from all accounts it served its purpose well.

Most of those interviewed were unable to separate the Old Community from the Mansion House. In their minds the two had become one, a fusion of the social and the structural, which, again, underscores the pervasiveness of the physical setting. Even today the building serves as a kind of community center. Most of the surviving members live there, and a good many of the direct descendants live within a block or two; in fact, as the descendants themselves age, they are likely to move into the Mansion House to spend their remaining years. In the words of one of the informants:

> We all love the old place. Many of our folks lived there, and most of us played there as kids. We know the building down to the last brick and board. It's odd, so many of the people who move away seem to come back when they get older and live in the Mansion House. It's because they had such good times and such happy memories.

It should not be thought that life in the old Community was a continual round of entertainment. The Oneidans built their own home, raised their own food, made all their own clothes (including shoes!), did their own laundry, ran their own school, and performed countless other collective tasks.

Virtually all of their activities were designed to accentuate the *we* rather than the *I*, and the economic sphere was no exception. Special abilities were recognized; indeed, wherever possible, occupational assignments were made on the basis of individual aptitudes. But at one time or another most of the work had to be rotated or shared, and so it was with Community life in general. The roles of the members were made crystal clear, and whether the activity in question was social, economic, sexual, or spiritual, the Oneida Perfectionists invariably turned against the *culte du moi* in favor of what to them was a **selfless collectivism**.

Human nature being what it is, of course, there were inevitable lapses on the part of certain members. Role conflicts sometimes did occur, and it was to counteract any tendency toward selfishness or ego-involvement that the much-publicized system of Mutual Criticism was inaugurated. Although details varied over the years, the general system involved a member who evidenced signs of personal aggrandizement being brought before a committee of peers who, frankly and objectively, attempted to pinpoint his social malfeasance. None of the persons talked with had undergone Mutual Criticism inasmuch as they were too young at the time. (Children were not included in this part of the Oneida program.) From all reports, however, the system of Mutual Criticism was well received. None of those interviewed could recall hearing of any adverse comments; in fact, it appears that as the membership increased, the system came to be applied not only to deviants but to any one who was seriously desirous of self-improvement. The following appeared during 1871–1872 in the *Oneida Circular*, the Community's weekly newspaper:

> I feel as though I had been washed; felt clean through the advice and criticism given. I would

call the truth the soap; the critics the scrubbers; Christ's spirit the water.

The followers of John Humphrey Noyes were hard-working, well-behaved citizens, among whom crime and delinquency were virtually unknown. Because of this, they were generally respected by the surrounding community and by most every one else who came into actual contact with them. Nevertheless, the Oneidans were different. They knew it and The World knew it. By way of illustration, the Oneida women wore a very distinctive attire: in a period of floor-length skirts the Perfectionist ladies wore short ones (knee length) with loose trousers or "pantalettes" down to the shoes. I was shown some of the original dresses, and my impression was that they would create quite a stir even today. How must they have been viewed by outsiders 100 years ago! Moreover, all the Oneida women bobbed their hair, a custom which the Community instituted in 1848—and which was not introduced into The World until 1922 (by dancer Irene Castle). At any rate, it is easy to see why secular differentiation of this kind strengthened group identity. The following comment is illustrative:

> Your asking of sociological questions about what held the Community together reminds me of something my aunt used to tell. The old Oneidans kept pretty much to themselves, but during the summer months they would sometimes permit visitors. Some Sunday afternoons whole trainloads of visitors would come. They were served picnic-style on the lawn of the Mansion House. I think they were charged $1.00 for the whole thing. Of course, the visitors couldn't get over the way the Oneida women dressed, and they kept staring. My aunt always felt that the way outsiders always looked at them and talked about them had a great deal to do with their feelings of closeness.

Another measure which apparently helped to integrate Community membership was their widely-publicized system of economic communism. Personal ownership of wealth and private property of any kind were taboo, down to and including children's toys. Several of the informants mentioned the fact that in the early days of the Community the Oneidans had rough going; in fact, around 1850 their agricultural economy was in such poor shape that it was necessary for them to sell their watches in order to make ends meet. Fortunately, one of their members developed a steel trap, the manufacture of which involved a secret process of spring tempering. Demand for the traps proved great, and before long it was commonplace for the entire Community to turn out in order to meet the deadline for a large order.

From 1855 on, the Oneidans were without financial worry; in fact, when they broke up around 1880, the treasury showed a balance of some $600,000, no small sum for the period in question.

A final force which served to unite the Perfectionists was their religion and their spiritual devoutness; indeed, it would not be far from the mark to say that the Oneida Community was basically a religious organization. Their social, economic, and sexual beliefs all stemmed from the conviction that they were following God's word as expounded by John Humphrey Noyes. Noyes preached that Christ had already returned to earth and that redemption or liberation from sin was an accomplished fact. It followed, therefore, that the spiritual world was autonomous, free, and quite independent of the temporal order. From this perspective, it is easy to see why Noyes was often antagonistic to temporal or "external" law.

What was the net result of all of the above measures? From what was said, it appears that the Oneidans were able to maintain a remarkably cohesive form of family and social organization. Those interviewed were nearly unanimous in their belief that the old Oneida Community was an effectively organized, well integrated, and happy group. The following three comments speak for themselves:

I was a child in the old Community, and I can tell you that they were a happy group. Of course, I was only a child at the time—they disbanded before I was 10—and children like to glorify their childhood. Still, when anybody asks me about the old days, my dominant memory is one of contentment and happiness.

I was too young to remember much. But as I grew older and asked my relatives about the Community days, their faces would light up.

I was not born in the old Community, although many of my relatives were. But from the way they all talked about life in the Mansion House, they were living life to the fullest. They were able to combine the spiritual, the economic, and the social, and make it really work.

Sexual Practices

PART 6

Although their family and social organization were unique, it was the Community's bizarre sexual system which attracted national and international attention. Just as Mormonism is invariably linked with polygyny, so the Oneida Community seems destined to be associated with group marriage. John Humphrey Noyes believed neither in romantic love nor in monogamous marriage, such manifestations being considered selfish and smacking of possessiveness. He taught that all men should love all women and that all women should love all men, and while no attempt was made to impose this reciprocality on The World, group marriage (or "Complex Marriage," as it was called) continued throughout the whole of the Community's existence.

Sex relations within the group were reportedly easy to arrange inasmuch as the men and women all lived in the Mansion House. If a man desired sexual intercourse with a particular woman, he was supposed to make his wish known to a Central Committee, who would convey his desire to the woman in question. If the latter consented, the man would go to her room at bedtime and spend an hour or so with her before returning to his own room. No woman was forced to submit to a sexual relationship which was distasteful to her, and the committee system presumably afforded her a tactful method for turning down unwelcome suitors. It was understood by all concerned that their sexual latitude did not carry with it the rights of parenthood. Only the select were permitted to have children, a point which will be discussed later.

Although respondents were agreed that the men readily adjusted to a plurality of women partners, they were generally silent on the question of how the Oneida females adjusted to a variety of male partners. It is unfortunate that so little information was available on this point, for this issue—in my opinion, at least—is a crucial one. In effect, the Oneida women were encouraged to have sex relations with a variety of men, but were not supposed to become emotionally involved with any of the men with whom they were having these relations! The woman of today tends to emotionalize and romanticize her sexual experience, and it would be hard for her to have any empathetic understanding of the Oneida system, wherein neither romance nor monogamous love were supposed to play any part in the sex act. As for the Oneida women, themselves, one can but conjecture.

One thin clue was the belief by four of the interviewees that at least in terms of overt behavior the female refusal rate was not high. Another male respondent stated that he had been informed by an old Community member that the latter "had never been refused." Two female interviewees had been told by an older woman member that the refusal rate was probably low.

The question whether the Oneida women ever took the initiative in requesting sexual relations drew a generally negative response. Several interviewees reported that they knew of some coquetry on the part of certain women, but that they had never heard of anything more direct.

The Eugenics Program

A vital component of the Oneida sexual system was the **eugenics** program, usually referred to as **Stirpiculture**. Noyes had been impressed with the writings of Darwin and Galton, and from the very beginning had decided that the Community should follow the principles of scientific propagation. Accordingly, he requested the Perfectionists to refrain from having children until such time as adequate financial resources were built up, and published accounts make much of the fact that during the 20 years it took to achieve economic self-sufficiency the Oneidans were successful in their efforts at fertility control. The type [of] birth control used was *coitus reservatus*, sexual intercourse up to but not including ejaculation.

Male orgasm was permissible only with women who had passed menopause; in fact, it was with this group of females that the younger men were supposed to learn the necessary ejaculatory control. After the 20-year period, 53 women and 38 men were chosen to be parents, or stirps, and the eugenics program was officially inaugurated. During the ensuing ten years, 58 children were born into the Community, after which period the Perfectionists disbanded.

So much for the published accounts. From the information which could be pieced together, these accounts are somewhat inaccurate. To begin with, some children *were* born into the Community prior to 1869, the year the eugenics program was started. The technique of *coitus reservatus*, therefore, was not 100 per cent effective, though in view of its rather bizarre nature it seems to have worked reasonably well.[1]

The actual criteria and methods for selecting the stirps have never been revealed. It is known that committees were set up to make the selection, but what standards they used is something of a mystery. Noyes served on the committees, and it would seem that it was he who largely decided which of the Perfectionists were qualified for parenthood. It was said that Noyes, himself, fathered a dozen children, so that evidently he was not adverse to self-selection.

Whatever the criteria used, and whatever the relative contributions of heredity and environment, the Stirpiculture program was apparently a success. As a group, the children born of selected parents led a healthy and vigorous life. Their death rate was reportedly lower than that of the surrounding community;[2] in fact, as mentioned earlier, thirteen of the Stirpiculture children are still living, a figure substantially greater than actuarial expectancy. Interviews revealed that a number of the children had achieved eminence in the business and professional world, several had written books, and nearly all had in turn borne children who were a credit to the community.

It might be well at this point to clear up a misconception relative to the child-rearing program of the Community. It is true that the children were not raised by their parents. Infants were under the care of their mothers up to the age of 15 months, but thereafter were moved to the children's section of the Mansion House. And while the youngsters were treated with kindness by their parents, the Community made a conscious effort to play down feelings of sentimentality between parents and offspring, the feeling being that Perfectionists should treat all children as their own, and vice versa.

It is not true, however, that the child-rearing system was one of impersonality. Children were shown ample affection and kindness, and they apparently enjoyed the zest of group living; at least, all those interviewed felt certain that childhood in the Old Community was a happy and exhilarating experience. As one of the "children" put it.

> Well, I remember one little girl always wanted her mother. She'd stand outside her window and call to her, even though the mother wasn't supposed to answer. Other than that particular case, all the children seemed happy enough. Everybody was good to us. You know you were loved because it was like a big family. Also, there were so many activities for the youngsters, so many things to do, well—believe me—we were happy children. Everybody around here will give you the same answer on that!

As an example of historico-cultural investigation I have attempted to analyze an experimental form of family organization. Other forms are available for parallel study: celibate groups such as the Father Divine Movement and the Shakers; polygynist groups such as the Mormon Fundamentalists (who continue their practice of plural marriage in spite of severe legal obstacles). Still other groups with unique forms of family or social organization would include the Amana Society, the Black Jews, the Hutterites, the House of David, the Llano Colonies, and the Old Order Amish.

To the best of my knowledge, the present account of the Oneida Community is the first ever to appear in any family journal. Most of the other groups mentioned above have yet to make such an appearance. It would seem, certainly, that they are over-due. Students of the family have made effective use of cross-cultural data, both for teaching purposes and for typologies in theory building. I submit that modern historico-cultural research—as focused, for example, on unique forms of family organization such as those mentioned above—would be similarly effective.

PART 6

NOTES

1. It should be mentioned that in the minds of the Perfectionists the system was by no means bizarre. *Coitus Reservatus* was looked upon not only as an effective method of birth control but as a means of *emotionally elevating* sexual pleasure. Interestingly enough, in Aldous Huxley's recent best-selling *Island* (N.Y., Harper, 1962), *coitus reservatus* is the method used by the Utopian society of Pala: "Did you ever hear of the Oneida Community?" Ranga now asked. "Basically, *maithuna* is the same as what the Oneida people called *coitus reservatus*. . . . But birth control is only the beginning of the story. Maithuana is something else. Something even more important. Remember," he went on earnestly, "the point that Freud was always harping on. . .the point about the sexuality of children. What we're born with, what we experience all

through infancy and childhood, is a sexuality that isn't concentrated on the genitals; it's a sexuality diffused throughout the whole organism. That's the paradise we inherit. But the paradise gets lost as the child grows up. Maithuana is the organized attempt to regain that paradise" (pp. 86–87).

2. H. H. and G. W. Noyes, "The Oneida Community Experiment in Stirpiculture," *Eugenics, Genetics and the Family,* 1 (1932), pp. 374–386.

Critical Thinking Questions

1. What happened in the Oneida Community when conflict arose? How does this compare with how conflict is resolved in the community you live in?
2. Using your "sociological lens," why do you suppose alternatives to monogamy in the Western world are considered deviant and severely tabooed?
3. Did the use of eugenics in the Oneida community differ from the use of eugenics in Alberta (Chapter 7)? Please explain.

Chapter 16
Sex and Temperament

MARTHA C. WARD

As sociologists, when undertaking the study of gender, what is most interesting, as well as troubling, is that many still confuse *sex* (the biological and physical characteristics often associated with being male or female) with *gender* (the psycho-social behaviours and activities associated by society with males and females) or think that they are one and the same. The great value of anthropology along with sociology, is its ability to demonstrate that much of what we take as natural or innate in human beings, in fact, varies greatly from society to society. This is precisely why Margaret Mead's investigation of gender in three New Guinea societies has become one of the most-assigned readings in gender courses. Basically, what Mead found in New Guinea was one society (the Arapesh) where both males and females behaved in ways that might strike us as stereotypically feminine, a second society (the Mundugumor) where males and females behaved in ways that might strike us as stereotypically masculine, and a third society (the Tchambuli) where gender roles seemed to be a reversal of ours. This selection not only describes her findings in detail but also indicates some of the strengths and limitations of her analysis in light of later investigations. It also provides some insight (let's be honest: some gossip) about what can happen to Western anthropologists when they are thrown together in foreign climes.

1. What did Mead find with each of the following cultures in terms of gender and sex: Arapesh, Mundugumor, and Tchambuli?

PART 7

From 1931 to 1933, Margaret Mead and Reo Fortune mounted an anthropological expedition to the Sepik River region of New Guinea. What happened during this trip is an incredible story about four cultures, three anthropologists, two genders, and one river. This story is enormously significant to what anthropologists know about women, men, and culture. In fact, the story has achieved its own mythic status in the history of science.

The Sepik River is a land of mosquitos, crocodiles, cannibals, and floating corpses, Mead would write. People ate tasteless flour laboriously processed from sago palms, yams, bananas, and other produce from their garden plots and fish from the Sepik and its tributaries. Until the Australian government imposed a colonial peace a few years earlier, the peoples of the river region had been cannibals and headhunters. But memories and the social organizations that supported these activities remained potent.

In the first group Mead studied, the Arapesh, both men and women acted in a mild, parental, and responsible manner—like the stereotypes about females at various times in human history. In the second group, the Mundugumor, both men and women were fierce, sexually charged, assertive, and loud—a view some people hold about males from time to time. And in the third, the Tchambuli, men gossiped about each other and worried about their hairstyles, pretty costumes, or whether any women would marry them. The women in this region of beautiful dark lakes were competent and no-nonsense business managers. These three groups showed Mead that a culture may impose personalities and patterns on one gender or both genders that are only a subset of the whole spectrum of possibilities available to human beings.

THE ARAPESH

When they first arrived in New Guinea, Margaret and Reo were not certain where to go or which group to study. They hired carriers from the interior to help them up the slippery trails and across the rivers; these workers even had to carry Margaret because her ankle was broken. The decision was made for them when their carriers simply stranded them, with six-months' supplies, in a mountain village.

In the steep hills above the flood plain of the Sepik, level land is scarce. Collecting enough firewood and food is difficult. The women carry loads of sixty to seventy pounds suspended from their foreheads, often with a nursing baby in a bark sling or bag. Precious pigs die easily and yams grow poorly in shallow tropical soils. Mead described the sexual division of labor as a necessity for survival. Men were freer to assume authority, a necessary but evil responsibility. Men worked desperately hard to keep the dangerous secrets of the men's houses; women were excluded from ceremonies to protect them and unborn children from malignant spirits.

Mead called the Arapesh cooperative, oriented to the needs of the next generation, gentle, responsive, carefully parental, and willing to subordinate themselves in caring for those who were younger and weaker. She noted that the Arapesh would probably find the Western notion of parenting and paternity repulsive. They said that a man and a woman cannot make a baby from a moment of passion or a simple act of intercourse. Rather, sex is the strong purposeful work of feeding and shaping a baby during the early weeks in its mother's womb. Since the child is the product of both father's semen and mother's blood, combined in equal parts in the beginning weeks, both parents must work diligently to make the child both desire. This arduous labor begins when menstruation ceases. When this hard work is done, intercourse is strictly forbidden and a wide array of taboos are placed on the mother to protect the unborn child and insure a safe delivery.

An Arapesh man is strategically involved with various phases of his wife's labor. Immediately after birth and the careful disposal of the afterbirth, he brings her a bundle of soft absorbent leaves to line the little net bag in which the baby is suspended through its waking time, curled up as though still in its mother's tummy. He brings water to wash the baby and sweet smelling leaves to keep evil influences from the hut. Putting his wooden pillow (which men use to protect their hair styles) beside his resting wife, he is "in bed having a baby." Together they fast and perform small rituals to help their baby grow safely. His maternal and nurturant tasks continue in diminishing degrees through the baby's first year of life. Arapesh parents observe what we call a postpartum sex taboo: They don't have intercourse with each other or with others until their baby is walking around; then it is strong enough to withstand its parents' renewed sexuality.

Mead's descriptions of mothers nursing their babies are one of the most authentic and enduring images from *Sex and Temperament*. The emotional content of the culture for her came through in these ordinary moments. Always a skillful observer, she related how mother and infant nursed together to how men and women have sex later in life. She tells how Arapesh mothers, like mothers everywhere, have to go back to work at some point. By the time her child is walking, it may be too heavy for a mother to carry on long trips to her garden. So she may leave it with its father or her sister or mother.

But what about Arapesh individuals who do not conform to these cultural patterns she described? Mead was deeply concerned about people who did not "fit in" their culture; the term she used was "deviant." If the Arapesh insisted that everyone was gentle, maternal, and not sexually aggressive, then they would have trouble with others who did not fit these patterns. In fact, Mead said that egocentric, possessive, or jealous women suffered most from their deviation from the norms of Arapesh society. They were likely to act out violently because there were no boundaries or acceptance for them as part of the continuum of human culture.

But Margaret Mead left the Arapesh disappointed. She had not found temperamental differences between women and men. So how could she examine the differences between the sexes if both had roughly the same temperament or social personality?

Moreover, Margaret and Reo had other frustrations. Her bad ankle kept her confined to the unstimulating Arapesh while her restless and volatile husband went off on trips. It is clear from her autobiography that she found Arapesh values of nurturing over aggression compatible with her own personality, while her husband found them particularly shapeless and offensive. She attributed their marital troubles to differences in their respective temperaments. Reo, it seems, was equally disgruntled with both the Arapesh and his wife.

THE MUNDUGUMOR

Their second field site was equally arbitrary. Margaret and Reo looked on a map and selected the nearest group accessible by water, patrolled by the government but not visited by missionaries. The river-dwelling Mundugumor were in sharp contrast to the Arapesh. Both males and females acted like stereotypes of men we would probably like to avoid. In fact, until the early 1930s, the Mundugumor had been cannibals and headhunters.

Mead called both men and women of the Mundugumor virile, actively masculine, positively sexed, jealous, violent, hard, and arrogant. She witnessed many episodes of angry defiance, mutual hostility, and ruthless individualism. She said they could be charming but hypocritical.

The Mundugumor lived on high, fertile land between swift and treacherous tributaries of the Sepik River. Their neighbors and trading partners spoke of them as ferocious and reckless, and avoided crossing their lands. Rich by Sepik standards, the Mundugumor waterways were filled with fish, and with little effort, their gardens produced plenty of sago palms, coconut trees, and yams. The Mundugumor did not have to cooperate with each other to live well.

The rules of Mundugumor kinship and marriage were elaborate and harsh. In fact, they appeared made to be broken at the earliest opportunity. In their best possible kinship system, every man was supposed to acquire a wife by giving his sister in return for some other man's sister. But this principle never worked well. First of all, men wanted more than one wife; they also wanted to marry younger women who should have been properly married to a man in their sons' generation. So men competed with their sons for women because these young men wanted to use their sisters to make their own marriage alliances. Fathers used their daughters to make matches for themselves.

But Mundugumor women as sisters or daughters were never docile or cooperative in the marital schemes of their fathers or brothers. Furthermore, mothers plotted for themselves and against their daughters! A good Mundugumor mother wanted to see her daughter out of the way, replaced by a daughter-in-law living under her control. The best strategy of these two women was to become allies against their

PART 7

respective husbands. For obvious reasons, a Mundugumor woman preferred to have sons; a man preferred to have daughters.

The same atmosphere of jealousy and hostility prevailed after marriage. A man whose wife announced her pregnancy was a marked and unhappy man. He had to observe many public taboos while his peers taunted and teased him. He resented his wife and cursed the contraceptive magic which had so clearly failed him. A pregnant woman was deprived of sex and worried that her husband would desert her or take another wife altogether.

Mead wondered how any infant survived Mundugumor babyhood.

Mundugumor babies were not comforted with their mother's breasts; they were put in scratchy, harsh baskets until they learned to kick their way out of them. Once out of their baskets, they had to cling strongly to their mother's hair and make lots of noise to gain even the minimal attention necessary for survival. Mothers resented their smallest illness, accident, or weakness. Blows and cross words marked their weaning. They were surrounded by rules, a series of prohibitions: Don't go in the houses of your father's other wives and ask for food; don't cry or demand attention; don't wander out of sight, and so on.

It is not surprising that sex for Mundugumor adults potently mirrored their childhood experiences. Children who fought for every drop of milk and every ounce of nurturing would be unlikely candidates for romance, docility, or cooperation with parents' plans for arranged marriages. So girls put on their best jewelry or grass skirts and boys watched for the slightest sign of opportunity.

What would happen, Mead asked, to a Mundugumor couple who somehow invented long, languorous lovemaking, or to a Mundugumor man who rejoiced in his children's growth, or to a Mundugumor woman who cuddled and comforted her crying child? Too bad. They would be defined as deviates in Mundugumor society. While such individuals did not cause trouble in their communities, they were outsiders nonetheless. Who would marry a man who wished to be loyal or parental, or a woman who suckled a foster child?

The three months among the Mundugumor were troubled and discouraging for Mead. For starters, the group did not throw any light on her central theme of showing the contrast between female and male temperament since both sexes were so aggressive and assertive. As in the Arapesh, there were no behavioral styles that seemed to separate women and men. She hated the way they treated children and used them in conflict between the parents. The village flooded regularly and the mosquitos were even more hostile and aggressive than the Mundugumor.

Judging from her autobiography and their letters from the field, it is also clear that Margaret and Reo were getting on each other's nerves. She notes: "Reo was both repelled and fascinated by the Mundugumor. They struck some note in him that was thoroughly alien to me, and working with them emphasized aspects of his personality with which I could not empathize" (1976: 206). When she was ill with malaria, her husband offered no sympathy or assistance. When he was sick, he raged, fought the sickness, and climbed mountains.

So Margaret and Reo decided to leave this troubled field site. The government patrol boat took them upstream in time for Christmas. With the kind of luck, good and bad, that had so marked this trip, the boat deposited them on the doorstep of an English anthropologist named Gregory Bateson, who had been working in a dramatic culture called the Iatmul. This group set their tensions between the sexes into elaborate dances and ceremonials, using cross-dressing with costumes and makeup, and mock and ritual homosexuality.

THE TCHAMBULI

"You must be tired," Gregory said to Margaret tenderly as he pulled out a soft chair for her. She melted. Everything about this new anthropologist and the village was a relief for the aching **ethnographer**.

So Mead and Fortune decided to stay and finish their fieldwork with a group called the Tchambuli. They were neighbors to the Iatmul and had many similar practices. Both groups had splendid artistic traditions and complex cultures. Both lived in settled villages and traded fish with bush dwellers who made sago flour, the other staple of their diet. For both groups, women manufactured large, woven, mosquito-proof sleeping bags traded throughout the Sepik.

The Tchambuli lived on a blue-black lake. Small, sharp hills rose beyond the indistinct shores of the lake. In Mead's time a road wound near the lake margins. Men's houses, thirty to forty feet long, with painted, carved gables and figures of bird-men at the ends, lined the road. Paths ran from the ceremonial houses up the rocky hillsides to the women's houses. These were built to last three or four life-times and house three or four families.

For Mead, the Tchambuli dwelling house revealed the solidarity and solidity of women. Women, competent, collegial, and certain of themselves, occupied the center of the house. Men sat at the edges near the doors, uneasy, wary, ready to bolt back into their ceremonial houses. There they gathered their own firewood and cooked their own bachelor meals. While the women fished and wove, the men practiced dances, prepared extravagant costumes of feathers, fibers, and shells, or arranged each other's curls.

To men, the thing that mattered most in life was art. Every man knew at least one art: carving, weaving, painting, dancing, music, costume-making, drama productions, and the creation of a graceful pattern of social relations that allowed the unadorned women to draw sustenance and return to their work or trading activities. The women tolerated and even appreciated the games, dances, and theatricals the men staged. But the dance was valuable, not the dancer.

Tchambuli women weaned their children in the same careless, casual manner as they nursed them, stuffing their mouths with sweet delicacies to stop their crying.

Mead concluded that Tchambuli women had what she called dominance. She pointed out that the group practiced both patrilineal descent and polygyny (having two or more wives). These customs would seem to be oppressive or degrading to women. Yet these women had real power. While men bickered and reconciled, the women quietly carried on with their work. Mead spoke of women as impersonal, vigorous, and efficient.

Women, it is clear from her description, exercised their own choices for a mate despite patrilineal clans, polygyny, and a shallow mystique of arranged marriages.

Do not, however, be misled. Assuming that Mead presented a proper perspective on what she witnessed, women's freedom to ignore the rules of patriliny and arranged marriages still produced jealousy, conflicts, and soap opera dramas. For boys, there was a deeper discontinuity; a young man had no real training for his future role. By contrast, girls were thoroughly and practically trained in handicrafts, fishing, and the responsible, practical lives of women. The young men Mead saw in this society were confused; she says they were more maladjusted than any other group she had known. The patrilineal system justified a young man's wish or need to dominate, to initiate marriage choices, and to dictate economic decisions. But for reasons that are clear only in a later historic context, a man could not do these things. So some young men grew angry, violent, and neurotic. This was the primary example of deviancy she noted for the group.

DAUGHTERS OF SEX AND TEMPERAMENT

In the years that followed the publication of *Sex and Temperament*, many readers had trouble believing that within a 100-mile area of a remote

PART 7

and magnificent river region Mead conveniently found three societies that perfectly illustrated her points.

Mead always insisted that the sites selected for their three phases of fieldwork were only good luck. Ultimately, each was a theoretical bonus.

And, fortunately, we have the fieldwork of contemporary anthropologists, Nancy McDowell in the contemporary Mundugumor (now called the Biwat) and Deborah Gewertz among the Tchambuli (now called the Chambri). So we can ask these anthropologists and the host of excellent ethnographers who do fieldwork in this area: Was Margaret Mead losing it on the Sepik? Did she know what she was doing? Can we trust her conclusions? What can we really learn from studying sex and temperament in such settings?

Anthropologist Deborah Gewertz went to the Sepik River to do fieldwork in the early 1970s with the Chambri (Tchambuli). Although she was primarily concerned with trade and exchange networks, Deborah knew that she would be working in a group that had become an icon in women's studies. After all, Margaret Mead had labeled the women of Tchambuli "dominant."

Deborah concludes that Mead was essentially correct in what she saw, but she didn't stay long enough or have the viewpoint at that time to see the Chambri embedded in a long history of which 1933 was only a piece. Mead studied the Tchambuli as the group had just returned to the shores of the beautiful lake after a twenty-year exile in the hills above. While Mead was there, competition between males decreased temporarily while they rebuilt their base, the men's houses, the male rituals, and the symbolic equipment: slit drums, costumes, art and musical instruments. It is no wonder the men seemed strained and watchful, worried about marital prospects, or that they appeared preoccupied with artistic productivity and building activity. The women had already rebuilt their barter market system, trading fish for sago in the complementarity that ensured their food supply. So the women appeared "dominant."

According to Deborah Gewertz, Mead did not take complex regional histories into account nor push her own brilliant methodology to its fullest conclusions: She should have noted that women can move throughout a hierarchy without changing into men. Women can move through time taking on different attitudes and practices without losing basic functions. **Sex roles** (or gender roles) have enough flexibility to use in adjusting to changing circumstances. We cannot just label a group of women as dominant or submissive. Instead, we may find an underlying pattern of relationships that persists through time and provides us a range of negotiations for a complex variety of social situations.

With the blessings of Mead, anthropologist Nancy McDowell reworked the field notes from Margaret and Reo's sojourn among the Mundugumor in 1932 and compared them to her fieldwork with the group (now called the Biwat) in the early 1970s. Nancy concludes that "Mead's ethnographic skills, as well as her powers of observation and perception, were exceptional and clearly superseded the theory she espoused" "(McDowell 1991: 77). Unlike Mead, however, Reo Fortune never wrote up his notes from this trip. Margaret did some of them for him (as many academic wives have done for husbands), but the rest in his handwriting are useless.

What do we learn from these researchers? We see that gender roles are not fixed, rigid, or defined for all time. Sex roles are not divinely assigned nor inherent in something we call "nature." They are flexible; they can be used as problem-solving devices. For example, the Arapesh believed that women should avoid the yam gardens because the yams did not grow well around females; both women and gardens were believed to be protected by this belief. By contrast, Mundugumor couples took advantage of a similar mindset and deliberately copulated in other people's gardens just to ruin them.

What Mead called sex roles are only a script, not a prescription. She quoted Ruth Benedict, who said culture is "personality writ large." In Benedict's view, writes Mead,

It is possible to see each culture, no matter how small and primitive or how large and complex, as having selected from the great arc of human potentialities certain characteristics and then having elaborated them with greater strength and intensity than any single individual could ever do in one lifetime. (Mead 1959: v)

Their view of culture as a pattern or configuration of homogenous and integrated elements, often linked with a unified theme, lacks the dimensions of contemporary theories. Now anthropologists think that culture is never simple, uniform, or well integrated. It is a messy, complicated, and often contradictory set of differences or oppositions that may exist side by side within the same group claiming the same territory, history, or worldview. This is why, today, we can talk of a female culture and a male culture within complex and contradictory ethnic, national, and world cultures.

REFERENCES

McDowell, Nancy. 1991. *The Mundugamor: From the Field Notes of Margaret Mead and Reo Fortune.* Washington, D.C.: Smithsonian Institution Press.

Mead, Margaret. 1972. *Blackberry Winter: My Earlier Years.* New York: William Morrow.

Mead, Margaret. 1959. "Preface" to Ruth Benedict, *Patterns of Culture.* New York: Mentor (originally published in 1934).

Critical Thinking Questions

1. Can we take Mead's impressions as good measures of the three tribes?
2. From this article, what is the difference between sex and gender? What is the significance of this difference?

PART 7

Chapter 17

If Men Could Menstruate

GLORIA STEINEM

Gloria Steinem is a journalist, activist, and feminist most identified for going undercover as a Playboy Bunny at the Manhattan Playboy Club in the 1960s and exposing how poorly the women were treated. Since then, she has been a pillar in the feminist movement, championing rights not only for women, but for men as well. This selection is a classic in gender studies. Although meant to be funny, Steinem's brief essay makes a serious point. Although biology does not determine gender, it is often the case that cultural attitudes about gender shape attitudes about biology. In this article, she is suggesting that in a **patriarchial** society like ours, we would think quite differently about menstruation if it was associated with the dominant group (men) rather than the subordinate group (women).

While the topic of menstruation is still strongly **tabooed**, and often evokes strong reactions in sociology students, try to address and understand why this subject is still so tabooed and how this may lend itself toward understanding Steinem's overall message.

1. How do the characteristics of the powerful compare to the characteristics of the powerless? Does the critique of gender in the article bring to mind other examples of inequality?
2. Through the article, how does Steinem envision a world where men could menstruate and women could not? Would this resolve issues of gender inequality?

A white minority of the world has spent centuries conning us into thinking that a white skin makes people superior—even though the only thing it really does is make them more subject to ultra-violet rays and to wrinkles. Male human beings have built whole cultures around the idea that penis-envy is "natural" to women—though having such an unprotected organ might be said to make men vulnerable, and the power to give birth makes womb-envy at least as logical.

In short, the characteristics of the powerful, whatever they may be, are thought to be better than the characteristics of the powerless—and logic has nothing to do with it.

What would happen, for instance, if suddenly, magically, men could menstruate and women could not?

The answer is clear—menstruation would become an enviable, boastworthy, masculine event:

Men would brag about how long and how much.

Boys would mark the onset of **menses**, that longed-for proof of manhood, with religious rituals and stag parties.

Congress would fund a National Institute of Dysmenorrhea to help stamp out monthly discomforts.

Source: "If Men Could Menstrate" from the book *Outrageous Acts and Everyday Rebellions* by Gloria Steinem, Copyright ©1983 by Gloria Steinem, ©1984 by East Toledo Productions, Inc., ©1995 by Gloria Steinem. **Reprinted by permission of Henry Holt and Company, LLC.**

Sanitary supplies would be federally funded and free. (Of course, some men would still pay for the prestige of commercial brands such as John Wayne Tampons, Muhammad Ali's Rope-a-dope Pads, Joe Namath Jock Shields "For Those Light Bachelor Days," and Robert "Baretta" Blake Maxi-Pads.)

Military men, right-wing politicians, and religious fundamentalists would cite menstruation ("*men*-struation") as proof that only men could serve in the Army ("you have to give blood to take blood"), occupy political office ("can women be aggressive without that steadfast cycle governed by the planet Mars?"), be priests and ministers ("how could a woman give her blood for our sins?"), or rabbis ("without the monthly loss of impurities, women remain unclean").

Male radicals, left-wing politicians, and mystics, however, would insist that women are equal, just different; and that any woman could enter their ranks if only she were willing to self-inflict a major wound every month ("you *must* give blood for the revolution"), recognize the preeminence of menstrual issues, or subordinate her selfness to all men in their Cycle of Enlightenment.

Street guys would brag ("I'm a three-pad man") or answer praise from a buddy ("Man, you lookin' *good*!") by giving fives and saying, "Yeah, man, I'm on the rag!"

TV shows would treat the subject at length. ("Happy Days": Richie and Potsie try to convince Fonzie that he is still "The Fonz," though he has missed two periods in a row.) So would newspapers. (SHARK SCARE THREATENS MENSTRUATING MEN. JUDGE CITES MONTHLY STRESS IN PARDONING RAPIST.) And movies. (Newman and Redford in "Blood Brothers"!)

Men would convince women that intercourse was *more* pleasurable at "that time of the month." Lesbians would be said to fear blood and therefore life itself—though probably only because they needed a good menstruating man.

Of course, male intellectuals would offer the most moral and logical arguments. How could a woman master any discipline that demanded a sense of time, space, mathematics, or measurement, for instance, without that in-built gift for measuring the cycles of the moon and planets—and thus for measuring anything at all? In the rarefied fields of philosophy and religion, could women compensate for missing the rhythm of the universe? Or for their lack of symbolic death-and-resurrection every month?

Liberal males in every field would try to be kind: the fact that "these people" have no gift for measuring life or connecting to the universe, the liberals would explain, should be punishment enough.

And how would women be trained to react? One can imagine traditional women agreeing to all these arguments with a staunch and smiling masochism. ("The ERA would force housewives to wound themselves every month": Phyllis Schlafly. "Your husband's blood is as sacred as that of Jesus—and so sexy, too!": Marabel Morgan.) Reformers and Queen Bees would try to imitate men, and *pretend* to have a monthly cycle. All feminists would explain endlessly that men, too, needed to be liberated from the false idea of Martian aggressiveness, just as women needed to escape the bonds of menses-envy. Radical feminists would add that the oppression of the nonmenstrual was the pattern for all other oppressions. ("Vampires were our first freedom fighters!") Cultural feminists would develop a bloodless imagery in art and literature. Socialist feminists would insist that only under capitalism would men be able to monopolize menstrual blood. . . .

In fact, if men could menstruate, the power justifications could probably go on forever.

If we let them.

PART 7

Critical Thinking Questions

1. Steinem writes on gender inequality by drawing on the strongly tabooed subject of menstruation. Does the discussion of such a tabooed subject make the discussion of gender inequality easier to understand, or does it alienate the reader from Steinem's ideas?

2. Despite popular belief, feminism is about achieving equality for women, as well as men. Thinking beyond Steinem's argument, what do you suppose the world would look like if *both* men and women could physically bear children?

Chapter 18

The National Conversation in the Wake of Littleton Is Missing the Mark

JACKSON KATZ AND SUT JHALLY

The high schools may be in Littleton, Colorado; Tabor, Alberta; Montreal, Quebec; or Blacksburg, Virginia, but the pattern is now all too familiar—students with guns opening fire on other students. Naturally, we want to know the causes of this violence, and there has been no dearth of articles speculating on what those causes might be. The usual suspects include things like violent video games, social maladjustment, jock culture, a breakdown in family, and so on. In this selection Jackson Katz and Sut Jhally make an interesting point: Most discussions of these school shootings pay little or no attention to the one social pattern that is constant across cases—the shooters are male. At the very least, they suggest, we need to consider the possibility that the way our culture defines what it means to "be male" might be an important element in predisposing males toward this sort of violence. A useful supplement to this reading is the film Tough Guise, narrated by Jackson Katz and available from the Media Education Foundation.

1. What is missing from public discussions of school shootings? Does this impact our capacity to prevent such horrific acts?

PART 7

The events at Columbine High School 12 days ago have plunged us into a national conversation about "youth violence" and how to stop it. Proposals came last week from all corners. That we are talking about the problem is good; but the way we are talking about it is misdirected.

It is tempting to look at the murderous attack in Littleton as a manifestation of individual pathologies, an isolated incident involving deeply disturbed teenagers who watched one too many video games. That explanation ignores larger social and historical forces, and is dangerously shortsighted. Littleton is an extreme case, but if we examine critically the cultural environment in which boys are being socialized and trained to become men, such events might not appear so surprising.

Political debate and media coverage keep repeating the muddled thinking of the past. Headlines and stories focus on youth violence, "kids killing kids," or as in the title of a CBS "48 Hours" special, "Young Guns." This is entirely the wrong framework to use in trying to understand what happened in Littleton—or in Jonesboro, Ark., Peducah, Ky., Pearl, Miss., or Springfield, Ore.

This is not a case of kids killing kids. This is boys killing boys and boys killing girls.

What these school shootings reveal is not a crisis in youth culture but a crisis in masculinity. The shootings—all by white adolescent males—are telling us something about how we are doing as a society, much like the canaries in coal mines, whose deaths were a warning to the miners that the caves were unsafe.

Consider what the reaction would have been if the perpetrators in Littleton had been girls. The first thing everyone would have wanted to talk about would have been: Why are girls—not kids—acting out violently? What is going on in the lives of girls that would lead them to commit such atrocities? All of the explanations would follow from the basic premise that being female was the dominant variable.

But when the perpetrators are boys, we talk in a gender-neutral way about kids or children, and few (with the exception of some feminist scholars) delve into the forces—be they cultural, historical, or institutional—that produce hundreds of thousands of physically abusive and violent boys every year. Instead, we call upon the same tired specialists who harp about the easy accessibility of guns, the lack of parental supervision, the culture of peer-group exclusion and teasing, or the prevalence of media violence.

All of these factors are of course relevant, but if they were the primary answers, then why are girls, who live in the same environment, not responding in the same way? The fact that violence—whether of the spectacular kind represented in the school shootings or the more routine murder, assault, and rape—is an overwhelmingly male phenomenon should indicate to us that gender is a vital factor, perhaps the vital factor.

Looking at violence as gender-neutral has the effect of blinding us as we desperately search for clues about how to respond.

The issue is not just violence in the media but the construction of violent masculinity as a cultural norm. From rock and rap music and videos, Hollywood action films, professional and college sports, the culture produces a stream of images of violent, abusive men and promotes characteristics such as dominance, power, and control as means of establishing or maintaining manhood.

Consider professional wrestling, with its mixing of sports and entertainment and its glamorization of the culture of dominance. It represents, in a microcosm, the broader cultural environment in which boys mature. Some of the core values of the wrestling subculture—dominant displays of power and control, ridicule of lesser opponents, respect equated with physical fear and deference—are factors in the social system of Columbine High, where the shooters were ridiculed, marginalized, harassed, and bullied.

These same values infuse the Hollywood action-adventure genre that is so popular with boys and young men. In numerous films starring iconic hypermasculine figures like Arnold Schwarzenegger, Sylvester Stallone, Wesley Snipes, Bruce Willis, and Mel Gibson, the cartoonish story lines convey the message that masculine power is embodied in muscle, firepower, and physical authority.

Numerous other media targeting boys convey similar themes. Thrash metal and gangsta rap, both popular among suburban white males, often express boys' angst and anger at personal problems and social injustice, with a call to violence to redress the grievances. The male sports culture features regular displays of dominance and one-upsmanship, as when a basketball player dunks "in your face," or a defensive end sacks a quarterback, lingers over his fallen adversary, and then, in a scene reminiscent of ancient Rome, struts around to a stadium full of cheering fans.

How do you respond if you are being victimized by this dominant system of masculinity? The lessons from Columbine High—a typical suburban "**jockocracy**," where the dominant male athletes did not hide their disdain for those who did not fit in—are pretty clear.

The 17- and 18-year-old shooters, tired of being ridiculed or marginalized, weren't big and strong and so they used the great equalizer: weapons. Any discussion about guns in our society needs to include a discussion of their function as equalizers. In Littleton, the availability of weapons gave the shooters the opportunity to exact a twisted and tragic revenge: 15 dead, including themselves, and 23 wounded.

What this case reinforces is our crying need for a national conversation about what it means to be a man, since cultural definitions of manhood and masculinity are ever-shifting and are particularly volatile in the contemporary era.

Such a discussion must examine the mass media in which boys (and girls) are immersed, including violent, interactive video games, but also mass media as part of a larger cultural environment that helps to shape the masculine identities of young boys in ways that equate strength in males with power and the ability to instill fear—fear in other males as well as in females.

But the way in which we neuter these discussions makes it hard to frame such questions, for there is a wrong way and a right way of asking them. The wrong way: "Did the media (video games, Marilyn Manson, 'The Basketball Diaries') make them do it?" One of the few things that we know for certain after 50 years of sustained research on these issues is that behavior is too complex a phenomenon to pin down to exposure to individual and isolated media messages. The evidence strongly supports that behavior is linked to attitudes and attitudes are formed in a much more complex cultural environment.

The right way to ask the question is: "How does the cultural environment, including media images, contribute to definitions of manhood that are picked up by adolescents?" Or, "How does repeated exposure to violent masculinity normalize and naturalize this violence?"

There may indeed be no simple explanation as to why certain boys in particular circumstances act out in violent, sometimes lethal, ways. But leaving aside the specifics of this latest case, the fact that the overwhelming majority of such violence is perpetrated by males suggests that part of the answer lies in how we define such intertwined concepts as "respect," "power" and "manhood." When you add on the easy accessibility of guns and other weapons, you have all the ingredients for the next deadly attack.

PART 7

Critical Thinking Questions

1. How does violence relate to masculinity? How is violence constructed as a social norm (and what role does the media play)?
2. Are there possibilities for a masculine alternative that does not involve violence and physicality? Can some of these alternatives be outlined from lessons from the previous two articles on gender (Ward, Chapter 16, and Steinem, Chapter 17)?

Chapter 19

Sexual Assault in Canada: Gendered Expectations, Myths, and Resistances

LAURA MURPHY

The issue of sexual assault is ever present in our daily lives, yet most of us have little knowledge about what rape and sexual assault is. This is a complex and difficult social problem. Often, the focus and even at times the blame, is placed on the survivor rather than on the perpetrator. This can make it difficult to understand the underlying conditions and culture that propagate sexual assault. Without these understandings, sexual violence cannot be properly addressed. This article will focus on sexual assault, rape, and sexual violence committed against women and how the expression of masculinity in our culture (and others) can influence the number and severity of sexual assaults and how they are dealt with by society. The author will introduce the reader to new terms such as "rape culture" in order to explain how violence can become accepted through the acquisition and perpetuation of "norms."

1. How has the legal system changed its view of sexual assault over the last three decades?
2. What is the sociological milieu of sexual assault? **Please note: If you are grappling with any of the issues raised in this reading, there are avenues for support. Please contact your campus sexual assault centre, or your local sexual assault centre at http://www.casac.ca/content/anti-violence-centres. This website may also be of use: http://www.consented.ca.

It has been argued that we live in a 'rape culture,' which is described by Jacelyn Friedman here: http://yesmeansyesblog.wordpress.com/2009/07/23/this-is-what-rape-culture-looks-like/. More directly, rape culture is the notion that **rape** and **sexual assault** is commonplace through dominant norms, beliefs, stereotypes, and commonsense notions that excuse, justify, and normalize sexual violence (particularly against women).

For the purpose of this article, the focus of sexual assault and rape will be that which is committed against women given the prevalence of women as survivors of these crimes. This is not intended to ignore the seriousness of sexual assault for men or transgendered individuals, however, statistics indicate women experience rape at five times the rate of men (Brennan & Taylor-Butts 2008, 12) and it is estimated that one of every four women in Canada will experience sexual assault in their adult lives (Statistics Canada 2006, 24). As well, 97 percent of those accused of sexual assault are men (Brennan & Taylor-Butts 2008). While the vast majority

Source: Murphy, Laura. "Sexual Assault in Canada." Unpublished Manuscript, 2011. Reproduced with permission of the author.

of men are not perpetrators of sexual violence this article will examine how the expression of masculinity in our culture (and others) can increase the number and severity of sexual assaults and how they are dealt with by society.

One of the strongest misconceptions about sexual assault and rape is that it is about sex. What sexual assault is really about is power: power that is distributed throughout our culture, and often held in the hands of men. The issue of rape and sexual assault can only be understood in the context of normative gender relations where men are dominant, hold the control, and are expected to be aggressive. In complement, women are meant to be submissive and passive.

Rape is sex (penetration) without voluntary consent. **Consent** is a freely made choice that is clearly communicated. Rape is a form of sexual assault and abuse. Sexual assault may include rape, but it is defined as any sexual contact without consent and/or involving the use of force. Sexual assault includes a wide spectrum of sexual violence.

ACCORDING TO THE LAW

Historically, women in Canada were acknowledged as chattel (movable property), owned by their husbands (Stanley 1987). Therefore, when a woman was raped it was a crime against her husband's property. Prior to 1983 rape was considered to be penetration of the vagina with a penis without the consent of the woman outside of marriage. Therefore, husband rape was not recognized in Canadian law as a crime.

Women's advocacy groups pressured the government for changes and The Charter of Rights and Freedoms set a new tone for sexual assault. Bill C-127 (1983) aimed to make it easier for survivors to report attacks. The law recognized there could be rape and abuse in marriage, men could be raped, different forms of coercion could indicate denial of consent, and most importantly the survivor's lifestyle could not be put on trial as a defence for the accused nor could the survivor's name be made public (rape shield law).[1]

Prior to Bill-C-127, Canadian laws only addressed rape, and did so under narrow terms. Under the new legislation there was a three-tiered definition of sexual assault, which set out a continuum of "types of sexual assault" that involved different levels of violence and attached different penalties. These included unwanted or forced touching to forced intercourse, sexual assaults by threat of bodily harm, and aggravated sexual assault where the survivor[2] was injured (Stanley 1987; House of Commons Debates).

No longer were Canada's laws particular to rape only, but now were set in place to provide recourse for survivors of all types of sexual violence. There is evidence that reporting of sexual assaults has increased dramatically since the new legislation was put into place (Schissel 1996). However, more recently according to Statistics Canada, and through information from victimization surveys, less than one in ten sexual assault survivors report the crimes committed against them to the police (Brennan & Taylor-Butts 2008, 8). Consequently, sexual assaults remain severely underreported (Dauvergne & Turner 2010). Despite the changes set in place in the Canadian Criminal Code, why are reports of sexual assault not only extremely low, but now on the decline (Brennan & Taylor-Butts 2008, 8)? And further, what does this mean?

To address this question, the remainder of this paper will discuss persistent rape myths. This article will then look to grassroots organizations and activities that provide alternatives to the status quo and attempt to change the current state of how sexual assault is interpreted and understood in Canada.

THE HARM OF RAPE MYTHS: PRODUCTION AND REPLICATION OF GENDERED VIOLENCE

Rape myths are powerful and pervasive "false beliefs used mainly to shift the blame of rape from perpetrators to victims . . . [which] in many ways contribute toward the pervasiveness of rape" (Suarez & Gadalla 2010). Rape myths can often illicit negative reactions from those closest to a survivor (Suarez & Gadalla 2010), which in turn contributes toward low reporting rates. Further, such myths are so strong that they may cause a survivor to feel personally responsible for the crime committed against them and they may internalize the trauma they have experienced. Not only does this prevent an individual from seeking out help and assistance in dealing with such a difficult and sensitive issue, but the individual may develop symptoms such as post-traumatic stress, chronic pain syndromes, "depression, anxiety, substance abuse, and eating disorders . . ." (Luce, Schrager, & Gilchrist 2010, 493–494) amongst other problems. Without proper support, these issues and the trauma from the experience can become extremely difficult to overcome. Even worse, rape myths justify and normalize sexual violence, paving the way for perpetrators to commit these violent acts with little or no recourse for the survivor. In addition, some of the contributors that lead to negative and inefficient policing regarding the crime of sexual assault "stem directly from rape myths that are deeply embedded in our general culture" (Tomlinson 1999, 86).

Rape myths are rooted in gendered norms and expectations, and those beliefs are embedded with expectations of sexuality. Rape myths support male privilege regarding heteronormative sexuality and open access to women's bodies. Under gendered norms, men are expected to be extremely physical, virile, and dominant. The expectations placed on men's sexual desire are made tangible when compared to the expectations placed upon women, which include sexual submissiveness, chasteness, and vulnerability. Male privilege can be difficult to interrogate resulting in unexamined feelings of superiority over women. Male privilege and its relation to rape culture was examined in a study conducted by the Ontario Women's Directorate (1995).

College-aged men were asked if they would participate in activities we know as sexual assault if they would not be caught: *60 percent responded they would commit the crime of sexual assault if they could get away with it.*

Rape Myth One: Survivors Engage in 'Risky Behaviour'

One of the most harmful rape myths constantly reproduced is that the rape survivor engaged in 'risky behaviour.' Such behaviours are often attributed to those who frequent nightclubs and bars, as well as those who engage in drinking (Mont, Miller, & Myhr 2003, 470). It has been embedded within our culture that those who engage in the aforementioned behaviours, and/or those dressed in bar-type clothing, are deserving of (or at least encouraging) men to assault them. However, when an individual chooses to wear a certain outfit, regardless of what that is, they are only consenting to wearing that outfit, not to being raped. This is further articulated by a recent anti-rape campaign put in place by Rape Crisis Scotland (http://www.youtube.com/watch?v=h95-IL3C-Z8&feature=player_embedded).

Rape Myth Two: Strangers are Rapists

In approximately 80 percent of sexual assault cases, the perpetrator is *known to the survivor* (Brennan & Taylor-Butts 2008, 13). Additionally, the majority of sexual assault attacks take place in private residences (Brennan & Taylor-Butts 2008, 14). This demonstrates that most assaults and rapes most likely occur in the home of the survivor, the perpetrator, or in the home of an individual known to either party. So in reality, engaging in risky behaviour translates to spending time with people that you know in your own home or in a private residence most likely known to you. Therefore stranger rapes, while they do happen, are not nearly as common as rapes and sexual assaults committed by those known to the survivor. Perhaps this myth of 'stranger rape' is reproduced as it creates the idea of a rapist as an 'other': an individual outside of our communities, our neighbourhoods, our families, and our relationships. Having an outsider to blame for rape and sexual assault is much easier than taking a hard look at some of the contributing factors of sexual assault, factors which our culture creates and replicates, through gendered norms and beliefs, the normalization of violence against women, whether in music videos, in movies, or in the sexist and derogatory language used to discuss and describe women.

Rape Myth Three: Causes

While alcohol and drugs may increase the incidences of sexual assault and rape (Brennan & Taylor-Butts 2008), they *do not cause* sexual assault and rape. Rather, they can provide an opportunity for a perpetrator to commit the crime of sexual assault. When an individual consents to partaking in alcohol consumption or the use of drugs, that is all that they are consenting to: they are not consenting to being raped.

As well, women who are most vulnerable (those who are pregnant, disabled, Indigenous, and/or who live in poverty) experience elevated rates of sexual assault (Statistics Canada 2006; Brennan & Taylor-Butts 2008). Sociologists would say that if you are vulnerable or included in a vulnerable population socially or economically you are also more vulnerable to sexual exploitation.[3] Women who are vulnerable, or in threatening circumstances, may not be able to give consent.

Yes Means Yes

Sexual consent can only be given freely, free from threat, and/or harm. Consent cannot be given by somebody who is unconscious, coerced, or unable to communicate. Consent can be given, and can subsequently be revoked. The act of revoking one's consent can happen verbally or

physically. Proper ongoing communication and agreed boundaries between both partners leaves room for an individual to give, refuse, or revoke their consent.

As well, women may revoke consent, but this may not be acknowledged. Again, as most sexual assaults occur with someone known to the survivor, a common reaction may be disbelief in the moment. While it is commonly expected that when a woman is attacked the 'normal' reaction is for her to fight or react, however, individuals react in varied ways. Other reactions include the survivor freezing up, and/or mentally separating themselves from the situation to avoid being emotionally and viscerally present in the rape or sexual assault. The myth that a 'true' survivor would fight back, combined with the fact they most likely know the perpetrator may make the survivor feel they were not actually raped, or that they may have given the wrong signals.

Rape myths are troubling as they leave little room to question the perpetrator's activities: rather they demonstrate that rape happens, it is inevitable, and it is the responsibility of those vulnerable to take it upon themselves to avoid it from happening to them. Some may see this as sexual terrorism, where the onus is placed upon potential victims, and results in women being afraid to walk alone at night, restrained in the activities they may want to pursue, being afraid of being attacked, and feeling helpless and responsible when they do.

BACKLASH TO THE STATUS QUO: THE GARNEAU SISTERHOOD AND THE RISE OF THE SLUTWALK

The three most common reported reactions amongst survivors of sexual assault are anger, confusion, and frustration (Brennan & Taylor-Butts 2008, 14). While police officers may not take the survivor's complaint seriously (Mont, Miller, & Myhr 2003), neither may the court.

PART 7

In 2008, a rash of violent sexual assaults and rapes began in Edmonton's Garneau neighbourhood (Gotell forthcoming). Reportedly, the police did not take the first woman's word seriously about her sexual assault, and a second woman was violated. Despite the first two reported assaults occurring in the same neighbourhood, the police did not notify the community. Finally, when a third woman came forward, the police finally released some information, sparingly and vaguely, on the sexual assaults (Gotell forthcoming). Eventually, with the rape of an older woman in a more middle class area, the police issued warnings to women to be vigilant, to lock up their homes properly, and to be aware of who is around them (Gotell forthcoming). In short, the police placed the onus on women in Edmonton to take proper care of themselves, limit their activities, and to be aware of who may be around them, which transferred the responsibility of the rapist for their actions onto women who could be potentially sexually assaulted. A group of women who lived in the area responded to this. They labelled themselves the Garneau Sisterhood (http://garneausisterhood. weebly.com) and "mounted a poster and media campaign challenging [the] disciplinary and individualizing thrust of police warnings . . . calling upon women to actively reject their assigned role as safety-conscious victims-in-waiting" (Gotell forthcoming, 2). This anonymous group most notoriously postered the Garneau neighbourhood with signs addressed specifically to the rapist, calling him out for his actions, and making him the subject of focus, rather than potential victims.

Most recently, in February 2011, Manitoba Court of Queen's Bench Justice (Judge) Robert Dewar commented in the sentencing of a man convicted of sexual assault that the woman who was attacked was 'dressed for it' and had questionable behaviour that was misinterpreted by a "clumsy Don Juan" (CBC News 2011a). Further, the judge made light of the woman's sexual assault by claiming "sex was in the air," and rather than jail time, sentenced the perpetrator to community service and released him right back into the community (CBC News 2011a).

In the same month a Toronto police officer informed female students at University of Toronto's Osgoode Hall Law School (during a campus safety information session) that the best way to avoid being sexually assaulted was to avoid dressing as a "slut" (CBC News 2011b).

Unfortunately, examples such as these are not a rarity and assist in contributing to the low levels of reported sexual assaults (Mont, Miller, & Myhr 2003). The comments made by the police officer advising women to avoid dressing like 'sluts' garnered a lot of attention, and in response several 'Slutwalks' were organized in cities across Canada, with the intention of demonstrating turning the notion of blaming a survivor's clothing on their sexual assault on its head. While the rise of the slutwalk seemed to be partially celebrated, partially misunderstood, the walk was cultivated around an ironic response to the blame placed upon the victim for their own assault because of their choice of clothing. Many slutwalks featured women dressing in all types of clothing (whether 'slutty' or not), and was intended for women reappropriating public spaces and their bodies from rape myths and sexual assault.

The rise of the Garneau Sisterhood and the Slutwalk demonstrate a backlash and vigorous response to the societal norms and expectations that intricately ignore rapists and focus on demonizing the survivor of rape. These movements, made up of strong empowered women, can be difficult to understand given how the women actively involved do not fit into the gendered norms and expectations placed upon them. Perhaps these misunderstandings and confusions are most powerful of all, as they demonstrate the improbability, impossibility, and danger of gendered norms, and how they extend to false and harmful expectations of sexuality.

NOTES

1. The "rape shield" provision was struck down in the early 1990s, but was reintroduced in amended form somewhat later.
2. While often those who have experienced sexual violence and/or rape have been referred to as 'victims,' as the connotations associated with victim are problematic. Instead, I have chosen to primarily employ the much more empowered and positive term of 'survivor.'
3. See http://www.metrac.org/programs/safety/downloadswhy.safety.for.women.marginalized.groups.pdf.

REFERENCES

Brennan, S., & Taylor-Butts, A. 2008. *Sexual Assault in Canada: 2004 and 2007.* Ottawa, ON: Statistics Canada, Canadian Centre for Justice Statistics.

Bumiller, K. 2008. *In an Abusive State: How Neoliberalism Appropriated the Feminist Movement Against Sexual Violence.* Durham: Duke University Press. pp. 79–90.

Carol S. 1989. *Feminism and the Power of Law.* London: Routledge.

CBC News. 2011a. Judge's Sex-Assault Remarks Under Review, February 25, 2011. Accessed at http://www.cbc.ca/news/canada/manitoba/story/2011/02/25/mb-dewar-comments-review-judicial-council-winnipeg.html. Toronto, ON: CBC News.

CBC News. 2011b. Toronto Officer To Apologize for 'Sluts' Remark: Advised Female Students to Dress More Modestly. Accessed at http://www.cbc.ca/news/canada/toronto/story/2011/02/17/toronto-officer-slut657.html. Toronto, ON: CBC News.

Dauvergne, M., & Turner, J. 2010. Police-reported crime statistics in Canada, 2009. *Juristat* 30 (2):1–37.

Gotell, L. Forthcoming 2011. Third Wave Antirape Activism on Neoliberal Terrain: The Garneau Sisterhood in *Sexual Assault Law, Practice & Activism in a Post-Jane Doe Era,* Elizabeth Sheehy, ed. Accessed at http://www.ruor.uottawa.ca/fr/handle/10393/19876. Ottawa, ON: University of Ottawa.

House of Commons Debates, XVII at 20039 (Hon. Jean Chrétien).

Luce, H., Schrager, S., and Gilchrist, V. 2010. Sexual assault of women. *American Family Physicia* 81(4): 489–495.

Mont, J., Miller, K.L., and Myhr, T. 2003. The role of "real rape" and "real victim": Stereotypes in the police reporting practices of sexually assaulted women. *Violence Against Women* 9(4): 466–486.

Ontario Women's Directorate (OWD). 1995. *Facts to Consider About Sexual Assault.* Toronto, ON: OWD.

Schissel, B. 1996. Law reform and social change: A time series analysis of sexual assault in Canada. *Journal of Criminal Justice* 24(2): 123–138.

Stanley, M. G. 1987. *The Experience of the Rape Victim with the Criminal Justice System Prior to Bill C-127.* Ottawa: Communications and Public Affairs, Department of Justice.

Statistics Canada. 2006. *Measuring Violence Against Women: Statistical Trends 2006.* Ottawa, ON: Statistics Canada.

Suarez, E. and Gadalla, T. 2010. Stop blaming the victim: A meta-analysis on rape myths. *Journal of Interpersonal Violence* 25: 2010–2035.

Tomlinson, D. 1999. *Police-reporting Decisions of Sexual Assault Survivors: An Exploration of Influential Factors.* Calgary, AB: Calgary Communities Against Sexual Assault.

PART 7

Critical Thinking Questions

1. Do you think the interventions like the Garneau Sisterhood and Slutwalks are effective? Why or why not? Can you suggest others kinds of interventions on this issue?
2. Why do survivors still have a difficult time "proving" that they were violated, despite the research showing the rate of false allegations of sexual assault are so low?

Chapter 20
Pornography and Violence: A New Look at the Research

MARY ANNE LAYDEN

With the advent of the Internet, pornography has become readily available to anyone who has a computer and Internet connection. Further, this ease of accessibility has driven the industry toward the exploration and exploitation of almost every sexual situation possible. This article discusses a disturbing trend, the link between violence and pornography. While most viewing is done in private, there are "commonsense" notions regarding the politics and social relations embedded within pornography that impact on those viewing it, particularly young people.

1. What are the consumers of pornography learning?
2. Does pornography empower some while denigrating others?

. . .

We learn better using images than words, because images carry more information in a more compact form. . . . The vast majority of **pornography** is visual.

We also learn better when aroused. If something activates our sympathetic nervous system, we are more prepared to remember the information received at that point. The arousal may come from excitement, fear, disgust, or sexual tension. Pornography can produce any of these emotions. We tend to remember any experience we have in those aroused states.

And learning is better if it is reinforced. Behavior that is rewarded is likely to be repeated while behavior that is punished is less likely to be repeated. Sexual arousal and orgasm are extremely rewarding experiences. We may be innately predisposed to enjoy the rewards of sexual arousal and orgasm, but we learn how and when and with whom we can experience those pleasures. . . .

Learning is also better if we see others perform a behavior and observe what happens. Seeing others who are modeling behaviors rewarded or punished will have some of the same effects on us as if we were rewarded or punished ourselves. . . . We learn to repeat or avoid those behaviors by seeing their effect on the models.

Imagery that contains role models who are demonstrating sexual behavior and being rewarded for it, that produces sexual arousal in the viewer and is followed by an orgasm, can be extremely effective in producing deeply learned beliefs and behaviors.

Pornography can offer all these elements—images, arousal, reinforcement, the example of others—so it is a potent teacher of both beliefs and behaviors. It provides the ideal conditions for learning.

Source: Layden, Mary Anne. "Pornography and Violence: A New Look at the Research." *The Social Costs of Pornography: A Collection of Papers.* Ed. James R. Stoner, Jr. and Donna M. Hughes. Princeton, NJ: 2010. Used with permission from The Witherspoon Institute.

One category of beliefs we learn is called "permissions-giving beliefs."[1] These beliefs give us permission to engage in a behavior we would like to engage in or are already engaging in. They tell us there is no need to stop, change, or reduce the behavior—they tell us, for example, that what we are doing is normal, that it doesn't hurt anyone, and that everyone is doing it.

Marshall has stated that "this may be pornography's most insidious influence; namely, the acceptance of the attitudes (some obvious, some more subtle) expressed in pornography. Pornographic depictions of sexuality distort the truth about desires of women and children, and legitimize men's sense of entitlement, and use of force, violence, and degrading by male actors."[2] In other words, pornography has the ability not only to teach social attitudes and behaviors, but also to give permission to engage in them. Permission-giving beliefs become releasers of behavior.

Pornography is an ideal teacher of these releaser beliefs. It can teach specific sexual behaviors and general attitudes toward women and children, teach what relationships are like, and teach the nature of sexuality, thus giving permission for a wide range of actions. For example, a male masturbating to the images of smiling children having sex with adults or of sexually aroused women being beaten, raped, or degraded, is learning that the subjects enjoy and desire this treatment and is thereby being taught that he has permission to act this way himself.

. . . Pornography can teach what to do, with whom to do it, when and how often to do it, that it's okay to do it, and then stimulate the urge to do it now.

. . .

Some of the messages of pornography teach beliefs and behaviors. Some of these behaviors are pathological, illegal, or both, and are toxic on many levels. . . . Some of pornography's messages about relationships, sexuality, and women may be damaging and pathological, even if the behaviors are not illegal.

. . .

PORNOGRAPHY AND ATTITUDES TOWARD SEXUAL VIOLENCE

The rape myth is a set of beliefs that women are responsible for rape, like to be raped, want to be raped, and suffer few negative outcomes because of it. A number of studies have looked at the acceptance of the rape myth after exposing the subjects to sexual imagery, both violent and non-violent, and one study also asked subjects about their typical pornography use.

Males shown imagery of a woman aroused by **sexual violence,** and then shown pornography that involved rape, were more likely than those who hadn't to say that the rape victim suffered less, that she enjoyed it, and that women in general enjoy rape. . . .[3]

Males who viewed sexual violence obtained higher scores on scales measuring acceptance of both interpersonal violence and the rape myth when compared with males who viewed either a physically violent or a neutral film.[4] The increase in attitudes supporting sexual violence following exposure to pornography is greater if the pornography is violent than if it is nonviolent.[5]

A similar effect is seen even when the pornography is not violent. Males who were shown non-violent scenes that sexually objectified and degraded women and were then exposed to material that depicted rape were more likely to indicate that the rape victim experienced pleasure and "got what she wanted."[6] Even *women* who were exposed to pornography as a child had a greater acceptance of the rape myth than those who were not exposed as children.[7] Both males and females who were exposed to pornography recommended a sentence for a rapist that was half that recommended by those who had been shown non-pornographic imagery. These subjects appear to have trivialized the crime of rape.[8]

. . .

These studies indicate that the use of pornography, even that which does not include

PART 7

sexual violence, changes beliefs about rape and sexual violence. If women like to be raped and deserve to be raped, there isn't any need for sexual restraint or frustration of sexual desire. Rape pornography teaches men that when a woman says no, the man does not need to stop. So a man may learn that there isn't any need to pay attention to a woman who is resisting, crying, screaming, struggling, or saying no, because ultimately she wants it and will enjoy it. He can conclude that her resistance is a sham and is part of a sex dance that leads to orgasm. He may assume that even her resistance is sexy and sexually arousing because it is part of the sexual template.

In other words, pornography makes violence sexy.[9]

PORNOGRAPHY AND SEXUAL VIOLENCE BEHAVIORS

. . .

Pornography's effect depends upon not just what you are exposed to, but also how often. The more frequently men use pornography and the more violent the pornography they used, the more likely they were to coerce others into sex, including to use physical coercion (i.e., rape).[10]

Pornography's effect also depends upon individuals' characteristics as well as how often they use pornography. Males who were high in hostile masculinity and sexual promiscuity and who used pornography frequently were significantly more likely to be physically and sexually aggressive than males who were low in these three factors.[11] However, this study was unable to determine if those individual characteristics of hostile masculinity and promiscuity might have been produced by pornography use at an earlier point in life.

Much of the research has focused on the males who perpetrate the behaviors. However, there are studies that have focused on the female victims. One study questioned 100 women who

presented to a rape crisis center. Twenty-eight percent said that their abuser used pornography. Of those whose abuser used pornography, 40% said the pornography was part of the abuse, being used either during the abuse or just prior to it, and 43% said that it affected the nature of the abuse. None of them thought it decreased the frequency of the abuse, but 21% thought it increased the frequency and 14% believed it increased the level of violence. In fact, 18% thought their abuser became more sadistic with the use of pornography. Of the total, 12% said the abuser imitated the pornography, and 14% said someone had tried to force them to do something he had seen in pornography.[12]

Another study found 24% of women surveyed indicated that they had been upset by someone trying to get them to do something they had seen in pornography. Those who said this were more likely to have been victims of threatened or actual sexual assault.[13]

. . .

PEDOPHILIA, SEXUAL HARASSMENT, AND DOMESTIC VIOLENCE

Being charged with a child pornography offense is a good predictor of who might get the diagnosis of pedophilia. It appears to be a better predictor of pedophilia than actually having raped a child. Individuals who have been charged with a child pornography offense, whether or not they have committed a sexual offense against children, are more likely to be pedophiles than are individuals who have offended against children but do not use child pornography. Fantasy may be a more accurate predictor than behavior because individuals may have more options and more control of their options in fantasies than in behaviors that depend upon the availability of others.[14]

Forms of sexual violence perpetrated against women other than rape are affected by the use of pornography. Many women will be sexually harassed on their jobs and elsewhere. The likelihood of sexually harassing another is significantly correlated with the volume of past exposure to sexually explicit materials.[15]

Domestic violence is another form of violence against woman. The violence may typically be physical and emotional, but these are often combined with sexual violence. Battered women experienced significantly more sexual violence than women who were not battered.[16] For example, 39% of the battered women said that their partners had tried to get them to act out pornographic scenes they had been shown, compared with 3% of other women.[17]

. . .

Forty percent of abused women indicated that their partner used violent pornography. Of those whose partners used pornography, 53% said that they had been asked or forced to enact scenes they had been shown, and 26% had been reminded of pornography by an abuser during the abuse. Of the 40% who had been raped, 73% stated that their partners had used pornography.

These studies may not indicate that pornography causes battering, but they do suggest that battering may be expanded to include sexual violence when pornography is involved.

. . . PARTNERS, AND DEVIANCE

. . .

Exposure to pornography leads men to rate their female partners as less attractive than they would have had they not been exposed.[18] They are less satisfied with their partners' attractiveness, sexual performance, and level of affection. They expressed a greater desire for sex without emotional involvement.[19] Undergraduate men who regularly viewed pornography spontaneously generated more sexual terms to describe the construct "women" than did those who viewed pornography less regularly.[20]

. . .

Sexual deviance can be learned. Some men may initially look at deviant pornography out of curiosity. Some may move up to harder kinds because softer material no longer arouses them. Either way they may learn deviant beliefs and behavior from it. . . .

NOTES

1. Aaron T. Beck, *Prisoners of Hate: The Cognitive Basis of Anger, Hostility, and Violence* (New York: HarperCollins, 1999).
2. William L. Marshall, "Revisiting the Use of Pornography by Sexual Offenders: Implications for Theory and Practice," *Journal of Sexual Aggression* 6, nos. 1 and 2 (2000): 67.
3. James Check and Neil Malamuth, "An Empirical Assessment of Some Feminist Hypotheses About Rape." *International Journal of Women's Studies* 8, no.4 (September-October 1985): 414–23.
4. Monica G. Weisz and Chistopher Earls, "The Effects of Exposure to Filmed Sexual Violence on Attitudes Toward Rape," *Journal of Interpersonal Violence* 10, no. 1 (1995): 71–84.
5. Mike Allen et al., "Exposure to Pornography and Acceptance of the Rape Myth," *Journal of Communication* 45, no.1 (1995): 5–26.
6. Michael Milburn, Roxanne Mather, and Sheree Conrad, "The Effects of Viewing Movie Scenes that Objectify Women on Perceptions of Date Rape," *Sex Roles* 43, no. 9 and 10 (2000): 645–64.
7. Shawn Corne et al., "Women's Attitudes and Fantasies About Rape as a Function of Early Exposure to Pornography," *Journal of Interpersonal Violence* 7, no.4 (1992): 454–61.
8. Dolf Zillman and Jennings Bryant, "Effects of Massive Exposure to Pornography," *Pornography and Sexual Aggression,* eds. Neil M Malamuth and Edward Donnerstein (New York: Academic Press, 1984).
9. Diana E.H. Russell, *Making Violence Sexy: Feminist Views on Pornography* (New York: Teachers College Press, 1933).
10. Mary Koss and Cheryl Oros, "Sexual Experiences Survey: A Research Instrument Investigating

PART 7

Sexual Aggression and Victimization," *Journal of Consulting and Clinical Psychology* 50, no. 3 (June 1982): 455–57.

11. Neil M. Malamuth, Tamara Addison, and Mary Koss, "Pornography and Sexual Aggression: Are There Reliable Effects and Can We Understand Them?" *Annual Review of Sex Research* 11 (2000): 26–68.

12. Raquel Bergen and Kathleen Bogle, "Exploring the Connection Between Pornography and Sexual Violence," *Violence and Victims* 15, no. 3 (2000): 227–34.

13. Charlene Senn, "The Research on Women and Pornography: The Many Faces of Harm," *Making Violence Sexy,* ed. Diana E. H. Russell (New York: Teachers College Press, 1993).

14. Michael C. Seto, James Cantor, and Ray Blanchard, "Child Pornography Offenses Are a Valid Diagnostic Indicator of Pedophilia," *Journal of Abnormal Psychology* 115, no. 3 (2006): 610–15.

15. Azy Barak et al., "Sex, Guys, and Cyberspace: Effects of Internet Pornography and Individual Differences on Men's Attitudes Toward Women,"

Journal of Psychology and Human Sexuality 11, no. 1 (1999): 63–91.

16. Evelyn Sommers and James V.P. Check, "An Empirical Investigation of the Role of Pornography in the Verbal and Physical Abuse of Women," *Violence and Victims* 2, no. 1 (1987): 189–209.

17. Evelyn Sommers and James V.P. Check, "An Empirical Investigation of the Role of Pornography in the Verbal and Physical Abuse of Women," *Violence and Victims* 2, no. 1 (1987): 189–209.

18. James B. Weaver, Jonathan L. Masland, and Dolf Zillmann, "Effect of Erotica on Young Men's Aesthetic Perception of Their Female Sexual Partners," *Perceptual and Motor Skills* 58 (1984): 929–30.

19. Dolf Zillman and Jennings Bryant, "Pornography's Impact on Sexual Satisfaction," *Journal of Applied Social Psychology* 18, no.5 (1988): 43.

20. Deborrah E. S. Frable, Anne E. Johnson, Hildy Kellman, "Seeing Masculine Men, Sexy Women, and Gender Differences: Exposure to Pornography and Cognitive Constructs of Gender," *Journal of Personality* 65, no. 2 (1997): 311–55.

Critical Thinking Questions

1. How has the use of the Internet impacted the consumption and demand for pornography?
2. Is all pornography "bad"? If not, what distinguishes "harmful" from "positive" pornography?

Chapter 21

Population and Politics: Voodoo Demography, Population Aging, and Canadian Social Policy

ELLEN M. GEE

As baby boomers enter retirement, there is a growing fear that they will increasingly and quite unfairly come to be supported by younger generations who themselves are struggling to make ends meet. This argument is based upon common sense, little else. As we have already come across in previous chapters, it is important as sociologists to interrogate such "commonly held" or "obvious" notions to see where they may come from, and why they persist. As this selection demonstrates (at least with regard to Canada), stereotypes of seniors do not hold up under closer scrutiny. For example, there is a misconception that most retired Canadians are well-off, which is simply not true. Further, this commonly encountered argument incorrectly sees "demography" as the primary cause of certain issues, like lack of pension funds, dramatic increases in the costs of health care, etc. Note the author's contention that this is not the first time that "demographics" has been seen as a threat to society. It also happened in the early 20th century and gave rise to the Eugenics Movement (see Chapter 7 in this book). The author suggests that people who saw high birth rates among non-Nordic populations as a threat to society were as flawed in their thinking as people who today see aging baby boomers as a threat. Reading through their arguements, does the author convince you of this?

1. What is the relationship between social scientific evidence and the creation of public policy?

We are constantly bombarded with words and images informing us that our changing demographics—in particular, our aging population—are the cause, and will continue to be the cause, of a leaner and meaner Canada. These words and images reflect the ideology of voodoo—or apocalyptic—demography[1] that has come to frame Canadians' views of their society, now and in the future. What is voodoo/apocalyptic demography? It is the oversimplified idea that population aging has catastrophic consequences for a society. More specifically, it embraces the view that increasing numbers (or 'hordes') of older people will bankrupt a society, due to their incessant demands on the health-care system and on public pensions. A closely aligned idea is that an aging society exacts an unfair price on younger segments of the population who have to pay to meet the needs of the burgeoning numbers of elders. This idea has

Source: "Population and Politics: Voodoo Demography, Population Aging, and Canadian Social Policy," in *The Overselling of Population Aging: Apocalyptic Demography, Intergenerational Challenges, and Social Policy*, edited by Ellen M. Gee and Gloria M. Gutman © Oxford University Press Canada 2000. Reprinted by permission of the publisher.

come to be labeled 'intergenerational equity' (or 'inequity') (Longman, 1987). Intertwined in the intergenerational equity concept is an image of the elderly as well-off leisurers who golf and cruise, partly at public expense, and who have no regard for the situation of younger people. This image, too, comes with a label—the elderly are 'greedy geezers' (Binstock, 1994). Also, this generational unfairness is viewed as leading to intergenerational conflict, straining the Canadian social fabric.

My analysis of apocalyptic demography will encompass both its numerical or data side and its political consequences and agenda. However, as a preface, I present actual examples of it, as culled from Canadian newspapers.

Painful Decisions Must Be Made to Ensure Future of Social Programs

If you think we are having a hard time affording our social programs today, just wait a few years. What is little understood is how the demographic clock is working against us and how fast it is ticking.

> Peter Hadekel, *Montreal Gazette*, 10 Dec. 1994

Grandma! Grandpa! Get Back to Work!

Retirement isn't a birthright. Those who enjoy it haven't earned it. Canadians enjoy retirement, and why not? Most retirees are having the time of their lives: long, lazy summers at the cottage, gambling jaunts to Vegas in the winter, golf all year round.

> Peter Shawn Taylor, *Saturday Night*, June 1995

Raise Seniors' Taxes

Ottawa should hit older people and their estates with new taxes to pay down the national debt, says a top lawyer. Seniors have benefited from a lifetime of economic growth boosted by government spending and it is now time for them to pay the country back. . . . The

$400 billion federal debt 'belongs' to older Canadians, but younger generations are being asked to pay for it.

> *Toronto Star*, 11 Nov. 1994

Greyer Horizons

. . . the deal between the generations is under severe threat, as the costs of state pensions rise. Many countries are running out of people to pay those contributions. . . . But the argument between the generations is not just about pensions. Medical expenses, too, will burgeon as people get older.

> Barbara Beck, *Globe and Mail*, 29 Dec. 1995

Value for Money

Canadians have rarely received so few benefits for their tax dollars, and the difficult times are just beginning. The consequences of this will be profound: tense interregional conflict, *clashes between young and old people*, and, if things get really bad, class warfare. [italics added]

> Edward Greenspoon, *Globe and Mail*, 3 Oct. 1996

Pension Plan Pins Prospects on Market

Faced with the daunting demographic challenges of an aging baby-boom . . . Canadians— younger ones in particular—are skeptical . . . the CPP will be around for their retirement. And they have every reason to worry.

> Shawn McCarthy and Rob Carrick, *Globe and Mail*, 11 Apr. 1998

Paying for the Boomers

Blame it on the baby boomers. Last week, Finance Minister Paul Martin announced that Canada Pension Plan contributions will increase to 9.9 percent of pensionable earnings.

> *Maclean's*, 24 Feb. 1997

Letter to the Editor

The old women lugging their pension-laden purses from store to store aren't suffering. It's the people who are too young for the pension who are hard up.

Toronto Star, 5 Dec. 1994

At least five themes can be detected in this material. One theme is the *homogenization* of persons on the basis of age, e.g., old people are basically the same—they are comfortably well off. A second theme is *age blaming*. A third theme is that the shifting age structure is considered to be a significant *social problem* (e.g., 'a daunting demographic challenge'; 'the demographic clock is working against us'). A fourth, and very prominent, theme is *intergenerational injustice*—an aging population exacts an unfair toll on its younger members. The last theme is the *intertwining of population aging and social policy* concerns: for example, demographic aging will make it hard for us to afford our social programs; the federal debt is the fault of seniors; public pension sustainability is threatened by the baby boomers.

POPULATION AND POLITICS

Apocalyptic demography demonstrates that population can become intertwined with politics to serve a political agenda. This is not the first time that this unhappy mixture has occurred; in this century, two other examples come to mind. One is the cause of the eugenics movement in Canada, in which the control of reproduction was viewed as a way to preserve and improve the white race. Non-whites and less 'socially desirable' whites became the target of a campaign to lower their fertility. This movement gained its impetus from scientists and physicians; for example, E.W. McBride, McGill University's Strathcona Professor of Zoology in the early 1900s, wrote that 'All attempts to favour the slum population by encouraging their habits of reckless reproduction is throwing the support of their children on the State [which] places a heavier burden on

the shoulders of the Nordic race, who form the bulk of the taxpayers' (McLaren, 1990: 24).

These ideas may seem foolish to us now, but their transformation into legislation is much more difficult to brush off. The eugenics movement led to sterilization legislation in British Columbia and Alberta that remained on the books until 1972 in both provinces. The Alberta legislation was more stringent, and we only have hard data for that province (because of lost and destroyed files in BC). We know that between 1928 and 1971, nearly 3,000 sterilizations occurred in Alberta; that teenage girls were the most likely to be sterilized; that Anglo-Saxons were under-represented among those sterilized; and that in the last 27 years of the legislation, Indians and Métis, who comprised 2.5 per cent of Alberta's population, accounted for more than 25 per cent of the persons who were sterilized (ibid.).

At first glance, all of this may seem very remote from the issues involved in apocalyptic demography. But there are important points of parallelism: the problems of the day were conceptualized in strictly demographic terms, these demographic problems were deemed to be costly to the public purse; and, accordingly, 'remedies' were sought to lower public costs.

A second example of the intertwining of population and politics can be found in the formulation of the 'population bomb' problem in the three decades or so after World War II. It is true that populations in many Third World countries were growing rapidly after the war—largely due to the introduction of technologies that lowered the death rate. However, it was the industrialized North that defined the problem as a 'bomb' that had to be detonated, with massive birth control aid as the detonating device. Millions of Western dollars (both public and private monies, with the private sources large US-based foundations like the Rockefeller Foundation) were spent on the delivery of birth control to (largely) women in Third World countries, based on the assumption that lower rates of population growth would positively influence economic development.

PART 8

APOCALYPTIC DEMOGRAPHY AND SOCIAL POLICY

Let us now turn to some of the direct ways in which apocalyptic demography has informed Canadian public policy—and how these claims stack up against empirical evidence.

Pensions and Population Aging

Most of the public debate around population aging has focused on pensions. The pension area brings out two of the strongest images of apocalyptic demography—the elderly as well-heeled 'greedy geezers' and the intergenerational injustice that will be brought on by the baby boomers.

Income and income security in later life are a huge topic. Here, I just want to highlight important points with regard to apocalyptic demography.

First, the 'greedy geezer' stereotype is unwarranted. While we do have a small portion of highly visible well-off seniors, the Canadian aged as a whole are not rich. In a recent analysis of 1996 Survey of Consumer Finance data, Lochhead (1998) shows that 20 per cent of Canadian senior-headed households have less than $65 in annual pre-transfer income, i.e., income before the Old Age Security (OAS), Guaranteed Income Supplement (GIS), and Canada/Quebec Pension Plan (C/QPP), and that 40 per cent have less than $5,179 in pre-transfer income. It should also be remembered that the GIS was put in as a temporary measure in the late 1960s and was expected not to be needed when the C/QPP matured. However, the incomes of many seniors have remained so low that the GIS has never been rescinded and it is important in keeping many older Canadians out of poverty. Nearly 40 per cent of the elderly have such meager incomes that they qualify for the GIS, and the combined OAS/GIS benefit does not lift the elderly living in larger cities out of poverty, and it barely does for others. As well, poverty continues to plague older

unattached women, of whom nearly one-half live below the poverty line (Gee and Gutman, 1995).

Contribution rates to the Canada Pension Plan (shared equally by employers and employees) were increased in January 1998, with the goal of creating a five-year fund of money. This change has been presented as necessitated by our changing demographics. Let's see if the reason really is demographic.

The CPP operates on a 'pay-go' principle, with the contributions of today's workers paying the benefits of today's seniors, so there has never been a CPP fund in the same sense as there is with private pension plans. But there has been a potential fund, that is, the difference between what workers are contributing and what seniors are receiving. But that fund has been depleted over the years, not because of excessive benefits paid to seniors, but rather due to the borrowing of these funds by the provinces—at very low interest rates and generally not repaid—for all manner of things, such as building bridges and schools and preserving parks (Finlayson, 1988).

Thus, one problem is the transfer of potential pension benefits to other areas. This is not illegal; in fact, it was built into the original CPP legislation at the insistence of Ontario, which would not agree to sign this new pension scheme unless provincial borrowing was allowed. Such is the nature of Canadian federalism. Another problem is that the original contribution rates were set very low; in Myles's (1996: 55) words, our contribution rates are 'pitiably low' and 'by international and even American standards Canada is not even in the ballpark.'

These comments are not meant to imply that some increases in CPP contribution rates will not be required as the population ages. This is surely to be the case, and has been known for many years. The problem is that other causes are not mentioned. Another concern, highlighted by Prince (1996), is the political shift in pension reform from a focus on expanding coverage to one of 'heading for cover'. The federal government now concentrates on affordability, neglecting issues of expansion in benefits (desperately needed by many, as data on seniors' incomes show), as well as problems with private pensions, such as increasingly inadequate coverage, especially in the private sector, and lack of indexation. The Senior's Benefit would have done little, except save the federal government money. It would have added 17 cents a day to the incomes of poorer seniors and was projected to save the government $2.1 billion in 2011 and $8.2 billion in 2030 (Brown, 1997).

Clearly, the message is that we are not to depend on public pensions and must save for our own retirement. The preferred vehicle is RRSPs—a partially privatized system that benefits the highly paid—although all evidence suggests that RRSPs will not play a key role for many Canadians in replacing pre-retirement income (Baldwin, 1996). McDonald (1995: 451) warns that our pension reforms are placing us on 'the brink of entrenching a two-tiered retirement system: one for the rich and one for the poor'. Our model of later-life income as social insurance is being replaced with a social welfare model. The pension reforms that will affect tomorrow's elderly are being driven by a **neo-conservative ideology** that will create hardship.

The issue is not demography; rather, it is the failure of our policy-makers to recognize that the market-driven solutions that may have worked in the past will not work now. One could say that apocalyptic policy accompanies apocalyptic demography.

Today's workforce faces unemployment, downsizing and restructuring, and increased contract and part-time labour. As Marshall (1995: 48) states, 'rational individual-level planning for retirement is virtually impossible, [therefore] we must try to reverse the current trend of placing more and more responsibility for providing income security in retirement onto individuals.' This sentiment is echoed by demographers Rosenberg and Moore (1996), the authors of the 1991 Canadian census monograph on population aging. In my words, pension policy and economic realities for workers are on a collision course for reasons quite independent of demography. In more creative language, McDaniel (1996b) refers to the problem as one of 'serial employment and skinny government'.

Apocalyptic Demography and Health Care

There is no simple relationship between population age structure and health-care costs. While it seems obvious/intuitive that the older a population is, the more expensive are its health costs, the research evidence does not support this. For example, if we compare Canadian health costs and age structure with those of other developed countries, we see that while the Canadian population is quite 'young', we spend a higher proportion of our GDP on health than do many other 'much older' countries (Binstock, 1993).

Nevertheless, health-care costs have been escalating in the last few decades in Canada. The reason is not population aging. Barer et al. (1995) estimate that less than 5 per cent of the increase in BC health-care costs over a 12-year period is due to our changing age structure and that, overall, annual growth rates in the GDP of 1–2 per cent per year could accommodate the increases in costs. A major factor is increasing use of the health-care system. These increases have been substantial for all age groups, but have risen the most for persons aged 75 and over. Some ask if older people are receiving 'unnecessary' health care. Some evidence suggests that this might be the case, for example, Black et al. (1995), using Manitoba data for the period 1971–83, found that around one-half of the increase in consultations to specialist physicians was due to increased visits by elders in (self-reported) good health. But all gerontologists know that a very high proportion of the aged self-report they are in good health, meaning they are in good health 'for their age' (Gutman et al., 1999). Certainly, any 'overuse' of the medical/health system by elders (and others) should be curtailed, but we must be clear about

PART 8

what constitutes overuse and how much savings would be entailed. For example, one US–based study (Emanuel and Emanuel, 1994) finds that only 1 percent of total national health-care expenditures would be saved if all aggressive treatment, hospice care, and advance directives were eliminated for persons aged 65 and over in their last year of life. Marshall (1997) argues that health-care reform aimed at reducing unnecessary use should be targeted at servicing patterns and not at the elderly *per se*.

But let us not forget two things. First, the Canadian health-care system is—despite, not because of, our demographics—very expensive. (This is in direct contrast to our income security system, which has minimal administrative costs; see Brown, 1997.) The reasons for this are complex, having to do with the multiple linkages among needs, delivery, financing, organization, and management (Angus, 1996). This topic is outside the realm of what is being addressed here, but one point is important to emphasize. Available evidence shows that the successful control of health-care expenditures is more likely to occur in centralized health-care fiscal systems (ibid.). However, Canada and its provinces are committed to decentralization in health care, so we will have to be very careful that we are not making a costly policy error.

Second, despite our expensive formal health-care system, the large bulk of health care to the elderly is provided informally, largely by women. Attempts to reduce the formal costs of caring will thus place an even greater burden on women, who may themselves be frail and lack the financial resources to cope. Rosenthal (1994) argues that the health-care reform that is shifting elder care from institutions to the community carries along with it the yet unaddressed need for support for caregivers—support in the workplace, support in the form of formal services, and support with regard to available and high-quality institutions. And Aronson (1992) reminds us that many women caregivers really do not have a choice in the matter, given the prevailing gendered division of care labour. Health-care reform that traps and overworks women in an effort to save government dollars is not much of a bargain.

CONCLUSION

It is important to recognize voodoo/apocalyptic demography (and its components) for what it is— an ideology based on beliefs that do not hold up to the test of empirical research and that is leading us in regressive policy directions. It is attractive because (1) it provides a simple and intuitively plausible explanation for present-day problems and (2) it places blame on inexorable demographic change that we cannot do anything about. Together, these two qualities allow us to take what seems to be a simple path, even though it may be a path that creates a much degraded Canadian society. In many ways, voodoo demography can be considered as a kind of 'moral panic' (Thompson, 1998)—the consequences of population aging are being exaggerated to serve a political agenda.

NOTE

1. The terms 'voodoo demography' and 'apocalyptic demography' are used synonymously.

REFERENCES

Angus, Douglas E. 1966. 'Future Horizons for Health and Health Care: A Policy Perspective', in Canadian Federation of Demographers, *Towards the XXIst Century: Emerging Socio-Demographic Trends and Policy Issues in Canada*. Ottawa: Canadian Federation of Demographers, 11–22.

Aronson, Jane. 1992. 'Women's Sense of Responsibility for the Care of Old People: "But Who Else is Going to Do It?"', *Gender and Society* 6: 8–29.

Baldwin, Bob. 1996. 'Income Security Prospects for Older Canadians', in A. Joshi and E. Berger, eds., *Aging Workforce, Income Security, and Retirement: Policy and Practical Implications*. Hamilton, Ont.: Office of Gerontological Studies, McMaster University, 69–74.

Barer, Morris L., Robert G. Evans, and Clyde Hertzman. 1995. 'Avalanche or Glacier?: Health Care and Demographic Rhetoric', *Canadian Journal of Aging* 14: 193–224.

Bengtson, Vern L., and R. A. Harootyan. 1994. *Intergenerational Linkages: Hidden Connections in American Society.* New York: Springer.

Binstock, Robert H. 1993. 'Healthcare Costs Around the World: Is Aging a Fiscal "Black Hole"?', *Generations* 17, 4: 37–42.

___. 1994. 'Changing Criteria in Old-Age Programs: The Introduction of Economic Status and Need for Services', *Gerontologist* 34: 726–30.

Black, Charlene, P. Noralou Roos, Betty Havens, and Linda McWilliam. 1995. 'Rising Use of Physician Services by the Elderly: The Contribution of Morbidity', *Canadian Journal on Aging* 14: 225–44.

Brown, Robert L. 1997. 'Economic Security for an Aging Canadian Population', Ph.D. thesis, Simon Fraser University.

Clark, R. L., and J. J. Spengler. 1980. 'Dependency Ratios: Their Use in Economic Analyses', in J.L. Simon and J. DaVanzo, eds, *Research in Population Economics,* vol. 2. Greenwich, Conn.: JAI Press, 63–76.

Corak, Miles, ed. 1998. Government Finances and Generational Equity. Ottawa: Statistics Canada Catalogue No. 68-513-XPB.

Denton, Frank T., Christine H. Fever and Bryon G. Spencer. 1998. "The Future Population of Canada: Its Age Distribution and Its Dependency Relations", *Canadian Journal on Aging* 17: 83–109.

Emanuel, E. J. and L. L. Emanuel. 1994. "The Economics of Dying: The Illusion of Cost Savings at the End of Life," *New England Journal of Medicine* 330: 540–4.

Finlayson, Anne. 1988. *Whose Money Is It Anyway? The Showdown on Pensions.* Markham, Ont.: Viking/Penguin.

Foot, David K. 1989. 'Public Expenditure, Population Aging and Economic Dependency in Canada, 1921–2021', *Population Research and Policy Review* 8: 97–117.

Fortin, Pierre. 1996. 'The Canadian Fiscal Problem: The Macroeconomic Connection', in Osberg and Fortin (1996a) 26–38.

Gee, Ellen M., and Gloria M. Gutman. 1995. 'Introduction', Gee and Gutman, eds., *Rethinking Retirement.* Vancouver: Geronology Research Centre, Simon Fraser University, 1–12.

Gillespie, W. Irwin. 1996. 'A Brief History of Government Borrowing in Canada', in Osberg and Fortin (1996a: 1–25).

Good, Christopher. 1995. 'The Generational Accounts of Canada', *Fraser Forum* (Aug.: special issue). Vancouver: Fraser Institute.

Gutman, G.M., A. Stark, A. Donald, and B.L. Beattie. 1999. 'The Contribution of Self-reported Health Ratings to Predicting Frailty, Institutionalization and Death Over a 5 Year Period', unpublished paper.

Hodgson, Dennis. 1988. 'Orthodoxy and Revisionism in American Demography', *Population and Development Review.* 14: 541–69.

Hunsley, Terrance. 1997. *Lone Parent Incomes and Social Policy Outcomes: Canada in International Perspective.* Kingston, Ont.: Queen's University School of Policy Studies.

Kotlikoff, Lawrence J. 1993. *Generational Accounting: Knowing Who Pays, and When, For What We Spend.* New York: Free Press.

Kronebusch, Karl, and Mark Schlesinger. 1994. 'Intergenerational Transfers', in Bengtson and Harootyan (1994: 112–51).

Longman, Philip. 1987. *Born to Pay: The New Politics of Aging in America.* Boston: Houghton Mifflin.

Lochhead, Clarence. 1998. 'Who Benefits from Canada's Income Security Programs," *Insight* 21, 4: 9–12.

McDaniel, Susan A. 1996a. 'At the Heart of Social Solidarity', *Transition* 9 (Sept.): 9–11.

___. 1996b. 'Serial Employment and Skinny Government: Reforming Caring and Sharing in Canada at the Millennium', in Federation of Canadian Demographers, *Towards the XXIst Century: Emerging Socio-Demographic Trends and Policy Issues in Canada.* Ottawa: Canadian Federation of Demographers.

___. 1997. 'Intergenerational Transfers, Social Solidarity, and Social Policy: Unanswered Questions and Policy Challenges', *Canadian Journal on Aging/ Canadian Public Policy* (Supplement): 1–21.

McDonald, Lynn. 1995. 'Retirement for the Rich and Retirement for the Poor: From Social Security to Social Welfare', *Canadian Journal on Aging* 14: 447–51.

McLaren, Angus. 1990. *Our Own Master Race: Eugenics in Canada, 1845-1945.* Toronto: McClelland & Stewart.

McMullin, Julie A., and Victor W. Marshall. 1995. 'Social Integration: Family, Friends and Social Support', in Marshall, Mullin, P. J. Ballantyne, J. F. Daciuk, and B. T. Wigdor, eds, *Contributions to Independence Over the Life Course.* Toronto: Centre for Studies in Aging, University of Toronto.

Marshall, Victor W. 1995. 'Rethinking Retirement: Issues for the Twenty-First Century', in E. M. Gee and G. M. Gutman, eds, *Rethinking Retirement.* Vancouver: Gerontology Research Centre, Simon Fraser University, 31–50.

PART 8

___. 1997. 'The Generations: Contributions, Conflict, Equity', prepared for the Division of Aging and Seniors, Health Canada.

Murphy, Michael. 1996. 'Implications of and Aging Society and Changing Labour Market: Demographics', *Roundtable on Canada's Aging Society and Retirement Income System*. Ottawa: Caledon Institute of Social Policy.

Myles, John. 1995. 'Pensions and the Elderly', *Review of Income and Wealth* 41: 101–6.

___. 1996. 'Challenges Facing the Welfare State: Putting Pension Reform in Context', in A. Joshi and E. Berger, eds, *Aging Workforce, Income Security and Retirement Policy and Practical Implications*. Hamilton, Ont.: Office of Gerontological Studies, McMaster University, 51–6.

Osberg, Lars. 1998. 'Meaning and Measurement in Intergenerational Equity', in M. Corak, ed., *Government Finances and Generational Equity*. Ottawa: Statistics Canada Catalogue No. 68–513–XPB, 131–9.

___ and Pierre Fortin, eds. 1996a. *Unnecessary Debts*. Toronto: James Lorimar.

___ and ___ Pierre Fortin. 1996b. 'Credibility Mountain', in Osberg and Fortin (1996a: 157–72).

Pozo, Susan, ed. 1996. *Exploring the Underground Economy: Studies of Illegal and Unreported Activity*. Kalamazoo, Mich.: W.E. Upjohn Institute for Employment Research.

Prince, Michael J. 1996. 'From Expanding Coverage to Heading for Cover: Shifts in the Politics and Policies of Canadian Pension Reform', in A. Joshi and E. Berger, eds. *Aging Workforce, Income Security and Retirement Policy and Practical Implications*.

Hamilton, Ont.: Office of Gerontological Studies, McMaster University, 57–67.

___ and Neena L. Chappell. 1994. *Voluntary Action by Seniors in Canada*. Victoria, BC: Centre on Aging, University of Victoria.

Robertson, Ann. 1997. 'Beyond Apocalyptic Demography: Towards a Moral Economy of Interdependence', *Ageing and Society* 17: 425–26.

Rosenberg, Mark W., and Eric G. Moore, 1996. 'Transferring the Future of Canada's Aging Population', in Federation of Canadian Demographers, *Towards the XXIst Century: Emerging Socio-Demographic Trends and Policy in Canada*. Ottawa: Canadian Federation of Demographers, 35–41.

Rosenbluth, Gideon. 1996. 'The Debt and Canada's Social Programs', in Osberg and Fortin (1996a: 90–111).

Rosenthal, Carolyn J. 1994. 'Long-term Care Reform and "Family" Care: A Worrisome Combination', *Canadian Journal of Aging* 13: 419–27.

Statistics Canada. 1998. *The Daily*. http://www.statcan.ca/Daily/English/980512/d980512.pdf

Thompson, Kenneth. 1998. *Moral Panics*. London: Routledge.

US Department of Commerce. 1993. *An Aging World II*. Washington: Government Printing Office: International Population Report Series P-95 (Feb.).

Van Audenrode, Marc. 1996. 'Some Myths about Monetary Policy', in Osberg and Fortin (1996a: 112–23).

Wolfson, M. C., G. Rowe, X. Lin, and S. F. Gribble. 1998. 'Historical Generational Accounting with Heterogeneous Populations', in M. Corak, ed., *Government Finances and Generational Equity*. Ottawa: Statistics Canada Catalogue No. 68–513–XPB, 107–25.

Critical Thinking Questions

1. Provide some examples where apocalyptic demography informed politics/policy or political agendas. Were you surprised? Do we just expect policy-makers to be objective in the same way that we just expect researchers and health-care providers to be ethical (e.g., Tuskegee, the Eugenics Movement in Alberta, etc.)?

2. Our health-care system in Canada is primarily geared around diagnoses and subsequent treatment. If our system was more focused on prevention, do you think apocalyptic demography would have much of an effect on health-care policy?

3. In this article the author says, "the issue is not demography; rather, it is the failure of our policy-makers to recognize that the market-driven solutions that may have worked in the past will not work now." Do you think this statement may also hold for the recent worldwide recession, and its effect on Canada and Canadian jobs? If so, in what way and how may policy relieve recession?

Chapter 22
Aging Around the World: The Aged as Teachers

DONALD O. COWGILL

In some ways, this selection likely reinforces something that most readers already believe: in many traditional societies, the elderly are treated with respect (more respect than is associated with the elderly in our society) because they are repositories of valued knowledge. Certainly, the many examples presented here—drawn overwhelmingly from anthropological literature—suggest that this common belief is well grounded. There are, however, other lessons to be learned from this selection. For example, it seems clear that "storytelling" in traditional societies is a well-developed art and that the process of storytelling binds together grandparents and grandchildren in a way that does not happen in our society. Why is this the case? Partly, it is likely that the elderly in our society are less likely to have valuable knowledge to transmit, but it also seems obvious that there are other factors at work, for example, grandchildren are less likely to live near their grandparents; the "storytelling function" has been taken over by the mass media; and so on. Generally, this selection can serve as the starting point for thinking about the many reasons that the elderly in our society have lost ground relative to the elderly in traditional societies, and how roles within the family institution shift and change over time.

1. According to the article, why do some societies treat their elders with respect while other societies devalue their elders?

Almost forty years ago, Simmons (1945:40) asserted: "Few generalizations concerning the aged in primitive societies can be made with greater confidence than that they have almost universally been regarded as the custodians of knowledge *par excellence* and the chief instructors of the people." Maxwell and Silverman (1970) hypothesized that control of useful knowledge is a primary basis of the high esteem in which older people are held in such societies. Later, Watson and Maxwell (1977) confirmed this hypothesis after correlating an information control scale with a scale for esteem of elderly in 26 societies. This implies that control of useful information partially explains the high esteem of the elderly in primitive societies, but, conversely, the loss of such control in modern societies helps explain the decline in the status of the elderly in these societies.

Among the Aleuts in the late nineteenth century, every village reportedly had one or two men whose special function was to educate the children (Elliot, 1886). In many societies this becomes the particular prerogative of grandparents. Thus it is the grandparents, not the parents, who represent the chief transgenerational conveyors of a society's culture (Tomashevich, 1981:21). So it is among the !Kung Bushman, where the grandparents care for small children while their mothers are away on their gathering forays (Biesele and Howell, 1981:89). The elder generation spends much of its time in teaching the grandchildren the skills, traditions, and values of the society. In fact the Baganda define a good grandparent as "one who teaches, loves and cares for his or her grandchildren" (Nahemow, 1983:112). This is true also in Dahomean society, where older people spend much of their time educating their grandchildren, using **storytelling** as the chief medium (Tomashevich, 1981:28). But this is neither a matter of convenience nor of blood relationship; it is very much a matter of age and experience. Age and wisdom are so closely identified.

It is natural that such wise persons should be advisors as well as teachers.

Another area in which the knowledge of older people is extensive and relevant is the physical environment within which the people live. Fuller notes (1972:59) that among the Zulu, information supplied by him about the natural environment was distrusted because he "was not old enough to know." The only credible information came from their own elderly. The elderly of the Maori are a veritable storehouse of nature lore. The names of all living things are known and this represents only a fragment of the information stored in the memories of elderly Maori people (Simmons, 1945:138). The older men among the Aranda of Australia teach the young the tracks of various animals and the location of the best sources of food.

Perhaps even more notable among the teaching skills of the elderly are those in the realm of arts and crafts. These range broadly through music, art, pottery, weaving, tanning, dance, flower arranging, and calligraphy. Among them are the best technicians, the older women in pottery and basketry and the older men in weaving and tanning. In Japan the folk arts in which older people excel and which they in turn teach to the young include calligraphy, flower arranging, the tea ceremony, *bonsai* horticulture, and several stylized forms of poetry (Maeda,

1978:66–67). Among the Bantus of southern Africa, an elderly male or female usually initiated a dance, performing the first steps, and an elder began the first drumming (Fuller, 1972:63). The treasured knowledge of the elders of the Coast Salish included methods of construction and canoe making (Amoss, 1981a:227).

A favorite medium through which the elderly carry out their educator role is storytelling. Some develop this to a high art, and the education is at the same time amusement and entertainment. Such was the case with the old men of the Asmat tribe. Beginning at about the age of eight, boys would gather at the fireplace of their grandfather to listen to the adventures of fictional characters, or of animals. In the course of such stories, the children would learn much about their jungle environment and the natural resources of the area (Van Arsdale 1981b:116–117). The young defer to the elderly among the !Kung Bushmen, and the elderly take great delight in telling and retelling stories of their own exploits or those of mythical beings (Biesele and Howell, 1981:88–89). Oratory is a prized art form in Samoa, and the young orator chiefs often gather in the evening to listen to their elders as they discuss myths, legends, customs, family history, and genealogy. The aged are considered storehouses of information, and this is the customary method of imparting it (Holmes and Rhoads, 1983:123).

I observed an interesting variation in the use of older people for oral history in China in 1978. Here the elderly were encouraged to tell about their lives before the Revolution of 1949. The intent was the opposite of most oral history; instead of glorifying the past, the purpose was to portray the horrible conditions that obtained in China before the revolution and in the process to justify it and attest to the progress since then. The elderly often visit schools to tell their "bitterness stories." In performing this role, the elderly are presented as heroes in Chinese society (Missine, 1982:7).

What do older people get in return for these activities? Often the returns are very tangible and very practical. In fact the simplest answer to the question is: they get a living. In some societies this is supplied in a quid pro quo exchange; that is, in return for a given bit of valued information, the elder may receive definite remuneration. Aged men among the Navaho charged high prices for information about cures, sacred names, legends, secrets, and songs (Simmons, 1945:135). They were paid in sheep, cattle, or horses.

In other instances the exchange was less explicit and less crassly economic. Marshall (1976) reports that among the !Kung Bushmen, a hunter is expected to share any kill with his parents and with his wife's parents.

But apart from the economic rewards, which may be specific and explicit or quite general and implicit, there are other rewards. When the information imparted is valued, its possessors and teachers will also be valued, and this implies some other intangible dividends in the form of prestige, honor, respect, and a sense of importance to the community. The feeling of being a significant member of the society and having a secure and accepted role in it is certainly a part of the role of the aged in the preindustrial societies. It is a role that tends to be eroded in the process of modernization.

The fact of the matter is that rapid social change, such as the contemporary process of modernization, renders older people obsolete. Their classic role as conservators and transmitters of vital information is destroyed. Much that they know is no longer pertinent, and much that they don't know is essential.

The acceleration of social change—along with the developing technology of recording, storing, and retrieving information—has largely destroyed the traditional role of the elderly as teachers. The pace of social change is now so swift that one's knowledge and skills are obsolete by the time one is old, unless of course he or she participates in lifelong learning, as a few are belatedly coming to do. But even here the emphasis is upon the renewal of technical skills or the development of idiosyncratic forms of personal expression. There does not appear to be anything on the education horizon that would renew the grandparent-to-grandchild teaching-learning relationship.

REFERENCES

Amoss, Pamela T. 1981a. "Coast Salish Elders." Pp. 227–47 in P. T. Amoss and S. Harrell (eds.), *Other Ways of Growing Old*. Stanford, CA: Stanford University Press.

Biesele, Megan, and Nancy Howell. 1981. "The Old People Give You Life: Aging Among !Kung Hunter Gatherers." Pp. 77–98 in P. Amoss and S. Harrell (eds.), *Other Ways of Growing Old: Anthropological Perspectives*. Stanford, CA: Stanford University Press.

Elliott, H. W. 1886. *Our Arctic Province: Alaska and the Seal Islands*. New York: Scribner's.

Fuller, Charles Edward. 1972. "Aging Among Southern African Bantu." Pp. 51–72 in D. O. Cowgill and L. D. Holmes (eds.), *Aging and Modernization*. New York: Appleton-Century-Crofts.

Holmes, Lowell D., and Ellen C. Rhoads. 1983. "Aging and Change in Modern Samoa." Pp. 119–29 in J. Sokolovsky (ed.), *Growing Old in Different Cultures*. Belmont, CA: Wadsworth.

Maeda, Daisaku. 1978. "Ageing in Eastern Society." Pp. 45–72 in D. Hobman (ed.), *The Social Challenge of Ageing*. New York: St. Martin's Press.

Marshall, Lorna. 1976. "Sharing, Talking and Giving." Pp. 349–71 in R. B. Lee and I. DeVore (eds.), *Kalahari Hunter Gatherers: Studies of !Kung San and Their Neighbors*. Cambridge: MA: Harvard University Press.

Maxwell, Robert J., and Philip Silverman. 1970. "Information and Esteem: Cultural Considerations in the Treatment of the Elderly." *Aging and Human Development* 1: 361–92.

Missine, Leo E. 1982. "Elders Are Educators." *Perspective on Aging* 11 (No. 6, November–December): 5–8.

Nahemow, Nina. 1983. "Grandparenthood in Baganda: Role Option in Old Age?" Pp. 104–15 in J. Sokolovsky (ed.), *Growing Old in Different Societies: Cross-Cultural Perspectives*. Belmont, CA: Wadsworth.

Simmons, Leo. 1945. *The Role of the Aged in Primitive Society*. London: Oxford University Press.

Tomashevich, George Vid. 1981. "Aging and the Aged in Various Cultures." Pp. 17–41 in G. Falk, U. Falk, and G. V. Tomashevich (eds.), *Aging in America and*

PART 8

Other Cultures. Saratoga, CA: Century Twenty One Publishing.

Van Arsdale, Peter W. 1981. "The Elderly Asmat of New Guinea." Pp. 111–23 in P. T. Amoss and S. Harrell (eds.), *Other Ways of Growing Old: Anthropological*

Perspectives. Stanford, CA: Stanford University Press.

Watson, Wilbur H., and Robert J. Maxwell (eds.). 1977. *Human Aging and Dying: A Study in Sociocultural Gerontology.* New York: St. Martin's Press.

Critical Thinking Questions

1. Do you think our devaluation of elders can be linked to apocalyptic demography, as discussed in Chapter 21? If so, how?
2. Throughout history, other cultures have experienced "rapid social change." Do you agree with the author's statement that the most recent period of rapid social change has been a key factor in the devaluation of elders? Or do you think other social factors are at play?
3. Do you think all types of knowledge provided by elders have been rendered obsolete or just particular types of knowledge?

Chapter 23

On Being Sane in Insane Places

DAVID L. ROSENHAN*

It sounds like a movie: Sane people get admitted to mental institutions to investigate the bad guys, only to find that nobody believes them when they say that they are sane and try to get out. Luckily, the sane patients who sought admission to mental hospitals in the experiment reported here were all eventually released. Rosenhan's concern, however, is to use the data that they recorded in these hospitals to document the profound effect that the label of "insane" had on hospital professionals. As these data demonstrate, staff reactions to the simplest behaviours (like asking a question) differed dramatically from what happens outside the hospital. These particular "patients" being part of an experiment, did not have to carry their label with them when they left the hospital. Unfortunately, real patients typically do not have that option.

1. What is the goal of questioning normality and abnormality; sane and insane? Do you think these two labels are socially constructed? If so, what is the significance or implication of this?
2. Is Rosenhan correct in suggesting that the mentally ill have become the modern equivalent of lepers in our society?

If sanity and insanity exist, how shall we know them?

The question is neither capricious nor itself insane. However much we may be personally convinced that we can tell the normal from the abnormal, the evidence is simply not compelling. It is commonplace, for example, to read about murder trials wherein eminent psychiatrists for the defense are contradicted by equally eminent psychiatrists for the prosecution on the matter of the defendant's sanity. More generally, there are a great deal of conflicting data on the reliability, utility, and meaning of such terms as "sanity," "insanity," "mental illness," and "schizophrenia."

(1) Finally, as early as 1934, Benedict suggested that normality and abnormality are not universal (2). What is viewed as normal in one culture may be seen as quite aberrant in another. Thus, notions of normality and abnormality may not be quite as accurate as people believe they are.

To raise questions regarding normality and abnormality is in no way to question the fact that some behaviors are deviant or odd. Murder is deviant. So, too, are hallucinations. Nor does raising such questions deny the existence of the personal anguish that is often associated with "mental illness." Anxiety and depression exist. Psychological suffering exists. But normality and

*The author is professor of psychology and law at Stanford University, Stanford, California 94305. Portions of these data were presented to colloquiums of the psychology departments at the University of California at Berkeley and at Santa Barbara; University of Arizona, Tucson; and Harvard University, Cambridge, Massachusetts.

Source: From Rosenhan, D.L. "On Being Sane in Insane Places." *Science*, New Series, Vol. 179, No. 4070 (Jan. 19, 1973). Reprinted with permission from AAAS.

abnormality, sanity and insanity, and the diagnoses that flow from them may be less substantive than many believe them to be.

At its heart, the question of whether the sane can be distinguished from the insane (and whether degrees of insanity can be distinguished from each other) is a simple matter: Do the salient characteristics that lead to diagnoses reside in the patients themselves or in the environments and contexts in which observers find them? The belief has been strong that patients present symptoms, that those symptoms can be categorized, and, implicitly, that the sane are distinguishable from the insane. More recently, however, this belief has been questioned. Based in part on theoretical and anthropological considerations, but also on philosophical, legal, and therapeutic ones, the view has grown that psychological categorization of mental illness is useless at best and downright harmful, misleading, and pejorative at worst. Psychiatric diagnoses, in this view, are in the minds of observers and are not valid summaries of characteristics displayed by the observed (3–5).

Gains can be made in deciding which of these is more nearly accurate by getting normal people (that is, people who do not have, and have never suffered, symptoms of serious psychiatric disorders) admitted to psychiatric hospitals and then determining whether they were discovered to be sane and, if so, how. If the sanity of such pseudopatients were always detected, there would be prima facie evidence that a sane individual can be distinguished from the insane context in which he is found. Normality (and presumably abnormality) is distinct enough that it can be recognized wherever it occurs, for it is carried within the person. If, on the other hand, the sanity of the pseudopatients were never discovered, serious difficulties would arise for those who support traditional modes of psychiatric diagnosis. Given that the hospital staff was not incompetent, that the pseudopatient had been behaving as sanely as he had been outside of the hospital, and that it had never been previously suggested that he belonged in a psychiatric hospital, such an unlikely outcome would support the view that psychiatric diagnosis betrays little about the patient but much about the environment in which an observer finds him.

This article describes such an experiment. Eight sane people gained secret admission to 12 different hospitals (6). Their diagnostic experiences constitute the data of the first part of this article; the remainder is devoted to a description of their experiences in psychiatric institutions.

PSEUDOPATIENTS AND THEIR SETTINGS

The eight pseudopatients were a varied group. One was a psychology graduate student in his 20's. The remaining seven were older and "established." Among them were three psychologists, a pediatrician, a psychiatrist, a painter, and a housewife. Three pseudopatients were women, five were men. All of them employed pseudonyms, lest their alleged diagnoses embarrass them later. Those who were in mental health professions alleged another occupation in order to avoid the special attentions that might be accorded by staff, as a matter of courtesy or caution, to ailing colleagues. (7) With the exception of myself (I was the first pseudopatient and my presence was known to the hospital administration and chief psychologist and, so far as I can tell, to them alone), the presence of pseudopatients and the nature of the research program was not known to the hospital staffs (8).

The settings were similarly varied. In order to generalize the findings, admission into a variety of hospitals was sought. The 12 hospitals in the sample were located in five different states on the East and West coasts. Some were old and shabby, some were quite new. Some were research-oriented, others not. Some had good staff-patient ratios, others were quite understaffed. Only one was a strictly private hospital. All of the others were supported by state or federal funds or, in one instance, by university funds.

After calling the hospital for an appointment, the pseudopatient arrived at the admissions office complaining that he had been hearing voices. Asked what the voices said, he replied that they were often unclear, but as far as he could tell they said "empty," "hollow," and "thud." The voices were unfamiliar and were of the same sex as the pseudopatient. The choice of these symptoms was occasioned by their apparent similarity to existential symptoms. Such symptoms are alleged to arise from painful concerns about the perceived meaninglessness of one's life. It is as if the hallucinating person were saying, "My life is empty and hollow." The choice of these symptoms was also determined by the absence of a single report of existential psychoses in the literature.

Beyond alleging the symptoms and falsifying name, vocation, and employment, no further alterations of person, history, or circumstances were made. The significant events of the pseudopatient's life history were presented as they had actually occurred. Relationships with parents and siblings, with spouse and children, with people at work and in school, consistent with the aforementioned exceptions, were described as they were or had been. Frustrations and upsets were described along with joys and satisfactions. These facts are important to remember. If anything, they strongly biased the subsequent results in favor of detecting sanity, since none of their histories or current behaviors were seriously pathological in any way.

Immediately upon admission to the psychiatric ward, the pseudopatient ceased simulating *any* symptoms of abnormality. In some cases, there was a brief period of mild nervousness and anxiety, since none of the pseudopatients really believed that they would be admitted so easily. Indeed, their shared fear was that they would be immediately exposed as frauds and greatly embarrassed. Moreover, many of them had never visited a psychiatric ward; even those who had, nevertheless, had some genuine fears about what might happen to them. Their nervousness, then, was quite appropriate to the novelty of the hospital setting, and it abated rapidly.

Apart from that short-lived nervousness, the pseudopatient behaved on the ward as he "normally" behaved. The pseudopatient spoke to patients and staff as he might ordinarily. Because there is uncommonly little to do on a psychiatric ward, he attempted to engage others in conversation. When asked by staff how he was feeling, he indicated that he was fine, that he no longer experienced symptoms. He responded to instructions from attendants, to calls for medication (which was not swallowed), and to dining-hall instructions. Beyond such activities as were available to him on the admissions ward, he spent his time writing down his observations about the ward, its patients, and the staff. Initially these notes were written "secretly," but as it soon became clear that no one much cared, they were subsequently written on standard tablets of paper in such public places as the dayroom. No secret was made of these activities.

The pseudopatient, very much as a true psychiatric patient, entered a hospital with no foreknowledge of when he would be discharged. Each was told that he would have to get out by his own devices, essentially by convincing the staff that he was sane. The psychological stresses associated with hospitalization were considerable, and all but one of the pseudopatients desired to be discharged almost immediately after being admitted. They were, therefore, motivated not only to behave sanely, but to be paragons of cooperation. That their behavior was in no way disruptive is confirmed by nursing reports, which have been obtained on most of the patients. These reports uniformly indicate that the patients were "friendly," "cooperative," and "exhibited no abnormal indications."

THE NORMAL ARE NOT DETECTABLY SANE

Despite their public "show" of sanity, the pseudopatients were never detected. Admitted, except

PART 9

in one case, with a diagnosis of schizophrenia, (9) each was discharged with a diagnosis of schizophrenia "in remission." The label "in remission" should in no way be dismissed as a formality, for at no time during any hospitalization had any question been raised about any pseudopatient's simulation. Nor are there any indications in the hospital records that the pseudopatient's status was suspect. Rather, the evidence is strong that, once labeled schizophrenic, the pseudopatient was stuck with that label. If the pseudopatient was to be discharged, he must naturally be "in remission"; but he was not sane, nor, in the institution's view, had he ever been sane.

The uniform failure to recognize sanity cannot be attributed to the quality of the hospitals, for, although there were considerable variations among them, several are considered excellent. Nor can it be alleged that there was simply not enough time to observe the pseudopatients. Length of hospitalization ranged from 7 to 52 days, with an average of 19 days. The pseudopatients were not, in fact, carefully observed, but this failure speaks more to traditions within psychiatric hospitals than to lack of opportunity.

Finally, it cannot be said that the failure to recognize the pseudopatients' sanity was due to the fact that they were not behaving sanely. While there was clearly some tension present in all of them, their daily visitors could detect no serious behavioral consequences—nor, indeed, could other patients. It was quite common for the patients to "detect" the pseudopatient's sanity. During the first three hospitalizations, when accurate counts were kept, 35 of a total of 118 patients on the admissions ward voiced their suspicions, some vigorously. "You're not crazy. You're a journalist, or a professor (referring to the continual note-taking). You're checking up on the hospital." While most of the patients were reassured by the pseudopatient's insistence that he had been sick before he came in but was fine now, some continued to believe that the pseudopatient was sane throughout his hospitalization (10). The fact that the patients often

recognized normality when staff did not raises important questions.

Failure to detect sanity during the course of hospitalization may be due to the fact that physicians operate with a strong bias toward what statisticians call the **Type 2 error** (5). This is to say that physicians are more inclined to call a healthy person sick (a false positive, Type 2) than a sick person healthy (a false negative, Type 1). The reasons for this are not hard to find: it is clearly more dangerous to misdiagnose illness than health. Better to err on the side of caution, to suspect illness even among the healthy.

But what holds for medicine does not hold equally well for psychiatry. Medical illnesses, while unfortunate, are not commonly pejorative. Psychiatric diagnoses, on the contrary, carry with them personal, legal, and social stigmas (11). It was therefore important to see whether the tendency toward diagnosing the sane insane could be reversed. The following experiment was arranged at a research and teaching hospital whose staff had heard these findings but doubted that such an error could occur in their hospital. The staff was informed that at some time during the following three months, one or more pseudopatients would attempt to be admitted into the psychiatric hospital. Each staff member was asked to rate each patient who presented himself at admissions or on the ward according to the likelihood that the patient was a pseudopatient. A 10-point scale was used, with a 1 and 2 reflecting high confidence that the patient was a pseudopatient.

Judgments were obtained on 193 patients who were admitted for psychiatric treatment. All staff who had had sustained contact with or primary responsibility for the patient—attendants, nurses, psychiatrists, physicians, and psychologists—were asked to make judgments. Forty-one patients were alleged, with high confidence, to be pseudopatients by at least one member of the staff. Twenty-three were considered suspect by at least one psychiatrist. Nineteen were suspected by one psychiatrist and one other staff member. Actually, no genuine pseudopatient (at least from my group) presented himself during this period.

The experiment is instructive. It indicates that the tendency to designate sane people as insane can be reversed when the stakes (in this case, prestige and diagnostic acumen) are high. But what can be said of the 19 people who were suspected of being "sane" by one psychiatrist and another staff member? Were these people truly "sane" or was it rather the case that in the course of avoiding the Type 2 error the staff tended to make more errors of the first sort—calling the crazy "sane"? There is no way of knowing. But one thing is certain: any diagnostic process that lends itself too readily to massive errors of this sort cannot be a very reliable one.

THE STICKINESS OF PSYCHODIAGNOSTIC LABELS

Beyond the tendency to call the healthy sick—a tendency that accounts better for diagnostic behavior on admission than it does for such behavior after a lengthy period of exposure—the data speak to the massive role of **labeling** in psychiatric assessment. Having once been labeled schizophrenic, there is nothing the pseudopatient can do to overcome the tag. The tag profoundly colors others' perceptions of him and his behavior.

As far as I can determine, diagnoses were in no way affected by the relative health of the circumstances of a pseudopatient's life. Rather, the reverse occurred: the perception of his circumstances was shaped entirely by the diagnosis. A clear example of such translation is found in the case of a pseudopatient who had had a close relationship with his mother but was rather remote from his father during his early childhood. During adolescence and beyond, however, his father became a close friend, while his relationship with his mother cooled. His present relationship with his wife was characteristically close and warm. Apart from occasional angry exchanges, friction was minimal. The children had rarely been spanked. Surely there is nothing especially pathological about such a history. Indeed, many readers may see a similar pattern in their own experiences, with no markedly deleterious consequences. Observe, however, how such a history was translated in the psychopathological context, this from the case summary prepared after the patient was discharged.

> This white 39-year-old male ... manifests a long history of considerable ambivalence in close relationships, which begins in early childhood. A warm relationship with his mother cools during his adolescence. A distant relationship with his father is described as becoming very intense. Affective stability is absent. His attempts to control emotionality with his wife and children are punctuated by angry outbursts and, in the case of the children, spankings. And while he says that he has several good friends, one senses considerable ambivalence embedded in those relationships also ...

The facts of the case were unintentionally distorted by the staff to achieve consistency with a popular theory of the dynamics of a schizophrenic reaction (12). Nothing of an ambivalent nature had been described in relations with parents, spouse, or friends. To the extent that ambivalence could be inferred, it was probably not greater than is found in all human relationships. It is true the pseudopatient's relationships with his parents changed over time, but in the ordinary context that would hardly be remarkable—indeed, it might very well be expected. Clearly, the meaning ascribed to his verbalizations (that is, ambivalence, affective instability) was determined by the diagnosis: schizophrenia. An entirely different meaning would have been ascribed if it were known that the man was "normal."

All pseudopatients took extensive notes publicly. Under ordinary circumstances, such behavior would have raised questions in the

PART 9

minds of observers, as, in fact, it did among patients. Indeed, it seemed so certain that the notes would elicit suspicion that elaborate precautions were taken to remove them from the ward each day. But the precautions proved needless. The closest any staff member came to questioning those notes occurred when one pseudopatient asked his physician what kind of medication he was receiving and began to write down the response. "You needn't write it," he was told gently. "If you have trouble remembering, just ask me again."

If no questions were asked of the pseudopatients, how was their writing interpreted? Nursing records for three patients indicate that the writing was seen as an aspect of their pathological behavior. "Patient engaged in writing behavior" was the daily nursing comment on one of the pseudopatients who was never questioned about his writing. Given that the patient is in the hospital, he must be psychologically disturbed. And given that he is disturbed, continuous writing must be behavioral manifestation of that disturbance, perhaps a subset of the compulsive behaviors that are sometimes correlated with schizophrenia.

One tacit characteristic of psychiatric diagnosis is that it locates the sources of aberration within the individual and only rarely within the complex of stimuli that surrounds him. Consequently, behaviors that are stimulated by the environment are commonly misattributed to the patient's disorder. For example, one kindly nurse found a pseudopatient pacing the long hospital corridors. "Nervous, Mr. X?" she asked. "No, bored," he said.

The notes kept by pseudopatients are full of patient behaviors that were misinterpreted by well-intentioned staff. Often enough, a patient would go "berserk" because he had, wittingly or unwittingly, been mistreated by, say, an attendant. A nurse coming upon the scene would rarely inquire even cursorily into the environmental stimuli of the patient's behavior. Rather, she assumed that his upset derived from his pathology, not from his present interactions with other staff members. Occasionally, the staff might assume that the patient's family (especially when they had recently visited) or other patients had stimulated the outburst. But never were the staff found to assume that one of themselves or the structure of the hospital had anything to do with a patient's behavior. One psychiatrist pointed to a group of patients who were sitting outside the cafeteria entrance half an hour before lunchtime. To a group of young residents he indicated that such behavior was characteristic of the oral-acquisitive nature of the syndrome. It seemed not to occur to him that there were very few things to anticipate in a psychiatric hospital besides eating.

A psychiatric label has a life and an influence of its own. Once the impression has been formed that the patient is schizophrenic, the expectation is that he will continue to be schizophrenic. When a sufficient amount of time has passed, during which the patient has done nothing bizarre, he is considered to be in remission and available for discharge. But the label endures beyond discharge, with the unconfirmed expectation that he will behave as a schizophrenic again. Such labels, conferred by mental health professionals, are as influential on the patient as they are on his relatives and friends, and it should not surprise anyone that the diagnosis acts on all of them as a self-fulfilling prophecy. Eventually, the patient himself accepts the diagnosis, with all of its surplus meanings and expectations, and behaves accordingly (5).

THE EXPERIENCE OF PSYCHIATRIC HOSPITALIZATION

The term "mental illness" is of recent origin. It was coined by people who were humane in their inclinations and who wanted very much to raise the station of (and the public's sympathies toward) the psychologically disturbed from that of witches and "crazies" to one that was akin to the physically ill. And they were at least partially successful, for the treatment of the mentally ill has improved considerably over the years. But while treatment has improved, it is doubtful that people really regard the mentally ill in the same way that they view the physically ill. A broken leg is something one recovers from, but mental illness allegedly endures forever (*13*). A broken leg does not threaten the observer, but a crazy schizophrenic? There is by now a host of evidence that attitudes toward the mentally ill are characterized by fear, hostility, aloofness, suspicion, and dread (*14*). The mentally ill are society's lepers.

That such attitudes infect the general population is perhaps not surprising, only upsetting. But that they affect the professionals—attendants, nurses, physicians, psychologists and social workers—who treat and deal with the mentally ill is more disconcerting. Negative attitudes are there too and can easily be detected. Such attitudes should not surprise us. They are the natural offspring of the labels patients wear and the places in which they are found.

Consider the structure of the typical psychiatric hospital. Staff and patients are strictly segregated. Staff have their own living space, including their dining facilities, bathrooms, and assembly places. The glassed quarters that contain the professional staff, which the pseudopatients came to call "the cage," sit out on every dayroom. The staff emerge primarily for caretaking purposes—to give medication, to conduct therapy or group meeting, to instruct or reprimand a patient. Otherwise, staff keep to themselves, almost as if the disorder that afflicts their charges is somehow catching.

So much is patient-staff segregation the rule that, for four public hospitals in which an attempt was made to measure the degree to which staff and patients mingle, it was necessary to use "time out of the staff cage" as the operational measure. While it was not the case that all time spent out of the cage was spent mingling with patients (attendants, for example, would occasionally emerge to watch television in the dayroom), it was the only way in which one could gather reliable data on time for measuring.

The average amount of time spent by attendants outside of the cage was 11.3 percent (range, 3 to 52 percent). This figure does not represent only time spent mingling with patients, but also includes time spent on such chores as folding laundry, supervising patients while they shave, directing ward cleanup, and sending patients to off-ward activities. It was the relatively rare attendant who spent time talking with patients or playing games with them. It proved impossible to obtain a "percent mingling time" for nurses, since the amount of time they spent out of the cage was too brief. Rather, we counted instances of emergence from the cage. On the average, daytime nurses emerged from the cage 11.5 times per shift, including instances when they left the ward entirely (range, 4 to 39 times). Later afternoon and night nurses were even less available, emerging on the average 9.4 times per shift (range, 4 to 41 times). Data on early morning nurses, who arrived usually after midnight and departed at 8 a.m., are not available because patients were asleep during most of this period.

Physicians, especially psychiatrists, were even less available. They were rarely seen on the wards. Quite commonly, they would be seen only when they arrived and departed, with the remaining time being spent in their offices or in the cage. Consequently, it is understandable that attendants not only spend more time with patients than do any other members of the staff—that is required by their station in the hierarchy—but, also, insofar as they learn from their superior's behavior, spend as little time with patients as they can. Attendants are seen mainly in the cage, which is where the models, the action, and the power are.

I turn now to a different set of studies, those dealing with staff response to patient-initiated contact. It has long been known that the amount of time a person spends with you

PART 9

can be an index of your significance to him. If he initiates and maintains eye contact, there is reason to believe that he is considering your requests and needs. If he pauses to chat or actually stops and talks, there is added reason to infer that he is individuating you. In four hospitals, the pseudopatients approached the staff member with a request which took the following form: "Pardon me, Mr. [or Dr. or Mrs.] X, could you tell me when I will be eligible for grounds privileges?" (or " … when I will be presented at the staff meeting?" or "… when I am likely to be discharged?"). While the content of the question varied according to the appropriateness of the target and the pseudopatient's (apparent) current needs the form was always a courteous and relevant request for information. Care was taken never to approach a particular member of the staff more than once a day, lest the staff member become suspicious or irritated. In examining these data, remember that the behavior of the pseudopatients was neither bizarre nor disruptive. One could indeed engage in good conversation with them.

The data for these experiments are shown in Table 23.1, separately for physicians (column 1) and for nurses and attendants (column 2). Minor differences between these four institutions

were overwhelmed by the degree to which staff avoided continuing contacts that patients had initiated. By far, their most common response consisted of either a brief response to the question, offered while they were "on the move" and with head averted, or no response at all.

The encounter frequently took the following bizarre form: (pseudopatient) "Pardon me, Dr. X. Could you tell me when I am eligible for grounds privileges?" (physician) "Good morning, Dave. How are you today?" (Moves off without waiting for a response.)

It is instructive to compare these data recently obtained at Stanford University. It has been alleged that large and eminent universities are characterized by faculty who are so busy that they have no time for students. For this comparison, a young lady approached individual faculty members who seemed to be walking purposefully to some meeting or teaching engagement and asked them the following six questions.

1. "Pardon me, could you direct me to Encina Hall?" (at the medical school: "… to the Clinical Research Center?").
2. "Do you know where Fish Annex is?" (there is no Fish Annex at Stanford).
3. "Do you teach here?"

TABLE 23.1   SELF-INITIATED CONTACT BY PSEUDOPATIENTS WITH PSYCHIATRISTS AND NURSES AND ATTENDANTS, COMPARED TO CONTACT WITH OTHER GROUPS

CONTACT	PSYCHIATRIC HOSPITALS		UNIVERSITY CAMPUS (NONMEDICAL)	UNIVERSITY MEDICAL CENTER PHYSICIANS		
	Psychiatrists	Nurses and attendants	Faculty	"Looking for a psychiatrist"	"Looking for an internist"	No additional comment
Responses						
Moves on, head averted (%)	71	88	0	0	0	0
Makes eye contact (%)	23	10	0	11	0	0
Pauses and chats (%)	2	2	0	11	0	10
Stops and talks (%)	4	0.5	100	78	100	90
Mean number of questions answered (out of 6)	*	*	6	3.8	4.8	4.5
Respondents (No.)	13	47	14	18	15	10
Attempts (No.)	185	1283	14	18	15	10

* Not applicable.

From Rosenhan, D.L. "On Being Sane in Insane Places." *Science*, New Series, Vol. 179, No. 4070 (Jan. 19, 1973). Reprinted with permission from AAAS.

4. "How does one apply for admission to the college?" (at the medical school: "... to the medical school?")
5. "Is it difficult to get in?"
6. "Is there financial aid?"

Without exception, as can be seen in Table 23.1 (column 3), all of the questions were answered. No matter how rushed they were, all respondents not only maintained eye contact, but stopped to talk. Indeed, many of the respondents went out of their way to direct or take the questioner to the office she was seeking, to try to locate "Fish Annex," or to discuss with her the possibilities of being admitted to the university.

Similar data, also shown in Table 23.1 (columns 4, 5, and 6), were obtained in the hospital. Here too, the young lady came prepared with six questions. After the first question, however, she remarked to 18 of her respondents (column 4), "I'm looking for a psychiatrist," and to 15 others (column 5), "I'm looking for an internist." Ten other respondents received no inserted comment (column 6). The general degree of cooperative responses is considerably higher for these university groups than it was for pseudopatients in psychiatric hospitals. Even so, differences are apparent within the medical school setting. Once having indicated that she was looking for a psychiatrist, the degree of cooperation elicited was less than when she sought an internist.

POWERLESSNESS AND DEPERSONALIZATION

Eye contact and verbal contact reflect concern and individuation; their absence, avoidance and depersonalization. The data I have presented do not do justice to the rich daily encounters that grew up around matters of depersonalization and avoidance. I have records of patients who were beaten by staff for the sin of having initiated verbal contact. During my own experience, for example, one patient was beaten in the presence of other patients for having approached an attendant and

told him, "I like you." Occasionally, punishment meted out to patients for misdemeanors seemed so excessive that it could not be justified by the most rational interpretations of psychiatric canon. Nevertheless, they appeared to go unquestioned. Tempers were often short. A patient who had not heard a call for medication would be roundly excoriated, and the morning attendants would often wake patients with, "Come on, you m_ _ _ _ _ f _ _ _ _ _ s, out of bed!"

Neither anecdotal nor "hard" data can convey the overwhelming sense of powerlessness which invades the individual as he is continually exposed to the depersonalization of the psychiatric hospital. It hardly matters which psychiatric hospital—the excellent public ones and the very plush private hospital were better than the rural and shabby ones in this regard, but, again, the features that psychiatric hospitals had in common overwhelmed by far their apparent differences.

Powerlessness was evident everywhere. The patient is deprived of many of his legal rights by dint of his psychiatric commitment (*15*). He is shorn of credibility by virtue of his psychiatric label. His freedom of movement is restricted. He cannot initiate contact with the staff, but may only respond to such overtures as they make. Personal privacy is minimal. Patient quarters and possessions can be entered and examined by any staff member, for whatever reason. His personal history and anguish is available to any staff member (often including the "grey lady" and "candy striper" volunteer) who chooses to read his folder, regardless of their therapeutic relationship to him. His personal hygiene and waste evacuation are often monitored. The water closets have no doors.

At times, depersonalization reached such proportions that pseudopatients had the sense that they were invisible, or at least unworthy of account. Upon being admitted, I and other pseudopatients took the initial physical examinations in a semipublic room, where staff members went about their own business as if we were not there.

PART 9

On the ward, attendants delivered verbal and occasionally serious physical abuse to patients in the presence of others (the pseudopatients) who were writing it all down. Abusive behavior, on the other hand, terminated quite abruptly when other staff members were known to be coming. Staff are credible witnesses. Patients are not.

A nurse unbuttoned her uniform to adjust her brassiere in the presence of an entire ward of viewing men. One did not have the sense that she was being seductive. Rather, she didn't notice us. A group of staff persons might point to a patient in the dayroom and discuss him animatedly, as if he were not there.

THE CONSEQUENCES OF LABELING AND DEPERSONALIZATION

How many people, one wonders, are sane but not recognized as such in our psychiatric institutions? How many have been needlessly stripped of their privileges of citizenship, from the right to vote and drive to that of handling their own accounts? How many have feigned insanity in order to avoid the criminal consequences of their behavior, and, conversely, how many would rather stand trial than live interminably in a psychiatric hospital—but are wrongly thought to be mentally ill? How many have been stigmatized by well-intentioned, but nevertheless erroneous, diagnoses? On the last point, recall again that a "Type 2 error" in psychiatric diagnosis does not have the same consequences it does in medical diagnosis. A diagnosis of cancer that has been found to be in error is cause for celebration. But psychiatric diagnoses are rarely found to be in error. The label sticks, a mark of inadequacy forever.

Finally, how many patients might be "sane" outside the psychiatric hospital but seem insane in it—not because craziness resides in them, as it were, but because they are responding to a bizarre setting.

SUMMARY AND CONCLUSIONS

It is clear that we cannot distinguish the sane from the insane in psychiatric hospitals. The hospital itself imposes a special environment in which the meaning of behavior can easily be misunderstood. The consequences to patients hospitalized in such an environment—the powerlessness, depersonalization, segregation, mortification, and self-labeling—seem undoubtedly counter-therapeutic.

REFERENCES AND NOTES

1. P. Ash, J. Abnorm. Soc. Psychol. 44, 272 (1949); A. T. Beck, Amer. J. Psychiat. 119, 210 (1962); A. T. Boisen, Psychiatry 2, 233 (1938); N. Kreitman, J. Ment. Sci. 107, 876 (1961); N. Kreitman, P. Sainsbury, J. Morrisey, J. Towers, J. Scrivener, ibid., p. 887; H. O. Schmitt and C. P. Fonda, J. Abnorm. Soc. Psychol. 52, 262 (1956); W. Seeman, J. Nerv. Ment. Dis. 118, 541 (1953). For an analysis of these artifacts and summaries of the disputes, see J. Zubin, Annu. Rev. Psychol. 18, 272 (1967); L. Phillips and J. G. Draguns, ibid. 22, 447 (1971).
2. R. Benedict, J. Gen. Psychol., 10 59 (1934).
3. See in this regard H. Becker, Outsiders: Studies in the Sociology of Deviance (Free Press, New York, 1963); B. M. Braginsky, K. Ring, Methods of Madness: The Mental Hospital as a Last Resort (Holt, Reinhart & Winston, New York, 1969); G. M. Crocetti and P. V. Lemkau, Amer. Sociol. Rev. 30, 577 (1965); E. Goffman, Behavior in Public Places (Free Press, New York, 1964); R. D. Laing, The Divided Self: A Study of Sanity and Madness (Quadrangle, Chicago, 1960); D. L. Phillips, Amer. Sociol. Rev. 28, 963 (1963); T. R. Sarbin, Psychol. Today 6, 18 (1972); E. Schur, Amer. J. Sociol. 75, 309 (1969); T. Szasz, Law, Liberty and Psychiatry (Macmillan, New York, 1963); The Myth of Mental Illness: Foundations of a Theory of Mental Illness (Hoeber-Harper, New York, 1963). For a critique of some of these views, see W. R. Gove, Amer. Sociol. Rev. 35, 873 (1970).
4. E. Goffman, Asylums (Doubleday, Garden City, NY, 1961).
5. T. J. Scheff, Being Mentally Ill: A Sociological Theory (Aldine, Chicago, 1966).

6. Data from a ninth pseudopatient are not incorporated in this report because, although his sanity went undetected, he falsified aspects of his personal history, including his marital status and parental relationships. His experimental behaviors therefore were not identical to those of the other pseudopatients.

7. Beyond the personal difficulties that the pseudopatient is likely to experience in the hospital, there are legal and social ones that, combined, require considerable attention before entry. For example, once admitted to a psychiatric institution, it is difficult, if not impossible, to be discharged on short notice, state law to the contrary notwithstanding. I was not sensitive to these difficulties at the outset of the project, nor to the personal and situational emergencies that can arise, but later a writ of habeas corpus was prepared for each of the entering pseudopatients and an attorney was kept "on call" during every hospitalization. I am grateful to John Kaplan and Robert Bartels for legal advice and assistance in these matters.

8. However distasteful such concealment is, it was a necessary first step to examining these questions. Without concealment, there would have been no way to know how valid these experiences were; nor was there any way of knowing whether whatever detections occurred were a tribute to the diagnostic acumen of the hospital's rumor network. Obviously, since my concerns are general ones that cut across individual hospitals and staffs, I have respected their anonymity and have eliminated clues that might lead to their identification.

9. Interestingly, of the 12 admissions, 11 were diagnosed as schizophrenic and one, with the identical symptomatology, as manic-depressive psychosis. This diagnosis has more favorable prognosis, and it was given by the private hospital in our sample. On the relations between social class and psychiatric diagnosis, see A. deB. Hollingshead and F.C. Redlich, *Social Class and Mental Illness: A Community Study* (New York: John Wiley, 1958).

10. It is possible, of course, that patients have quite broad latitudes in diagnosis and therefore are inclined to call many people sane even those whose behavior is patently aberrant. However, although we have no hard data on this matter, it was our distinct impression that this was not the case. In many instances, patients not only singled us out for attention, but came to imitate our behaviors and styles.

11. J. Cumming and E. Cumming, *Community Ment. Health* 1, 135 (1965); A. Farina and K. Ring, *J. Abnorm. Psychol.* 70, 47 (1965); H. E. Freeman and O. G. Simmons, *The Mental Patient Comes Home* (Wiley, New York, 1963); W. J. Johannsen, *Ment. Hygiene* 53, 218 (1969); A. S. Linsky, *Soc. Psychiat.* 5, 166 (1970).

12. For an example of a similar self-fulfilling prophecy, in this instance dealing with the "central" trait of intelligence, see R. Rosenthal and L. Jacobson, *Pygmalion in the Classroom* (Holt, Rinehard & Winston, New York, 1968).

13. The most recent and unfortunate instance of this tenet is that of Senator Thomas Eagleton.

14. T. R. Sarbin and J. C. Mancuso, *J. Clin. Consult. Psychol.* 35, 159 (1970); T. R. Sarbin, ibid. 31, 447 (1967); J. C. Nunnally, Jr., *Popular Conceptions of Mental Health* (Holt, Rinehart & Winston, New York, 1961).

15. D. B. Wexler and S. E. Scoville, *Ariz. Law Rev.* 13, 1 (1971).

PART 9

Critical Thinking Question

1. Mental health may be heavily linked to social norms (particularly those which are deviant), whether or not this is outwardly acknowledged. By example, homosexuality was previously listed in the *DSM (Diagnostic and Statistical Manual of Mental Disorders)* as a "Sexual Deviation" under the category of "Personality Disorders and Certain Other Non-Psychotic Mental Disorders." This categorization no longer exists. With this knowledge and the information provided to you in the article, how has your understanding of what constitutes mental illness been impacted as a sociologist?

2. How might a sociologist understand the process involved in labelling an individual "feeble-minded" during the eugenics movement in Alberta (Chapter 7), drawing on labelling as presented in this chapter?

Chapter 24

Revisiting the Stanford Prison Experiment: A Lesson in the Power of Situation

PHILIP G. ZIMBARDO

The Milgram experiment is one of the best known experiments in social science. The goal was to find out how difficult it was to get otherwise decent people to obey an order to harm another human being. As Milgram found out in his experiment, it was quite easy, all it took was a few simple experimental manipulations and people who would "never" think of doing harm in fact obeyed an order to harm another. We have also read in the media about how guards committed brutal acts against prisoners in the infamous Abu Ghraib prison in Iraq. In this article you will look at another situation where we can draw similar lessons. Zimbardo discusses and reflects upon his famous experiment where he recreated William Golding's "Lord of the Flies" scenario by having university students act as guards in a make-shift prison. He had to abruptly end the experiment less than halfway through because the student "guards" were seriously abusing the volunteer "prisoners."

1. Why are people able to abandon their rational civility when following groups or when put in situations where they may not be held responsible?
2. Are there only special circumstances where people are able to abandon their rational civility and engage in abusive or brutal behaviours? Or is this some general human trait that is demonstrated in many circumstances?

By the 1970s, psychologists had done a series of studies establishing the social power of groups. They showed, for example, that groups of strangers could persuade people to believe statements that were obviously false. Psychologists had also found that research participants were often willing to obey authority figures even when doing so violated their personal beliefs. The Yale studies by Stanley Milgram in 1963 demonstrated that a majority of ordinary citizens would continually shock an innocent man, even up to near-lethal levels, if commanded to do so by someone acting as an authority. The "authority" figure in this case was merely a high-school biology teacher who wore a lab coat and acted in an official manner. The majority of people shocked their victims over and over again despite increasingly desperate pleas to stop.

In my own work, I wanted to explore the fictional notion from William Golding's Lord of the Flies about the power of anonymity to unleash violent behavior. In one experiment from 1969, female students who were made to feel anonymous and given permission for

Source: Philip G. Zimbardo, Inc. Zimbardo, Philip G. "Revisiting the Stanford Prison Experiment: A Lesson in the Power of Situation." *Chronicle of Higher Education*, Vol. 53.30 (2007): B6–B7.

aggression became significantly more hostile than students with their identities intact. Those and a host of other social-psychological studies were showing that human nature was more pliable than previously imagined and more responsive to situational pressures than we cared to acknowledge. In sum, these studies challenged the sacrosanct view that inner determinants of behaviour—personality traits, morality, and religious upbringing—directed good people down righteous paths.

Missing from the body of social-science research at the time was the direct confrontation of good versus evil, of good people pitted against the forces inherent in bad situations. It was evident from everyday life that smart people made dumb decisions when they were engaged in mindless groupthink, as in the disastrous Bay of Pigs invasion by the smart guys in President John F. Kennedy's cabinet. It was also clear that smart people surrounding President Richard M. Nixon, like Henry A. Kissinger and Robert S. McNamara, escalated the Vietnam War when they knew, and later admitted, it was not winnable. They were caught up in the mental constraints of cognitive dissonance—the discomfort from holding two conflicting thoughts—and were unable to cut bait even though it was the only rational strategy to save lives and face. Those examples, however, with their different personalities, political agendas, and motives, complicated any simple conceptual attempt to understand what went wrong with these situations.

I decided that what was needed was to create a situation in a controlled experimental setting in which we could array on one side a host of variables, such as role-playing, coercive rules, power differentials, anonymity, group dynamics, and dehumanization. On the other side, we lined up a collection of the "best and brightest" of young college men in collective opposition to the might of a dominant system. Thus in 1971 was born the Stanford prison experiment, more akin to Greek drama than to university psychology study. I wanted to know who wins—good people or an evil situation—when they were brought into direct confrontation.

First we established that all 24 participants were physically and mentally healthy, with no history of crime or violence, so as to be sure that initially they were all "good apples." They were paid $15 a day to participate. Each of the student volunteers was randomly assigned to play the role of prisoner or guard in a setting designed to convey a sense of the psychology of imprisonment (in actuality, a mock prison set up in the basement of the Stanford psychology department). Dramatic realism infused the study. Palo Alto police agreed to "arrest" the prisoners and book them, and once at the prison, they were given identity numbers, stripped naked, and deloused. The prisoners wore large smocks with no underclothes and lived in the prison 24/7 for a planned two weeks; three sets of guards each patrolled eight-hour shifts, throughout the experiment, I served as the prison "superintendent," assisted by two graduate students.

Initially nothing much happened as the students awkwardly tried out their assigned roles in their new uniforms. However, all that changed suddenly on the morning of the second day following a rebellion, when the prisoners barricaded themselves inside the cells by putting their beds against the door. Suddenly the guards perceived the prisoners as "dangerous"; they had to be dealt with harshly to demonstrate who was boss and who was powerless. At first, guard abuses were retaliation for taunts and disobedience. Over time, the guards became ever more abusive, and some even delighted in sadistically tormenting their prisoners. Though physical punishment was restricted, the guards on each shift were free to make up their own rules, and they invented a variety of psychological tactics to demonstrate their dominance over their powerless charges.

Nakedness was a common punishment, as was placing prisoners' heads in nylon stocking caps (to simulate shaved heads); chaining their legs; repeatedly waking them throughout the night

PART 9

for hourlong counts; and forcing them into humiliating "fun and games" activities. Let's go beyond those generalizations to review some of the actual behaviours that were enacted in the prison simulation. They are a lesson in "creative evil," in how certain social settings can transform intelligent young men into perpetrators of psychological abuse.

PRISON LOG, NIGHT 5

The prisoners, who have not broken down emotionally under the incessant stress the guards have been subjecting them to since their aborted rebellion on Day 2, wearily line up against the wall to recite their ID numbers and to demonstrate that they remember all 17 prisoner rules of engagement. It is the 1 a.m. count, the last one of the night before the morning shift comes on at 2 a.m. No matter how well the prisoners do, one of them gets singled out for punishment. They are yelled at, cursed out, and made to say abusive things to each other. "Tell him he's a prick," yells one guard. And each prisoner says that to the next guy in line. Then the sexual harassment that had started to bubble up the night before resumes as the testosterone flows freely in every direction.

"See that hole in the ground? Now do 25 push-ups [expletive] that hole! You hear me!" One after another, the prisoners obey like automatons as the guard shoves them down. After a brief consultation, our toughest guard (nicknamed "John Wayne" by the prisoners) and his sidekick devise a new sexual game. "OK, now pay attention. You three are going to be female camels. Get over here and bend over, touching your hands to the floor." When they do, their naked butts are exposed because they have no underwear beneath their smocks. John Wayne continues with obvious glee, "Now you two, you're male camels. Stand behind the female camels and hump them."

The guards all giggle at this double-entendre. Although their bodies never touch, the helpless prisoners begin to simulate sodomy by making thrusting motions. They are then dismissed back to their cells to get an hour of sleep before the next shift comes on, and the abuse continues.

By Day 5, five of the student prisoners have to be released early because of extreme stress. (Recall that each of them was physically healthy and psychologically stable less than a week before.) Most of those who remain adopt a zombielike attitude and posture, totally obedient to escalating guard demands.

TERMINATING THE TORMENT

I was forced to terminate the projected two-weeklong study after only six days because it was running out of control. Dozens of people had come down to our "little shop of horrors," seen some of the abuse or its effects, and said nothing. A prison chaplain, parents, and friends had visited the prisoners, and psychologists and others on the parole board saw a realistic prison simulation, an experiment in action, but did not challenge me to stop it. The one exception erupted just before the time of the prison-log notation on Night 5.

About halfway through the study, I had invited some psychologists who knew little about the experiment to interview the staff and participants, to get an outsiders' evaluation of how it was going. A former doctoral student of mine, Christina Maslach, a new assistant professor at the University of California at Berkeley, came down late Thursday night to have dinner with me. We had started dating recently and were becoming romantically involved. When she saw the prisoners lined up with bags over their heads, their legs chained, and guards shouting abuses at them while herding them to the toilet, she got upset and refused my suggestion to observe what was happening in this "crucible of human nature." Instead she ran out of the basement, and I followed, berating her for being overly sensitive and not realizing the important lessons taking place here.

"It is terrible what YOU are doing to those boys!" she yelled at me. Christina made evident in that one statement that human beings were suffering, not prisoners, not experimental subjects, not paid volunteers. And further, I was the one who was personally responsible for the horrors she had witnessed (and which she assumed were even worse when no outsider was looking). She also made clear that if this person I had become—the heartless superintendent of the Stanford prison—was the real me, not the caring, generous person she had come to like, she wanted nothing more to do with me.

That powerful jolt of reality snapped me back to my senses. I agreed that we had gone too far, that whatever was to be learned about situational power was already indelibly etched on our videos, data logs, and minds; there was no need to continue. I too had been transformed by my role in that situation to become a person that under any other circumstances I detest—an uncaring, authoritarian boss man. In retrospect, I believe that the main reason I did not end the study sooner resulted from the conflict created in me by my dual roles as principal investigator, and thus guardian of the research ethics of the experiment, and as the prison superintendent, eager to maintain the stability of my prison at all costs. I now realize that there should have been someone with authority above mine, someone in charge of oversight of the experiment, who surely would have blown the whistle earlier.

By the time Christina intervened, it was the middle of the night, so I had to make plans to terminate the next morning. The released prisoners and guards had to be called back and many logistics handled before I could say, "The Stanford prison experiment is officially closed." When I went back down to the basement, I witnessed the final scene of depravity, the "camel humping" episode. I was so glad that it would be the last such abuse I would see or be responsible for.

GOOD APPLES IN BAD BARRELS AND BAD BARREL MAKERS

The situational forces in that "bad barrel" had overwhelmed the goodness of most of those infected by their viral power. It is hard to imagine how a seeming game of "cops and robbers" played by college kids, with a few academics (our research team) watching, could have descended into what became a hellhole for many in that basement. How could a mock prison, an experimental simulation, become "a prison run by psychologists, not by the state," in the words of one suffering prisoner? How is it possible for "good personalities" to be so dominated by a "bad situation"? You had to be there to believe that human character could be so swiftly transformed in a matter of days—not only the traits of the students, but of me, a well-seasoned adult. Most of the visitors to our prison also fell under the spell. For example, individual sets of parents observing their son's haggard appearance after a few days of hard labor and long nights of disrupted sleep said they "did not want to make trouble" by taking their kid home or challenging the system. Instead they obeyed our authority and let some of their sons experience full-blown emotional meltdowns later on. We had created a dominating behavioral context whose power insidiously frayed the seemingly impervious values of compassion, fair play, and belief in a just world.

The situation won; humanity lost. Out the window went the moral upbringings of these young men, as well as their middle-class civility. Power ruled, and unrestrained power became an aphrodisiac. Power without surveillance by higher authorities was a poisoned chalice that transformed character in unpredictable directions. I believe that most of us tend to be fascinated with evil not because of its consequences but because evil is a demonstration of power and domination over others.

CURRENT RELEVANCE

Such research is now in an ethical time capsule, since institutional review boards will not allow social scientists to repeat it (although experiments like it have been replicated on several TV shows and in artistic renditions). Nevertheless,

PART 9

the Stanford prison experiment is now more popular than ever in its 36-year history. A Google search of "experiment" reveals it to be fourth among some 132 million hits, and sixth among some 127 million hits on "prison." Some of this recent interest comes from the apparent similarities of the experiment's abuses with the images of depravity in Iraq's Abu Ghraib prison—of nakedness, bagged heads, and sexual humiliation.

Among the dozen investigations of the Abu Ghraib abuses, the one chaired by James R. Schlesinger, the former secretary of defense, boldly proclaims that the landmark Stanford study "provides a cautionary tale for all military detention operations." In contrasting the relatively benign environment of the Stanford prison experiment, the report makes evident that "in military detention operations, soldiers work under stressful combat conditions that are far from benign." The implication is that those combat conditions might be expected to generate even more extreme abuses of power than were observed in our mock prison experiment.

However, the Schlesinger report notes that military leaders did not heed that earlier warning in any way. They should have—a psychological perspective is essential to understanding the transformation of human character in response to special situational forces. "The potential for abusive treatment of detainees during the Global War on Terrorism was entirely predictable based on a fundamental understanding of the principles of social psychology coupled with an awareness of numerous known environmental risk factors," the report says. "Findings from the field of social psychology suggest that the conditions of war and the dynamics of detainee operations carry inherent risks for human mistreatment, and therefore must be approached with great caution and careful planning and training." (Unfortunately this vital conclusion is buried in an appendix.)

The Stanford prison experiment is but one of a host of studies in psychology that reveal the extent to which our behavior can be transformed from its usual set point to deviate in unimaginable ways, even to readily accepting a dehumanized conception of others, as "animals," and to accepting spurious rationales for why pain will be good for them.

The implications of this research for law are considerable, as legal scholars are beginning to recognize. The criminal-justice system, for instance, focuses primarily on individual defendants and their "state of mind" and largely ignores situational forces. The Model Penal Code states: "A person is not guilty of an offense unless his liability is based on conduct that includes a voluntary act or the omission to perform an act of which he is physically capable." As my own experiment revealed, and as a great deal of social-psychological research before and since has confirmed, we humans exaggerate the extent to which our actions are voluntary and rationally chosen—or, put differently, we all understate the power of the situation. My claim is not that individuals are incapable of criminal culpability; rather, it is that, like the horrible behavior brought out by my experiment in good, normal young men, the situation and the system creating it also must share in the responsibility for illegal and immoral behavior.

If the goals of the criminal system are simply to blame and punish individual perpetrators—to get our pound of flesh—then focusing almost exclusively on the individual defendant makes sense. If, however, the goal is actually to reduce the behavior that we now call "criminal" (and its resultant suffering), and to assign punishments that correspond with culpability, then the criminal-justice system is obligated, much as I was in the Stanford prison experiment, to confront the situation and our role in creating and perpetuating it. It is clear to most reasonable observers that the social experiment of imprisoning society's criminals for long terms is a failure on virtually all levels. By recognizing the situational determinants of behavior, we can move to a more productive public-health model of prevention and intervention, and away from the individualistic medical and religious "sin" model that has never worked since its inception during the Inquisition.

The critical message then is to be sensitive about our vulnerability to subtle but powerful situational forces and, by such awareness, be more able to overcome those forces. Group pressures, authority symbols, dehumanization of others, imposed anonymity, dominant ideologies that enable spurious ends to justify immoral means, lack of surveillance, and other situational forces can work to transform even some of the best of us into Mr. Hyde monsters, without the benefit of Dr. Jekyll's chemical elixir. We must be more aware of how situational variables can influence our behavior. Further, we must also be aware that veiled behind the power of the situation is the greater power of the system, which creates and maintains complicity at the highest military and governmental levels—with evil-inducing situations, like those at Abu Ghraib and Guantánamo Bay prisons.

Critical Thinking Questions

1. Ethics committees at universities have put an end to these types of experiments because there is potential danger to participants. Is research like the Milgram or Zimbardo experiments important to conduct?
2. Does the existence of external authority or group-think absolve a person from responsibility for his or her acts?
3. What did you learn that was surprising from this article?
4. Does society mitigate this type of danger (blind obedience)?

PART 9

Chapter 25

Online Communication and Negative Social Ties

GUSTAVO S. MESCH AND ILAN TALMUD

It seems that bullying has always been a social problem, particularly among children and youth. While traditionally bullying seems to have been accepted as a right of passage, in recent years, it has been taken more seriously, particularly by the social institutions that serve our youth. However, with the rise of social networking, the capacity to bully has expanded. As legislation and regulation struggle to catch up with these technologies, bullying has become increasingly pervasive. This following article demonstrates how the Internet, while often a source of pro-social behaviour, has also enabled escalated bullying.

1. How has the use of social networking sites, instant messaging, and other online technologies transformed bullying?
2. While this article is written to address child and teen bullying, can adult bullying also be understood within these contexts?

CYBERBULLYING FROM A SOCIAL NETWORK PERSPECTIVE

In our understanding of the role of youth social networks it is positive outcomes that are almost always emphasized. From a normative social perspective, social networks have an important role on the individual and social levels. On the individual level, the existence of social ties is linked to the development of a positive social bond to social institutions. Having friends means developing social skills, as through social interaction we internalize social norms, expectations and social values. On the aggregate level, social ties link individuals to society and support the development of a common identity and social solidarity. Through social interaction, namely exposure to each other, individuals develop mutual obligations, trust and commitment. The existence of social ties affords the individual access to companionship, information and romantic involvement. In the literature on youth, social bonds with other peers have indeed been associated with compliance with social values and social norms, but with avoidance of deviant behaviour as well. Supportive and mutual ties have been linked to keeping clear of engagement in deviant and non-normative behaviour both offline and online, to avoid the negative consequences of suffering social sanctions at the hands of significant others.

At the same time we should recognize that social ties can carry negative outcomes, commonly thought to be the result of lack of social ties alone. Not belonging to a large network, not experiencing closeness to existing ties, or belonging to a low density network are all assumed conducive to deterioration in mental

---

health (Beraman and Moody, 2004). Note, however, that negative outcomes may result from being involved in negative social ties—negative in the sense of hostile, aggressive and humiliating interactions (Beran and Li, 1995; Berson *et al.*, 2002). . . .

FROM BULLYING TO CYBERBULLYING

Bullying is a serious social issue as it is a vicious threat to a welcoming and supportive educational environment. Grave consequences have been identified in victimized people, including suicide attempts, eating disorders, running away from home, depression, dropping out of school and aggressive behaviour in adulthood (Borg, 1998; Kaltiala-Heino *et al.*, 1999; Olweus, 1999; Hawker and Boulton, 2000).

Historically, bullying is a common form of youth violence that affects children and teenagers, mostly when engaged in age-related activities such as going to school and travelling to and from school or when in public places such as hangouts (Patchin and Hinduja, 2006). Accordingly, in the past bullying has been extensively studied as a behaviour enacted in children's and adolescents' natural habitats such as the neighbourhood and school and at social gathering places. As to the prevalence of bullying, the data show that 10 to 15 per cent of students aged 12 to 18 years had been bullied in the previous 30 days (Devoe *et al.*, 2002; Galinsky and Salmond, 2002).

Bullying is conceived as an act of aggression with the attempt to exert domination through inducing fear. According to dominance theory (Hawley, 1999), students use aggression against weaker fellows to gain access to resources, including high sociometric status among peers. Bullies will therefore occupy more central network positions and hold more physical and social power, while victims will probably not be at the centre but more peripheral on the network than their classmates. Mouttapa *et al.* (2004) found that

victims received fewer friendship nominations and occupied less central positions in the friendship network than other members. Socially, for different reasons, they were less integrated in the school groups and of an inferior social status in the school network.

An issue more relevant to our argument is the major importance of the youth network as a protective factor. During adolescence an attempt is made to attain social status in the peer network. Achieving good grades, participating in extra-curricular activities, socializing and displaying cultural symbols are in part tools for adolescents striving to achieve social status. Targets of bullying at school tend to be children who are not well integrated in their social networks and known to be lonely or isolated. Well-integrated children are not targeted, as their friends are more likely to be in their company and to intervene in threatening situations (Mesch *et al.*, 2003). Network analysis has been used to investigate whether school sociometric status is associated with bullying victimization. Centrality, an index of popularity, is linked to both pro-social and anti-social behaviours. In their study of fourth and sixth grade males, Rodkin *et al.* (2000) found that boys perceived as non-aggressive, cooperative and leaders, and boys perceived as aggressive, equally occupied a central position in their classmates' social network. Some studies have specifically examined bullies' and victims' sociometric characteristics. Victims were often found to be rejected by their peers and lonelier than other students (Graham and Juvonen, 1998). There is evidence that a display of reciprocal friendships (e.g. students nominate a friend and receive a friendship nomination from that friend) protects students against victimization (Boulton *et al.*, 1999). Thus many young people are able to avoid the experience of bullying at school mainly due to peer or parental support (Farrington, 1993; Nansel *et al.*, 2001; Mesch 2003). Peers represent a support system, and studies on social networks and bullying have shown that victims are more likely to have friends who are non-aggressive, and

PART 9

offenders have ties to others who are aggressors (Mouttapa *et al.*, 2004). Another notable result of these studies is the importance of closeness of children to parents. When children inform their parents of bullying experiences, they are able to intervene and inform the school authorities (Farrington, 1993; Mesch *et al.*, 2003). These findings indicate the relevance of studying social networks for the understanding of bullying.

. . .

By utilizing information and communication technologies, bullying enjoys the advantage of several characteristics of the medium that transform the essence of the phenomenon as we know it. First, online communication in its very nature might induce bullying behaviour (Giuseppe and Galimberti, 2001). Communication that lacks non-verbal cues, status symbols and proximity to the victim may produce a behaviour that is self-oriented and not concerned with the feelings and opinions of others. Self-orientation may lead to lack of inhibition and negative perceptions of others, resulting in an increase in online bullying. Second, offenders exploit the internet's relative anonymity, through the use of screens or nicknames, to hide their true identity. An overall feeling of fear is generated in the victim, not knowing the perpetrator's identity; he or she does not know whether the perpetrator is or is not a classmate or a person met online (Li, 2007). Fear of unknown cyberbullies harms the educational and accepting environment essential to the classroom. The school is perceived as a hostile environment where victims feel unsafe, and such a child might avoid this by not attending classes. Third, the online environment provides a potentially large audience for the aggressive actions. This might appeal to perpetrators and furnish them positive feedback for their actions. Fourth, the large audience may amplify the negative effects of online bullying on the victim, as the harassment is being watched by all known acquaintances even beyond the school and neighbourhood. In sum, we may conclude that a

salient difference between school and cyberspace is that in the latter a large number of perpetrators can be involved in the abuse, and classmates who eschew bullying at school will engage in it in cyberspace, hiding behind anonymity.

Past studies on real-life bullying have shown the importance of the audience, as 30 percent of bystanders were found to express attitudes supporting the aggressors rather than the victims. The longer the bullying persists, the more bystanders join, and the more bystanders joins the worst are the consequences (Boulton *et al.*, 1999).

PREVALENCE AND CONSEQUENCES OF CYBERBULLYING

An early survey in Canada showed that one quarter of young internet users reported they had experienced messages containing hateful things about others (Mnet, 2005). Ybarra and Mitchell (2004) conducted a large study of young internet users in the USA and found that 19 per cent of the adolescents reported being bullied. Victims of online bullying were more likely than non-victims to be the target of offline bullying as well, but the correlation was far from perfect. A more recent online study of young internet users found that 29 per cent were victims of online bullying (Patchin and Hinduja, 2006). Online bullying seems to be increasing over the years. A study by the Crimes Against Children research centre that compared the results from two US national youth internet surveys in 2000 and 2005 found that self-reported online victimization of bullying increased from 6 to 9 per cent. Also, the percentage of children reporting cyberbullying others online increased from 14 to 28 per cent. In that study, being cyberbullied was defined as receiving mean, nasty messages, being threatened with bodily harm, being called names and having others tell lies about the victim on the internet. Inspecting in more detail the types of online bullying to which youth are exposed online, a study in the USA found that 13 per cent had experienced a situation of others spreading a rumour online about them, 6 per cent a situation in which someone posted an embarrassing picture of them online without their permission, and 13 per cent had received a threatening or aggressive email or text message (Pew Internet and American Life, 2006).

As to risk factors, studies have indicated that the higher the frequency of internet use, the higher the risk of cyberbullying (Patchin and Hinduja, 2006; Mitchell *et al.*, 2007; Rosen, 2007). Victimization occurs more often in internet spaces used for communication with unknown individuals such as chat rooms and **social networking** sites than through email and IM (Hinduja and Patchin, 2008). . . . Online games were not found associated with the risk of online bullying (Mesch, 2009b). An online profile in social networking and clip-sharing sites provides personal characteristics, disseminates contact information and exposes the adolescent to potential contact with motivated offenders, probably unknown. This private information is the raw material that might be used by potential offenders to call youngsters names, threaten them and ridicule them. . . .

. . . Public disclosure of such information increases the risk of cyberbullying (Hinduja and Patchin, 2008). Not surprisingly, participation in chat rooms heightens the risk of cyberbullying still more, as participants are likely to engage in conversations with strangers, some of whom may be offenders. Studies have already found that online conversations tend to develop intimacy, and individuals are more likely to share private and personal information online because of the relative anonymity of the medium. . . .

. . .

OUTCOMES

For several reasons the effects of cyberbullying might be more pronounced than those of traditional bullying. . . . In traditional bullying the possibility exists of physical separation between the aggressor and the victim, but in cyberbullying physical separation does not guarantee cessation of acts such as sending text messages and emails to the victim. Second, with the internet the abuser has a sense of anonymity and often believes that there is only a slim chance of detection of the misconduct. Third. . . . Anonymity and absence of interaction may make the aggressor still less inhibited and increase the frequency and power of cyberbullying (Heirman and Walrave, 2008).

Being a victim of online bullying has negative effects on adolescents' well-being. Victims are more likely to engage in high risk behaviours such as low school commitment, neglect of grades and alcohol and cigarette consumption (Finkelhor *et al.*, 2000). An emotional aspect also exists. After a bullying event the victim reports feeling angry and upset, and has difficulty concentrating on schoolwork. Online bullying has proven to have a negative effect on parent–child relationships and on relations with friends (Patchin and Hinduja, 2006). . . .

. . .

EXPLAINING CYBERBULLYING

PART 9

. . .

Participation through social media (email, instant messaging, social networking sites, forums and chat rooms) have an effect on the size, composition and quality of social ties, increasing exposure of youth to them. The effect varies according to each application, and the risk of exposure to victimization varies accordingly. Participation in chat rooms and forums and exchange of emails expose youth to new ties with unknown others. With some of them the exposure can have positive consequences as youth are able to meet others who share their interests and concerns and are able to exchange resources that are not located in the existing network. At the same time, internet activity enlarges the youth network;

hence the risk to exposure to others with whom negative relationships may develop. The more unknown individuals become part of the social network, the greater the likelihood of meeting some who might become aggressors. . . . Some older individuals might express interest in associating with teens to harass them or solicit them sexually. Also, the addition of online ties to the youth network might temporarily decrease the strength of existing ties, reducing the sources of social support available to the individual. The extent that cyberbullying is carried out by strangers remains to be assessed as existing evidence is more anecdotal than based on large-scale studies. . . .

The use of social media such as IM to maintain existing ties and keeping a profile and communicating with friends through social networking sites expose youth to the risk of online victimization, but by a different mechanism. The incorporation of IM and social networking sites into adolescents' lives transforms their relationship with peers. When teens arrive home every day, rather than disconnecting from their friends they enter a state of perpetual connection as IM is all the time, text messages arrive and conversations continue. In this case online bullying becomes an extension of school bullying, conducted after school hours through electronic communication. Now the possibility of after-school disconnection from or avoidance of contact with aggressors decreases. Cyberbullying often starts at the school or in the neighbourhood and it continues online, as affirmed by adolescents themselves. . . . For teenagers, online bullying can be emotionally debilitating, particularly because it is mainly a continuation at home of the aggression in the playground by known others from their social network. With traditional bullying, on arriving home the youngster felt safe and there was a respite from the aggression; now the aggression follows the adolescent home and can go on 24 hours a day. There is no place for the youngster to hide, even at home, from the persistent aggression (Rosen, 2007). A study in Canada

(Li, 2007) investigated different forms of electronic bullying and found that the most frequently reported were email (20 per cent), chat rooms (33 per cent) and mobile phone texting (13 per cent). In the UK a study of the different channels of cyberbullying in greater depth found similar results. . . .

Important too is that online bullying requires some knowledge of the victim. When conducting online activities, individuals differ in their readiness to share personal information. Some are less willing to provide contact and personal information than others. Providing personal information can be considered a risk factor for victimization, particularly when it is given to strangers (Mesch, 2009b).

. . . Suler (2004) noted that cyberspace can be conducive to behaviours they may not be revealed in the offline world. Various factors contribute to creating a subjective perception that fosters the disinhibition effect. Among the most salient characteristics are anonymity, asynchronicity and dissociative imagination. Anonymity means that individual's subjective perception that the use of a nickname online separates him or her from the real world and his or her real identity is not known to others. This sense of anonymity might give rise to actions for which the actor does not feel responsible, at least not in the way he or she feels responsible for actions performed in a social circle in which his or her identity is known to friends, teachers and parents. Asynchronicity means that often individuals interact online not in real time, especially when communicating through email, forums and social networking sites. Not interacting in realtime means that individuals do not experience in real time the reactions of others, or get immediate negative feedback for their actions. . . .

Dissociative imagination means a situation in which some individuals evaluate online events differently and separately from face-to-face events. Certainly anonymity may reinforce this feeling that online norms of behaviour unacceptable in a face-to-face situation are acceptable online. This is sensed as a different sphere, less real, or with fewer real consequences, for the victims. . . . Accordingly, in the case of cyber-bullying the victim's emotional reactions are not present. The aggressor is unaware of the victim's distress, fear, tears and other emotional reactions. He or she is thus likely to increase the aggression attempts without setting limits on it that would otherwise derive from interpersonal contact and interactivity. . . .

LINKING TRADITIONAL BULLYING AND CYBERBULLYING

Is cyberbullying independent of bullying at school and in the neighbourhood? Some observers have advanced the idea that cyberbullying is a new phenomenon, largely the result of children and adolescents coming into contact with strangers and unknown individuals in open chat rooms online. In these spaces of conversation and social interaction strangers hold conversations with young people, making derogatory ethnic and sexual comments, or deriding their contributions. However, recent studies point more and more to a link between school bullying and cyberbullying. A study in Canada found that the most important predictor of cyberbullying victimization was victims being bullied at school (Li, 2007).

Bullying and cyberbullying are closely related, and in many cases the bullying possibly started at school and/or in the neighbourhood and then spread to cyberspace. In fact, cyberspace serves bullies as yet another venue in which to harass others, as they take advantage of the high rate of internet use among youth. Another possibility is that bullying starts online, and later the perpetrators take it into the real world, converting it into face-to-face bullying.

In trying to resolve this issue we face the problem of identifying the aggressor. As the internet often provides anonymity, victims do not always know who the perpetrator of the aggressive behaviour is. A study reported that 25.6 per cent of the respondents said that they were cyberbullied by schoolmates, 12.8 per cent by people outside school. The most surprising finding was that 46.6 per cent did not know who cyberbullied them (Li, 2006).

Over time, online bullying seems to be on the rise. The percentage of victims of cyberbullying has increased despite the decrease in participation in open chat rooms and forums and an increase in the participation in IM and social networking sites. These results provide an additional indication that cyberbullying is aggression by known others, such as schoolmates, taking advantage of social networking media (e.g. Instant Messenger, social network sites, SMS). As noted earlier, a study by the Crimes Against Children research centre compared the results of two national youth internet safety surveys in 2000 and 2005 and found that the amount of cyberbullying had increased. In Rosen's study (2007), although only 11 percent of the teens reported being harassed, 57 per cent of parents and 34 per cent of teens reported that they were concerned about harassment on MySpace. Clearly, the use of communication channels that link youth with friends and friends of friends is associated with an increase of cyberbullying; this supports the argument of a link between this and offline bullying. Rather than being new, cyberbullying seems to be a supplement to school aggression.

REFERENCES

Beraman, P. S. and Moody, J. (2004) Adolescents' suicidability. *American Journal of Public Health*, 94, 89–95.

Beran, K. M. and Li, A. (1995) Bully and victim problems in elementary schools and students beliefs about aggression. *Canadian Journal of School Psychology*, 11, 153–165.

Berson, I. R., Berson, M. J. and Ferron, J. M. (2002) Emerging risks of violence in the digital age. *Journal of School Violence*, 2, 51–71.

Borg, M. G. (1998) The emotional reaction of school bullies and their victims. *Educational Psychology*, 18, 433–444.

PART 9

Boulton *et al.,* (1999) Concurrent and longitudinal links between friendship and peer victimization: implications for befriending interventions. *Journal of Adolescence*, 22, 461–466.

Devoe *et al.,* (2001) *Indicators of Schooled Crime and Safety.* Washington, DC: US Department of Education.

Farrington, D. (1993) Understanding and preventing bullying. In M. Tony *Crime and Justice: A Review of Research.* Chicago: University of Chicago Press.

Finkelhor, D., Mitchell, K. and Wollak, J. (2000) *Online Victimization: A Report on the Nation's Youth.* Alexandria, VA: National Center for Missing and Exploited Children.

Galinsky, E. and Salmond, K. (2002) *Youth and Violence: Students Speak Out for a More Civil Society.* New York: Families and Work Institute.

Giuseppe, R. and Galimberti, C. (2001) *Towards Cyber-Psychology: Mind, Cognitions and Society in the Internet Age.* Amsterdam: IOS Press.

Graham, S. and Juvonen, J. (1998) Social-cognitive perspective on peer aggression and victimization. *Annals of Child Development*, 13, 23–70.

Hawker, D. S. J. and Boulton, M. J. (2000) Twenty years of research on peer victimization and psychological maladjustment: a meta analysis. *Journal of Child Psychology and Psychiatry*, 41, 441–445.

Hawley, P. H. (1999) The ontogenesis of social dominance: a strategy-based evolutionary perspective. *Development Review*, 19, 97–132.

Heirman, W. and Walrave, M. (2008) Assessing concerns and issues about the mediation of technology in cyberbullying. *Cyberpsychology: Journal of Psychosocial Research on Cyberspace*, 2(2), 1–12.

Hinduja, S. and Patchin, J. W. (2008) Personal information of adolescents on the internet: a quantitative content analysis of MySpace. *Journal of Adolescence*, 31, 125–146.

Kaltiala-Heino *et al.,* (1999) Bullying, depression, and suicidal ideation in Finnish adolescents. *British Medical Journal*, 319, 348–351.

Li, Q. (2006) Cyber bullying in schools: a research of gender differences. *School Psychology International*, 27, 157–170.

Li, Q. (2007) Bullying in the new playground: research into cyber-bullying and cyber-victimization.

Australasian Journal of Educational Technology, 23(3), 435–454.

Media Awareness Networks (Mnet) (2005) *Young Canadians in a Wired World.* http://www.media-awareness.ca/english/research/YCWW/phaseII (accessed 26 June 2009).

Mesch, G. S., Fishman, G. and Eisikovits, Z. (2003) Attitudes supporting violence and aggressive behavior among adolescents in Israel: the role of family and peers. *Journal of Interpersonal Violence*, 18, 1132–1148.

Mesch, G. S. (2009) Parental mediation, online activities and cyberbullying. *Cyberpsychology and Behavior*, 12(4), 387–393.

Mitchell, K. J., Ybarra, M. and Finkelhor, D. (2007) The relative importance of online victimization in understanding depression, delinquency, and substance use. *Child Maltreatment*, 12(4), 314–324.

Mouttapa *et al.,* (2004) Social network predictors of bullying and victimization. *Adolescence*, 39(154), 315–335.

Nansel *et al.,* (2001) Bullying behaviors among US youth: prevalence and association with psychological adjustment. *Journal of the American Medical Association*, 285, 2094–2100.

Olweus, D. (1999) *Bullying at School: Long-Term Outcomes for Victims and an Effective School-Based Intervention Program.* New York: Plenum.

Patchin, J. and Hinduja, S. (2006) Bullies move beyond the schoolyard. *Youth Violence and Juvenile Justice*, 4(2), 148–169.

Pew Internet and American Life Project (2006) *The Ever-shifting Internet Population.* Washington, DC: Pew Internet and American Life Project.

Rodkin *et al.,* (2000) Heterogeneity of popular boys: antisocial and prosocial configurations. *Developmental Psychology*, 36, 14–24.

Rosen, L. D. (2007) *Me, MySpace, and I: Parenting the Net Generation.* London: Palgrave Macmillan.

Suler, J. (2004) The online disinheriting effect. *Cyber-Psychology and Behavior*, 7, 321–326.

Ybarra, M. L. and Mitchell, K. J. (2004) Online aggressor/targets, aggressors and targets: a comparison of associated youth characteristics. *Journal of Child Psychology and Psychiatry*, 45(7), 1308–1316.

Critical Thinking Questions

1. Do you think that bullying is taken seriously enough as a generally recurring problem, or is it only properly addressed in extreme cases where the victims are physically harmed or harm themselves?
2. Does the article point to norms regarding bullying that delay or minimize prevention of this?

PART 9

Chapter 26

Religion: The Comeback

REGINALD BIBBY

In his article, Bibby argues that some religions survive because they successfully compete with others that decline. He does not think that religion is doomed, rather he argues that religion is about to make a "comeback." Bibby uses a framework to study religions as "firms" that compete in a market for "customers" who become their believers. In order to be competitive, a particular religion must be appealing and offer something different and enticing to potential members, while retaining current participants. Consider this analogy as you go through the reading and decide whether it is a useful way to understand the reality of religions today.

1. How are religious groups currently evolving in Canada?
2. How does the situation in Canada regarding religious groups compare worldwide?

Prophecy is not exactly a social science virtue.

. . .

It's not that we never try. When it comes to religion, we have had a good share of would-be social prophets. People like Auguste Comte (1798–1857), Karl Marx (1818–1883), and Sigmund Freud (1856–1939) saw religion's disappearance as inevitable. Comte said scientific thought would replace religious thinking, Marx felt the resolving of social and economic inequities would eliminate the need for religion as a pain-killing drug, and Freud maintained that science and personal resolve would combine to allow us to abandon our child-like fantasies about a father-like God and a future existence in heaven.

There obviously is much data that point to the fact that such thinkers were too quick to write off religion. In settings where religion is currently flourishing, a measure of **secularization** undoubtedly will take place. The historical precedents of Europe and North America suggest such a trend will be closely associated with heightened levels of development.

But in other places where polarization is prominent, or where secularity is pronounced, comebacks are in the works.

. . .

THE CANADIAN SITUATION

As we look at Canada, some general observations about the immediate future of some of the groups can be made with a high level of confidence.

Roman Catholics. Make no mistake about it—this is the big player in Canada. The 2001 census revealed that close to 13 million Canadians (43%) viewed themselves as Catholic—about 7 million outside Quebec (23%), 6 million in Quebec (20%). The median age of Catholics is 37.8, about the same as the Canadian population as a whole.

Source: Bibby, Reginald. *Beyond the Gods and Back: Religion's Demise and Rise and Why it Matters*. Lethbridge: Project Canada Books, 2011. Reprinted with permission of Project Canada Books.

As the Roman Catholic Church goes, so goes organized religion in the nation. Other groups may get much of the ink. Some might even believe they are the key to the country's religious health. But at the end of the day, Catholics rule. Don't fear for their future. Besides, this is not just a big regional or national company. This is a vast and powerful multinational corporation.

Seen in such perspective, the Catholic Church in Quebec is "merely" a problem spot on the Catholic global map. Yes, the provincial government plays no religious favourites.[1] Yes, Catholics have become selective consumers. But the research to date is definitive: most people in the province remain Catholic and are not going anywhere. Lack of commitment understandably troubles leaders. But widespread defection is not on the horizon. Religion à la carte, Catholic-style, rules in Quebec.

Elsewhere, Catholicism's vitality is fueled in part by new arrivals from other countries. But let's not minimize the importance of faith for earlier generations of people who were raised in Canadian Catholic homes.

The time is come to quit belittling the health of Canadian Catholicism. Large numbers may show up only occasionally for seasonal services, for rights of passage, or because they think they are overdue to share in a Mass. But they still show up. And they are still Catholic.

Large numbers also are open to greater involvement if they find it to be worthwhile. The challenge lies with the supplier. If the Catholic Church comes through, who knows what could happen?

Mainline Protestants. As I look at the four primary "firms" in this grouping—the United, Anglican, Lutheran, and Presbyterians churches. . . .

. . .

In short, the demographics have not been good. Limited growth through immigration, migration, and birth, coupled with mortality, add up to an obvious result: zero or negative growth. Given their global nature, Anglicans have the potential to be helped considerably by immigration. But to date their potential global gains have been neutralized considerably by divisive homosexuality and gender issues.

There is an additional problem. To the extent Stark and others are right in maintaining people will be drawn to groups which address questions that "only the gods can answer," it's not clear that Mainline Protestants have particularly strong ultimate answer "product lines." Tom Harpur doesn't mince his words. In the case of life after death, he says that many groups simply "avoid the topic completely."[2] And he's not talking about the evangelicals.

Unlike Catholics, for example, who give a fair amount of attention to things like heaven and the importance of "last rites" so that people are ready for life after death, the United Church—for example—rightly or wrongly is seen by many as focusing almost exclusively on life. Perhaps Anglicans, Presbyterians, and Lutherans are different.[3]

Beyond tirelessly debating the reasons for the decline, the bottom line is that Mainline numbers are down, with significant resource implications: good ministry is all the more difficult to accomplish.[4] Still, Diana Butler Bass could be right: it may yet be possible for Mainline churches to be renewed "by weaving personal spiritual quests" with a primary strength—"their more traditional forms of religious life."[5] David Harris, editor of the *Presbyterian Record*, comments that "the church desperately needs to find a way to move forward." But he cautions that flexibility and creativity can be hard to come by. In the words of one former moderator, "Zacchaeus was not a Presbyterian."[6]

Conservative Protestants. The "evangelicals," as they are commonly known collectively, are characterized by considerable vitality. Their major demographic accomplishment has been their ability to sustain a market share of approximately 8% (7% Baptist) from the first census in 1871 through to the present day.

Religious intermarriage alone should have decimated the Conservative Protestants. Yet,

PART 10

because of factors that include immigration, their emphasis on tight-knit communities and strong youth and family ministries, they have been able to sustain their market share. The thesis of Mainline Protestant executive Dean Kelley, put forth in the early 1970s, also knows increasing support. In his book, *Why Conservative Churches Are Growing*, Kelley maintained that two key factors of central importance were (1) the demands that evangelicals placed on their members, in the form of expectations such as participation, tithing, and lifestyles and (2) the provision of answers to ultimate questions, including life after death.[7]

My examination of Calgary evangelical church growth dating back to the late-1960s shows that, contrary to popular myth, Conservative Protestants know only modest growth through the recruitment of outsiders. Their numerical stability and growth are tied primarily to their ability to retain their own people—their children and their geographically-mobile members.[8]

To the extent they are outsiders, the key factor is relationships: they tend to either befriend or marry them.

. . .

Somewhat paradoxically, while Conservative Protestants tend to stay with their "Believers' Church" denominations, they move fairly freely between individual evangelical groups.[9] As a result, no single denomination in this "family" makes up even 3% of the Canadian population, nowhere near the 7% who identified themselves as "Baptist" when the first census was conducted in 1871. Many prefer to go simply by "Christian."[10]

Evangelicals, who typically are younger than Mainline Protestants, will continue to be a smaller player on the Canadian religious scene. But their steady market share of 8% is finally about to increase. Why? The explosive growth of evangelicals in many parts of the world will result in an increasingly robust immigration pipeline—and an increasingly multicultural church. . . .

Other Faith Entries. As people came to Canada from an array of countries, they brought other religions besides Christianity to Canada. At the time of Confederation, Jews made up about one-tenth of one percent of the population. With the arrival of increasing numbers of people from countries other than Europe and the United States, additional faiths also took root.

Through about 1981, the number of people identifying with faiths other than Christianity remained very small. Much of the difficulty such groups had, of course, was tied to the fact that they had difficulty holding on to their children: many married Protestants and Catholics.

The net result was that, by 1981, less than 3% of Canadians indicated they were either Jewish, Muslim, Buddhist, Hindu, or Sikh. Another 1% were either Jehovah's Witnesses or Mormons.

As we have seen, over the past three decades or so, immigration has seen the percentage of people who identify with the other major world religions double to about 6%. The largest of these is Islam at 2%.

The historical track records of the number of these faiths—Judaism, Buddhism, Hinduism, and Sikhism, along with the Latter Day Saints and Jehovah's Witnesses—suggest that they will continue to be part of the Canadian religious scene. But like the four Mainline Protestant groups, they will not be among the major religious firms.

Islam is another story. There already are more Muslims in Canada than Presbyterians, Pentecostals, and Jews, for example. They may well be on the verge of attaining the proverbial "critical mass"—such as the evangelicals have experienced—where their numbers reach a point where they are able to cut down on losses through intermarriage. Moreover, Islam obviously is a very powerful multinational religion. In light of the diverse number of countries in which it is prominent, the immigration pipeline that has been such a critically important component of religious group growth over the years will contain to produce new people for some time to come.

TABLE 26.1   CANADA'S 16 LARGEST RELIGIOUS GROUPS

		NUMBERS	%	MEDIAN AGE
1.	Roman Catholic	12,793,125	44	37.8
2.	United Church	2,839,125	12	44.1
3.	Anglican	2,035,500	8	43.8
4.	Christian *(unspecified)*	780,450	3	30.2
5.	Baptist	729,475	3	39.3
6.	Eastern Orthodox	606,620	2	40.1
7.	Lutheran	606,590	2	43.3
8.	Muslim	579,640	2	28.1
9.	Protestant *(unspecified)*	549,205	2	40.4
10.	Presbyterian	409,830	1	46.0
11.	Pentecostal	369,475	1	33.5
12.	Jewish	329,995	1	41.5
13.	Buddhist	300,345	1	38.0
14.	Hindu	297,200	1	31.9
15.	Sikh	278,410	<1	29.7
16.	Greek Orthodox	215,175	<1	46.1
	No Religion	*4,796,325*	*16*	*31.1*

SOURCE: Statistics Canada, 2001 Census.

In addition, a relatively high birth rate and an emphasis on the retention of children will further contribute to Islam's viability. It is worth noting that the median age of Muslims as of the 2001 census was 28.1. Some additions through proselytism—or what many social scientists call "switching"—also can be expected.

Finally, the two traits that observers such as Kelley and Stark see as essential to success—an emphasis on demands and rewards, as well as the ability to speak to ultimate questions—are major features of Islam.

In short, as we look to the future of religion in Canada, we can anticipate that the Roman Catholic Church will continue to be the dominant player. Other key market members will be the Conservative Protestants and Muslims.

The marketplace will not lack for other players, both old and new. But those groups will have to work hard just to retain—let alone expand—their market shares.

THE GLOBAL SITUATION

As with Canada, there are and will continue to be people all over the world who are not in the market for religion, old or new. But they will be in the minority.

At this point in history, some 6 billion of the planet's 7 billion people are identifying with a religion. They are led by Christians (2.1 billion), Muslims (1.5 million) and Hindus (900 million).

Like the auto multinationals, including Toyota, GM, Volkswagen, Ford, and Hyundai, these religious powerhouses will continue to lead the way as the most prominent religious "suppliers" on earth.

To the extent that markets in any country become open to their presence and that of other smaller suppliers—in part because their existing clienteles simply move to new places—religions will make national inroads.

Collectively, the religious companies have been performing very well of late. In the words of Harvey Cox, "Instead of disappearing, religion is now exhibiting new vitality all around the world."[11]

Christianity's Growth. In recent years Christianity has experienced more worldwide growth than any religion. Such a reality of the faith's global health will come as news to many people. After all, as Philip Yancey noted recently, it's not making the headlines of CNN.[12] *Globe and Mail* columnist

PART 10

Neil Reynolds similarly wrote in early 2010, "You could call it the greatest story never told."[13]

Reynolds drew on two prominent observers of the global religious scene, U.S. political scientist Walter Russell Mead and British scholar Scott M. Thomas. Their thoughts are worth retrieving in detail.[14]

The flamboyant Mead has noted that Christianity is now "on its biggest roll" in its 2000-year history.[15] It is both the world's largest faith and the world's fastest growing faith. Its absolute numbers and market share are at all-time highs. In the last fifty years, Mead says, "It has surpassed Islam as the most popular religion in sub-Saharan Africa and as the leading Abrahamic religion in China." The Christian faith, he asserts, "claims almost twice as many adherents as Islam worldwide."[16] By 2050, the worldwide Christian population could top three billion.

- Roman Catholic commentator John Allen would note that, between 1950 and 2000, the number of Catholics worldwide grew from just under 500 million to over one billion. The church suffered serious losses in the global North (Europe and North America), but grew dramatically in the global South (Africa, Asia, and Latin America).[17]
- In a country like Russia, Orthodox Christianity is enjoying a revival after seventy years of communist suppression.[18]
- But of particular significance, Pentecostals have experienced the fastest growth of any religious movement in history, says Mead, "from zero to something like half a billion members in the last 100 years." Growth has been pronounced in Africa, Asia, and Latin America.[19]

Thomas likewise maintains that "around the world, religion is on the rise, and notes that, "the most dramatic religious explosion is the spread of evangelical Protestantism, led by Pentecostalism." After Catholics, he says, Pentecostals represent the largest single group of Christians worldwide.[20] It typically crosses class lines.

What perhaps is startling to learn is not only that evangelicals now number close to 700 million people worldwide; it's that they have achieved strategic masses in such places as China, Indonesia, India, Nigeria, the Philippines, South Africa, and Brazil.

For example, it is estimated that, by 2050, there could be 220 million Christians in China—about 15% of the population.[21]

In many instances, Thomas notes, Christianity is "returning to its roots by becoming a post-Western religion dominated by the peoples, cultures, and countries of the global South."[22] While having a strong personal focus, it also has become increasingly politically active, especially in Latin America.[23]

These expansion patterns, of course, have not been without conflict. Thomas points out that "three countries with substantial Muslim communities—India, Indonesia, and Nigeria—also have large Pentecostal populations and sizable minorities of Christians more broadly." Tensions have been rising, resulting in violence such as the conflict in Nigeria in 2010 that left over 500 people dead.[24]

In addition, competition with Catholicism in various parts of the world is frequently intense. John Allen writes that as "Pentecostals march across the planet," they have been "siphoning off significant numbers of Catholics." He notes that "the Catholic Church is itself being 'Pentecostalized' through the Charismatic movement.[25]

A massive shift in population growth from the developed countries of the North to the developing countries of the global South will result in a changing global religious landscape. Thomas points out that the developed countries of the North accounted for 32% of the world's population in 1900 and 18% in 2000. By 2050, that figure will drop to just 10%.[26] "A new kind of world is in the making," he says, "and the people, states, and religious communities that compose the global South are making it."[27]

In the case of Roman Catholics, Allen notes that the church was dominated in the last century by the global North. Today, two in three Catholics are found in Africa, Asia, and Latin America.[28] One obvious result? An unprecedented number of Catholic leaders are coming from all over the world[29]—often, in the Canadian instance, to a parish near you.

Mead and Thomas both draw attention to the fact that the rise in evangelical Christianity in particular can be expected to bring with it a concomitant increase in Protestant ideals, such as the work ethic, entrepreneurial aspirations, and personal freedom.[30] Thomas sees global Christianity as becoming more conservative than European Christianity, but more liberal than the Catholic model which, in some Latin American settings, will be replaced by evangelicalism. Sometimes it will be a hybrid with Catholicism, sometimes not.[31]

In addition, both Mead and Thomas maintain that the spread of evangelical Christianity will have important social consequences. Globally, "Evangelicals will be a major religious, social, and political force in the coming century," Thomas writes.[32] In China, for example, he maintains that the government tacitly allows the established religions of Christianity and neo-Confucianism "to operate relatively freely, believing that they can promote social harmony amid rapid social changes." He suggests that if Christianity achieves the culture permeation in China that it knows in South Korea—at around 25%—it could fundamentally alter China's political fabric.[33]

Islamic Growth. Observers maintain that Islam also is experiencing a revival that extends well beyond the more extreme Islamic fundamentalist movements. As we have seen with the global Gallup data, large proportions of people in predominantly Muslim countries are saying that religion is an important part of their daily lives. In reminding readers that Islamic renewal is extending far beyond the Arab world, Thomas writes that "more Muslim women are wearing the veil, more Muslim men are growing beards, and more Muslims are attending mosques more often."[34]

- Russia now has more Muslims and any other country in Europe.
- Northwestern China "is home to over 20 million Muslims and is now in the grip of an Islamic reawakening."[35] Many young Chinese Muslims are studying across the Middle East.
- Sheer numbers alone mean that Christian-Islam relations will, in John Allen's words, "be a major driver of world history in the twenty-first century."[36]

One cannot underestimate the role that the Internet is playing in connecting Christians, Muslims, and people of many other faiths who, because of geographical separation, were isolated religious diasporas.

Yet, ironically, notes Thomas, globalization in general simultaneously contributes to "a more unified and yet more fragmented world."[37]

ASSESSMENT

Obviously the receptivity levels to religion vary considerably around the world. In Stark's parlance, settings are variously religiously "regulated" and "deregulated." They have open as well as closed markets, robust competition as well as long-standing monopolies.

But because of both (1) the ongoing demand and (2) the ongoing availability of global suppliers, one thing is clear: religion will persist as far as the social scientific eye can see, individually and organizationally.

The scope of the market for religion is so vast that, apart from the gods, entrepreneurial human beings would find its potential too great to ignore.

Religions, major and minor, well-established and freshly minted, will continue to be at work, attempting to increase their local, national, and global market shares.

Individuals will continue to explore the options, and will usually opt for one—or more. After all, for some, religion enriches life. For all, it offers market entries when it comes to death.

PART 10

And as for the gods, if they actually exist and people ignore them for very long, they can be expected to shake things up from time to time.

NOTES

1. deSouza, Father Raymond J. (2010, December 30). "Quebec worships the idol of secularism." *National Post*.
2. Harpur, Tom. (1991). *Life after death*. Toronto: McClelland and Stewart.
3. Nicolisi, Gary. (2010, November 1). "Guest reflections: What happens when we die?" *AnglicanJournal.com*.
4. Bagnell, Kenneth. (2010). "Secular shift." *The United Church Observer*. January.
5. Butler Bass, Diana. (2006) *Christianity for the rest of us*. New York: HarperOne.
6. Harris, David. (2009, October 1). "Start something unthinkable: The church needs to be flexible." *Presbyterian Record*.
7. Kelley, Dean. (1972). *Why conservative churches are growing*. New York: Harper and Row.
8. Bibby, Reginald W. and Brinkerhoff, Merlin B. (1973). "The circulation of the saints: A study of people who join conservative churches." *Journal for the Scientific Study of Religion* 12: 273-83; and Bibby, Reginald. (2003). "The circulation of the saints: One final look at how conservative protestant churches grow." Presented at the annual meeting of the Pacific Sociological Association, San Diego, April.
9. Bibby, Reginald W. and Brinkerhoff, Merlin B. (1973). "The circulation of the saints: A study of people who join conservative churches." *Journal for the Scientific Study of Religion* 12: 273-83; and Bibby, Reginald. (2003). "The circulation of the saints: One final look at how conservative protestant churches grow." Presented at the annual meeting of the Pacific Sociological Association, San Diego, April.
10. Clarke, Brian and Macdonald, Stuart. (2007). "Simply christian: Canada's newest major religious denomination." *Toronto Journal of Theology* 23(2): 109-25.
11. Cox, Harvey. (2009). The future of faith. New York: HaperOne.
12. Yancy, Philip. (2010) *What good is God?* New York: FaithWords/Hatchett Book Group. 4
13. Reynolds, Neil. (2011, January 10). "The globalization of God in the 21st century." *Globe and Mail*.
14. Mead, Walter Russell. (2010, May 28). "Pentecostal power." A blog in *The American Interest*.
15. Mead, Walter Russell. (2010, May 28). "Pentecostal power." A blog in *The American Interest*.
16. Mead, Walter Russell. (2010, May 28). "Pentecostal power." A blog in *The American Interest*.
17. Allen, John L., Jr. (2009). *The future church*. New York: Doubleday. 20.
18. Thomas, Scott M. (2010). "A globalized god." *Foreign Affairs*, November/December 89: 93–101.
19. Mead, Walter Russell. (2010, May 28). "Pentecostal power." A blog in *The American Interest*.
20. Thomas, Scott M. (2010). "A globalized god." *Foreign Affairs*, November/December 89: 93–101.
21. Thomas, Scott M. (2010). "A globalized god." *Foreign Affairs*, November/December 89: 93–101.
22. Thomas, Scott M. (2010). "A globalized god." *Foreign Affairs*, November/December 89: 93–101.
23. Thomas, Scott M. (2010). "A globalized god." *Foreign Affairs*, November/December 89: 93–101.
24. Thomas, Scott M. (2010). "A globalized god." *Foreign Affairs*, November/December 89: 93–101.
25. Allen, John L., Jr. (2009) *The future church*. New York: Doubleday.
26. Thomas, Scott M. (2010). "A globalized god." *Foreign Affairs*, November/December 89: 93–101.
27. Thomas, Scott M. (2010). "A globalized god." *Foreign Affairs*, November/December 89: 93–101.
28. Allen, John L., Jr. (2009) *The future church*. New York: Doubleday.
29. Allen, John L., Jr. (2009) *The future church*. New York: Doubleday.
30. Mead, Walter Russell. (2010, May 28). "Pentecostal power." A blog in *The American Interest*.
31. Brinkerhoff, Merlin B. and Reginald Bibby. (1985). "Circulation of the saints in South America." *Journal for the Scientific Study of Religion* 24: 253–262.
32. Thomas, Scott M. (2010). "A globalized god." *Foreign Affairs*, November/December 89: 93–101.
33. Thomas, Scott M. (2010). "A globalized god." *Foreign Affairs*, November/December 89: 93–101.

34. Thomas, Scott M. (2010). "A globalized god." *Foreign Affairs,* November/December 89: 93–101.

35. Thomas, Scott M. (2010). "A globalized god." *Foreign Affairs,* November/December 89: 93–101.

36. Allen, John L., Jr. (2009) *The future church.* New York: Doubleday.

37. Thomas, Scott M. (2010). "A globalized god." *Foreign Affairs,* November/December 89: 93–101.

Critical Thinking Questions

1. Why has organized religion persisted?
2. Will religious groups be maintained in the future in Canada?

PART 10

Chapter 27

Islamophobia: A New Racism?

VIC SATZEWICH

Islam is the second-largest religion worldwide, but, as Satzewich notes, many still know very little about its practices and its followers. Often, Westerners hold stereotyped and uninformed notions about Muslims. The article argues that a limited public knowledge of Islam, supplemented by snippets of extremist activities and stereotypes, have created a culture of distrust and discrimination of those affiliated, or assumed to be affiliated with, Islam. Satzewich titles this form of discrimination as "Islamophobia."

1. How does Islamophobia differ from other forms of racism and discrimination in Canada (or does it)?

. . .

At first blush, it seems odd to describe **Islamophobia** as a form of racism. After all . . . . racism involves the negative evaluation of groups defined and constructed by reference to their perceived biological makeup and/or physical appearance. It is about the social construction and social evaluation of physical differences like skin colour and presumed race. But. . . racism has taken on new forms. Today, code words and seemingly neutral language are sometimes used to express negative attitudes toward a group. These code words allow individuals or organizations to discriminate against a given group, and at the same time allow them to deny that they are racist. As a result, the former criticisms sometimes stand in for racially based criticisms.

The term Islamophobia first came into widespread use in Britain in the 1990s. Even before the attacks of September 11, 2001, sections of British society were concerned about the apparent rise in Islamophobia in that country. Sparked in part by the negative treatment of Muslims in Britain as a consequence of the Rushdie affair, an organization called The Runnymede Trust—a think tank mandated to deal with matters of ethnic and racial equality and justice—issued a report in 1997 titled *Islamophobia: A Challenge for Us All*. The Trust made a distinction between what is called closed and open views of Islam.

The Runnymede Trust report characterized closed views of Islam as "Islamophobia." In a follow-up report, Islamophobia was specifically defined as a form of racism. The report suggested that the definition of racism required expansion

to refer to a wide range of intolerance, not just to intolerance where the principal markers of difference is physical difference and skin colour. For example, the term should encompass patterns of prejudice and discrimination such as anti-semitism and sectarianism, where the markers of supposed difference are religious and cultural rather than to do with physical appearance. . . . There are clear similarities between antisemitism, sectarianism, and Islamophobia, and between these and other forms of intolerance. The plural term "racisms" is sometimes used to evoke this point. (Commission on British Muslims and Islamophobia 2004, 12)

In the British political context, this broadened definition of racism was used to justify the inclusion of discrimination against Muslims within the wider purview of the country's Race Relations legislation. . . .

Some social scientists argue that defining Islamophobia as a form of racism may stretch the definition of the term too far (Miles and Brown 2003); this disagreement will most likely continue (Arat-Koc 2006). What is clear, however, is that Muslims have become targets of hostility and discrimination in Canada and in other countries around the world. Let us examine some of the forms that this has taken in this country.

MUSLIMS AS "THE NEW POLITICAL BLACK"

In many Western countries, one of the areas of public life where Islamophobia has surfaced most often is crossing borders, either among visitors to other countries or permanent residents. The term "flying while Muslim" captures this new form of discrimination. Many of the public debates about immigration in Western countries in the 1980s and 1990s focused on black immigrants, particularly Caribbean and African immigrants, and their perceived failure to fully integrate into British society. These immigrants were defined as problem populations threatening the stability of British society. In other Western European countries at the same time, debates about "third-world" migrants were largely coded terms for black immigration; many countries regarded this issue with alarm. . . .

. . .

. . . [M]oral panic about the negative consequences of immigration is nothing new. The demonization of black immigration in the 1980s and 1990s also occurred in Canada, focused on black immigration in general, and immigrants from Jamaica in particular. Francis Henry and Carol Tator (2010) argue that the Canadian media tended to "Jamaicanize" crime, pointing to the apparent overrepresentation of Jamaicans in criminal ranks.

Muslims more recently have nudged black people aside and have moved up the list of "risk" groups. While the debate about "reasonable accommodation in Quebec" in 2008 and 2009 was ostensibly related to a variety of religious and ethnic communities, much of the concern was really about Muslims, and the apparently unreasonable demands that they were placing on Quebec society.

There is considerable evidence behind the perception that Arabs and Muslims are targeted when they cross international borders, including the border into this country. In a 2007 survey, 22 percent of respondents reported that Border Services Officers do not treat all travellers equally. Of this 22 percent, almost half reported that the Canada Border Services Agency used racial, ethnic, and/or religious profiling (EKOS Research Associates 2007, 91, 94).

In 2008 a University of British Columbia Faculty of Law research group conducted a study on the impact of racial profiling of Muslims in Canada. Like the Ontario Human Rights Commission study . . . the research was particularly interested in exploring the consequence for Muslims of September 11, 2001. They conducted a small number of face-to-face interviews with Muslim Canadians who reported that their experiences of profiling mainly took place during international airplane travel. . . .

. . . One respondent who works with international humanitarian organizations explains:

> [A] climate of fear that exists within these organizations.... I make sure there's absolute fiscal transparency to ensure that every single penny

PART 10

is accounted for. We have to ensure that no one on the board has any religious affiliation. . . . (Gova and Kurd 2008, 38)

The consequences of profiling at borders seem to also spread into the wider economy. Reem Bahdi's (2003) analysis of stereotyping Muslims as potential terrorists found that Arab employers in Windsor refused to hire Arab employees, or even "Arab-looking" employees out of fear that they were more likely to be stopped and detained when crossing the border (Bahdi 2003, 309–310); as a result, some Arab employers hired mostly white workers. Bahdi also analyzes how lost and ruined reputations are another part of the psychological costs of racial profiling (309).

Bahdi characterizes Muslim profiling as a counterproductive policing strategy. Rather than enhancing security, this kind of profiling leads to increased distrust of authority figures, even when individuals do nothing wrong. It sends a message to Muslims that they are not fully Canadian; the result is that profiled individuals may be less likely to interact with the justice system, less inclined to seek remedies if in need.

. . .

MUSLIMS AND THE MEDIA

After it became clear that the terrorist attacks of September 11 had been carried out in the name of Islam, leaders of many Western governments appealed for calm. There was an upsurge of attacks in Canada, the United States, and elsewhere against Muslims and others who were mistaken for Muslims. A Hindu temple in Hamilton, Ontario, was burned; police believe the attackers mistook the temple for a mosque. In the US, Muslims and people mistaken for Muslims were assaulted. Mosques were vandalized.

Political leaders in the two countries publicly came out in defence of their resident Muslim populations, pointing out that the vast majority of Muslims were peaceful citizens who condemned the attacks as much as did non-Muslims.

Leaders warned against vigilante-type retaliation against their Muslim neighbours. . . .

Despite these appeals for calm, however, governments have contributed to the perception that Muslims are inherently prone to terrorism through their apparent sanctioning of extra vigilance over Muslims who cross international borders. The media is also implicated. A 2000 study of press images over a 10-year period between 1972 and 1982 found that Arabs were portrayed in the Canadian media as "irrational, backward, bloodthirsty, amoral and ignorant" (Bullock and Jafri 2000). In the aftermath of the events of September 11, 2001, "terrorist" was added to this list and "Arabs" morphed into "Muslims."

Many of the debates about Islamophobia in Canada, and in the West more generally, take place in the context of media representations of Muslims. Controversies have generated significant public debates about the meaning of hate speech, Islamophobia, and racism. These debates demonstrate among other things that Muslims and non-Muslims alike are far from passive in the face of Islamophobia.

In the case of a controversial *Maclean's* magazine article, discussed below, claims about Islamophobia are well grounded; elsewhere, however, the claim seems exaggerated.

Maclean's and Islamophobia

In October 2006 *Maclean's* published an article titled "The New World Order" featuring excerpts from author Mark Steyn's (2006) book *America Alone*. The book was highly critical of Islam and painted an unflattering picture of the dangers posed by Muslim immigrants and their children to Western civilization. The excerpts from Steyn's book focused on the demographic crisis facing many Western societies, including Canada, and how the future of these societies "belonged to Islam." "Everything starts with demography," he claimed, pointing out that Western countries are aging and birth rates are falling. He contrasts this to Muslim societies in the West and in Asia, Africa, and the Middle East, where the birth rate is higher. Growing numbers of Muslims in the West provide what he calls "jihadist" cover for their anti-democratic agenda of terror and chaos. Where native Western populations are aging demographically, they are being "remorselessly" replaced by a young Muslim demographic. Steyn notes that there are "obligatory 'of courses'" to insert, such as "of course" not all Muslims are terrorists; nevertheless, he insists that there are enough Muslims who are "hot for Jihad" to create a network of mosques throughout the West.

Though Steyn is careful to say that not all Muslims support terrorism, he thinks that many do share the basic long-term objectives of terrorists, which in his view is to impose Islamic law in Western democracies. Thus, even if they do not outwardly support terrorist causes, moderate Muslims and their communities in the West nonetheless provide a supportive environment within which "jihad" operates. Steyn contrasts the Irish Republican Army tactics in Northern Ireland in the 1970s and 1980s with "European jihadist" tactics in western Europe today to seemingly differentiate between "good terrorists and bad terrorists." He suggests that "despite the nuttiness of the terrorists' demands," the IRA bombings of public places occurred in defiance of democracy; for "Jihadists," on the other hand, terrorist attacks on public places are the way they practice democracy.

Further, in excerpts of the book reproduced by *Maclean's*, Muslim immigrants are portrayed as a foreign presence in Western societies. Muslims are seen as having no loyalty to their Western countries of residence or citizenship. Their loyalties are primarily to other places, and ideas: "Western Muslim's pan-Islamic identity is merely the first great cause in a world where globalized pathologies are taking place of old school nationalism." As a result, Steyn predicts a future of violence and disorder in the West coming largely from its Muslim population. He also characterized Muslims, particularly youth,

as naturally violent, recounting media and government authorities' characterization of the unrest as "youth" violence. According to Steyn, these sources lacked the courage to name the violence for what it really was—"Muslim youth violence."

In Steyn's view, Western governments and many of their well-meaning citizens and institutions are bending over backwards to accommodate Muslims and to avoid insulting Muslim sensibilities.

> How does the state react? In Seville, King Ferdinand III is no longer patron saint of the annual fiesta because his splendid record in fighting for Spanish independence from the Moors was felt to be insensitive to Muslims. In London, a judge agreed to the removal of Jews and Hindus from a trial jury because the Muslim defendant's counsel argued he couldn't get a fair verdict from them. The Church of England is considering removing St. George as the country's patron saint on the ground that, according to various Anglican clergy, he's too "militaristic" and "offensive to Muslims." They wish to replace him with St. Alban, and replace St. George's cross on the revamped Union Flag, which would instead show St. Alban's cross as a thin yellow streak. (Steyn 2006a)

Steyn argues that governments and institutions are taking these tacks because of a fear of backlash from their respective Muslim communities. He alleges that Western governments live in fear of Muslim violence and are too willing to accommodate themselves to Islam. In his view, radicalized Islamists are experts at exploiting the tolerance of Western societies (Steyn 2006a). "Multiculturalism" is not an ideology that constitutes an effective glue to keep Western societies together. Like other critics of multicultural policy in this country, he suggests that it fosters division, separation, and new forms of fundamentalism.

Maclean's was taken before the British Columbia Human Rights Tribunal in 2008.

PART 10

Mohammad Elmasry, President of the Canadian Islamic Congress, and Naiyer Habib, a cardiologist from Abbotsford, British Columbia, lodged a complaint before the Tribunal. The specific complaint was that the *Maclean's* article exposed Muslims in British Columbia to hatred and contempt, which is contrary to Section 7 of the Human Rights Code of the province. In its judgment, the BC tribunal did recognize that the article contained "historical, religious and factual inaccuracies" and that it "used common Muslim stereotypes" (*Elmasry and Habib v. Rogers Publishing and MacQueen* 2008, 33). The tribunal was reluctant to admit that the article was a form of Islamophobia, though, because the complainants and their witnesses offered no definition of the term. In the end, however, the tribunal rejected the complaint on the grounds that the article was a legitimate contribution to public debate and that while it may have raised fears in readers' minds about Muslims, "fear is not synonymous with hatred and contempt" (*Elmasry and Habib v. Rogers Publishing and MacQueen* 2008, 37).

Allegations that *Maclean's* promotes Islamophobia and fear of Muslims continue. A report prepared by graduates of Osgood Hall Law School argues that a number of articles published by the magazine between 2005 and 2007 "demonstrates that *Maclean's* is engaging in a discriminatory form of journalism that targets the Muslim community, promotes stereotypes, misrepresents fringe elements as the mainstream Muslim community, and distorts facts to present a false image of Muslims" (Awam et al. 2009, 4).

REFERENCES

Arat-Koc, S. 2006. Whose Transnationalism? Canada, "Clash of Civilizations" Discourse, and Arab and Muslim Canadians, in *Transnational Identities and Practices in Canada*, eds. V. Satzewich and L. Wong. Vancouver: University of British Columbia Press.

Awam, K., et al. 2009. *Maclean's Magazine: A Case Study of Media-Propagated Islamophobia.* Unpublished manuscript.

Bahdi, R. 2003. No Exit: Racial Profiling and Canada's War Against Terrorism. *Osgood Hall Law Journal* 41 (2-3): 293-316.

Bullock, K., and G. J. Jafri. 2000. Media (Mis)representations: Muslim Women in the Canadian Nation. *Canadian Woman Studies* 20 (2): 35-40.

Commission on British Muslims and Islamophobia. 2004. *Islamophobia: Issues, Challenges, Action: A Report by the Commission on British Muslims and Islamophobia.* Stoke-on-Trent: Trentham Books.

EKOS Research Associates. 2007. *Canada Border Services Agency: Baseline Study.* Ottawa: EKOS Research Associates.

Elmasry and Habib v. Rogers Publishing and MacQueen. 2008. British Columbia Human Rights Tribunal (4): 378.

Gova, A., and R. Kurd. 2008. *The Impact of Racial Profiling.* Working Paper 08-14. Vancouver: Metropolis British Columbia.

Henry, F., and C. Tator. 2010. *The Colour of Democracy: Racism in Canada,* 4th ed. Toronto: Thomson Nelson.

Miles, R., and M. Brown. 2003. *Racism, 2nd ed.* London: Routledge.

Steyn, M. 2006. *American Alone: The End of the World as We Know It.* Washington: Regnery Publishing.

Critical Thinking Questions

1. Why do you suppose the stereotype of Muslims being "terrorists" is so persistent, while other groups, such as Irish Catholics and Protestants, seemed to escape this global branding despite the activities of the IRA (Irish Republican Army) and Protestant paramilitary in Northern Ireland and England?
2. The murder of nearly 100 people by Anders Breivik in Norway in 2011 was horrifying. Why do you suppose his acts were described by the world media primarily as "acts of terror," rather than "acts of terrorism," despite the fact that he was reported to be a member of a Norwegian political extremist right-wing group?

Chapter 28

McJobs: McDonaldization and Its Relationship to the Labor Process

GEORGE RITZER

In this selection, Ritzer wants to expand on his core arguments regarding **McDonaldization** (where society adopts the features of a fast-food restaurant and becomes a highly rationalized division of de-skilled labour). For example, while it is easy to understand how, say, the process by which food is produced in fast-food restaurants has been shaped by an emphasis on efficiency, calculability, predictability, and control, what is less obvious, but nevertheless true, is that even the interactions between workers and customers are also shaped by these emphases. In some cases, as Ritzer points out, these emphases function to blur the line between "worker" and "customer" so that customers become unpaid workers. Finally, he confronts what might be a puzzle: Why is there so little discontent among the workers whose lives have been affected by McDonaldization? Ritzer's answer is that any discontent that might arise in some particular organization is blunted by the fact that we live in a society that is being McDonaldized on so many different levels. Do you agree that McDonaldization produces little discontent? Isn't the popularity of Ritzer's argument itself some evidence to the contrary?

1. Who takes McJobs, and how are they exploited by the McDondaldized system?

In recent years the spread of McDonaldized systems has led to the creation of an enormous number of jobs. Unfortunately, the majority of them can be thought of as McDonaldized jobs, or "**McJobs.**" While we usually associate these types of positions with fast-food restaurants, and in fact there are many jobs in that setting, McJobs have spread throughout much of the economy. . . .

It is worth outlining some of the basic realities of employment in the fast-food industry in the United States since those jobs serve as a model for employment in other McDonaldized settings. The large number of people employed in fast-food restaurants accounts for over 40 percent of the approximately 6 million people employed in restaurants of all types. Fast-food restaurants rely heavily on teenage employees—almost 70 percent of their employees are 20 years of age or younger. For many, the fast-food restaurant is likely to be their first employer. It is estimated that the first job for one of every 15 workers was at McDonald's; one of every eight Americans has worked at McDonald's at some time in his or her life. The vast majority of employees are part-time workers: the average

Source: Republished with permission of SAGE Publications, from *McDonaldization: The Reader*, George Ritzer, Thousand Oaks: Pine Forge Press, 2002; permission conveyed through Copyright Clearance Center, Inc.

PART 11

workweek in the fast-food industry is 29.5 hours. There is a high turnover rate: Only slightly more than half the employees remain on the job for a year or more. Minorities are overrepresented in these jobs—almost two-thirds of employees are women and nearly a quarter are non-white. These are low-paid occupations, with many earning the minimum wage or slightly more. As a result, these jobs are greatly affected by changes in the minimum wage: An upward revision has an important effect on the income of these workers. However, there is a real danger that many workers would lose their positions as a result of such increases, especially in economically marginal fast-food restaurants. . . .

McJobs are characterized by the…dimensions of McDonaldization. The jobs tend to involve a series of simple tasks in which the emphasis is on performing each as efficiently as possible. Second, the time associated with many of the tasks is carefully calculated and the emphasis on the quantity of time a task should take tends to diminish the quality of the work from the point of view of the worker. That is, tasks are so simplified and streamlined that they provide little or no meaning to the worker. Third, the work is predictable; employees do and say essentially the same things hour after hour, day after day. Fourth, many nonhuman technologies are employed to control workers and reduce them to robot-like actions. Some technologies are in place, and others are in development, that will lead to the eventual replacement of many of these "human robots" with computerized robots. Finally, the rationalized McJobs lead to a variety of irrationalities, especially the dehumanization of work. The result is the extraordinarily high turnover rate described above and difficulty in maintaining an adequate supply of replacements.

The claim is usually made by spokespeople for McDonaldized systems that they are offering a large number of entry-level positions that help give employees basic skills they will need in order to move up the occupational ladder within such systems (and many of them do). This is likely to be true in the instances in which the middle-level jobs to which they move—for example, shift leader in or assistant manager or manager of a fast-food restaurant—are also routinized and scripted. . . . However, the skills acquired in McJobs are not likely to prepare one for, help one to acquire, or help one to function well in, the far more desirable postindustrial occupations which are highly complex and require high levels of skill and education. Experience in routinized actions and scripted interactions do not help much when occupations require thought and creativity. . . .

McJobs are not simply the de-skilled jobs of our industrial past in new settings; they are jobs that have a variety of new and distinctive characteristics. . . . There have also emerged many distinctive aspects of the control of these workers. Industrial and McDonaldized jobs both tend to be highly routinized in terms of what people do on the job. However, one of the things that is distinctive about McDonaldized jobs, especially since so many of them involve work that requires interaction and communication, especially with consumers, is that what people *say* on the job is also highly routinized. To put this another way, McDonaldized jobs are tightly scripted: They are characterized by *both* routinized actions . . . and scripted interactions (examples include "May I help you?"; "Would you like a dessert to go with your meal?"; and "Have a nice day!"). Scripts are crucial because many of the workers in McDonaldized systems are interactive service workers. This means that they not only produce goods and provide services, but they often do so in interaction with customers.

The scripting of interaction leads to new depths in the **de-skilling of workers**. Not only have employee actions been de-skilled; employees' ability to speak and interact with customers is now being limited and controlled. There are not only scripts to handle general situations but also a range of subscripts to deal with a variety of contingencies. Verbal and interactive skills are being taken away from employees and built into the scripts in much the same way that manual skills were taken and built into various technologies. At one time distrusted in their ability to *do* the right thing, workers now find themselves no longer trusted to *say* the right thing. Once able to create distinctive interactive styles, and to adjust them to different circumstances, employees are now asked to follow scripts as mindlessly as possible. . . .

McDonaldized systems have little interest in how their mainly part-time, short-time employees feel about and see themselves. These systems are merely interested in controlling their employees' overt behavior for as long as they work in such a system.

One very important, but rarely noted, aspect of the labor process in the fast-food restaurant and other McDonaldized systems is the extent to which customers are being led, perhaps even almost required, to perform a number of tasks without pay that were formerly performed by paid employees. For example, in the modern gasoline station the driver now does various things for free (pumps gas, cleans windows, checks oil, and even pays through a computerized credit card system built into the pump) that were formerly done by paid attendants. In these and many other settings, McDonaldization has brought the customer *into* the labor process: The customer *is* the laborer! This has several advantages for employers, such as lower (even nonexistent) labor costs, the need for fewer employers, and less trouble with personnel problems. Customers are far less likely to complain about a few seconds or minutes of tedious work than employees who devote a full workday to such tasks. Because of its advantages, as well as because customers are growing accustomed to and accepting of it, I think customers are likely to become even more involved in the labor process.

This is the most revolutionary development, at least as far as the labor process is concerned, associated with McDonaldization. . . . The analysis of the labor process must be extended to what customers do in McDonaldized systems.

The distinction between customer and employee is eroding, or in postmodern terms "imploding," and one can envision more and more work settings in which customers are asked to do an increasing amount of "work." More dramatically, it is also likely that we will see more work settings in which there are no employees at all! In such settings, customers, in interaction with non-human technologies, will do *all* of the human labor. A widespread example is the ATM in which customers (and the technology) do all of the work formerly done by bank tellers.

In a sense, a key to the success of McDonaldized systems is that they have been able to supplement the exploitation of employees with the exploitation of customers. In Marxian terms, customers create value in the tasks they perform for McDonaldized systems. And they are not simply paid less than the value they produce, they are paid *nothing at all*. In this way, customers are exploited to an even greater degree than workers. As is true of the exploitation of workers, owners are unaware of the fact that they are exploiting customers. But knowledge of exploitation is not a prerequisite to its practice.

While we have been focusing on the exploitation of customers in McDonaldized systems, this is not to say that employers have lost sight of the need to exploit workers. Beyond the usual exploitation of being paid less than the value of what they produce, McDonald's employees are often not guaranteed that they will work the number of hours they are supposed to on a given day. If business is slow, they may be sent home early in order that the employer can economize on labor costs: This reduces their take-home pay. As a result, employees often find it hard to count on a given level of income, meager as it might be, each week. In this way, and many others, employees of McDonaldized systems are even more exploited than their industrial counterparts.

This discussion brings together the two great theories in the history of sociology—Weber's theory of rationalization and Marx's

PART 11

theory of capitalist expansion and exploitation. **Rationalization** is a process that serves the interest of capitalists. They push it forward (largely unconsciously) because it heightens the level of exploitation of workers, allows new agents (e.g., customers) to be exploited and brings with it greater surplus value and higher profits. . . .We can see here how rationalization not only enhances control but also heightens the level and expands the reach of exploitation.

In various ways, McDonaldization is imposed on employees and even customers. They often have no choice but to conform, even if they would prefer things to be done in other ways. However, it would be a mistake to look at McDonaldization as simply being imposed on workers and customers. As discussed above, the basic ideas associated with McDonaldization are part of the value system. Many workers and customers have internalized them and conform to them of their own accord.

The emphasis on the McDonaldization of work (like that on de-skilling) tends to emphasize only one side of the dialectic between structural changes, especially those imposed by management, and the significance of the responses of employees, which are consistently downplayed. But . . . the employees of McDonaldized systems often exhibit a considerable amount of independence, perhaps even creativity, on the job. . . . Also, . . . in our rush to condemn, we must not ignore the advantages to both employees and customers of the routinization, even the scripting, of work. . . .

There is also a dialectic between living one's life in a McDonaldized society and working in a McDonaldized job. These are mutually reinforcing, and the net result is that if most of one's life is spent in one McDonaldized system or another, then one is less likely to feel dissatisfied with either one's life or one's job. This helps to account for . . . [the] finding that McDonald's workers do not evidence a high level of dissatisfaction with their work. This, perhaps, is one of the most disturbing implications of the McDonaldization thesis. If most of one's life is spent in McDonaldized

systems, then there is little or no basis for rebellion against one's McDonaldized job since one lacks a standard against which to compare, and to judge, such a job.

This also undermines one of Marx's fundamental assumptions that when all is said and done workers remain at odds with the kind of work that is being imposed on them and are a threat to those who are imposing the work. To Marx, there is a creative core (species being, for example) lying just below the surface that is ever-ready to protest, or rebel against, the rationalized and exploitative character of work. However, can that creative core survive intact, or even at all, in the face of growing up in a McDonaldized world, being bombarded by media messages from McDonaldized systems, and being socialized by and educated in McDonaldized schools?

It has been argued that the kinds of trends discussed above and in Marx's work are occurring not only among the lower layers in the occupational hierarchy but also among the middle layers. McDonaldization is something that those at the top of any hierarchy seek to avoid for themselves but are willing and eager to impose on those who rank below them in the system. Initially, it is the lowest level employees who have their work McDonaldized, but it . . . eventually creeps into those middle layers.

While guilty of exploiting and controlling employees, franchise operators are, in turn, controlled and exploited by franchise companies. Many franchise operators have done well, even becoming multimillionaires controlling perhaps hundreds of franchises, but many others have staggered or failed as a result of high start-up costs and continuing fees to the franchise companies. (The inducement to the franchisor to open as many outlets as possible threatens the profitability and even the continued existence of extant franchise owners.) The operators take much of the financial risk, while the franchise companies sit back and (often) rake in the profits. In addition, the franchise companies frequently have detailed rules, regulations, and even inspectors that they use to control the operators.

While no class within society is immune to McDonaldization, the lower classes are the most affected. They are the ones who are most likely to go to McDonaldized schools; live in inexpensive, mass-produced tract houses; and work in McDonaldized jobs. Those in the upper classes have much more of a chance of sending their children to non-McDonaldized schools, living in custom-built homes, and working in occupations in which they impose McDonaldization on others while avoiding it to a large degree themselves.

Also related to the social class issue is the fact that the McDonaldization of a significant portion of the labor force does not mean that all, or even most, of the labor force is undergoing this process. In fact, the McDonaldization of some of the labor force is occurring at the same time that another large segment is moving in a postindustrial, that is, more highly skilled, direction. Being created in this sector of society are relatively high-status, well-paid occupations requiring high levels of education and training.

McDonaldization and postindustrialization tend to occur in different sectors of the labor market. However, the spread of McJobs leads us to be dubious of the idea that we have moved into a new postindustrial era and have left behind the kind of de-skilled jobs we associated with industrial society.

It could be argued, as many have, that the focus in modern capitalism has shifted from the control and exploitation of consumption. While that may well be true, the fact is that capitalists do not, and will not, ignore the realm of production. . . . The nature of work is changing and capitalists are fully involved in finding new ways of controlling and exploiting workers. Further, they have discovered that they can even replace paid employees not only with machines, temporary workers, and so on but also with customers who are seemingly glad do the work for nothing! Here, clearly, is a new gift to the capitalist. Surplus value is now not only to be derived from the labor time of the employee but also from the leisure time of the customer. McDonaldization is helping to open a whole new world of exploitation and growth to the contemporary capitalist.

Critical Thinking Questions

1. Are there any ties between the discussion of exploitation in this article and the discussion of exploitation in the Tuskegee (Chapter 6) and Eugenics (Chapter 7) articles?

2. Can you draw a link between the "powerlessness" and "depersonalization" of patients mentioned in the Rosenhan article ("On Being Sane in Insane Places," Chapter 23) and the experience of people in McJobs?

PART 11

Chapter 29

The Disneyization of Society

ALAN BRYMAN

Most North Americans have childhood memories that include some element of the Walt Disney enterprise, whether it be the films, merchandise, or even memories of visiting one of the theme parks (or a combination of the three). In this article, Bryman argues that the spread of "the principles of the Disney theme parks" are influencing elements of our social lives. Also tackling the topic of globalization of consumption, he picks up where George Ritzer (see Chapter 29) leaves off. Make note of the similarities and differences between McDonaldization and Disneyization, as both can be helpful when trying to understand the increasing influence and consequences of our global economies and marketplaces (production and consumption).

1. How does the author define Disneyization, and how does it differ from McDonaldization?

I make the case that more and more sectors of society and the economy are being infiltrated by a process I call **Disneyization.** By Disneyization I mean simply:

> the process by which *the principles* of the Disney theme parks are coming to dominate more and more sectors of American society as well as the rest of the world.

. . .

. . . In much the same way that Walt Disney did not invent modern animation,[1] he did not invent Disneyization through the Disney theme parks.

Disneyization parallels Ritzer's[2] notion of **McDonaldization,** which was concerned with the diffusion of the principals associated with the fast-food restaurant. Indeed, the definition of Disneyization offered above is meant to be slightly ironic but nevertheless serious adaptation of Ritzer's definition of McDonaldization. 'Disneyization' is meant to draw attention to the spread of *principles* exemplified by the Disney theme parks.

In the sense, Disneyization takes up where McDonaldization leaves off. McDonaldization is frequently accused of creating a world of homogeneity and sameness. One of the main foundations for Disneyization is that of increasing the appeal of goods and services and the settings in which they are purveyed in the increasingly homogenized environments that are the products of McDonaldization. In essence, Disneyization is about consumption. Consumption and, in particular, increasing the inclination to consume, is Disneyization's driving force. Disneyization seeks to create variety and difference, where McDonaldization wreaks likeness and similarity. It exchanges the mundane blandness of homogenized consumption experiences with frequently spectacular experiences. In addition,

Disneyization seeks to move consumers' need for the prosaic fulfilling of basic needs and to entice them into consumption beyond mere necessity. To take a simple and somewhat stereotyped illustration: eating in a standard McDonald's or Burger King may have the advantage of filling a basic need (hunger) cheaply and in a predictable environment,[3] but Disneyization restaurants are likely to provide an experience that gives the impression of being different and even a sense of the dramatic while being in a location that perhaps increases the likelihood that the consumer will engage in other types of consumption, such as purchasing merchandise or participating in other activities in a hybrid consumption setting. Hybrid consumption environments themselves frequently take on the characteristics of the spectacular because of the sheer variety of consumption opportunities they offer and especially when accompanied by theming. To a significant extent, then, Disneyization connects with a post-Fordist world of variety and choice in which consumers reign supreme.

. . .

Inevitably, readers familiar with Ritzer's influential work on McDonaldization[4] will draw comparisons with his concept, especially since, as noted above, the definition of Disneyization is an adaptation of his definition. In fact, Disneyization and McDonaldization can be thought of as parallel processes rather than as in any sense competing. They both provide viable accounts of some of the changes occurring in modern society. Neither provides a complete account but each is meant to offer a springboard for understanding some of the processes that are going on around us and to present capsule accounts of those processes. In this chapter, Disneyization has been painted as a set of principles that address a consumerist world in which McDonaldization has wrought homogeneity and in its place projects an ambience of choice, difference, and frequently the spectacular. Both Disneyization and McDonaldization are concerned with consumption, but whereas McDonaldization is rooted in rationalization and its associations with the Fordism, scientific management and bureaucracy, Disneyization's affinities are with a post-Fordist world of variety and consumer choice. . . .

IMPLICATIONS OF DISNEYIZATION

. . .

In describing Disneyization as a globalizing force, there is a risk of a simplistic globalization or Americanization thesis that depicts symbols of American culture spreading by design across the globe and riding roughshod over local conditions and practices, creating an homogenized world in their wake. As writers on globalization who prefer to emphasize the accommodations that global tendencies have to make to local contexts and conditions observe, the principles underlying apparently global forces do not necessarily spread without adaptation. . . .

Although the following distinction is crude, globalization can be said to meet the forces of the local in several ways but two basic forms seem to stand out. First, there is *anticipatory localization*, whereby firms adapt the principles of Disneyization (or indeed any globalizing force) to local conditions in anticipation of how they are likely to be received. Thus, when entering a new market, based on their knowledge of local conditions and customs, a service firm anticipates the likely receptiveness to its services and how they are to be delivered by fine-tuning them to the host culture. Secondly, there is *responsive localization*, whereby as a result of its contact with local conditions and culture, a firm feels compelled or inclined to adapt its services and how they are to be delivered. The firm may have engaged in anticipatory localization, but perhaps feels that it has not gone far enough or feels it has misread the local culture.

PART 11

The Disney Theme Parks Encounter the Local

. . .

The Disney theme parks have themselves been forced to adapt to foreign sensibilities when they have been transported abroad to Tokyo and Paris. . . . In many ways, the designers of the two foreign Disney theme parks have been caught in a pincer movement between, on the one hand recognizing that visitors are likely to be attracted to a piece of Americana in their own countries and therefore not wanting to adapt too much, and on the other hand realizing that the American parks cannot be transplanted wholesale and without consideration of overseas customs and feelings.

In the case of Tokyo Disneyland, Eisner asserts that Disney were under pressure not to Japanize the park,[5] so a clear sense of wanting to give visitors the impression of visiting a park that was clearly American was retained. Similarly, a spokesperson told one writer on the park: 'We really tried to avoid creating a Japanese version of Disneyland. We wanted the Japanese visitors to feel they were taking a foreign vacation by coming here.'[6] More and more of such 'foreign' lands within Japan have been built in the wake of Disneyland.[7] However, although this sense of taking an American vacation without leaving Japan is often conveyed in publicity and in public statements about the park (as in Eisner's and the spokesperson's remarks quoted above), there are grounds for thinking that more adaptation has taken place than such statements acknowledge.

Certain attractions were altered in anticipation of Japanese needs and preoccupations. For example, the Hall of Presidents was dropped because of its extreme foreignness, but the case for dropping others is less obvious; for example, Main Street, USA was replaced by World Bazaar. Raz observes that, although Tokyo Disneyland is invariably claimed to be a copy of the American original, it has in fact been Japanized. Thus, the Mystery Tour in the castle in Tokyo Disneyland is a Disney version of the Japanese ghost-house. The Meet the World show is described by Raz as 'a show about and for the Japanese.'[8] Changes such as these would seem to be token anticipatory localization but in addition responsive localization has taken place. This is particularly apparent in connection with food, with the opening of a Japanese restaurant catering for local tastes and allowing visitors to have picnics in the park, something very much in tune with Japanese lifestyle but unimaginable in the American parks where importing one's own food is discouraged. Also, Brannen notes that ride operators' commentaries are translations of the American originals but are invariably peppered with modifications in the form of 'Japan-specific puns, jokes, and creative explanations.'[9] In addition, Raz argues that the hiring, orientation and training of regular employees are very different from in the US (but not of part-time employees for whom these three phases of becoming a cast member are the same as in the US).[10] For example, there is less emphasis in training on Disney traditions and on learning about and imbibing the Disney corporate culture; instead, there tends to be greater emphasis at Tokyo Disneyland on helping the trainee to become accustomed to his or her work area.

In Disneyland Paris, Disney were keen to keep an essentially American format and ambience. Michael Eisner has written: 'for the most part we were determined to make [Disneyland Paris] every bit as American as Tokyo Disneyland and our domestic parks.'[11] The comment is interesting in part because of the conviction that it was important not to surrender the parks' sense of America, but also because it depicts the Tokyo Park as American. Eisner notes that the American qualities are particularly apparent with the Paris park's hotels, all of which are themed on American places or symbols of American culture.

However, local adaptation can be seen in Disneyland Paris, where after a disappointing beginning, the company was forced to adapt the park to European tastes.[12] Anticipatory localization was not a prominent feature of the park. The Jungle Cruise was dropped, perhaps in part because of its potential to offend in post-colonial times and the more American attractions, such as Hall of Presidents, were also not included. Responsive localization was more in evidence though this also demonstrates the difficult balancing act that firms like Disney are engaged in. The alcohol ban, in particular, was soon dropped. There is some evidence that the company does not seek to insist on emotional labour among cast members to the degree that occurs in the US.[13] But in fact, it has been difficult to fine tune the balance of the American and the European. A year after it opened, the then new chairman of the Park was quoted as saying:

> Each time we tried to Europeanise the product we found it didn't work. Europeans want America and they want Disney, whether French intellectuals like it or not.[14]

This quotation brings out the dilemmas that globalizing firms are involved in when they seek to engage in both anticipatory and responsive localization.

Disneyization and Local Conditions

However, while reassuring, these indications of the continued relevance of the local for the Disney theme parks should not blind us to the fact that while Tokyo Disneyland and Disneyland Paris have adapted many attractions and other aspects of the parks to local sensibilities, this is not what Disneyization is about. As previously argued, it is about *principles* to do with the production and delivery of goods and services. In a sense, Disneyization could be regarded as more worrying for the critics of the notion of globalization as a homogenizing force than the transplanting of Disney theme parks abroad. It is potentially more worrying because Disneyization, like McDonaldization, is a more insidious process: it is less conspicuous

in its emergence than the appearance of magic kingdoms (and the various other symbols of globalization, such as McDonald's, Starbucks coffee shops, Coca-Cola, and so on) on nations' doorsteps. In other words, finding adaptations and local uses of Disney theme parks should not lead us to think that they denote or necessarily entail adaptations to and local uses of Disneyization.

. . .

Disneyization is a less visible process than the arrival of brand names on foreign shores. It is a set of processes designed to maximize consumers' willingness to purchase goods and services that in many cases they might not otherwise have been prompted to buy or that they might have bought from a competitor. Theming provides the consumer with a narrative that acts as a draw by providing an experience that lessens the sense of an economic transaction and increases the likelihood of purchasing merchandise. Hybrid consumption is meant to give the consumer as many opportunities as possible to make purchases and therefore to keep them as long as possible in the theme park, mall, or whatever. Emotional labour is the oil of the whole process in many ways: in differentiating otherwise identical goods and services, as an enactment of theming, and as a means for increasing the inclination to purchase merchandise.

Structures of Similarity

The direction that these reflections are pointing is to suggest that systemscapes like Disneyization and McDonaldization constitute templates for the way goods and services are presented and delivered in modern society. When exported abroad they are capable of being adapted to local conditions, circumstances and culture in numerous ways by both corporations and consumers. They do not determine the forms that institutions will assume. Instead, they provide templates that allow variation in the concrete forms that institutions can take on. However, there is a crucial difference here between Disneyization and

PART 11

McDonaldization. While there is evidence from studies of the export of McDonald's abroad and its reception among overseas consumers to suggest that McDonaldization should not automatically be associated with homogeneity of appearance and reaction,[15] it also needs to be recognized that McDonaldization is considerably more prone to creating a sense of homogeneity than Disneyization. In fact, one of the dimensions of McDonaldization—predictability—is very much associated with the drift towards standardization. As Ritzer puts it:

> Rationalization involves the increasing effort to ensure predictability from one time or place to another. In a rational society people prefer to know what to expect in all settings and at all times. They neither want nor expect surprises. … In order to ensure such predictability over time and place, a rational society emphasizes such things as discipline, order, systemization, formalization, routine, consistency, and methodical operation.[16]

. . .

ANTI-DISNEYIZATION

. . .

That Disneyization is less likely to engender such criticism then transnational companies and their brands does not render it immune to ideological criticism. It is vulnerable on several fronts. . . .

- *Distortion of history and place.* The widespread use through theming of historical periods and events as the foundation for commercial activity has been criticized for the frequently sanitized and bowdlerized images that are served up as capsule accounts of the past. . . . Similarly, images of place are prone to distortion and frequently produce patronising representations sometimes with colonial overtones. . . .

- *Manipulation of children.* Disneyization is strongly associated with the manipulation of children. . . . [T]he use of such techniques as giving toys away with meals and the widespread merchandising directed at children are blatant marketing appeals to get children to spend money via their parents. . . .
- *Manipulation of consumers.* The use of various tactics for getting consumers to stay longer, to purchase items they had not intended to buy by positioning outlets strategically, using theming to create a ludic atmosphere to make them more likely to spend, and directing their movements towards the purchase of merchandise are all features of Disneyization that might be criticized. . .
- *Manipulation of workers' emotions.* The extensive use of emotional labour as a means of differentiating services means that workers are increasingly being expected to display certain emotions but to suppress others. . . .

. . . However, the possible grounds for an ideological critique of Disneyization do not end there and the following additional points are worthy of consideration.

Sweated Labour

Much of the apparently benign merchandise that is sold in theme parks, themed restaurants, and similar outlets is often likely to be the product of sweated labour. In August 1996, Tracy participated in a market survey of merchandise licensed by Disney for *The Hunchback of Notre Dame* in various retail outlets in Tucson, Arizona.[17] The survey entailed noting the place of manufacture and the price and type of item. It was found that 47% of the products were from what he calls 'dependent countries.' Of these products, 16% were made in countries where the average wage per worker was just under $4,000. These items are often produced in working conditions that are extremely unpleasant and at wage rates that are very low. . . .

Moreover, even the merchandise produced in the United States, which formed 48% of all *Hunchback* merchandise, is frequently manufactured under sweatshop conditions. This is particularly the case with clothing items, which, Tracy suggests, are frequently manufactured in sweatshops regardless of the country of origin. These factories do not pay the minimum wage or overtime in the US. The owners of these factories frequently take advantage of the fact that the workers do not have proper immigration status and are therefore less likely to complain. He argues that because Disney charge so much for licensing agreements, contractors are compelled to find the least expensive manufacturers possible and it is this pressure that results in frequent use of sweated labour. . . .

Destruction of Land and Natural Habitats

Disneyization frequently requires large-scale building projects that are extremely destructive as land and the natural habitats of animals are brought to heel by bulldozers. This is especially likely to be the case with theme parks and large themed malls. Certainly the Disney theme parks themselves serve as a reminder of this undesirable aspect of Disneyization which is likely to be at least partly generalizable to other large-scale projects underpinned by its principles. Disney World serves as a reminder of the environmental hazards involved. . . . The tinge of guilt about the impact of Disneyland on the local environment is palpable in the following passage written by the founder of the University of Disneyland:

> Those of us working on the Disneyland project felt that we were bringing 'progress' to a farming community. In the name of progress we replaced the fragrance of orange groves with the smell of smog, two-lane roads with freeways and comfortable homes with motels, shopping centres and fast-food restaurants.[18]

Relatedly, the expansion of massive developments of the kind that Disneyization frequently entails can create a situation in which the state becomes preoccupied with assisting theme parks and entertainment-cum-retail projects to the exclusion and ultimately neglect of natural or indigenous attractions. Cartier has shown how in the small Malaysian state of Melaka a tendency to encourage *faux* leisurescapes has led to an abandonment of authentic attractions of both historical and natural interest in favour of these more high profile projects.[19] Not only has this resulted in a distortion of the nature of tourism in the region but it has also created problems for the local ecology.

Running Down of Cities

The growth of out of town shopping- and entertainment-based destinations has often led to a deterioration in the fabric of many cities. . . . [C]ities have often come to be seen as dangerous areas and Disneyized developments such as these have capitalized on these fears to create the impression of safety. As a result, many downtowns have suffered as they have come to be seen as dangerous 'no go' areas.[20] Orlando again acts as a salutary reminder. When a British journalist visited downtown Orlando, he reported: 'Downtown … is now downbeat. Derelict shops, homeless people sleeping on benches, police signs warning "TV surveillance is in operation," piles of litter.'[21]

. . . While there are several factors that contribute to the decline of city downtown areas, of which Disneyization is merely one, it nonetheless constitutes an important factor, especially in terms of its contribution to the perception of downtowns as dangerous and to be avoided.

. . .

THE ECONOMIC MEETS THE CULTURAL

. . . Commercially appropriated thematic narratives feed back into culture and are reinforced by enterprise.

PART 11

Equally, culture becomes more and more economically inflected when commercial organizations create idioms that find their way into culture. These cultural elements are representations that frequently sanitize and distort. Nowhere is distortion more apparent than in the frequent appeals to feelings of nostalgia concerning a lost but revered time when life was supposedly more exotic, simpler or more varied. . . .

A further aspect of the way in which culture becomes increasingly economically inflected occurs in connection with merchandising, where items bearing commercial logos come to infiltrate culture's sense of what a souvenir is. . . .

In addition, we find that the very notion of culture has come to have a prominent economic component. . . . The notion that 'companies with a record of outstanding financial performance often have powerful corporate cultures'[22] led to a fashion for managing cultures to make them more distinctive that received a further boost from the growing use of TQM initiatives where cultural change is a key ingredient.[23] . . . Culture thus became central to the business sphere as something that can be enlisted for commercial ends and indeed almost inseparable from it. Such a view radically alters our perception of what cultures are, where they come from and how they arise, but most importantly they revise our understanding of them by investing them with an economic aspect.

CONCLUSION

. . . I have sought to outline some of the broader ramifications of Disneyization and some of the wider theoretical issues with which I see it as being entangled. In a sense, it becomes a useful lens through which to view a number of issues that are of concern in contemporary social sciences, such as globalization and the fusion of the economic and the cultural. More fundamentally, I have sought to outline how I perceive Disneyization, namely, as a set of processes that are circling the globe and which are to do with

the provision of a framework for making goods, and in particular services, desirable and therefore more likely to be bought. . . .

NOTES

1. Bryman, A. (1997). 'Animating the pioneer versus late entrant debate: an historical case study.' *Journal of Management Studies,* 34: 415–38.
2. Ritzer, G. (1998). *The McDonaldization Thesis.* London: Sage.
3. Twitchell, J. B. (1999). *Lead Us Into Temptation: The Triumph of American Materialism.* New York: Columbia University Press.
4. Ritzer, G. (1998). *The McDonaldization Thesis.* London: Sage.
5. Eisner, M. D. (1998). *Work In Progress,* London: Penguin.
6. Brannen, M. Y. (1992). '"Bwana Mickey: constructing cultural consumption at Tokyo Disneyland,' in J. J. Tobin (ed.) *Re-made In Japan: Everyday Life and Consumer Taste in a Changing Society,* New Haven, CT: Yellow University Press.
7. Hendry, J. (2000). *The Orient Strikes Back: A Global View of Cultural Display,* Oxford: Berg.
8. Raz, A. E. (1999). *Riding the Black Ship: Japan and Tokyo Disneyland.* Cambridge, Mass: Harvard University Press.
9. Brannen, M. Y. (1992). '"Bwana Mickey: constructing cultural consumption at Tokyo Disneyland,' in J. J. Tobin (ed.) *Re-made In Japan: Everyday Life and Consumer Taste in a Changing Society,* New Haven, CT: Yellow University Press.
10. Raz, A. E. (1999). *Riding the Black Ship: Japan and Tokyo Disneyland.* Cambridge, Mass: Harvard University Press.
11. Eisner, M. D. (1998). *Work In Progress,* London: Penguin.
12. Lainsbury, A. (2000). *Once Upon an American Dream: The Story of EuroDisneyland,* Lawrence, KA: University of Kansas Press.
13. Warren, S, (1999). 'Cultural contestation at Disneyland Paris,' in D. Crouch (ed.), *Leisure/ Tourism Geographies: Practices and Geographical Knowledge,* London: Routledge.
14. Skapinker, M. and Rawsthorn, A. (1993). 'An older, wiser Mickey Mouse,' *Financial Times,* April 10: 18.
15. Watson, J. L. (1997). 'Introduction: transnationalism, localization, and fast foods in East Asia,' in J. L. Watson (ed.), *Golden Arches East: McDonald's in East Asia,* Stanford, CA: Stanford University Press.

16. Ritzer, G. (1993). *The McDonaldization of Society.* Thousand Oaks, CA: Pine Forge.

17. Tracy, J. F. (1999). 'Whistle while you work: The Disney Company and the global division of labor,' *Journal of Communication Inquiry,* 23: 374–89.

18. France, V. A. (1991). *Window on Main Street,* Nashua, NH: Laughter Publications.

19. Cartier, C. (1998). 'Megadevelopment in Malaysia: from heritage landscapes to "leisurescapes" in Melaka's tourism sector,' *Singapore Journal of Tropical Geography,* 19: 151–76.

20. Hubbard, P. (2002). 'Screen-shifting: consumption, "riskless risks" and the changing geographies of cinema,' *Environment and Planning A,* 34: 1239–58.

21. Chesshyre, T. (2002). 'Under threat: the real face of Florida,' *The Times* (Travel section), May 25: 1–2.

22. Uttal, B. (1993). 'The corporate culture vultures,' *Fortune,* October 17: 66–72.

23. Powell, T. C. (1995). 'Total quality management as competitive advantage: A review and empirical study," *Strategic Management Journal,* 16(1): 15–37.

Critical Thinking Questions

1. How does Disney avoid critique and retain its image as "wholesome" and "family-friendly"?
2. Check out the documentary entitled *Mickey Mouse Monopoly.* Several versions are available online. How does the film with the article in their perceptions of the Disney enterprise?

PART 11

Chapter 30

Alienated Labour

KARL MARX

This will likely be a difficult selection. We have included it, however, so that you can read firsthand something written by Karl Marx, someone who undeniably has had a tremendous influence on sociology. As a start, take note of what is missing from this essay. In contrast to popular images of Marx, there is no call here for revolution, no telling workers to rise up and seize the factories, and so on. Marx's goal here, as in most of his writing in fact, is to analyze. In this case, he wants to understand how the logic of work under capitalism has impoverished the human experience. Perhaps the best way to read this selection is to make a list of the things that (according to Marx) workers confront as "alien" (separate and distinct from themselves and over which they have little or no control) and then ask why Marx believes these processes of 'alienation' may diminish us as human beings.

1. In the following article Marx discusses factory wage labour in the 19th century. Do these forms of alienation apply to today's workworld?

We shall begin from a *contemporary* economic fact. The worker becomes poorer the more wealth he produces and the more his **production** increases in power and extent.

The worker becomes an ever cheaper commodity the more goods he creates. The *devaluation* of the human world increases in direct relation with the increase *in value* of the world of things. Labour does not only create goods; it also produces itself and the worker as a *commodity*, and indeed in the same proportion as it produces goods.

This fact simply implies that the object produced by labour, its product, now stands opposed to it as an *alien being*, as a *power independent* of the producer. The product of labour is labour which has been embodied in an object and turned into a physical thing; this product is an *objectification* of labour. The performance of work is at the same time its objectification. The performance of work appears in the sphere of political economy as a *vitiation* of the worker, objectification as a *loss* and as *servitude to the object*, and appropriation as *alienation*.

So much does the performance of work appear as vitiation that the worker is vitiated to the point of starvation. So much does objectification appear as loss of the object that the worker is deprived of the most essential things not only of life but also of work. Labour itself becomes an object which he can acquire only by the greatest effort and with unpredictable interruptions. So much does the appropriation of the object appear as alienation that the more objects the worker produces the fewer he can possess and the more he falls under the domination of his product, of capital.

Source: Marx, Karl. *Early Writings*. Trans. and Ed. T.B. Bottomore. New York: McGraw-Hill Book Company, 1963. Reproduced with permission of The McGraw-Hill Companies, Inc.

All these consequences follow from the fact that the worker is related to the *product of his labour* as to an *alien* object. For it is clear on this presupposition that the more the worker expends himself in work the more powerful becomes the world of objects which he creates in face of himself, the poorer he becomes in his inner life, and the less he belongs to himself. The worker puts his life into the object, and his life then belongs no longer to himself but to the object. The greater his activity, therefore, the less he possesses. What is embodied in the product of his labour is no longer his own. The greater this product is, therefore, the more he is diminished. The *alienation* of the worker in his product means not only that his labour becomes an object, assumes an *external* existence, but that it exists independently, *outside himself*, and alien to him, and that it stands opposed to him as an autonomous power. The life which he has given to the object sets itself against him as an alien and hostile force.

Let us now examine more closely the phenomenon of *objectification*, the worker's production and the *alienation* and *loss* of the object it produces, which is involved in it. The worker can create nothing without *nature*, without the *sensuous external world*. The latter is the material in which his labour is realized, in which it is active, out of which and through which it produces things.

But just as nature affords the *means of existence* of labour, in the sense that labour cannot *live* without objects upon which it can be exercised, so also it provides the *means of existence* in a narrower sense; namely the means of physical existence for the *worker* himself. Thus, the more the worker appropriates the external world of sensuous nature by his labour the more he deprives himself of *means of existence*, in two respects: first, that the sensuous external world becomes progressively less an object belonging to his labour or a means of existence of his labour, and secondly, that it becomes progressively less a means of existence in the direct sense, a means for the physical subsistence of the worker.

In both respects, therefore, the worker becomes a slave of the object; first, in that he receives an *object of work*, i.e. receives *work*, and secondly, in that he receives *means of subsistence*. Thus the object enables him to exist, first as a *worker* and secondly, as a *physical subject*. The culmination of this enslavement is that he can only maintain himself as a *physical subject* so far as he is a *worker*; and that it is only as a *physical subject* that he is a worker.

(The alienation of the worker in his object is expressed as follows in the laws of political economy: the more the worker produces the less he has to consume; the more value he creates the more worthless he becomes; the more refined his product the more crude and misshapen the worker; the more civilized the product the more barbarous the worker; the more powerful the work the more feeble the worker; the more the work manifests intelligence the more the worker declines in intelligence and becomes a slave of nature.)

Political economy conceals the alienation in the nature of labour in so far as it does not examine the direct relationship between the worker (work) and production.

Labour certainly produces marvels for the rich but it produces privation for the worker. It produces palaces, but hovels for the worker. It produces beauty, but deformity for the worker. It replaces labour by machinery, but it casts some of the workers back into a barbarous kind of work and turns the others into machines. It produces intelligence, but also stupidity and cretinism for the workers.

The direct relationship of labour to its products is the relationship of the worker to the objects of his production. The relationship of property owners to the objects of production and to production itself is merely a consequence of this first relationship and confirms it. We shall consider this second aspect later.

Thus, when we ask what is the important relationship of labour, we are concerned with the relationship of the *worker* to production.

PART 12

So far we have considered the alienation of the worker only from one aspect; namely, *his relationship with the products of his labour*. However, alienation appears not merely in the result but also in the *process of production*, within *productive activity* itself. How could the worker stand in an alien relationship to the product of his activity if he did not alienate himself in the act of production itself? The product is indeed only the *résumé* of activity, of production. Consequently, if *the product of labour is alienation, production* itself *must be active alienation*—the alienation of activity and the *activity of alienation*. The alienation of the object of labour merely summarizes the alienation in the work activity itself.

What constitutes the alienation of labour? First, that the work is *external* to the worker, that it is not part of his nature, and that, consequently, he does not fulfil himself in his work but denies himself, has a feeling of misery rather than well-being, does not develop freely his mental and physical energies but is physically exhausted and mentally debased. The worker, therefore, feels himself at home only during his leisure time, whereas at work he feels homeless. His work is not voluntary but imposed, *forced labour*. It is not the satisfaction of a need, but only a *means for satisfying other needs*. Its alien character is clearly shown by the fact that as soon as there is no physical or other compulsion it is avoided like the plague. External labour, labour in which man alienates himself, is a labour of self-sacrifice, of mortification. Finally, the external character of work for the worker is shown by the fact that it is not his own work but work for someone else, that in work he does not belong to himself but to another person.

We arrive at the result that man (the worker) feels himself to be freely active only in his animal functions—*eating*, *drinking* and *procreating*, or at most also in his *dwelling* and in *personal* adornment—while in his human functions he is reduced to an animal. The *animal becomes human* and the *human becomes animal*.

Eating, drinking and procreating are of course also genuine human functions. But abstractly considered, apart from the environment of human activities, and turned into final and sole ends, they are animal functions.

We have now considered the act of alienation of practical human activity, labour, from two aspects: (1) the relationship of the worker to the *product of labour* as an alien object which dominates him. This relationship is at the same time the relationship to the sensuous external world, to natural objects, as an alien and hostile world; (2) the relationship of labour to the *act of production* within *labour*. This is the relationship of the worker to his own activity as something alien and not belonging to him, activity as suffering (passivity), strength as powerlessness, creation as emasculation, the *personal* physical and mental energy of the worker, his personal life (for what is life but activity?), as an activity which is directed against himself, independent of him and not belonging to him. This is self-alienation as against the above mentioned alienation of the thing.

We have now to infer a third characteristic of *alienated labour* from the two we have considered.

Man is a species being not only in the sense that he makes the community (his own as well as those of other things) his object both practically and theoretically, but also (and this is simply another expression for the same thing) in the sense that he treats himself as the present, living species, as a universal and consequently free being.[1]

Species-life, for man as for animals, has its physical basis in the fact that man (like animals) lives from inorganic nature, and since man is more universal than an animal so the range of inorganic nature from which he lives is more universal. Plants, animals, minerals, air, light, etc. constitute, from the theoretical aspect, a part of a human consciousness as objects of natural science and art; they are man's spiritual inorganic nature, his intellectual means of life, which he must first prepare for enjoyment and perpetuation. So also, from the practical aspect, they form a part of human life and activity.

In practice man lives only from these natural products, whether in the form of food, heating, clothing, housing, etc. The universality of man appears in practice in the universality which makes the whole of nature into his inorganic body: (1) as a direct means of life; and equally (2) as the material object and instrument of his life activity. Nature is the inorganic body of man; that is to say nature, excluding the human body itself. To say that man *lives* from nature means that nature is his *body* with which he must remain in a continuous interchange in order not to die. The statement that the physical and mental life of man, and nature, are interdependent means simply that nature is interdependent with itself, for man is a part of nature.

Since alienated labour: (1) alienates nature from man; and (2) alienates man from himself, from his own active function, his life activity; so it alienates him from the species. It makes *species-life* into a means of individual life. In the first place it alienates species-life and individual life, and secondly, it turns the latter, as an abstraction, into the purpose of the former, also in its abstract and alienated form.

For labour, *life activity*, *productive life*, now appear to man only as *means* for the satisfaction of a need, the need to maintain his physical existence. Productive life is, however, species-life. It is life creating life. In the type of life activity resides the whole character of a species, its species-character; and free, conscious activity is the species-character of human beings. Life itself appears only as a *means of life*.

The animal is one with its life activity. It does not distinguish the activity from itself. It is *its activity*. But man makes his life activity itself an object of his will and consciousness. He has a conscious life activity. It is not a determination with which he is completely identified. Conscious life activity distinguishes man from the life activity of animals. Only for this reason is he a species-being. Or rather, he is only a self-conscious being, i.e. his own life is an object for him, because he is a species-being. Only for this reason is his activity free activity. Alienated labour reverses the relationship, in that man because he is a self-conscious being makes his life activity, his *being*, and only a means for his *existence*.

The practical construction of an *objective world*, the *manipulation* of inorganic nature, is the confirmation of man as a conscious species-being, i.e., a being who treats the species as his own being or himself as a species-being. Of course, animals also produce. They construct nests, dwellings, as in the case of bees, beavers, ants, etc. But they only produce what is strictly necessary for themselves or their young. They produce only in a single direction, while man produces universally. They produce only under the compulsion of direct physical needs, while man produces when he is free from physical need and only truly produces in freedom from such need. Animals produce only themselves, while man reproduces the whole of nature. The products of animal production belong directly to their physical bodies, while man is free in face of his product. Animals construct only in accordance with the standards and needs of the species to which they belong, while man knows how to produce in accordance with the standards of every species and knows how to apply the appropriate standard to the object. Thus man constructs also in accordance with the laws of beauty.

It is just in his work upon the objective world that man really proves himself as *a species-being*.

PART 12

NOTE

1. In this passage Marx reproduces Feuerbach's argument in *Das Wesen des Christentums.*

Critical Thinking Questions

1. Discuss the following aspects of worker alienation: a) Alienation from production; b) Alienation from one's own labour; c) Alienation from the labour of others; and d) Alienation from one's own humanity.
2. As a university student, can you identify with any or all of the four types of worker alienation? Do any of these forms of alienation impact you?

Chapter 31

A New Barrier: Extra-Credential Inflation

WOLFGANG LEHMANN

As post-secondary education levels continue to rise in Canada, so do expectations. A post-secondary degree used to be more rare and, with that, highly valued. Now that many youth go on to complete post-secondary education, competition to enhance those degrees has increased. Consequently, students are not only expected to do well in their courses, but there are expectations of diverse and impressive experiences outside of scholastic endeavours. As well, there is increased pressure for students to go on to do professional programs, earn diplomas, or to go to graduate school, in order to attain that "rarity" of knowledge and/or skill that appeals to employers. Those rare opportunities (pursuing additional education or supplementary experiences) are often out of reach for students who come from less-privileged backgrounds. This article discusses the realities that face students from less privileged backgrounds and points to systemic and systematic inequalities set in place that launch some individuals ahead of others due to their ascribed statuses and awarded privileges.

1. What groups are overrepresented in post-secondary institutions? Underrepresented? Why?
2. What creates unequal access to post-secondary education?
3. Why is it more difficult for some groups to succeed in post-secondary programs?

INTRODUCTION

Education in Canada appears to be fulfilling its meritocratic promise. Secondary students are performing well in international assessment tests, such as the Program for International Student Assessment (PISA).[1] Canada has one of the highest rates of labour market participants with postsecondary education in the world (OECD 2010), which means we are preparing young people for participation in a knowledge economy. With a few notable exceptions (African Canadians and First Nation Canadians), members of visible minority groups in Canada perform exceptionally well at secondary schools, colleges, and universities. Finally, women have outpaced men in educational achievement, and an increasing number of low-income and working-class youth attend university (Canadian Association of University Teachers 2011). In fact, more than 50 percent of a graduating high school cohort now begins studies at university (Canadian Council on Learning 2006).

This educational success of individuals who were historically excluded from higher education would suggest that the status structure of Canadian society is also changing. In other words, one might assume that positions of power and status are no longer occupied by members of families who have traditionally been in these

PART 12

Source: Lehmann, Wolfgang. "Access and Barriers to Post-Secondary Education." Unpublished work, 2011. Reproduced with permission from the author.

positions. Yet, Richard Wanner, a sociologist at the University of Calgary, has shown that this is not the case (Wanner 2004). There has been very little movement in Canada in the distribution of power and status. Powerful positions in politics and industry are largely held by individuals from already established and powerful backgrounds. For instance, compared to 30 or 40 years ago, we do not see significantly more people from working-class backgrounds becoming judges, lawyers, doctors and CEOs. Brown, Lauder and Ashton (2011) have shown that the situation is similar in other Western, industrial nations like the U.S., the U.K., Germany, or France, to name only a few. Given the shifts in educational attainment described above, how can this be explained?

CREDENTIAL INFLATION

More than 30 years ago, Randall Collins, a prominent U.S. sociologist, wrote about **credential inflation**, a concept that still has a powerful explanatory value today (Collins 1976).

We can argue that educational credentials, such as a university degree, function very much like money or other forms of capital. The more there is of it, the less worth it will hold. In other words, if more and more young people enter the labour market with a Bachelor degree, a BA or BSc will no longer distinguish the holder of this degree from other individuals with similar credentials. As a consequence, individuals are looking for other ways to distinguish themselves on the labour market. Collins (1976) argued that this is generally achieved by getting further and higher levels of education. A Master degree will distinguish a job candidate vis-à-vis a competitor who only holds a Bachelor. Furthermore, degrees from prestigious universities will offer advantages over degrees from less prestigious institutions. For instance, a law degree from Harvard will open doors to top law firms in the U.S. or Canada in a way that a law degree from a minor university will not. How then is this related to the promise of meritocracy and an

open and just society? After all, if an increasing number of minority or working-class students get Bachelor degrees, what should keep them from achieving equally well at higher levels? The problem, as Collins sees it, is related to cost and limited access opportunities. Additional years of schooling, especially in costly professional programs and expensive elite universities, is out of reach of most students from families with modest or low incomes. Parallel to this development in education, employers have been raising credential requirements, so that you now need a Master degree to get a job for which in the past a Bachelor would have been sufficient, you need a Bachelor degree for a job that only used to require a high school diploma, and so forth. If we add together higher credential requirements for employment and access issues for advanced levels of higher education, we have an explanation for the persistence of status differences and hierarchies, despite the fact that more young people than ever, from diverse backgrounds, attend university for a first degree.

EXTRA-CREDENTIAL INFLATION

The dynamics of credential inflation are well understood and researched. Less obvious, but equally important, is the influence of what I shall call "extra-credential" inflation. Take, for instance, two students who graduated from the same university with the same degree. Valuable extra-credential experiences are those that allow one of the two students to stand out compared to the other, such as career-related employment, internships, volunteer work, study abroad, or travel. For instance, studies have shown that career-related work experiences are much more important for the employability of university graduates than casual, income-supporting jobs (Moreau & Leathwood 2006; Smetherman 2006).

Extra-credential involvement can also be a factor in achieving credentials in the first place. Most professional programs (e.g., law, medicine, dentistry, teaching, and so forth) not only set increasingly high tuition fees that are out of reach for low-income students, but also have admission criteria that emphasize non-academic experiences and involvement. For example, admission websites of U.S. and Canadian law and medical schools state that they want applicants who have 'personal strengths that predict professional distinction,' 'evidence of leadership,' 'demonstration of above-average non-academic qualities,' and 'personal qualities substantiated by examples of life experiences' to simply pick a few statements. The question is: why are these kinds of extra-credential experiences so unevenly distributed and how does this contribute to the persistence of social inequality?

Take the above-mentioned requirements for professional programs, for instance. Not everybody has equal access to opportunities that allow you to demonstrate capacity for professional distinction or leadership. Growing up in families that have many academic and cultural resources (such as books or travel opportunities) likely means that individuals will have had "richer" personal experiences to describe in their applications, at least in the sense that seems to appeal to admission committees at professional schools. The late French sociologist Pierre Bourdieu referred to these resources as cultural capital (Bourdieu 1986).

One might argue that valuable extra-credential opportunities are always limited. After all, internships with hospitals or top law firms are likely to be rare. Obviously, this is a problem that affects all students, regardless of their social backgrounds. Yet, working-class students also often face a relative lack of financial resources, connections, and valuable forms of cultural capital. To give a few examples: having first-hand experience as an intern—who is most likely unpaid—in a prestigious law firm will provide a person with substantial advantages upon graduation. Yet, for a student to gain this type of experience, he/she will likely have to have connections to the firm (e.g., through family networks), and not be forced to spend his/her summer holidays

working retail in order to simply afford being at university. Similarly, studying a year abroad does not only require the financial means to do so, but also a level of comfort with travel and experience of other cultures, which is a form of cultural capital students from middle-class backgrounds are more likely to have.

Extra-Credential Inflation in Action: A Research Example

To illustrate these arguments, I will draw on research I carried out with **first-generation students** at a large, research intensive university in Ontario (see e.g., Lehmann 2009a, b; 2011).

All the students in the study were the first in their family to attend university and came from working-class or low-income backgrounds. I interviewed the students in their first few weeks at university about their reasons for coming to university and their expectations, fears and hopes as first-generation students. They were then re-interviewed about their experiences in their second and fourth year at university. In the interview excerpts below, I will be using pseudonyms to protect the anonymity of the study participants.

Worries about extra-credential inflation became very clear in the fourth-year interviews, especially for the high-achieving students in the study. Take Alison for example, who was an exceptional student, with outstanding marks and high levels of involvement on campus. Yet, she was worried whether her lack of career related extra-credential experience will negatively affect her goal of attending medical school and becoming a doctor:

Alison: People that have more money have such an advantage in terms of what they can do. Like, they can just volunteer with the professor in a lab in the summer, and spend their whole summer doing that, and they don't have to work 60 hours a week. And then there's people like me that can't do that because they have to work 'cause they have to [pay for] school.

PART 12

The experience of Alison is not unique. Throughout the study, almost all participants indicated that they had spent the summer working in jobs unrelated to their academic study or career goal. Most also worked in unrelated jobs during the academic year.

I want to return to Alison's story once more. As I mentioned above, Alison was a truly outstanding and very ambitious student who felt that her need to engage in long hours of off-campus employment restricted her ability to accumulate extra-credential experiences. Similarly, here she describes her inability to become involved in an aid project that would have very likely boosted her chances to be considered an outstanding applicant to medical schools:

> Alison: I was going to [volunteer in a clinic in Nepal] in second year, and then I ended up not having enough money to go. A whole bunch of my friends from residence went to Nepal to go do medical work there and they loved it, but I ended up not having enough money to go. Which is alright, but when I'm applying to med school or grad school, it gives those people who were able to do those things in the summer a leg up, so when I'm writing my med school application, I don't look as good.

These findings reflect other, institutional data from the Canadian university at which the study was conducted.[2] These data show that first-generation students come to university with ambitions to attain extra-curricular, enriching experiences that are as high, if not higher than their non-first-generation peers, but that most cannot fulfill these ambitions. For instance, nearly 40 percent of first-generation students in their first-year stated that they intended to spend time studying abroad as part of their undergraduate education. Yet, only 4 percent of students in their final year had actually been able to do so.

Furthermore, for many working-class students, the financial struggle to gain access to career-related experiences is made worse by their lack of networks into their respective career areas. Sociologists refer to these networks and connections as **social capital**.

Sometimes, a social capital disadvantage can be as trivial as knowing somebody who can write you a reference letter, as this quotation by Sally shows:

> Sally: It's when I do need help, like, I guess a reference letter—my parents won't know people who can help me out with that. So the networking isn't that great with my parents, they're both in completely different fields than anything that requires so much education.

More often, however, the students talked about limited access to volunteer and career opportunities, because they didn't know the "right people" as the following two quotations show:

> Bruce: Finding a good job, just on the basis of having really good academic achievements doesn't really help you get a job at all. It's just about knowing someone who's hiring. And that's really frustrating.

> Marilyn: [Other students] have parents who know friends that could just get them right in. 'Oh yeah, I know this guy and he can hook you up and he gets you into the company'. Versus me, my parents have no networks in the community. And it kinda sucks, 'cause you realize, I'm actually doing better than them, but, you know, you still don't get these opportunities.

The most explicit personal experiences about social capital disadvantages were provided by Ian, a student who came to university from a rural region of Ontario and is determined to become a dentist. Here, Ian discusses his concerns about his lack of social capital and being shut out of important volunteer experiences:

> Ian: [Dental schools] look at volunteer hours and things like that, and I would love to get into a dental office and volunteer, just be a dental

assistant, just be in the back cleaning tools. I'll clean toilets. I just want to be in the building. My one friend he works with his Dad's best friend in the summer. And he sees every procedure and gets to do everything like that. And that looks really good on a resume, right? And I can't see me get that opportunity, and I've been hounding dentists all over [the city]. [. . .] People who have these connections will not give up these connections. It's like they have the upper hand. It's just so frustrating.

The students in this study had already overcome access barriers to higher education and completed their four years of undergraduate studies, some with outstanding success. Yet, their concerns about their restricted abilities to gain increasingly important extra-credential experiences suggest that social inequalities are not only maintained through the inflation of credential requirements, but also through the inflation of extra-credential requirements. Although the students in this study desired internships in medicine and dentistry, law firm volunteer placements, and international study and work experiences, these opportunities were out of their reach. As a consequence, many students actually revised their initial career goals. Rather than attend medical or law schools, for example, they decided to study biochemistry or criminology in graduate school instead. Others who wanted to enter the labour market after their undergraduate studies were very concerned about their ability to "exchange" their Bachelor degree for a good job.

CONCLUDING OBSERVATIONS

This study did not follow the students beyond their first four years at university. I therefore do not know if Alison was admitted to medical school, Ian became a dentist, or Bruce and Marilyn found jobs that match their high achievement at university. Nonetheless, the concerns they expressed about extra-credential inflation in these interviews suggest that universities and employers need to seriously look at how they select and reward students. Disadvantaging first-generation, working-class or low-income students on the basis of extra-credentials not only is an issue of social equality, but also leads to a waste of talent.

NOTES

1. For information regarding the PISA surveys and Canada's international ranking, see: http://www.pisa.oecd.org.
2. The university participates in the National Survey of Student Engagement (NSSE). The data in this section is taken from the 2008 survey. To protect the anonymity of the participants, I cannot identify the specific institutional source of this data; however, for further information about NSSE, please see http://nsse.iub.edu/html/about.cfm.

REFERENCES

Bourdieu, P. (1986). The Forms of Capital. In J. G. Richardson (Ed.), *Handbook of Theory and Research for the Sociology of Education* (pp. 241–258). New York: Greenwood Press.

Brown, P., Lauder, H., & Ashton, D. (2011). *The Global Auction: The Broken Promises of Education, Jobs and Incomes*. Oxford & New York: Oxford University Press.

Canadian Association of University Teachers (2011). CAUT Almanac of Post-Secondary Education in Canada 2010–11. Ottawa: Canadian Association of University Teachers (CAUT).

Canadian Council on Learning. (2006). *Canadian Post-secondary Education: A Positive Record—An Uncertain Future*. Ottawa: Canadian Council on Learning.

Collins, R. (1979). *The Credential Society: An Historical Sociology of Education and Stratification*. San Diego: Academic Press.

Lehmann, W. (2009a). Becoming middle class: How working-class university students draw and transgress moral class boundaries. *Sociology, 43*(4), 631–647.

Lehmann, W. (2009b). Class Encounters: Working-class Students at University. In C. Levine-Rasky (Ed.), *Canadian Perspectives on the Sociology of Education* (pp. 197–212). Don Mills, ON: Oxford University Press.

PART 12

Lehmann, W. (2011). Extra-credential experiences and social closure: Working-class students at university. *British Educational Research Journal.* First published on: 23 February 2011 (iFirst).

Moreau, M.P., & C. Leathwood. (2006). Graduates' employment and the discourse of employability: A critical analysis. *Journal of Education and Work* 19(4), 305–324.

OECD (2010). *Education at a Glance 2010.* Paris: OECD.

Smetherham, C. (2006). Firsts among equals? Evidence on the contemporary relationship between educational credentials and the occupational structure, *Journal of Education and Work*, 19(1), 29–45.

Wanner, R. (2004). Social Mobility in Canada: Concepts, Patterns and Trends. In J. Curtis, E. Grabb and N. Guppy (Eds); *Social Inequality in Canada: Patterns, Problems and Policies. Fourth Edition* (pp. 131–147). Toronto: Pearson.

Critical Thinking Questions

1. What could universities do to help first-generation students who lack financial resources and social capital? What could employers do?
2. Does extra-credentialism impact you in any way?

Chapter 32

The Gender Income Gap and the Role of Education

DONNA BOBBITT-ZEHER

One of the criticisms, or backlashes to feminism, is the notion that, since women have "already achieved parity with men," why do they continue to raise a fuss? As this article demonstrates, while women's rights have improved, we still have a long way to go before women achieve even economic parity of men. The monetary differences in income between men and women is a complex process, and Bobbitt-Zeher provides an analysis that teases apart some of the main reasons for the income gap, beginning with gendered educational selection processes. The foundation of the article is the idea that all humans are inherently equal, thus deserving of equal rights and treatment.

1. What are some of the reasons for the income gap between men and women?

Given the obvious connection between educational success and labor market outcomes, many consider education to be key to reducing group inequalities. In particular, schooling is thought to play a pivotal role in the success of racial/ethnic groups, such as Asian Americans, and the continuing struggles of others (e.g., blacks, Native Americans, and Hispanics). But what role does education play in lessening gender disparities in the larger society? With women's educational attainment and achievement patterns now matching or surpassing those of men on many measures, are women on their way toward gender equality more broadly?

Few studies have systematically analyzed the mediating role of education in gender disparities in earnings, along with the potentially confounding family and employment factors. In addition, little attention has been paid to the current level of gender disparities in earnings among the beneficiaries of these changing patterns of educational accomplishment or to the prospects of education contributing to further reductions in such inequalities should the patterns of women's educational success persist.

BACKGROUND

Consequences of Changing Educational Patterns

While scholars in the 1970s and 1980s highlighted ways in which schools shortchanged girls (Sadker and Sadker 1994), the focus has shifted in the past decade because young women now outperform young men on many indicators of educational achievement (National Center for Education Statistics (NCES) 2005;

PART 12

Riordan 2003). Not only are women enrolling in college in greater numbers than men, they are also outpacing men in graduating from high school, attending college, and attaining college degrees (NCES 2004; Sum, Fogg, and Harrington 2003). In addition, gender gaps in enrollment and degree attainment favoring women are expected to widen further in the next decade (NCES 2003:6; Sum et al. 2003).

These dramatic and well-documented educational changes have been fodder for much public debate regarding a "war against boys" (Riordan 2003); however, the pressing issue that has been overlooked in the literature is the degree to which the educational success of young women today leads to gender equality later in life. In particular, there has been little research on the implications of changing patterns in higher education for gender equality in labor market outcomes. A notable exception is Loury's (1997) work, which suggested that women's educational success had a direct effect on the narrowing **gender gap in earnings** in the early to mid-1980s.

Such work connecting women's educational accomplishments to the declining gender gap in income suggests an optimistic picture for young, college-educated women at the time of their entry into careers.

However, to what extent do young college-educated women reap equal returns in the labor market? The weight of the empirical evidence suggests lingering inequality, with women earning about 15 percent less than men early in their careers (e.g., Blau 1998:129; Marini and Fan 1997). Understanding the degree of gender inequality in earnings in the early years of careers is important because initial income disparities tend to grow over time (Marini 1989). And for those who are interested in examining the equalizing effects of education, it is during these early years of a career—when differences in employment histories, life experiences, and accumulated skills are minimized—that educational credentials and school experiences are likely to matter the most.

Educational Explanations for the Gender Income Gap

The recent focus on women's educational advances, which are both impressive and deserving of scholarly attention, tends to obscure the ways in which women remain disadvantaged on several educational measures. Gender differences on four of these measures, in particular, are implicated in the gender income gap: (1) choice of a college major, (2) skills as measured by standardized tests, (3) amount of education, and (4) selectivity of the college attended.

The most persuasive educational explanation of gender income inequality is that women major in fields that lead to jobs that are not rewarded with higher incomes (Bradley 2000; Davies and Guppy 1997; Gerber and Schaefer 2004). Individuals who major in such fields as engineering and computer science tend to earn more than do those who major in education and the humanities (Daymont and Andrisani 1984; Gerber and Schaefer 2004). However, in spite of the trend toward the integration of fields of study,   college majors are still quite gender segregated (Bradley 2000; Charles and Bradley 2002; Jacobs 1995, 1996). For example, women received 20 percent of the engineering degrees and 77 percent of the education degrees in 2000-01 (NCES 2004:78). Given that men are more concentrated in the higher-earning fields and women are more concentrated in the less rewarded ones, gender segregation in fields of study appears to contribute to gender differences in income.

Indeed, studies that have considered fields of study have found that the choice of college majors explains between roughly one-quarter to one-half of the gender gap in wages for college graduates (Brown and Corcoran 1997; Daymont and Andrisani 1984). Bradley (2000) concluded that this horizontal dimension of gender segregation is pivotal in understanding gender inequality in wages globally.

It is possible that "certain majors and courses may develop more valuable job-related human capital than do other majors and courses" (Brown and Corcoran 1997:432, citing Paglin and Rufolo 1990). In this view, the labor market rewards this investment in human capital with higher earnings. NCES (1998; see also Joy 2000) considered women's proportional representation in each field. It found that among the college educated, workers with female-dominated majors averaged 20 percent less in annual earnings in the first year after graduation than did workers with male-dominated majors. Such research suggests that the gender composition of fields should not be overlooked when considering why college majors matter for gender disparities in income.

Another education-related explanation for income inequalities concerns gender differences in cognitive skills. Measured using standardized test scores, cognitive skills are thought to affect the gender gap directly as well as indirectly through the choice of college major and access to jobs (Farkas et al. 1997; Paglin and Rufolo 1990). Research has suggested that as the U.S. economy has transformed since the 1970s, math and science abilities have become more predictive of salaries (Murnane, Willett, and Levy 1995), and math skills translate into higher earnings for all types of workers (Mitra 2002). Indeed, Mitra's (2002) study found that the gender gap in income disappears among professional men and women with the highest math skills. Thus, the gender income differential is a result of differences in highly valued skills—generally math skills—which lead to lower-paying jobs for women. Although evidence suggests that differences in boys' and girls' performance on standardized math and science tests are shrinking (Willingham and Cole 1997), persistent differences on standardized tests, including the SAT, favoring men (College Board 2003; NCES 2004) may continue to play a role in gender disparities in income, particularly in today's economy, in which skills are increasingly predictive of salaries (Murnane et al. 1995).

While the strongest educational influences on gender disparities in income are likely to be gender segregation in college majors and differences in standardized test scores, two additional schooling-related factors may contribute to these disparities to a lesser extent. The first is the vertical dimension of gender segregation, or the level of degree attainment. Although women now surpass men in undergraduate degrees that are awarded (NCES 2005), gender parity in the highest degrees has yet to be realized. Women receive approximately 45 percent of all professional and doctoral degrees (NCES 2004:82). Although this is not a large difference, the reality that greater educational attainment leads to higher wages for both women and men (Blau 1998; Kilbourne et al. 1994) suggests that men's advantage in receiving the highest degrees may contribute in a small way to women's lower average earnings.

College prestige has a positive relationship with earnings later in life (Jacobs 1999), and men are significantly more likely to attend selective postsecondary institutions than are women, net of background and academic factors (Davies and Guppy 1997, replicating the findings of Hearn 1991). Women's attendance at less selective postsecondary educational institutions may be the result of institutional bias favoring men, more selective schools tending not to offer traditionally female-dominated programs, and/or parental choices to invest more financially in sons (Davies and Guppy 1997; see also Jacobs 1999). Although there have been declines in gender differences in the selectivity of postsecondary institution attended (see Jacobs 1999; Karen 1991), institutional selectivity remains a potentially salient influence on gender disparities in income for today's college graduates.

With regard to young adults graduating from college and entering the labor market today, these findings suggest that lingering gender differences in schooling (e.g., fields of study, measured cognitive skills, college selectivity) may explain persistent gender disparities in earnings. With women's postsecondary education rates surpassing men's, participation in higher

PART 12

education is not likely to contribute to earnings disparities, except at the highest levels, where men's degree attainment continues to surpass that of women.

Education's Limited Role in the Gender Income Gap

The effects of family formation, particularly marriage and parenthood and their impact on participation in paid labor, are implicated in gender income disparities. For example, net of other factors, such as education, women with children make 10 percent to 15 percent less than do women without children (Korenman and Neumark 1992; Waldfogel 1998), and there is a 7 percent wage penalty for each child that a young woman has (Budig and England 2001). The penalty for having children is greater for married women than for non-married women (Budig and England 2001:218). The same patterns do not hold for men; fathers experience no comparable wage penalty for their parental status (Waldfogel 1998). Furthermore, married men receive higher pay than do unmarried men, while there is some evidence of a wage disadvantage for married women (Kilbourne et al. Gender Income Gaps 1994).

The impact of family formation on gender differences in earnings appears to operate through women's decreased labor force participation (Korenman and Neumark 1992). Both length of job experience and part-time employment contribute to lower earnings (Budig and England 2001; Shelton and Firestone 1989). And women historically have had less job experience and have engaged in part-time work more often than have men (Blau and Kahn 1997; Rosenfeld and Birkelund 1995).

Perhaps the most thoroughly discussed explanations for the gender income gap are occupational sex segregation and women's concentration in female-dominated occupations (e.g., Blau and Kahn 1997; England 1992; Huffman 2004; Kilbourne et al. 1994; Macpherson and Hirsch

1995). England (1992:181) found that "the sex composition of an occupation affects the pay it offers, such that both men and women earn less if they work in a predominantly female occupation." Given that women are concentrated in traditionally female occupations, the gender gap in wages can be partially explained by women's overrepresentation in jobs that pay less.

In addition to occupational sex segregation, other work-related factors contribute to inequality in earnings. Men tend to have longer tenure with their employers, greater full-time work experience, and more training, all of which contribute to their higher earnings relative to women (Blau and Kahn 1997; Marini 1989; Wellington 1994). Similar trends hold true for young workers: Women's first jobs tend to be of a lesser quality than men's, and women are more likely than men to be employed part time (Joy 2000). While occupations have received the most attention in studies of income disparities, research on wage differentials across sectors (Moulton 1990) and industries (Fields and Wolff 1995; Groshen 1991), along with gendered patterns of labor force participation, suggest the need to consider gender variations at these broader levels when explaining gender differences in income (see Fields and Wolff 1995; Macpherson and Hirsch 1995; Marini 1989).

Furthermore, as a result of gender socialization, young men and women have different values and occupational aspirations, and these gender differences appear to influence the gender income gap via occupational choices (Daymont and Andrisani 1984; Wilson and Boldizar 1990; see also Corcoran and Courant 1985; Reskin 1993; Shu and Marini 1998). These different occupational aspirations affect decisions regarding higher education, which, in turn, affect the occupations that these young adults enter (Wilson and Boldizar 1990).

Much of the research on educational contributions to earnings disparities has not considered work and family factors, while much of the work and family literature has deemphasized the role of education, which makes it difficult to understand the two sets of influences relative to one another. Also, much of this literature has offered little insight into women and men in the early years of their careers.

Gender differences in family responsibilities, labor market participation, and other human capital-related characteristics that grow over time are greatly minimized for this group of workers. However, little empirical work has examined the impact of such factors specifically on young workers.

DATA AND METHODS

NELS (National Educational Longitudinal Survey) offers a rich database for exploring the relationships between educational factors and the earnings gap between young working men and women. It followed students who were eighth graders in 1988 through high school and into their early adult lives. The baseline data are nationally representative, based on a sample of almost 25,000 students from 1,052 public and private schools. The 2000 data contain interviews with 12,144 of these individuals.

For comparison with national data from the Current Population Survey on the gender wage gap and to avoid part-time and inconsistent workers from biasing the analysis, I limited my analysis to college graduates who were full-time, year-round workers (that is, those with four-year degrees who were working 35 or more hours per week for all 52 weeks in 1999) and had annual income data available for 1999 (N = 1,946). I focused on college graduates for two reasons. First, postsecondary educational attainment is one area in which women have made the greatest gains. Given the relationship between postsecondary educational success and labor market outcomes, it is especially important to know to what degree college-educated women enjoy income equity with their male counterparts. Second, many educational characteristics, such as institutional selectivity, are meaningful

or applicable only to the college educated. In supplementary analyses, I found that the gender gap in income is larger among those without a college degree. By focusing on college graduates, therefore, I deliberately concentrated on a group for which educational characteristics arguably have the greatest chance of explaining gender gaps in earnings.

The findings of this study suggest that education continues to contribute to gender stratification in a meaningful way despite women's overall success in educational realms. The educational factor that appears to matter most is college major, and college major appears to affect inequality in earnings in two ways. As one may expect, field of study contributes to earnings inequality via occupational choices: People tend to work in jobs that are related to their fields of study, and some occupations are better rewarded than are others. Yet, the regression decomposition presented here suggests that college majors play a meaningful role in women's lesser income independent of later work factors. Indeed, even when work-, family-, and values-related factors are considered alongside education, 14 percent of the gender gap in income is still attributable to field of study.

It is often argued that some fields are more highly compensated because they develop skills that are more valued in the labor market. Although the content of the field of study seems to have an important relationship with earnings inequality, the gender composition of the field appears to be much more salient. This devaluation of majors associated with women is consistent with the finding of a general devaluation of jobs associated with women (England 1992). And it appears that the lesser value assigned to majors in which women are more heavily concentrated continues to affect one's earnings even when young workers enter comparable occupations. This pattern indicates that educational sex segregation by field of study continues to be an impediment to gender equality beyond its relationship to occupational sex segregation and will

PART 12

have to be addressed directly if gender disparities are to be eliminated.

In their mid-20s, college-educated women make about $4,400 less per year than do men even when they have the same level of education, college major, cognitive skills, and selectivity of the college from which they graduated. Here, it seems that gender differences in types of employment—occupations, industries, and sectors—are especially important. For this group of workers, aspirations for earning lots of money appear to matter only modestly for the income gap, and family formation matters not much at all.

The denial of opportunities for women to attend college and attain a degree on the basis of their sex is inconsistent with the contemporary gender ideology of equality of opportunity. Yet, as this vertical dimension of segregation has declined, fields of study—the horizontal dimension—remain resistant to integration. Because gender differences in college majors are viewed more as differences than as inequality, the segregation of fields of study can persist despite a more egalitarian gender ideology and the decline of vertical segregation (Charles and Bradley 2002). Thus, the overall positive picture of women's educational patterns can mask lingering gender differences that have important consequences for gender inequality later in life.

Similarly, occupational sex segregation persists and may increase despite the greater presence of women in the labor market (Charles and Grusky 2004).

Unfortunately, the ongoing debate over women's growing "advantage" in schooling has, by and large, overlooked the consequences of these patterns of educational attainment and performance. A look at one important outcome—the earnings of young women and men—should temper the optimism that is generally generated by trends toward girls' educational success. On the whole, the findings of this study suggest little reason to be optimistic that further educational changes will lead to large declines in gender inequality in income. If women maintain their current trajectory of improving their educational credentials relative to men, they will still face the barrier of sex segregation in college majors. And while the integration of majors could generate important reductions in the gender gap in income, research has found a general stagnation of integration of fields of study since the mid-1980s (Jacobs 1995). Even larger barriers to income equity are related to gendered patterns of employment, and today's young college-educated adults continue to confront these obstacles. Indeed, in spite of women's educational progress, the gendered organization of both higher education and employment remain substantial impediments to equality in earnings.

REFERENCES

Blau, Francine D. 1998. "Trends in the Well-Being of American Women, 1970–1995." *Journal of Economic Literature* 36:112–65.

Blau, Francine D., and Lawrence M. Kahn. 1997. "Swimming Upstream: Trends in the Gender Wage Differential in the 1980s." *Journal of Labor Economics* 15:1–42.

Bradley, Karen. 2000. "The Incorporation of Women into Higher Education: Paradoxical Outcomes" *Sociology of Education* 73:1–18.

Brown, Charles, and Mary Corcoran. 1997. "Sex Based Differences in School Content and the Male-Female Wage Gap." *Journal of Labor Economics* 15:431–65.

Budig, Michelle J., and Paula England. 2001. "The Wage Penalty for Motherhood." *American Sociological Review* 66:204–25.

Charles, Maria, and Karen Bradley. 2002. "Equal but Separate? A Cross-National Study of Sex Segregation in Higher Education." *American Sociological Review* 67:573–99.

Charles, Maria, and David B. Grusky. 2004. *Occupational Ghettos: The Worldwide Segregation of Women and Men.* Stanford, CA: Stanford University Press.

College Board. 2003, August 26. "SAT Verbal and Math Scores Up Significantly as a Record Breaking Number of Students Take the Test: Average Math Score at Highest Level in More than 35 Years." Press release. Available online at http://www.collegeboard.com/press/article/0?26858,00.html.

Corcoran, Mary E., and Paul N. Courant. 1985. "Sex Role Socialization and Labor Market Outcomes." *American Economic Review* 75:275–78.

Davies, Scott, and Neil Guppy. 1997. "Fields of Study, College Selectivity, and Student Inequalities in Higher Education." *Social Forces* 75:1417–38.

Daymont, Thomas N., and Paul J. Andrisani. 1984. "Job Preferences, College Major, and the Gender Gap in Earnings." *Journal of Human Resources* 19:408–28.

England, Paula. 1992. *Comparable Worth: Theories and Evidence.* New York: Aldine De Gruyter.

Farkas, George, Paula England, Keven Vicknair, and Barbara Stanek Kilbourne. 1997. "Cognitive Skill, Skill Demands of Jobs, and Earnings among Young European American, African American, and Mexican American Workers." *Social Forces* 75:913–38.

Fields, Judith, and Edward N. Wolff. 1995. "Interindustry Wage Differentials and the Gender Wage Gap." *Industrial and Labor Relations Review* 49(1):105–120.

Gerber, Theodore P., and David R. Schaefer. 2004. "Horizontal Stratification of Higher Education in Russia: Trends, Gender Differences, and Labor Market Outcomes." *Sociology of Education* 77: 32–59.

Groshen, Erica L. 1991. "The Structure of the Female/Male Wage Differential: Is It Who You Are, What You Do, or Where You Work?" *Journal of Human Resources* 23:457–72.

Hearn, James C. 1991. "Academic and Nonacademic Influences on College Destinations of 1980 High School Graduates." *Sociology of Education* 64:158–71.

Huffman, Matt L. 2004. "Gender Inequality Across Local Wage Hierarchies." *Work and Occupations* 31:323–44.

Jacobs, Jerry. 1995. "Gender and Academic Specialties: Trends Among College Degree Recipients During the 1980s. *Sociology of Education* 68:81–98.

— . 1999. "Gender and the Stratification of Colleges." *The Journal of Higher Education* 70:161–87.

Joy, Lois. 2000. "Do Colleges Shortchange Women? Gender Differences in the Transition from College to Work." *American Economic Review* 90:471–75.

Karen, David. 1991. "The Politics of Class, Race, and Gender: Access to Higher Education in the United States, 1960–1986." *American Journal of Education* 99:208–37.

Kilbourne, Barbara, Paula England, and Kurt Beron. 1994. "Effects of Individual, Occupational, and Industrial Characteristics on Earnings: Intersections of Race and Gender." *Social Forces* 72:1149–76.

Korenman, Sanders, and David Neumark. 1992. "Marriage, Motherhood, and Wages." *Journal of Human Resources* 27:233–55.

Loury, Linda Datcher. 1997. "The Gender Earnings Gap among College-Educated Workers." *Industrial and Labor Relations Review* 50:580–93.

Macpherson, David A., and Barry T. Hirsch. 1995. "Wages and Gender Composition: Why Do Women's Jobs Pay Less?" *Journal of Labor Economics* 13:426–71.

Marini, Margaret Mooney. 1989. "Sex Differences in Earnings in the United States." *Annual Review of Sociology* 15:343–80.

Marini, Margaret Mooney, and Pi-Ling Fan. 1997. "The Gender Gap in Earnings at Career Entry." *American Sociological Review* 62:588–604.

Mitra, Aparna. 2002. "Mathematics Skill and Male Female Wages." *Journal of Socio-Economics* 31:443–56.

Moulton, Brent R. 1990. "A Reexaminaron of the Federal-Private Wage Differential in the United States." *Journal of Labor Economics* 8:270–93.

Murnane, Richard J., John B. Willett, and Frank Levy. 1995. "The Growing Importance of Cognitive Skills in Wage Determination." *Review of Economics and Statistics* 77:251–66.

National Center for Education Statistics. 1998. *Gender Differences in Earnings Among Young Adults Entering the Labor Market* (NCES 98-086). By Suzanne B. Clery, John B. Lee, and Laura G. Knapp. Washington, DC: U.S. Government Printing Office.

— . 2003. *The Condition of Education 2003 in Brief (NCES 2003-068).* By Andrea Livingston and John Wirt. Washington, DC: U.S. Government Printing Office.

— . 2004. *Trends in Educational Equity of Girls and Women: 2004 (NCES 2005-016).* By Catherine E. Freeman. Washington, DC: U.S. Government Printing Office.

— . 2005. *Gender Differences in Participation and Completion of Undergraduate Education and How They Have Changed Over Time (NCES 2005-169).* By Katharin Peter and Laura Horn. Washington DC: US Government Printing Office.

Paglin, Morton, and Anthony M. Rufolo. 1990. "Heterogeneous Human Capital, Occupational Choice, and Male-Female Earnings Differences." *Journal of Labor Economics* 8:123–44.

Reskin, Barbara. 1993. "Sex Segregation in the Workplace." *Annual Review of Sociology* 19: 241–70.

PART 12

Riordan, Cornelius. 2003. "Failing in School? Yes; Victims of War? No." *Sociology of Education* 76:369–72.

Rosenfeld, Rachel A., and Gunn Elisabeth Birkelund. 1995. "Women's Part-Time Work: A Cross-National Comparison." *European Sociological Review* 11:111–34.

Sadker, Myra, and David Sadker. 1994. *Failing at Fairness: How Our Schools Cheat Girls.* New York: Simon & Schuster.

Shelton, Beth Anne, and Juanita Firestone. 1989. "Household Labor Time and the Gender Gap in Earnings." *Gender and Society* 3:105–12.

Shu, Xiaoling, and Margaret Mooney Marini. 1998. "Gender Related Change in Occupational Aspirations." *Sociology of Education* 71:43–67.

Sum, Andrew, Neeta Fogg, and Paul Harrington with Ishwar Khatiwada, Shelia Palma, Nathan Pond, and Paulo Tobar. 2003. "The Growing Gender Gaps in College Enrollment and Degree Attainment in the U.S. and Their Potential Economic and Social Consequences." Prepared for the Business Roundtable, Washington, DC. Boston: Center for Labor Market Studies. Available online at http://www.brtable.org/pdf/943.pdf.

Waldfogel, Jane. 1998. "Understanding the 'Family Gap' in Pay for Women with Children." *Journal of Economic Perspectives* 12:137–56.

Wellington, Alison J. 1994. "Accounting for the Male/Female Wage Gap Among Whites: 1976 and 1985." *American Sociological Review* 59:839–48.

Willingham, Warren W., and Nancy S. Cole. 1997. *Gender and Fair Assessment.* Mahwah, NJ: Lawrence Erlbaum.

Wilson, Kenneth L, Janet P. Boldizar. 1990. "Gender Segregation in Higher Education: Effects of Aspirations, Mathematics Achievement, and Income." *Sociology of Education* 63:62–74.

Critical Thinking Questions

1. Despite the continuing income gap between men and women, as demonstrated in the article, why do some assume that women have achieved parity? What impact might this assumption have?

2. According to Statistics Canada (Chapter 14), 68.6 percent of families are composed of different-sex marriages with most of them having both adults working in the paid labour force. Since the gender wage gap negatively impacts partners and family income, it is detrimental to men as well as women. Why then do you suppose the income gap between men and women continues even though it impacts most families?

Chapter 33

Why Do Skilled Immigrants Struggle in the Labor Market? A Field Experiment with Six Thousand Résumés

PHILIP OREOPOULOS

In Canada, overt racism may be difficult to see on a day to day basis, particularly in urban centres. This does not mean that overt discrimination of certain groups in society does not exist, it just means that such discrimination has taken on a different form, known as "covert racism." While covert racism can be difficult to measure, let alone research, Oreopoulos ingeniously created a means of accessing discrimination through a study of how employers behave in job application processes. The results of his experiment are compelling and provide a much needed insight into some of the systemic inequalities that newcomers, and others, continue to face.

1. What are some of the barriers that immigrants face in the Canadian labour market?

INTRODUCTION

Recent immigrants to Canada struggle in the labor market. Their unemployment rates compared to similarly aged non-immigrants are twice as high. Median wages of recent immigrant workers are also about 35 percent lower compared to native-born workers. While the immigrant-native wage gap used to disappear (and sometimes even reverse sign) after ten to fifteen years for immigrants arriving prior to the 1970s, wages of immigrants arriving in the 1990s are still about 25 percent lower than wages of non-immigrants even after 2005 (Frenette and Morissette 2005).

Recent immigrants to other countries such as the United States also experience similar labor market disadvantages (e.g. Lubotsky 2007), but what is noteworthy in the Canadian case is that their immigration policy focuses on attracting immigrants with superior levels of education, experience, and industry demand to offset an anticipated skilled labor force shortage. More than half of today's immigrants enter Canada under a point system, which rates applicants based on their highest degree, language ability, age, whether they have work experience at occupations deemed "in demand," and whether they already have a job offer, have worked or studied in Canada previously, and have cash at hand.

The international competition to attract skilled immigrants is evidently increasing and more attention is being devoted to a point-system approach to evaluate the desirable characteristics

PART 12

Source: Oreopoulos, Philip. "Why Do Skilled Immigrants Struggle in the Labor Market? A Field Experiment with Six Thousand Resumes." *American Economic Journal* 3.4 (2011): 148–71. Reprinted with Permission of the Author and the American Economic Association.

of prospective immigrants. While the United States has traditionally emphasized more the role of family reunification in its immigration policy, some debate has initiated over possible adoption of a point system.

The usual suspects to explain the gap include the possibility that employers do not value foreign education as much as they value Canadian education. The point system treats any degree from any institution the same. Foreign experience may also be treated as inferior to Canadian experience, since less is known about the employer and tasks involved. Another possibility is that cultural and language differences have grown as the proportion of applications from Europe has decreased and the proportion from Asia and the Pacific Coast has increased. There is general consensus around the conclusion that the immigrant-versus-Canadian-born wage gap exists mostly because of lower returns to foreign experience, especially among immigrants from Asia and the Pacific.

This study adopts a completely different methodology to investigate why Canadian immigrants arriving under the point system struggle in the labor market. Thousands of résumés were sent online in response to job postings across multiple occupations in the Greater Toronto Area after randomly varying characteristics on the résumé to uncover what affects employer's decisions on whether to contact an applicant. The résumés were constructed to plausibly represent recent immigrants under the point system from the three largest countries of origin (China, India, and Pakistan) and Britain, as well as non-immigrants with and without ethnic-sounding names. In addition to names, I randomized where applicants received their undergraduate degree, whether their job experience was gained in Toronto or Mumbai (or another foreign city), whether they listed being fluent in multiple languages (including French), whether they had additional education credentials, and whether they listed active extracurricular activities. The approach provides a way to estimate what résumé

elements affect callback rates and compare different theories behind the immigrant-native gap. I also recorded characteristics of the job and employer to determine whether the effects vary across type of firm or evaluator.

I find almost as much name-**discrimination** in my study as Bertrand and Mullainathan (2004) find between black- and white-sounding names. Applicants with English-sounding names who also had Canadian education and experience received callbacks 40 percent more often than did applicants with Chinese, Indian, or Pakistani names who had similar Canadian education and experience. Conditional on listing four to six years of Canadian experience, being foreign-educated (whether at a highly ranked school or not) did not affect callback rates substantially. But changing only the location of the applicant's job experience, from Canadian to foreign, lowered the callback rate further from about 10 percent to 5 percent. Adding more language credentials, additional Canadian education, or extracurricular activities had little impact on these overall results. The effects were almost the same regardless of whether the jobs applied to required more or fewer social or language skills. Callback differences mostly went away when comparing Canadian-born applications to British immigrants. Overall, the results suggest considerable employer discrimination against ethnic Canadians and immigrants.

RESEARCH DESIGN

Thousands of randomly created résumés were sent by email to job postings across multiple occupations in the Greater Toronto Area between April and November 2008. The résumés were designed to represent immigrants that arrived under the Canadian Point System from China, Pakistan, India, and Britain, as well as non-immigrants with and without ethnic-sounding names. They were constructed after consulting actual résumés of recent immigrants and online submissions. The sample of jobs I applied to represent all jobs posted accepted applications via email and required three to seven years of experience plus an undergraduate degree.

With few exceptions, four résumés were sent to each employer over a two- to three-day period in random order. The first represented an applicant with an English-sounding name, Canadian undergraduate education, and Canadian experience (Type 0). The second résumé had a foreign-sounding name (Chinese, Indian, or Pakistani) but still listed Canadian undergraduate education and Canadian experience (Type 1). The third résumé included a foreign-sounding name, foreign undergraduate degree, and Canadian experience (Type 2). The fourth included a foreign-sounding name, foreign education, and some (Type 3) or all (Type 4) foreign experience. I also randomized each applicant's alma mater, whether the applicant listed being fluent in multiple languages (including French), whether they had additional Canadian education credentials, and whether they listed active extracurricular activities.

Work experiences were constructed from actual résumés accessible online. The descriptions were sufficiently altered to create distinct sets that would not be associated with actual people, but I also tried to maintain original overall content and form. Each résumé listed the job title, job description, company name, and city location for an applicant's three most recent jobs covering four to six years, with the first job beginning in the same year as the applicant's undergraduate degree completion. The city listed was always the same (except for Type 3). Within each category, I created four different experience sets, whose job titles and corresponding job descriptions were randomly assigned to one of four résumés sent to a single employer. International companies were chosen to keep the experience sets identical across immigrant and non-immigrant résumés except for location (for example ABC Inc., Toronto versus ABC Inc., Mumbai). In cases where no obvious international company was available,

I picked closely related companies in size and industry. Interestingly, the overall results using identical company names were the same as those using different names.

Since virtually all immigrants that have arrived recently under the point system have at least a bachelor's degree, all résumés generated in this study did as well. Alma mater was picked randomly from a list of about four universities in the same country as the applicant's corresponding name and in the same proximity to the applicant's location of experience. About half of the universities were listed in the 2008 QS World University Rankings' top 200. The other universities were less prestigious. It is interesting to note that under the point system, an applicant receives the same number of points for a bachelor's degree, regardless of where he or she received it.

To assess whether additional Canadian educational credentials may offset lower callback rates, 20 percent of the résumés, except those of Type 4, were randomly assigned Canadian master's degrees from universities near Toronto. Master's degrees were occupation-specific and completed during the same three-year period as the applicants' most recent (Canadian) experience. For job postings that required a particular certificate (13 percent), I listed this credential on each of the four résumés sent.

Clearly, résumés had to look different when being sent to the same employer, so I randomized each applicant's cover letter, email subject line, and résumé file name. layout, residential address and telephone number email address and résumé profile. Five telephone numbers and two email accounts for each name were set up to collect employer responses. Responses were classified as requests for interviews if one was specifically mentioned. Research assistants also guessed the contact's gender and ethnicity based on accent or name. If the person calling back was likely the person who assessed the résumés, this information allowed me to analyze interaction effects between résumé type and assessor's

PART 12

characteristics. Employers that contacted an applicant twice were contacted during off-hours by email or phone message and told the applicant had accepted another position.

RESULTS

Overall, résumés with English-sounding names are 40 percent more likely to receive callbacks than résumés with Indian, Chinese, or Pakistani names. For comparison, Bertrand and Mullainathan (2004) find that résumés with similar white-sounding names are 50 percent more likely to receive callbacks than résumés with black-sounding names sent to employers in Boston and Chicago.

There does not appear to be any difference in callback rates between Type 1 and Type 2 résumés, which systematically differ only by whether they list a bachelor's degree from a Canadian (Type 1) or foreign (Type 2) university. Thus, conditional on listing four to six years of Canadian experience, employers do not seem to care whether an applicant's education is from a foreign institution. In contrast, the callback rate for résumés that list almost all job experience from India, China, or Pakistan drops 2.6 percentage points compared to résumés with all Canadian experience (from 11.4 to 8.8 percent). Callback rates drop 6.2 percentage points for résumés listing only foreign job experience. Interestingly, the résumés that list only British experience do not generate any significant fall in callback rates compared to Type 0 Canadian résumés (14.1 percent compared to 15.8 percent).

For the remaining results, Type 2, 3, and 4 résumés exclude applicants with British experience and education, to focus on comparisons with the three largest immigrant groups from India, China, and Pakistan.

Callback rates for résumés listing female are marginally higher than those listing male, but rates between résumés listing and not listing active extracurricular activities and between résumés listing and not listing fluency in multiple languages (including French) are about the same. Even résumés with master's degrees do not generate more callbacks than résumés without. I interpret these results as suggesting that experience plays far more an important role when applying to jobs requiring three to seven years experience. Or, perhaps employers do not look beyond an applicant's general experience and education when determining whether or not to call back. Unfortunately, the results also imply that an applicant's name matters considerably more than his additional education, multiple language skills, and extracurricular activities.

Females with English-sounding names are 3.3 percentage points more likely to receive a callback than males with English-sounding names. For applicants with foreign-sounding names, gender did not make a difference. This may be because employers could not distinguish gender from some of the names listed. Notably, callback rates are no different between applicants with foreign degrees from high-ranking universities and applicants from lesser-known schools.

There is some evidence that callback rates for programming jobs are not very different among the types of résumés submitted. These jobs require strong cognitive abilities but do not require as much social interaction skills.

As mentioned in Section II, certificates (such as Certified General Accountant) were added to all four résumés when a job posting noted they were required, and added randomly to one or two of the four résumés sent to an employer when a job posting noted they were preferred. Overall, obtaining additional Canadian education credentials appears to do little to offset the lower callback rates that result from listing foreign education or experience.

Among the set of résumés receiving at least one callback, male evaluators are 82 percent more likely to contact Type 0 résumés over résumés with foreign-sounding names. Females are 86 percent more likely to contact Type 0 résumés. Evaluators with Asian or Indian backgrounds are more likely to call back résumés with Asian or Indian names but still favor résumés with English-sounding names. Similarly, evaluators with no accent or ethnic name are about twice as likely to call back a résumé with an English-sounding name over a foreign one, while evaluators with an ethnic accent or name are still 67 percent more likely to call back a résumé with an English-sounding name.

The results hint that employers discriminate more for some jobs with higher speaking and writing skill requirements. Perhaps this implies that employers do not particularly discriminate by name ethnicity for jobs such as computer programmers and web developers. Overall, lower callback rates for résumés with foreign names occurs over occupations requiring different language and social skill requirements.

DISCUSSION AND CONCLUSION

In this paper, I conduct an audit-study to explore why immigrants, allowed into Canada based on skill, fare so poorly in the labor market.

The study leads to three main conclusions. First, Canadian-born individuals with English-sounding names are more likely to receive a callback for a job interview after sending their résumés compared to foreign-born individuals, even among those with foreign degrees from highly ranked schools or among those with the same listed job experience but acquired outside of Canada. More specifically, the study finds that 16 percent of résumés sent with English-sounding names, Canadian education and experience received a callback from an employer, compared to only 5 percent for résumés with foreign-sounding names from China, India, or Pakistan, and foreign experience and education. The callback gap corresponds with overall unemployment differences—in 2006, for example, the national unemployment rate for immigrants was 11.5 percent, more than double the rate of 4.9 percent for the Canadian-born population (Zietsma 2007). Much of the difference in

unemployment rates may therefore be due to immigrants not even making it to the interview stage in the job application process.

The second conclusion is that employers value Canadian experience far more than Canadian education when deciding to interview applicants with foreign backgrounds. Among résumés with foreign names and foreign education, the callback rate climbs from 5 percent to 8 percent by listing just one previous job with a company located inside Canada rather than outside. Listing all job experience with companies located inside Canada leads the callback rate to increase further to 11 percent. These substantial increases are noteworthy, especially in light of the fact that only job location differs while job descriptions and company names remain constant (e.g. ABC Inc., Toronto versus ABC Inc., Beijing). Employers are much more interested in foreign-born applicants with more Canadian experience. Letting in more of these immigrants or helping recent arrivals find initial work that matches their previous background may help to boost immigrants' wage trajectories.

While Canadian experience plays a crucial role in determining the likelihood of a callback, having a degree from a more prestigious foreign institution or acquiring additional schooling in Canada does not impact the chances of a callback significantly. Conditional on listing four to six years of Canadian experience on a résumé, callback rates do not differ by whether a résumé lists a bachelor's degree from a nearby Canadian university or from a foreign university. I also find little effect from indicating an applicant graduated from a top-ranking school compared to a low-ranking one, even among résumés with degrees from Canadian institutions. This surprises me, since admission criteria varies widely by school. It may indicate employers do not pay close attention to education qualifications for résumés with several years of experience. The one exception is Canadian résumés with foreign names. While there is no effect for similar applicants with English names, applicants with

PART 12

foreign names receive about 40 percent more callbacks if they list a higher-ranked Canadian university. Including credentials listed as required or desired for a job naturally raises callback rates, but more so for non-immigrant résumés with English names than for immigrant résumés with foreign names. I find no effect from listing a Canadian master's degree. Recruiters I discussed these results with are not surprised; all said that education plays only a minor role in deciding whether to call an applicant back for an interview once he or she has accumulated four to six years of experience.

The third conclusion is that employers discriminate substantially by the name provided on the résumé. More specifically, employer contact falls 40 percent when switching from a Canadian résumé with a common English name to one with a common Indian, Chinese, or Pakistani name. This difference is substantial and almost as large as that found by Bertrand and Mullainathan (2004) who used résumés with black- or white-sounding names in a similar study in the United States.

A potential explanation for these different callback rates is that employers statistically discriminate by name and location of experience because they believe these characteristics signal a greater chance of inadequate language and cultural skills for the job. Foreign-named applicants with Canadian experience and education are more likely second-generation immigrants than first, especially when only the last name sounds foreign (e.g. Amy Wang). Employers should not expect these applicants to face significant language or social difficulties, yet callback differences between them and résumés with all English-sounding names remain.

I find similar callback differences by name when comparing résumés sent to jobs requiring extensive communication skills to those sent to jobs that don't. If discrimination occurs primarily because employers believe ethnic applicants might lack adequate communication skills, we would expect to see larger differences in callback rates among ethnic and non-ethnic résumés sent in response to job openings that require more of these skills. As further evidence against the statistical discrimination story, I also find no difference in callback rates between immigrant or non-immigrant résumés listing fluency in French and other languages.

Another possibility behind these results is that employers prefer to hire individuals of similar ethnic or language backgrounds (this behavior is sometimes referred to as taste-based discrimination). I report evidence, however, to suggest that this type of discrimination also cannot fully explain the findings. For example, recruiting agencies are slightly less likely to respond to résumés with ethnic names compared with employers that sort through résumés themselves. Since agencies do not have to interact with individuals that get the job, they should not care about ethnicity as much as employers when deciding whom to interview. Furthermore, I also find that evaluators with Asian or Indian accents or names are less likely to call back résumés with Asian or Indian names (although these results are imprecise).

Regardless of what behavior underlies these results, deciding whether to interview an applicant based solely on his or her name is illegal under the Ontario Human Rights Act. Discrimination causes immigrants to miss out on hiring opportunities where they are qualified for a job. In turn, employers may miss out by hiring less qualified workers. The costs to employers from not interviewing an immigrant are likely not as large as the costs to immigrants from not being selected.

A number of researchers suggest that the conditions by which employers sort through résumés make it more likely that name discrimination is unintentional (Stanley Phelps, and Banaji 2008). Social psychologists differentiate between explicit attitudes, one's expressed views, and implicit attitudes, unconscious mental associations. Implicit attitudes may operate subconsciously, and cause people to make decisions that oppose their own deliberative views (Ranganath, Smith, and Nosek 2006). Chugh (2004) argues time pressure, stress, and ambiguity surrounding whether to place résumés on the "yes" pile or the "no" pile make it likely that employers use automatic implicit attitudes to decide.

If discrimination is unintentional, then employers would benefit from taking action to adjust their own practices. Correcting accidental tendencies to favor native-born Caucasian candidates may lead to better hires. Ethnic applicants would also benefit. Whatever the contributing factors might be, further research is clearly needed to investigate exactly why employers are much less interested in interviewing candidates with foreign-sounding names.

REFERENCES

Bertrand, Marianne and Sendhil Mullainathan. 2004. Are Emily and Greg more employable than Lakisha and Jamal? A field experiment on labor market discrimination. *American Economic Review* 94 (4): 991–1013.

Chugh, D. 2004. Societal and managerial implications of implicit social cognition: Why milliseconds matter. *Social Justice Research* 17 (2): 203–22.

Frenette, Marc and René Morissette. 2005. Will they ever converge? Earnings of immigrant and Canadian-born workers over the last two decades. *International Migration Review* 39 (1): 228–58.

Lubotsky, Darren. 2007. Chutes or ladders? A longitudinal analysis of immigrant earnings. *Journal of Political Economy* 115 (5): 820–67.

Ranganath, K. A., C. T. Smith and B. A. Nosek. 2008. Distinguishing automatic and controlled components of attitudes from indirect and direct MBC: Why Do Skilled Immigrants Struggle in the Labor Market? *Journal of Experimental Social Psychology* 44: 386–96.

Stanley, D., E. A. Phelps and M. R. Banaji. 2008. The neural basis of implicit attitudes. Special Issue, ed. R. Poldrack and A. Wagner, *Current Directions in Psychological Science* 17 (2): 164–70.

Zietsma, Danielle. 2007. The Canadian immigrant labour market in 2006: First results from Canada's labour force survey. The Immigrant Labour Force Analysis Series. *Research Paper.* Catalogue no. 71-606-XIE2007001. Ottawa: Statistics Canada.

Critical Thinking Questions

1. How does the article challenge the old adage, "If a person works hard enough they will be successful?"
2. In addition to the issues presented in the paper, many newcomer immigrants are not aware that their professional degrees may not be recognized in Canada until they have landed. What are the implications of this? And does this point influence your answer to the previous question?

PART 12

Chapter 34

Aboriginal People, Resilience and the Residential School Legacy

MADELEINE DION STOUT AND GREGORY KIPLING

In the summer of 2011, a historical event took place in Canada. Stephen Harper, the current Prime Minister of Canada, made a national apology on behalf of the Canadian government to Indigenous peoples who were students in the Residential School Programs, programs which were founded upon "killing the Indian in the child." These schools were often physically, socially, and sexually abusive, which has had implications for the generations following. To access Harper's full apology, see http://www.cbc.ca/news/canada/story/2008/06/11/pm-statement.html. Despite this public recognition, many Canadians have little knowledge of what Residential Schools were, what impact they had, and continue to have, on Indigenous peoples. The following article is a small excerpt adapted from the Aboriginal Healing Foundation Research Series, which was set in place to record the experiences of students, staff, and others, within Residential Schools. Many accounts acknowledge abuses, overt racism, and harsh assimilation practices. While these accounts are often harrowing, they offer insights into many of the difficulties Indigenous peoples continue to face.

1. What effect did the implementation of Residential Schools have on survivors? Their families? Social networks? Communities? Future generations?

RESILIENCE AND THE RESIDENTIAL SCHOOL EXPERIENCE

Many thousands of **Aboriginal** children were taken from their homes and placed in the **residential school** system over the past 100 years. As recently as 1991 and more than a decade after most of the schools had closed their doors, 13 per cent of the country's Aboriginal population were residential school Survivors (DIAND, 1998). While figures such as these give one an idea of how many lives have been touched by the

residential school Legacy, they cannot begin to capture the physical, psychological, spiritual and cultural harm the schools inflicted on Survivors, their families and communities.

However, despite evidence of a link between residential school attendance and all manner of negative life outcomes, including elevated rates of suicide, substance abuse and poor physical health (Deiter, 1999), there are also many Survivors whose resilience has allowed them to achieve remarkable happiness and success in their adult lives. Their stories, along with those of many others who resisted the assimilative

Source: Stout, Madeleine Dion and Gregory Kipling. *Aboriginal People, Resilience and the Residential School Legacy.* Ottawa, ON: Aboriginal Healing Foundation, 2003. Reproduced with Permission of the Aboriginal Healing Foundation.

practices imposed on them by school authorities, provide the focus for discussion in the following pages. First, however, a brief history of the residential school system is warranted.

Residential School System in Context

Although the pain and suffering endured by generations of Aboriginal children in the residential school system is shocking by any measure, their experiences cannot be divorced from the wider logic underlying origins and subsequent evolution of the schools. In effect, these origins lie in the very earliest days of European colonization of North America.

Even as diseases brought by the settlers decimated Aboriginal communities, with some researchers suggesting that close to 90 per cent of the continent's original population died as a direct or indirect result of contact (Culture and Mental Health Research Unit, 2000), various religious orders opened boarding schools in an early attempt to "Christianize" local people. . . .

While the schools were generally unpopular and attracted few students, the religious institutions were not to be dissuaded. Believing that education was the best means of moulding Aboriginal individuals into good Christians with an appreciation for settler mores and values, churches persevered in their efforts, opening the first Indian industrial schools at the beginning of the 19th century (Claes and Clifton, 1998).

By the 1840s, the attempts by the churches to "civilize" Aboriginal people became a matter of official state policy (Claes and Clifton, 1998). This was an era of westward expansion and the government was anxious to prevent any Aboriginal interference with its colonization plans. Subscribing to an ideology that constructed Aboriginal people as backward and savage, government officials believed assimilation was in the population's best interests (1998; Culture and Mental Health Research Unit, 2000). . . .

Faith in the principle of Aboriginal assimilation would guide government interventions to this day. On the one hand, this is seen in the desire to stamp out traditional cultural practices like the potlatch and Sun Dance. On the other hand, the government's treaty-making of the mid-19th century included commitments to provide each First Nation community with its own school (1998). However, these promises were not kept, with the government choosing to commit itself instead to a system of church-operated residential schooling in which Aboriginal children were given an education while being protected from their parents' "backward" influence (Culture and Mental Health Research Unit, 2000).

. . . Thus, while 11 such schools were operating in 1880, by 1896, the number had risen to 45 (Claes and Clifton, 1998).

The 1884 amendments to the Indian Act served as a particularly important impetus for growth. On the one hand, they made boarding school attendance mandatory for Native children under 16 years of age. On the other hand, the revised Act gave authorities the power to arrest, transport and detain children at school, while parents who refused to cooperate faced fines and imprisonment (Claes and Clifton, 1998).

Despite their claim to offer an education to Aboriginal children, industrial schools generally reserved only half days to academic subjects and the rest of the time was devoted to religious instruction and the development of vocational skills. Moreover, because the suppression of Aboriginal cultures was a priority of first order, the schools were characterized by a disciplinary regime that restricted interaction with family members, prohibited the use of Aboriginal languages and denigrated all aspects of Aboriginal life and customs (Claes and Clifton, 1998).

. . .

. . . By 1930, 75 per cent of First Nations children between the ages of 7 and 15 years were enrolled in one of 80 such schools across the country and in the 1940s, attendance was expanded to include Inuit children as well. . . .

PART 13

However, the ability of residential schools to fill classrooms was not matched by a similar success in giving students a decent education. For example, of approximately nine thousand Aboriginal children enrolled in the system in 1945, "only slightly more than 100 are beyond grade 8, and none beyond grade 9" (Claes and Clifton, 1998:13). . . .

While some Aboriginal students were enrolled in secular day schools as early as 1951, many children, particularly those from isolated communities, remained in the residential school system because no alternative was available. With time, however, more and more Aboriginal children gained access to provincial day schools. By 1969, the year the federal government ended church partnerships and assumed direct control of residential schools, 60 per cent of First Nations students were enrolled in provincial school systems (Claes and Clifton, 1998).

. . . [T]he last federally-run residential school closed its doors in Saskatchewan in 1996 (Indian and Northern Affairs Canada, n.d.).

. . . Aboriginal people across the country have paid a high price, both individually and collectively, for the government's misguided experiment in cultural assimilation.

Impact on Individuals

. . . Although some former residential school students have described their experiences in favourable terms, citing the useful skills and positive attitudes they learned, it is far more common to hear stories of loneliness, harsh discipline and abuse.

For many Survivors, the first trauma they endured was the sudden separation from their parents and family. Leaving behind the familiar world in which they had been raised, children suddenly found themselves far from home, confronting a new culture, language and role expectations without any support whatsoever. Furthermore, the deliberate policy of establishing industrial schools far from the home communities of students only served to reinforce their isolation, as did the active discouragement by school officials of contact between children and their parents.

However, the physical separation of students and their families was merely the first step in a more generalized attempt to sever any connection children had with their culture and history. . . .

In effect, students were made to feel ashamed of their ancestry, while teachers and other authority figures constantly sought to reinforce the innate superiority of "white" society and values. On the one hand, this indoctrination involved the devaluing of parents and all aspects of Aboriginal culture. On the other hand, schools attempted to disconnect children from their background by prohibiting communication in an Aboriginal language. A variety of punishments were reserved for those who failed to observe this rule, ranging from beatings to the shaving of one's head.

Indeed, the enforcement of a disciplinary regime where even minor transgressions were met with verbal, physical or sexual assault is one of the most shocking aspects of the residential school system. Characterizing this regime as one that was frequently severe and even abusive, Miller (1996) documents cases of children being beaten, confined in dark closets, sexual assaulted or forced to remain kneeling with arms outstretched for a prolonged period of time.

While the most severe punishments were usually reserved for children who attempted to run away (Miller, 1996), the capricious nature of the discipline administered in residential schools contributed to a generalized climate of fear within the student body. . . .

When one considers these abuses alongside the fact that residential schools were often characterized by an extremely high incidence of tuberculosis-related mortality among the children, it is understandable why many Survivors feel they were robbed of their childhood. Further contributing to this sense were the extensive work duties children had to fulfill. . . .

Given the discussion in preceding pages, it comes as no surprise that former residential school students rate their school years as significantly less happy than their non-residential counterparts (Claes and Clifton, 1998). . . .

. . . For example, many Survivors reported symptoms reminiscent of post-traumatic stress disorder, including nightmares, sleep problems, blackouts, apathy and depression.

Moreover, many also indicated that they found it difficult to relate to others as they were less loving, fearful of being touched and more likely to resort to violence or misdirect their anger towards loved ones. Others reported low self-esteem, feeling alienated from their parents and communities, ashamed of their Aboriginal heritage and consumed by anger and guilt (Claes and Clifton, 1998).

The impact of residential school is also seen in the destructive patterns of behaviour adopted by many Survivors. These range from an inability to say "no" and always putting oneself last to alcoholism, compulsive gambling and substance abuse (1998; Knockwood, 1992). Furthermore, researchers also point to the high incidence of sexual problems among former students of residential schools, including cases of sexual abuse and incest (Claes and Clifton, 1998).

However, perhaps the most telling legacy of the residential school system is the frequency with which Survivors have died an early death. This is seen not only in the high incidence of suicide, but also in the large number of deaths due to violence or alcohol-related causes (1998). . . .

Impact on Families

Like a pebble dropped in a pond, the effects of trauma tend to ripple outwards from victims to touch all those who surround them, whether parents, spouses, children or friends. There is ample evidence to support this view among residential school Survivors, where the consequences of emotional, physical and sexual abuse continue to be felt in each subsequent generation.

. . . Forced to accept their children's removal from the home under threat of legal action, parents were devastated by the separation and all the more so when they knew their children were likely to experience abusive treatment at the hands of school officials. Further suffering was inflicted because of the lack of subsequent contact with sons or daughters. Indeed, in some cases children became sick and died while attending a residential school, yet the parents never received any notification to this effect, only finding out when the child failed to return home at the appointed time (Claes and Clifton, 1998).

. . .

Furthermore, many former students indicate that their confinement in the residential school system has left them ill-prepared to become parents in their own right. Raised in an institutional setting characterized by rigidity, authoritarianism and lack of emotional support, Survivors report problems such as difficulty showing affection to their children or use of harsh discipline methods. At the same time, former students also express regret that they never had the chance to learn child-rearing techniques from their parents, leaving them without a strong base of knowledge as they raise children of their own. . . .

. . . [S]everal writers have noted how dysfunctional patterns of behaviour may be seen in the adult children of former students, leading them to conclude that: "native child-rearing patterns have been indelibly marked by residential schools in ways that will last for generations" (Claes and Clifton, 1998:43).

Impact on Communities

Despite the fact that abuses committed at residential schools were directed towards specific individuals, one must not forget that they were part of a larger project to suppress Aboriginal culture and identity in its entirety. Although this effort was not successful, Aboriginal communities continue to feel the impact of what some

PART 13

call attempted "cultural genocide" (Claes and Clifton, 1998).

Most evident among these effects is the loss of connectedness with Aboriginal languages and traditions. With several generations of children having grown up in a setting where any manifestation of Aboriginality was disparaged and devalued, it is scarcely surprising that the cultures and languages of many communities are now under severe threat. The implications of this state of affairs for community members are far-reaching. As one observer puts it:

> If people suddenly lose their 'prime symbol', the basis of their culture, their lives lose meaning. They become disoriented, with no hope. A social disorganization often follows such a loss, they are often unable to [e]nsure their own survival ... The loss of human suffering of those whose culture has been healthy and is suddenly attacked and disintegrated are incalculable (Claes and Clifton, 1998:38).

However, Aboriginal people are dealing not only with the harm done to their linguistic and cultural traditions, but also with a legacy of widespread sexual and physical abuse within the residential school system. Taken together, these issues have contributed to the development of serious social problems in some communities, including a lack of initiative, dependency on others and high rates of alcoholism and communal violence (Furniss, 1995).

While these problems are reinforced by the racist attitudes that continue to permeate Canadian society, they have also developed a self-perpetuating logic of their own: the existence of social pathologies has become an obstacle in the way of effective communal healing efforts.

Still, there are reasons to be hopeful, particularly when one considers study findings that show confinement in a residential school has, in fact, strengthened rather than weakened a sense of Aboriginal identity in some individuals (Furniss, 1995). . . .

At a more general level, communities have found strength in another unanticipated residential school impact; namely, the friendships and alliances built among students from different communities, nations and people. . . .

. . .

Life at School: Resistance and Coping Strategies

When discussing patterns of abuse, neglect and cultural domination within the residential school system, it is important to remember that the children attending these schools were not only victims, but also agents who consciously implemented strategies and tactics to cope with the difficult circumstances in which they found themselves. . . . Although some coping strategies were clearly self-destructive, many of those cited by Survivors are more akin to the flexible, problem-solving behaviours that Gilgun (1999) considers to be the hallmarks of a resilient individual.

This assessment is underscored in a 1994 Assembly of First Nations report, which argues that although children attending residential school were in a vulnerable position, they were not powerless. Among the coping strategies cited were the cultivation of a sense of solidarity among the children, refusing to inform on other students, speaking their language surreptitiously and protecting smaller children. In this way, children coped with the residential school experience by creating and maintaining their own world from which others were excluded. . . .

REFERENCES

Claes, R. and D. Clifton (1998). *Needs and expectations for redress of victims of abuse at residential schools*. Ottawa: Law Commission of Canada.

Culture and Mental Health Research Unit (2000). The mental health of Indigenous peoples. In L. Kirmayer, M. Macdonald and G. Brass (eds.).

Proceedings of the Advanced Study Institute, McGill Summer Program in Social and Cultural Psychiatry and the Aboriginal Mental Health Research Team, 29–31 May 2000. Montreal: Advanced Studies Institute. Retrieved 20 August 2002 from: http://www.mcgill.ca/psychiatry/transcultural/pdf/Report10.pdf.

Deiter, C. (1999). *From our mothers' arms: The intergenerational impact of residential schools in Saskatchewan.* Toronto: United Church Publishing House.

Department of Indian Affairs and Northern Development (DIAND) (1998). *Indian residential schools (IRS) Data Project.* Ottawa: DIAND.

Furniss, E. (1995). *Victims of benevolence: The dark legacy of the Williams Lake Residential School.* Vancouver: Arsenal Pulp Press.

Gilgun, J. (1999). Mapping resilience as process among adults with childhood adversities. In H. McCubbin, E. Thompson, A. Thompson and J. Futrell (eds.). *The dynamics of resilient families.* Thousand Oaks: Sage, 41–70.

Indian and Northern Affairs Canada (n.d.). *Backgrounder: The residential school system.* Retrieved 21 August 2002 from: http://www.ainc-inac.gc.ca/gs/schl_e.html.

Miller, J. R. (1996). *Shingwauk's vision: A history of native residential schools.* Toronto: U of T Press.

Critical Thinking Questions

1. Why did the government and churches seek to assimilate Indigenous peoples? Why did they fail?
2. Aboriginal people, their communities, and advocates say Residential Schools were like a cultural genocide that has led to social problems, powerlessness, and difficult conditions that we see today in Canada. Please discuss.
3. Is it surprising that educational attainment among First Nations, Métis, and Inuit is so low, given the Residential School experience?

PART 13

Chapter 35

Stolen Sisters, Second Class Citizens, Poor Health: The Legacy of Colonization in Canada

WENDEE KUBIK, CARRIE BOURASSA, AND MARY HAMPTON

Building upon the background provided by Chapter 34 (Stout and Kipling), this article reveals that while Residential Schools and overt assimilation processes have formally ended, the consequences and remnants of those processes still persist. In particular, the most vulnerable of Indigenous peoples, the women, are most harshly marginalized. Often it can be difficult to understand the implications and consequences of widespread forced assimilation and discrimination. This article will help you to understand those consequences in a tangible way through examining how Indigenous women are perceived and treated.

1. How does colonialism continue to impact Indigenous peoples and, in particular, Indigenous women?

MULTIPLE SOCIAL STRESSES, ECONOMIC, AND POLITICAL BARRIERS

Compared to their grandmothers, contemporary women have experienced remarkable improvements in their lives, particularly in literacy and education. However, many women around the world have experienced an absolute decline in their quality of life. The global gap between rich and poor has widened (UN 2000) and women remain the poorest of the poor. Women still experience a wage gap[1] and are typically paid less than men for their labour. Even today, the nature of women's participation in the waged labour force is shaped by factors such as marriage, reproductive rights and the expectation that women have primarily responsibility for family care (Seager 2003, p. 66). Overall, women work more hours each day than men, rest less, and perform a greater variety of tasks (Seager 2003:70). Women, because of their sex and gender, have different experiences than men as workers, parents and as members of their families and communities. These differences affect their health and well being in different ways than men and has led to a general awareness among researchers that gender is a determinant of health (Kaufert 2005).

Aboriginal women, however, are doubly marginalized. First, because they are Aboriginal and second because they are women, they experience a lesser status than men. Cora Voyageur (2000, p. 82) notes that some sociologists refer to this as "multiple jeopardy" because **colonialism** has created multiple economic, social and political barriers both within Aboriginal and outside Aboriginal communities. Aboriginal women

Source: Kubik, Wendee, Carrie Bourassa, and Mary Hampton. "Stolen Sisters, Second Class Citizens, Poor Health: The Legacy of Colonization in Canada." *Humanity and Society* 33 (February/May 2009): 18–34. Used with permission from the Association for Humanist Sociology, Inc.

have lower incomes, less formal education, poorer housing, lower health status and a greater chance of becoming lone parents. Indeed, when looking at the impact of racism, sexism and colonization on Aboriginal women, gaps exist between Aboriginal women and Aboriginal men as well as non-Aboriginal men and women, but also among and between Aboriginal women themselves. For example, Métis women are more likely to be employed than status Indian[2] women, but less likely than non-Aboriginal women (Saskatchewan Women's Secretariat 1999).

The two historic policies that particularly affected Aboriginal women negatively were the dispossession of Aboriginal women who married outside their communities and the removal of children to be educated in residential schools. The federal government in Canada would also use colonial policy, legislation and religion (via missionaries) to oppress Aboriginal women in ways that did not apply to men. Historically, in traditional Indian communities, women were removed from their roles as advisers and respected community members. Voyageur (2000) states that "Indian women and their egalitarian system were replaced by a male-dominated hierarchical system at the behest of Jesuit missionaries [and] in return, Indian men were given authority and social standing" (p. 82). As the Canadian Research Institute for the Advancement of Women (CRIAW) notes, "racism and sexism combine to produce more economic inequalities for racialized women than experienced by either white women or racialized men (2000, p. 4).

Today, Aboriginal women face the highest poverty and violence rates in Canada. Statistics Canada (2006, p. 195) data suggest that violence in marriages and common-law unions is a reality that many Aboriginal women face. Twenty-four percent of Aboriginal women, three times the figure for their non-Aboriginal counterparts (8%), experienced spousal violence from either a current or previous marital or common-law

partner in the five-year period prior to the survey. Aboriginal women are also twice as likely (36%) as other women (17%) to experience emotional abuse from either a current or previous marital or common-law partner.

In addition, status Indian women are five times as likely as non-Aboriginal women to be non-participants in the labour force, and Indian women have lower and less equitably distributed incomes than registered Indian and other Aboriginal men (Hull 2001). The income of other Aboriginal women (Inuit, Métis, non-status Indians) is "less favourable than Aboriginal men and much less favourable than non-Aboriginals" (Hull 2001, p. 57). Overall, the health status of Aboriginal women is lower than that of Aboriginal men and non-Aboriginal men and womens. Low income and social status as well as exposure to violence are among the major factors that contribute to the low health status of Aboriginal women.

A study conducted by the Saskatchewan Women's Secretariat (1999) notes: "Studies have shown that health differences are reduced when economic and status differences between people, based on things such as culture, race, age, gender and disability are reduced" (p. 44). Indeed, a more recent study undertaken by the Prairie Women's Health Centre of Excellence (2004) in Manitoba noted Aboriginal women have lower life expectancy, elevated mortality and morbidity rates and elevated suicide rates in comparison to non-Aboriginal women. However, Aboriginal women's poor health status can be truly understood in the context of a range of health determinants, including socio-economic status, education and employment conditions, social support networks, physical environments, healthy child development and access to health services.

Violence against women, often ignored on the grounds that it is a private matter, is one of the constants faced by women around the world regardless of race, class, or age. Rape is often underreported because of the stigma attached

PART 13

to victim (Seager 2003). Moreover, the fear of rape influences and constricts women's behaviour. A factor that leads to sexual victimization of First Nation women is the continued dominance of negative stereotypes of First Nations women as "squaw," "princess," or "sexually promiscuous" which were historically perpetuated by European colonizers (LaRocque 2005; Maltz and Archambault 1995). Media stereotypes continue to dominate images of Aboriginal women; prairie women in particular suffer from a negative stereotype (McLean 1970; Steckley 1999). Martin-Hill (2003) states that the media disseminates the ideology of the subservient and sexually available Aboriginal women leading to the internalization of colonial stereotypes and offers a cultural justification of sexual violence against Aboriginal women.

Victims of sexual assault suffer psychological, physical, and behavioural consequences that have long-term impact on women's health and well-being. Research conducted cross-culturally suggests that women of "minority" ethnic status are more vulnerable to sexual victimization than Caucasian women (Howard and Wang 2005; Koss 1993). In addition to sexual victimization, research suggests that gender-based violence is a learned behaviour, linked to male power, privilege and dominance in the family and society (Tolman 1999).

Recent research conducted in a Canadian urban setting found adolescent girls who identify as First Nations or Métis report higher rates of sexual victimization than non-Aboriginal adolescent girls (Hampton et al. 2002). Identifying as Aboriginal increased the odds of physically forced intercourse by 2.59 times. There was a significant difference between Métis youth and Non-Aboriginal youth with young Métis females at an increased risk for physically forced intercourse in high school settings. Almost half of the female participants (45.1%) reported that they didn't want to have sex the first time. Aboriginal females were 3.12 times more likely than Aboriginal males to report ever having had sex against their will at first intercourse. These results suggest that young Aboriginal females today in both high school and community settings suffer from sexual violence at higher rates than non-Aboriginal youth and Aboriginal males. These results can be interpreted as continued evidence of multiple oppressions as a result of colonialism (Hampton et al. 2002:201).

In Canada, the mortality rate due to violence for Aboriginal women is three times the rate experienced by of all other Canadian women. Aboriginal women with status under the Indian Act and who are between the ages of 25 and 44 are five times more likely to experience a violent death than other Canadian women in the same age category (Indian and Northern Affairs Canada 1996).

The legacy of colonization is apparent in a myriad of ways: socially, economically, culturally and politically. Poverty and poor health are embedded in a social structure that has deep colonial roots. Women's status was changed within the family because they played domestic roles and were defined as men's (Tuhiwai Smith 2002). Aboriginal women have poorer health outcomes than both Aboriginal men and non-Aboriginal men and women. In fact, women who have experienced physical or sexual abuse, as children or adults, are at greater risk of health problems, such as injury, chronic pain, gastrointestinal disorders, anxiety and clinical depression. Violence also undermines health by increasing self-destructive behaviors, such as smoking and substance abuse. The influence of abuse can persist long after the abuse has stopped. Over their lifetimes, survivors of abuse average more surgeries, physician and pharmacy visits, hospital stays and mental health consultations than other women even after accounting for other factors affecting health care use and discounting emergency room visits (CRIAW 2002). In addition, life expectancy for Aboriginal women is 76.2 years compared to 81.0 for non-Aboriginal women. Aboriginal women experience higher rates of circulatory problems, respiratory problems, diabetes, hypertension and cancer of the cervix than the rest of the general female population. Women who are the victims of family dysfunction and violence often turn to alcohol or substance abuse. Hospital admissions for alcohol related accidents are three times higher among Aboriginal females than they are for the general Canadian population (NWAC 2002).

SISTERS IN SPIRIT AND STOLEN SISTERS

The Native Women's Association of Canada (NWAC)[3] and other advocacy organizations have long spoken out against this "epidemic" of violence against Aboriginal women and children. Moreover, the level of violence against Aboriginal women is significantly higher than that experienced by other women. Stolen Sisters: A Human Rights Response to Discrimination and Violence Against Indigenous Women in Canada (Amnesty International 2004) tells the stories of Aboriginal women and girls who have gone missing or who have been killed in Canada.

The Report notes that violence towards Aboriginal women is often met with official indifference and systematic prejudice by police forces, government and society in general.. The result is many of the disappearances and murders of Native women and girls go unsolved and are forgotten.

In March 2004, NWAC launched the Sisters in Spirit (SIS) campaign (http://www.sistersin spirit.ca/) to raise awareness of the extremely high rates of violence perpetrated against Aboriginal women in Canada. NWAC has estimated more than 500 Aboriginal women have gone missing in the last 20 years. Data from Indian and Northern Affairs (1996) support this claim, noting that Aboriginal women with status were five times more likely to die as a result of violence than any other group in Canada.

The apparent widespread indifference to the welfare and safety of Aboriginal women has spurred families and non-governmental organizations working on their behalf, to bring these issues before the police, media and government officials. A number of high profile cases of assaulted, missing or murdered Aboriginal women and girls have also helped focus greater public attention on the violence Aboriginal women face. The Robert Pickton case in Vancouver and the large number of deaths and disappearances along Northern British Columbia's Highway 16 are grisly proof that a proportionally larger number of Aboriginal women as compared to non-Aboriginal women were among the missing and dead. Robert Pickton, the former Port Coquitlam pig farmer, has been charged with the first-degree murder of 27 women who have gone missing from Vancouver's Downtown Eastside. More than 60 women from the city's downtown eastside have been reported missing over the last two decades (Matas and Fong 2005). Many of the women were sex workers and drug addicts working in one of the city's toughest and poorest neighbourhoods. Amnesty International notes that 16 of the missing women are Indigenous, a number far in excess of the proportion of Indigenous women living in Vancouver (Amnesty International 2004: 23).

Highway 16, a 500 mile stretch of highway in northern British Columbia, became notorious during the 1990s and has been renamed the "Highway of Tears" because of the deaths and disappearances of more than 32 women and girls. Most of these deaths or disappearances have gone unsolved. In November 2005, a "Take back the Highway" demonstration organized by NWAC was held where hundreds of women, men and children, Native and non-Native Native prayed, sang, danced and marched along the highway to bring recognition to the lost women.

In Canada today, many Aboriginal women are exploited by Indigenous and non-Indigenous men and extreme acts of brutality are often perpetrated against these women. Because of the historical (and continuing) racism, sexism and discrimination, Aboriginal women have entered a cycle of poverty that is very difficult to

PART 13

escape. Struggling with poverty, many women are forced to work in the sex trade to provide for themselves and their families. Women in the sex trade are entitled to protection and the same human rights as everyone else. International human rights treaties have been signed and committed to by numerous countries around the world (including Canada). NWAC and Amnesty note that many times acts of violence against Aboriginal women may be carried out in the expectation that societal indifference to the welfare and safety of women will allow the perpetrators to escape justice.

NOTES

1. The wage gap is the difference in earning between women and men. It is measured by a ratio that compares average earnings for women and men who have worked full-time or a full-year.
2. Indian is the legal and historical term, however, First Nations is a term that is emerging from Canada's First Peoples and we will endeavor to be respectful in the use of the term(s).
3. The Native Women's Association of Canada (NWAC) is an aggregate of organizations of representing and advocating on behalf of First Nations and Métis women in Canada.

REFERENCES

Amnesty International. 2004. Stolen Sisters: A Human Rights Response to Discrimination and Violence against Indigenous Women in Canada. Retrieved November 4, 2005. (http://www.amnesty.ca/campaigns/sisters_overview.php).

Canadian Research Institute for the Advancement of Women. 2002. CRIAW fact sheet, "Women's experience of racism: How race and gender interact." Retrieved January 27 2005. (http://www.criaw-icref.ca/factSheets/Race%20and%20Gender/racegender _e.htm).

Hampton, Mary R. and Bonnie Jeffery, Barb McWatter, Sheri Farrell-Racette, Kim McNabb and Lyndsay. Foster. 2002. "Strengthening and Building Sexual Health of Aboriginal Youth and Young Adults." Retrieved November 4, 2005. (http://uregina.ca/hamptoma).

Howard, Donna E. and Min Qi Wang. 2005. "Psychosocial Correlates of US Adolescents Who Report a History of Forced Sexual Intercourse." *Journal of Adolescent Health* 36: 372–379.

Hull, Jeremy. 2001. "Aboriginal People and Social Classes in Manitoba." Winnipeg: CCPA—Manitoba. Retrieved January 27, 2006. (http://www.policyalternatives.ca/mb).

Indian and Northern Affairs Canada. 2007. *Report of the Ministerial Representative Matrimonial Real Property Issues On-Reserve.* Ottawa: Indian and Northern Affairs Canada.

Kaufert, Patricia. 2005. *Gender as a Determinant of Health: A Canadian Perspective.* Health Canada. Ottawa: Health Canada.

Koss, Mary P. 1993. "Detecting the Scope of Rape: A Review of Prevalence Research Methods." *Journal of Interpersonal Violence* 8: 98–112.

Maltz, Daniel and JoAllyn Archambault. 1995. "Gender and power in Native North America." Pp. 230–249 in *Women and Power in Native North America,* edited by L. F. Klein & L. A. Ackerman Norman: University of Oklahoma Press.

Martin-Hill, Dawn. 2003. "She No Speaks and Other Colonial Constructs of 'The Traditional Woman'." Pp. 16–120 in *Women of the First Nations: Power, Wisdom and Strength* edited by C. Miller & P. Chuchryk. Winnipeg, MB: University of Manitoba Press.

Matas, Robert and Petti Fong. 2005. "'27' Robert PicktonNow Stands Accused of 27 Counts of Murder After 12 New Charges were Laid Against Him in the Disappearance of Women From Vancouver's Downtown Eastside" *Globe and Mail,* May 26, 1A.

McLean, John. 1970. *The Indians of Canada: Their Manners and Customs.* Toronto, ON: Coles Publishing.

Royal Commission on Aboriginal Peoples. 1996, online version. Retrieved January 27, 2006. (http://www.ainc-inac.gc.ca/ch/rcap).

Saskatchewan Women's Secretariat. 1999. *Profile of Aboriginal Women in Saskatchewan.* Regina SK: Saskatchewan Women's Secretariat.

Seager, Joni 2003. *The Penguin Atlas of Women in the World.* New York: Penguin Books.

Sisters in Spirit. Online. Retrieved May 4, 2006. (http://www.sistersinspirit.ca).

Steckley, John. 1999. *Beyond Their Years: Five Native Women's Stories.* Toronto, ON: Canadian Scholars' Press.

Tolman, Deborah L. 1999. "Female Adolescent Sexuality in Relational Context: Beyond Sexual Decision Making." Pp. 227–247 in *Beyond Appearance: A New Look at Adolescent Girls* edited by

N. G. Johnson and M. C. Roberts. Washington, D.C.: American Psychological Association.

Tuhiwai Smith, Linda. 2002. *Decolonizing Methodologies: Research and Indigenous Peoples.* New York: Zed Books Ltd.

Voyageur, Cora 2000. "Contemporary Aboriginal Women in Canada." Pp. 81–106 in *Visions of the Heart: Canadian Aboriginal Issues* edited by D. Long and O. P. Dickason. Toronto: Harcourt Canada.

Critical Thinking Questions

1. Some may say that status quo stereotypes of Indigenous women continue to persist in Canada. If so, what are the consequence of this and how may this create inequality?

2. Looking back to the Oreopoulos article (Chapter 33), how do the barriers and inequalities that Indigenous women face compare with the Canadian ideal that "anyone can succeed if they work hard enough?"

PART 13

Chapter 36

Aboriginal Well-Being: Canada's Continuing Challenge

JERRY WHITE AND DAN BEAVON

You have likely read a news report suggesting that Canada has consistently scored at or near the top of the United Nation's Human Development Index. Such a result suggests that Canada is a great place to live. But suppose that the standard of living here deteriorated so that Canada fell from the top of the list to, say, 48th in the world. Would that be a cause for concern? Of course it would! This selection about Aboriginal well-being in Canada discusses how Aboriginal peoples have a much lower standard of living, have lower educational attainment, and suffer a host of inequalities in comparison to other peoples in Canada. This selection demonstrates, using the very same measure that suggests that the standard of living in Canada (generally) is so high, that a clearly identifiable segment of the Canadian population—Registered Indians—are currently ranked 48th in the world. It also suggests that if this inequality persists it will undermine every Canadian's standard of living; it may lead to social unrest, and tear at the fabric of this country. The authors argue that we cannot afford to shut our eyes to the problems any longer.

1. What is relative deprivation, and how does it impact society? Is it important to address this relative disadvantage directly? If so, how?
2. How do conditions for Aboriginal peoples in Canada compare to non-Aboriginal Canadians? Do these differences create problems and impact society?
3. Is it reasonable that a group in Canada can have a common experience of disadvantage?

Canada was founded on the principles of peace, order and good government.[1] It would be fair to say that most Canadians view our society as peaceful, civil, and just. As Canadians, we are often shocked or dismayed when we see civil unrest in other countries, particularly when police or military force are used against civil populations in order to quell popular uprisings or to restore order. When we see such events unfolding in the news, we breathe a collective sigh of relief and count our blessings that we live where we do. However, it may be that our collective memories are quite short and our knowledge of history quite limited because police forces and the military have intervened thousands of times against many different segments of civil society in Canada. Some of these interventions have been against protestors (e.g., the police action during 1997 Asia-Pacific Economic Cooperation summit meeting in Vancouver),

Source: White, J. and D. Beavon. *Aboriginal Well-Being: Canada's Continuing Challenge*. Toronto: Thompson Educational Publishers, 2007. Reproduced with permission.

unruly sports fans (e.g., the 1955 Rocket Richard riot in Montreal), unions (e.g., the 1919 Winnipeg general strike), and sometimes against Aboriginal peoples.

Some of the more recent and notable police and military interventions against Aboriginal peoples would include: **Oka** (1990), **Gustafsen Lake** (1995), and **Ipperwash** (1995).

The Oka crisis of 1990[2] is particularly noteworthy because it represents the last time in Canadian history that the military was used against a segment of civil society.[3] The Oka crisis resulted in the death of Sûreté du Québec Corporal Marcel Lemay and it led to the Royal Commission on Aboriginal Peoples.[4] The Gustafsen Lake siege represented the largest paramilitary operation in the history of British Columbia,[5] and the incident at Ipperwash resulted in the death of Aboriginal protestor Dudley George.

Usually these police and military interventions are the result of Aboriginal occupations and protests. As the Ipperwash inquiry noted (Linden, 2007, p. 15):

> Aboriginal occupations and protests can be large or small, short or long, peaceful or violent. They occur in urban areas, rural areas, and in the remote north. . . . The immediate catalyst for most major occupations and protests is a dispute over a land claim, a burial site, resource development, or harvesting, hunting and fishing rights. The fundamental conflict, however, is usually about land.

Aboriginal occupations and protests are quite common and the vast majority of these events are resolved peacefully, without violence or property damage.[6] Many of these incidents, however, garner considerable media coverage, especially when these events expose major fault lines within Canadian society. For example, the Burnt Church crisis of 1999 and 2000 resulted in angry non-Aboriginal fishermen damaging and destroying a number of Mi'kmaq lobster traps. The local Mi'kmaq retaliated by destroying non-Aboriginal fishing boats and buildings. The Caledonia dispute (2006 and on-going at press time) has been the catalyst for several confrontations between Aboriginal protestors, local non-Aboriginal residents, and the Ontario Provincial Police. While such incidents make for good news stories, they often expose the underlying racist underbelly that still permeates some segments of Canadian society. While many critics may question the economic effectiveness of Aboriginal occupations and protests, they clearly do not understand the intrinsic value that Aboriginal peoples place on their traditional lands and how this attachment is integral to their culture and identity (Burrows, 2005).

While Aboriginal occupations of land will continue in the foreseeable future, Canadians witnessed an entirely new type of Aboriginal protest on June 29, 2007. On this date, the **Assembly of First Nations (AFN)** organized a National Day of Action. This one-day event was part of a broader strategy of the AFN, launched in the fall of 2006 to create awareness of First Nations issues; more specifically, it was a call for action against poverty.[7] This book deals with this same issue, not from an advocacy or political viewpoint, but from an empirical and scientific perspective.

The "Make Poverty History for First Nations" campaign was initiated to highlight the struggles facing First Nations people and communities. The "National Day of Action" was unique for several reasons.

First, the event was one of the largest rallies in Canadian history based on the sheer number of events and locations across the country.

Second, the event was peaceful. There was considerable tension before the event, and some in the media and less sympathetic groups were anticipating confrontations between the Aboriginal peoples and the general public or police. But many of the anticipated tensions were reduced prior to the event through a series of actions. Minister Prentice made a major announcement for an action plan to reform and speed up the specific

PART 13

claims process. The slow pace with which specific claims were resolved has often created tensions between many First Nations and the government. He also defused the threat of blockades at one potential hot spot, by conferring official reserve status to 75 acres of land recently purchased by the Roseau River First Nation in Manitoba. AFN Grand Chief Phil Fontaine also did his part to calm the waters. He repeatedly urged Aboriginal people to make the Day of Action a peaceful demonstration aimed at generating public awareness of, and support for, Aboriginal issues. Chief Fontaine also signed a protocol between the AFN and the RCMP that set out ground rules for dealing with any crisis that might occur during the day of action. In summary, the event was so peaceful that it was anticlimactic.

Third, the event was not an occupation of a specific piece of land. In fact, the protest was not really about land at all. What we witnessed was a shift from a *rights-based agenda* (e.g., specific and comprehensive claims, self-determination, self-government, Indian status, membership, citizenship), which have dominated the Aboriginal political landscape over the last thirty years, to a *needs-based agenda*. While all of these latter rights-based issues are important, there is no direct evidence to suggest that the disproportionate attention that has been paid to them has improved the quality of life of Aboriginal people or their communities. That is not to say we will not see improvements coming from these actions, but to date such gains have not been measurable. . . .

Aboriginal issues will clearly present Canada with some of its most complex challenges in the twenty-first century. Will this century be the one where we finally address the issues of poverty, lack of educational attainment, poor health, and social problems that beset Aboriginal peoples? Or, will it be one that replicates the past, maintains the status quo, and condemns the next generation of Aboriginal children to a life of mediocrity, suicides, substance abuse, and poverty?

The National Day of Action reminded us that there is a growing understanding and impatience with respect to the **relative deprivation** that Aboriginal peoples face in Canada. The well-being of the general population far exceeds that of its Aboriginal population. Now instead of turning that inequality into despair and internal violence, it is being channelled outward.

We decided to title this book *Aboriginal Well-being: Canada's Continuing Challenge*. We had even considered calling it *Canada's Shameful Legacy*; however, shame is not what is needed. What is needed is better policies developed from solid research evidence created in partnership with the Aboriginal peoples themselves.

In our 2003 book *Aboriginal Conditions*, we said that "we need to develop better measures of the First Nation communities and tailor our programs and policies to match the reality of the country." In that book we discussed our preliminary attempts to adapt the United Nations Human Development Index (HDI) to the First Nations in Canada (Beavon and Cooke, 2003). We also presented a "Community Capacity Index" which aimed to assess the relative capacity of Aboriginal communities to accept and handle their socio-economic development. As we have repeatedly argued we cannot download programs to communities that have not got the capacity to take them on. It serves no one's interests to dump programs as fast as people can fail at managing them (Maxim and White, 2003).

We also argued that there are real differences between Aboriginal communities. Some are thriving and relatively self-reliant, while others are facing or have suffered virtual collapse. Within many communities there are vast differences in the resources that families have available. In *Aboriginal Conditions* we also presented research on the intra-Aboriginal inequalities that plague the populations. We concluded that we needed better ways of understanding capacity and well-being and that we also needed to develop Canada-wide initiatives that target the intra-Aboriginal differences.

This book is our next generation of models and tools that are developed to give us a better understanding of the levels of development and well-being of the Aboriginal peoples of Canada. Some might ask why we are doing this (see Salée, 2006). We would argue that it is our responsibility, as social scientists, to try and improve our understanding of the world. That in itself is true. However, we have a selfish reason as well. Our own well-being is tied to the well-being of the others who inhabit this great country. In order to keep the high standards of living, level of prosperity, relative social calm, and exceptional living conditions, we have to recognize that there is an important, on-going disadvantage that is experienced by the Aboriginal peoples of Canada. Unless we address this central problem, Aboriginal relative deprivation will lead to the erosion of the well-being of all those living in Canada.

WHAT IS AT STAKE IN THIS RELATIVE DEPRIVATION?

One of the most powerful of human motivators is relative deprivation. Sociologists, have argued that relative differences in well-being and resources, including wealth, are often more important than the absolute differences in determining the perceived quality of life (Gurr, 1970; Griffin, 1988). This means that policies that increase the societal wealth but leave relative inequalities may not actually increase the overall well-being of a country.

An understanding of deprivation develops as people compare themselves to those around them. If the comparison group is reasonable, then people will react to differences. It is not some absolute level that is used in comparisons. Inequalities that remain even as the absolute levels of prosperity increase still lead to group resistance. If we think of a village of subsistence farmers that has only their crops and a small amount of generated income to live on, it may be that they develop a lifestyle where they are happy despite limited resources. If that village

is moved to the outskirts of a big city or is integrated through digital means to the wider world, it will begin to assess its relative position. In this case the villagers will become angry about their circumstances and may begin to protest.

Feeling deprived as an individual differentiates from feeling deprived as a group . . . particularly if there are strong identifiers for that group (see Walker and Smith, 2002). We also know that social identity, social comparison, and understandings of distributive justice are involved in relative deprivation (ibid). These are collective or social theories and when we integrate them with relative deprivation we get what we call integrated relative deprivation theory.

This integrated theory is important because it captures how a group sees itself, how an individual belongs or identifies their place in the group, whether there is or could be any explanation for their similar treatment and whether there is a measure of fairness or lack of fairness in their deprivation.

We have argued in other works (White and Beavon, 2003) that understanding the collective identity of Aboriginal peoples is important. The world today is composed of peoples bound together in groups that share some characteristics that create bonds between them. These groups coalesce for a variety of reasons. More often than not, these bonds of cohesion have some relationship to cultural and physical similarities. Social scientists have spent countless research hours studying these ethnic and racial ties. Ties that bind groups together also create differences with others. These differences between collectivities can often involve the development of hierarchies and inequalities. Socio-economic conditions, sometimes measured and sometimes assumed, are used to rank peoples. The roots of some of the most complex social problems are the differential development of ethnic groups and the social ranking that comes with these variations. Public policy in this era of human development is confronted by these social problems and the set of questions that issue from them.

PART 13

If we look at this racialized and ethnicized understanding of differences in resources and resulting hierarchies and overlay this understanding with an appreciation of the integrated relative deprivation theory we can understand the import of the current situation. Aboriginal people, seeing and experiencing the differences in their lives in comparison with other groups in Canada, will inevitably draw conclusions about their relative worth. At an individual level this can result in a lack of respect for themselves, which leads to intra-group violence and self-abuse (drugs, alcohol, suicide, marital violence, etc.). The individual might blame society and strike out individually against that society (through crime or violence). Most assuredly, over time, the ties that create the collective identity will assert themselves in a collective understanding. Those who share history, culture, territory, and common understandings, who become bound together in groups that share some characteristics that create bonds between them, will assess that they are not treated fairly. Collective response to relative deprivation can become a challenge to the fabric of a country that has multiple collectivities, such as ethnic or racial groups.

This book is about identifying clearly that there is relative deprivation. It is also about wanting to spur us to move forward in dealing with that deprivation.

It was Francis Bacon who argued for an understanding of the world free from theologically distorted realities. We would concur that there should be a drive to develop the most appropriate and accurate assessments of the well-being and development of different peoples as is possible.

. . .

ABORIGINAL CONDITIONS *TODAY*

While many Canadians are aware that the First Nations peoples face certain hardships, they are not aware of the extent of the problems nor how persistent these differences are over time. There was a disturbing indication of this in the results of a poll conducted shortly after The Royal Commission on Aboriginal Peoples Report, which was released in the mid-1990s. In that survey nearly half of the Canadians polled thought that Indian reserves had similar standards of living and well-being as non-Aboriginal communities (Insight Canada, 1996). This is a problem for everyone. Unless we understand the real situation we can never confront it and make real improvements.

In Table 36.1, we summarize some trends that we have observed over the 1981 to 2001 period, comparing some basic indicators between Registered Indians and the Canadian population.

Registered Indian life expectancy improved from 65.7 years in 1981 to 72.9 years in 2001, an increase of 7.2 years, compared with an increase of 3.1 years for the Canadian population. This means that there has been a narrowing of the gap; however, the Registered Indian population remains nearly 6 years behind the Canadian population.

We find that educational attainment also lags behind the Canadian population. While we can see overall improvement for Registered Indians between 1981 and 2001, improvement in educational attainment has not been continuous. In the 1981 to 1991 period there was a narrowing of the gap with the Canadian population in terms of the proportion with high school or higher, whereas in the 1991 to 2001 period the gap actually increased.

The average annual income of both the Registered Indian population and the Canadian population increased over the 1981 to 2001 period. In terms of dollars, there was much less improvement in the average annual income of Registered Indians between 1981 and 2001. The income gap between Registered Indians and other Canadians grew over the entire period, from $9,714 in 1981 to $12,395 in 2001. It is interesting to note that over the twenty-year

TABLE 36.1 COMPARING LEVELS OF DEVELOPMENT: REGISTERED INDIANS IN CANADA AND THE CANADIAN POPULATION

		1981	1991	2001
Life Expectancy at Birth (years)	Registered Indians	65.7	70.6	72.9
	Canadian Population	75.6	77.9	78.7
Proportion Completed High School or Higher[1]	Registered Indians	0.33	0.55	0.57
	Canadian Population	0.60	0.68	0.75
Proportion Completed Grade 9 or Higher[2]	Registered Indians	0.60	0.72	0.83
	Canadian Population	0.80	0.86	0.90
Average Annual Income (2000$)[3]	Registered Indians	6,840	8,243	10,094
	Canadian Population	16,554	20,072	22,489

NOTES:

[1] The proportion completed high school or higher is estimated by the population with a secondary school graduation certificate, some post secondary or trades education, or some university with or without degree, divided by the population aged 19 years and over.

[2] The proportion completed grade 9 or higher is the population aged 15 years and over that has completed grade 9 or higher, divided by the total population aged 15 years and over.

[3] The average annual income is the average income from all sources for the year before the census enumeration, adjusted by the Statistics Canada Consumer Price Index to year 2000 constant dollars (Statistics Canada 2005b).

SOURCES: Statistics Canada Census Data custom tabulations; Statistics Canada 1984, 1990, 1995, 1998, 2005a; Rowe and Norris 1995; Nault et al. 1993; Norris, Kerr, and Nault 1996; DIAND 1998; Verma, Michalowski and Gauvin 2003; Authors' calculations.

period we see a slight improvement in the relative annual income. As a proportion of the Canadian population's average income, the Registered Indian population narrowed the average income gap over the twenty-year period from 0.413 to 0.449, although this proportion decreased slightly from 1981 to 1991, to 0.411.

If we look at labour force participation, we can see the same patterns of disadvantage.

Compared to the non-Aboriginal population, many more Registered Indians have chosen (or been forced) not to seek employment, as reflected in the substantially lower labour force participation rates. As well, of those seeking employment, nearly three times as many Registered Indians are unemployed.

TABLE 36.2 KEY LABOUR MARKET INDICATORS FOR ABORIGINALS AND NON-ABORIGINALS IN CANADA 2001

	NON ABORIGINAL	REGISTERED INDIAN
Not in the labour force	28.0%	42.0%
Unemployed	7.6%	22.4%

SOURCE: Based on the 2001 Census Public Use Microdata File.

We argued above that there is a relative disadvantage for Aboriginal people compared to the Canadian population, and it would appear to us that the patterns of relative disadvantage extend much further than most people understand. In fact, the disadvantage we note here captures only a portion of the issues. For example, we have seen that there is a serious and on-going problem with potable water (Chapters 8 and 9 in White et al., 2006), higher rates of suicide (Chandler and LaLonde, 2004), and high rates of self-reported health problems (Spence, 2007; Chapter 10).

EDUCATIONAL ATTAINMENT: A DETAILED PERSPECTIVE

We generally agree that the development of human capital is very important in the self-actualization of a person. It allows one to choose when and how to integrate into the economic enterprise of the country, region, or community in which one lives, and it also contributes to the production of citizenship.

There is a long scientific tradition in sociology and economics that has established that

PART 13

educational attainment, that is, the acquisition of human capital, is highly correlated with income, wealth, occupational diversity, and a host of other positive outcomes (see Becker, 1964; Coleman, 1988). This relationship has been demonstrated to hold for Aboriginal people as well (Spence et al., 2007; Spence, 2007; White, Maxim, and Spence, 2004; White, Spence, and Maxim, 2005).

If we look closely at the situation for education we see two trends. The Registered Indian population (measured in 2001) has a high school completion rate roughly equal to the rate of non-Aboriginals in 1981; thus, the former are twenty years behind the latter.

When we look at post-secondary education the story is even less positive. The Aboriginal population are at the same levels as the general population was in the 1950s. In fact, we have shown in our research that the gap has been increasing in the last decade (see Hull, 2005). . . . In a knowledge-based economy such as Canada's, this means that the chances for economic integration and higher well-being are going to be reduced as the century moves forward.

We wanted to raise one final disturbing issue. When we look at how Aboriginals, aged 18–29, compare in terms of educational attainment, when compared to a range of other ethnic groups in Canada in 2001, we can see that all Aboriginal groups have much lower rates of high school completion than the other ethnic groups. This indicates to us that there is an exceptional problem facing Aboriginal populations.

This is not the only exceptional problem that faces Aboriginal people. In a study of economic development projects on reserves, by the Strategic Research and Analysis Directorate of Indian and Northern Affairs Canada (INAC), it was found that, compared to the average, it takes between three and four times as long to get businesses developed on reserves.

Scientists and policy-makers have been faced with the on-going problem of understanding the relative levels of human development and predicting the capacity of a community (or nation or people) to develop given the resources they have at their disposal. Those interested in development have long sought to discover techniques for measuring social and economic progress. Even more challenging is trying to pinpoint the weaknesses in the mix of resources in order to increase the likelihood of success.

Despite the fact that Canadian social policy has, for the last half-century, focused on reducing inequalities through the removal of economic barriers, First Nations and other Aboriginal people face serious issues, as we noted in our brief description of the relative deprivation facing Aboriginal people in Canada. . . .

We are calling on Aboriginal and non-Aboriginal leaders, policy-makers, and researchers to make the tough questions part of our dialogue.

Our book raises some very important and controversial issues. Here are a few of them.

We are not saying "spend more" or "spend less." We have no idea whether $8 billion or $16 billion is what is necessary to solve the problems plaguing Aboriginal conditions. We are saying, "let us figure out what is best." What is the proper way to approach the government transfers and claims settlements to communities? We would say that is not clear right now. . . . [T]ransfers are not, on the surface, creating equality between communities, which is what they are supposed to do. They are supposed to make up for the shortfalls experienced by communities that are suffering some disadvantage. This raises two very complex and controversial questions. Should we be subsidizing the "worst-off" communities or stratifying our transfers to reward those that are making gains?

The second question is even more controversial. Are there some communities that are simply not sustainable? As hard a discussion as this would be, it is certainly not one we can avoid forever. The Kasatchewan story most certainly raised the spectre of this issue. Indeed, the suggestion was made to move the community.[8]

The demand for tools to be able to assist all of us, Aboriginal and non-Aboriginal, to make these choices is heartbreakingly obvious. It is not that people are incapable in some individual way; instead, it may be that history has passed some communities by. If we think of non-Aboriginal communities where a natural resource is the driving force behind the local economy, there are cases in which this resource becomes exhausted. The result is that these communities may slowly disappear in the absence of the necessary capacity for long-term sustainability. In the face of climate change, cultural change, and the corresponding change in ways of life in some Aboriginal communities, there may be communities that simply cannot be sustainable, productive, successful places to build families and live one's life.

This whole discussion requires great care. Some Canadians might say, "Why can't Aboriginal people simply move to another town or city if their home community is not working?" We are well aware that this is not the solution. Aboriginal people have a strong attachment to the land, they desire to have proximity to their families and clans, and many hold to the traditions and cultures of their past. Their home communities are part of their identity. This makes simply dispersing as individuals, when troubles increase, a difficult, if not impossible, choice. However, our research indicates that nearly half of all reserve band members (recognized citizens of First Nations communities) live off-reserve in non-Aboriginal towns and cities (see Norris et al., 2003).

We do not know which, if any, of the First Nations and Inuit communities might be unsustainable, but we do know that we must have the tools to supplement our understanding so that we can discuss the problem. *This is an issue that must be debated by Aboriginal people themselves. Solutions can never work if they are imposed.* There must be a widespread buy-in to whatever course of action is decided. Intra-Aboriginal debate would be paralleled by dialogue between the Aboriginal people and the Canadian government.

The foundation of such a debate must be empirical evidence, otherwise we rest on nothing but ideologies and pre-conceived ideas, including prejudice.

NOTES

1. This phrase is often abbreviated as "POGG." These principles form the introduction to section 91 of the *Constitution Act,* 1867.

2. The Oka crisis was the result of a land dispute between the Mohawk community of Kanesatake and the town of Oka in Quebec during the summer of 1990. This crisis was sparked by a decision taken by the Municipality of Oka to extend a nine-hole golf course on land that the Mohawks claimed was, and had always been, theirs. The 39 hectares of land in question included a Native cemetery and parts of a pine forest. Several books provide detailed accounts of the Oka crisis (e.g., MacLaine et al., 1991; Alfred, 1995).

3. During the 65-year period following confederation (1867–1933), Canada's military was engaged 132 times in law enforcement activities in order to restore civil order (Pariseau, 1973; Haslip, 2006). However, since 1933, Canada's military has been used only twice to restore civil order: the October crisis of 1970 and the Oka crisis of 1990. It is interesting to note that the Canadian Army mobilized over 2,000 troops to restore order in Oka, yet during that same summer in 1990, Canada sent slightly less than 1,000 soldiers to fight in Iraq. The Oka crisis drew worldwide attention, catapulting native land rights into the spotlight.

4. This Royal Commission was established in 1991 to address many of the Aboriginal issues that had come to light as a result of the Oka crisis and the failed Meech Lake Accord. The Commission culminated in a final report published in 1996. The final report consisted of five volumes and the 4,000 pages represent the most in-depth study ever undertaken of the historical relations between the Canadian government and Aboriginal peoples.

5. After failed negotiations, 400 tactical assault members of the RCMP, backed by helicopters and armoured personnel carriers supplied by

PART 13

the military, were deployed against the Aboriginal occupants and their supporters. In one particularly tense moment, the RCMP fired thousands of rounds during a 45-minute blaze of gunfire (Steele, 1997).

6. Wilkes (2004) analyzed media reports and noted that there were roughly 100 Aboriginal occupations or protests between 1968 and 2000. Using the same methodology, but different criteria, Clairmont and Potts (2006) found 616 incidents between 1951 and 2000. Chapter two of the Ipperwash Inquiry provides an excellent primer on Aboriginal occupations (Linden, 2007).

7. In some respects, this call for action against poverty was probably an off-shoot of the Kelowna Accord. The Kelowna Accord is the common name given to a working paper entitled "Strengthening Relationships and Closing the Gap" which resulted from 18 months of roundtable consultations cumulating at the First Ministers' Meeting in Kelowna in November, 2005. This working paper established targets to improve the education, employment, and living conditions for Aboriginal peoples through additional governmental funding. This accord was never signed, nor were monies ever budgeted for it, before the minority government of Paul Martin fell. The subsequent minority government of Stephen Harper identified different priorities with respect to Aboriginal affairs. While the Kelowna Accord is clearly a political hot potato, Wikipedia provides a brief, but balanced discussion of it.

8. This has unsuccessfully been tried in the past. See White (2003) for a discussion of the Davis Inlet and Port Harrison relocations.

REFERENCES

Alfred, G. R. 1995. *Heeding the Voices of Our Ancestors: Kahnawake Mohawk Politics and the Rise of Native Nationalism.* Oxford University Press.

Beavon, D. and M. Cook. 2003. "An Application of the United Nations Human Development Index to Registered Indians in Canada, 1996." Pp. 201–221 in *Aboriginal Conditions: Research as a Foundation for Public Policy,* edited by White, J. P., Maxim, P., and D. Beavon. Vancouver: University of British Columbia Press.

Becker, G. 1964. *Human Capital.* New York: The National Bureau of Economic Research.

Burrows, J. "Crown and Aboriginal Occupations of Land: A History & Comparison," background paper prepared for the Ipperwash Inquiry, October, 2005.

Clairmont, D. and Potts, J. "For the Nonce: Policing and Aboriginal Occupations and Protests," background paper prepared for the Ipperwash Inquiry, May, 2006.

Chandler, M. and C. Lalonde. 2004. "Transforming Whose Knowledge? Exchanging Whose Best Practices? On Knowing about Indigenous Knowledge and Aboriginal Suicide." Pp. 111–124 in White, J., Maxim, P., and D. Beavon (eds). *Aboriginal Policy Research: Setting the Agenda for Change.* Vol. 2. Toronto: Thompson Educational Publishing, Inc.

Coleman, J. 1988. "Social Capital in the Creation of Human Capital." *American Journal of Sociology* 94 Supplement.

Department of Indian Affairs and Northern Development. 1993. *Population Projections of Registered Indians, 1996–2121.* Ottawa: DIAND.

Fiscal Realities, "Expanding Commercial Activity on First Nations Land: Getting First Nation Land Development Regulations Right," Strategic Research and Analysis Directorate, Indian and Northern Affairs Canada, 1999.

Griffin, D. (Editor). 1988. *Spirituality and Society: Postmodern Visions.* New York: State University of New York Press.

Gurr, T. R. 1970. *Why Men Rebel.* Princeton: Princeton University Press.

Haslip, S. *The Bisons Now Hunt the Indians: A Critical Consideration of Contemporary Provisions Providing for the Use of Military Force Against Aboriginal Peoples (in Canada).* LL.M., University of Ottawa, Faculty of Law, 2002.

Hull, J. 2005. *Post-secondary Education and Labour Market Outcomes: Canada, 2001.* Ottawa: Department of Indian and Northern Affairs Canada.

Insight Canada Research Inc. 1996. *Perspectives Canada* 5(1).

Linden, S. B. *Report of the Ipperwash Inquiry,* Publications Ontario, 2007.

MacLaine, C. and M. S. Boxendale. 1991. *This Land Is Our Land: The Mohawk Revolt at Oka.* Optimum Publishing International Inc.

Maxim, P. and J. White. 2003. "Toward an Index of Community Capacity: Predicting Community Potential for Successful Program Transfer." Pp. 248–263 in *Aboriginal Conditions: Research as a Foundation for Public Policy,* edited by White, J., Maxim, P., and D. Beavon. Vancouver: University of British Columbia Press.

Maxim, P., White, J., and D. Beavon. 2003. "Dispersion and Polarization of Income among Aboriginal and Non-Aboriginal Canadians." In *Aboriginal Conditions: The Research Foundations for Public Policy.* Vancouver: University of British Columbia Press.

Nault, F., Chen, J., George, M. V., and M. J. Norris. 1993. Population Projections of Registered Indians, 1991-2016. Report prepared by the Population Projections Section, Demography Division, Statistics Canada. Ottawa: Indian and Northern Affairs Canada.

Norris, M. J., Cooke, M., and S. Clatworthy. 2003. "Aboriginal Mobility and Migration Patterns and the Policy Implications." Pp. 108–130 in *Aboriginal Conditions: Research as a Foundation for Public Policy,* edited by White, J., Maxim, P., and D. Beavon. Vancouver: University of British Columbia Press.

Norris, M. J., Kerr, D., and F. Nault. 1995. *Projections of the Population with Aboriginal Identity in Canada, 1991-2016.* Report prepared by the Population Projections Section, Demography Division, Statistics Canada, for the Royal Commission on Aboriginal Peoples. Ottawa: Canada Mortgage and Housing Corporation and the Royal Commission on Aboriginal Peoples.

Pariseau, J. J. B. Major. 1973. *Disorders, Strikes and Disasters: Military Aid to the Civil Power in Canada, 1867-1933.* Ottawa: Directorate of History, National Defence Headquarters.

Report of the Royal Commission on Aboriginal Peoples. 1996. Canada Communication Group Publishing, Ottawa, Ontario.

Rowe, G. and M. M. Norris. 1995. *Mortality Predictions of Registered Indians, 1982 to 1996.* Ottawa: Indian and Northern Affairs Canada.

Sallee, D. 2006. "Quality of Life of Aboriginal People in Canada." *IRPP Choices.* Vol 12, no 6. November.

Spence, N. 2007. *New Vistas on the Income Inequality-Health Debate: The Case of Canada's First Nations Reserve Population.* PhD Dissertation, Department of Sociology, The University of Western Ontario, London, Ontario.

Spence, N., White, J., and P. Maxim. (2007). "Modeling Community Determinants of Canada's First Nation's Educational Outcomes." *Canadian Ethnic Studies.* (Forthcoming)

Statistics Canada. 1984. *Life Tables, Canada and Provinces 1980–82.* Catalogue no. 84-532. Ottawa: Statistics Canada.

Statistics Canada. 1990. *Life Tables, Canada and Provinces, 1985–87.* Health Reports Supplement 13. Ottawa: Statistics Canada.

Statistics Canada. 1995. *Life Tables, Canada and Provinces, 1990–92.* Catalogue no. 84-537. Ottawa: Statistics Canada.

Statistics Canada. 1998. *Life Expectancy Abridged Life Tables, at Birth and Age 65, by Sex, for Canada, Provinces, Territories, and Health Regions.* CANISM Table 102-0016. Ottawa: Statistics Canada.

Statistics Canada. 2000. *The Consumer Price Index.* Catalogue no. 62-010-X1B. Ottawa: Statistics Canada.

Statistics Canada. 2005b. *Consumer Price Index, Historical Summary.* Ottawa: Statistics Canada.

Statistics Canada Census Data custom tabulations; Statistics Canada 1984, 1990, 1995, 1998, 2005a.

Steele, S. 1997. "Gustafsen Lake Standoff: 15 Charged," *Maclean's* Magazine, June 2.

Verma, R., Michalowski, M., and R. P. Gauvin. 2003. *Abridged Life Tables for Registered Indians in Canada, 1976–80 to 1996–2000.* Paper presented at the annual meeting of the Population Association of American, May 103, Minneapolis.

Walker, I. and H. Smith (Editors). 2002. *Relative Deprivation: Development, Specification and Integration.* Cambridge: Cambridge: Cambridge University Press.

White, J. P., Beavon, D., and P. Maxim. 2003. *Aboriginal Conditions: The Research Foundations for Public Policy.* Vancouver: University of British Columbia Press.

White, J. P., Maxim, P., and N. Spence. 2004. *Permission to Develop: Aboriginal Treaties, Case Law and Regulations.* Toronto: Thompson Educational Press.

White, J. P., Maxim, P., and D. Beavon (eds). 2004. *Aboriginal Policy Research: Setting the Agenda for Change.* Vol. 1. Toronto: Thompson Educational Press.

White, J. P., Maxim, P., and D. Beavon (eds). 2004. *Aboriginal Policy Research: Setting the Agenda for Change.* Vol. 2. Toronto: Thompson Educational Press.

White, J., Wingert, S., Beavon, D., and P. Maxim. 2006. *Aboriginal Policy Research: Moving Forward, Making a Difference.* Vol. 3. Toronto: Thompson Educational Publishing.

White, J., Wingert, S., and D. Beavon. 2007. *Aboriginal Policy Research: Moving Forward, Making a Difference.* Vol. 4. Toronto: Thompson Educational Publishing.

White, J. P., Anderson, E., and W. Cornett (eds). 2007. *Aboriginal Policy Research: Aboriginal Policy Research: Moving Forward, Making a Difference.* Vol. 5. Toronto: Thompson Educational Publishing.

White, J., Spence, N., and P. Maxim. 2005. "Social capital and educational attainment among Aboriginal peoples: Canada, Australia and New Zealand."

PART 13

Pp. 66–81 in *Policy Research Initiative Social Capital Project Series, Social Capital in Action: Thematic Studies,* edited by Policy Research Initiative. Ottawa: Policy Research Initiative, Government of Canada.

White, J., Maxim, P., and N. Spence. 2004. "A Educational Attainment of Aboriginal Canadians." In White, J., Maxim, P., and D. Beavon (eds). *Aboriginal Policy Research: Setting the Agenda for Change.* Vol. 1. Toronto: Thompson Educational Press.

Critical Thinking Question

1. Compare the overall trends and social indicators for Aboriginal versus non-Aboriginal peoples in Canada. Do these trends indicate social exclusion of Indigenous peoples? Why should non-Aboriginal Canadians be concerned about these differences?

Chapter 37

Stars and Bars

DANIEL LAZARE

How to eliminate racism in society? Common answers to this question call attention to the need for educational campaigns that emphasize tolerance and an appreciation of diversity, in addition to implementing laws that make it illegal to discriminate on the basis of race or ethnicity and/or to promote hatred against particular social groups. While we can all agree that these approaches are laudable, what they have in common is an emphasis on the individual and the beliefs that individuals hold. Sociologists concerned with race and ethnicity have long argued that these "individualistic" approaches to racism, however well intentioned, have little impact on the forms of **institutionalized racism** in society that most dramatically affect people's lives.

Indeed, some sociologists have argued that a focus on individuals in studying racism actually diverts attention from institutionalized racism in a society and thus helps maintain it. What is institutionalized racism? Basically, the term refers to the fact that society is organized in ways that function to disadvantage particular social groups. Glassner (2000), for example, reviews sociological works that argue that the criminal justice system in the United States has functioned as a mechanism of **internal colonialism** in regard to Native Americans.

In this selection, Daniel Lazare makes a similar—and updated—argument in regard to African-Americans. Basically, he argues that racial and class biases in the U.S. have produced "the largest detention system in the advanced industrial world," one that functions to disenfranchise a racial underclass. If Lazare's argument is correct (and addressing that issue in itself should provoke some lively discussion), then ask yourself if it seems likely that this form of institutionalized racism will be eliminated in the near future.

1. Why is there such a high level of incarceration in the United States, and what are the implications of this situation?

How can you tell when a democracy is dead? When concentration camps spring up and everyone shivers in fear? Or is it when concentration camps spring up and no one shivers in fear because everyone knows they're not for "people like us" (in Woody Allen's marvelous phrase) but for the others, the troublemakers, the ones you can tell are guilty merely by the color of their skin, the shape of their nose or their social class?

Questions like these are unavoidable in the face of America's homegrown gulag archipelago, a vast network of jails, prisons and "supermax" tombs for the living dead that, without anyone quite noticing, has metastasized into the largest

PART 14

Source: Lazare, Daniel. "Stars and Bars." Reprinted with permission from the August 27, 2007 issue of *The Nation*. For subscription information, call 1-800-333-8536. Portions of each week's Nation magazine can be accessed at http://www.thenation.com.

detention system in the advanced industrial world. The proportion of the US population languishing in such facilities now stands at 737 per 100,000, the highest rate on earth and some five to twelve times that of Britain, France and other Western European countries or Japan. With 5 percent of the world's population, the United States has close to a quarter of the world's prisoners, which, curiously enough, is the same as its annual contribution to global warming. With 2.2 million people behind bars and another 5 million on probation or parole, it has approximately 3.2 percent of the adult population under some form of criminal-justice supervision, which is to say one person in thirty-two. For African-Americans, the numbers are even more astonishing. By the mid-1990s, 7 percent of black males were behind bars, while the rate of imprisonment for black males between the ages of 25 and 29 now stands at one in eight. While conservatives have spent the past three or four decades bemoaning the growth of single-parent families, there is a very simple reason some 1.5 million American children are fatherless or (less often) motherless: Their parents are locked up. Because they are confined for the most part in distant rural prisons, moreover, only about one child in five gets to visit them as often as once a month.

What's that you say? Who cares whether a bunch of "rapists, murderers, robbers, and even terrorists and spies," as Republican Senator Mitch McConnell once characterized America's prison population, get to see their kids? In fact, surprisingly few denizens of the American gulag have been sent away for violent crimes. In 2002 just 19 percent of the felony sentences handed down at the state level were for violent offenses, and of those only about 5 percent were for murder. Nonviolent drug offenses involving trafficking or possession (the modern equivalent of rum-running or getting caught with a bottle of bathtub gin) accounted for 31 percent of the total, while purely economic crimes such as burglary and fraud made up an additional

32 percent. If the incarceration rate continues to rise and violent crime continues to drop, we can expect the nonviolent sector of the prison population to expand accordingly. A normal society might lighten up in such circumstances. After all, if violence is under control, isn't it time to come up with a more humane way of dealing with a dwindling number of miscreants? But America is not a normal country and only grows more punitive.

It has also been extremely reluctant to face up to the cancer in its midst. Several of the leading Democratic candidates, for example, have recently come out against the infamous 100-to-1 ratio that subjects someone carrying ten grams of crack to the same penalty as someone caught with a kilo of powdered cocaine. Senator Joe Biden has actually introduced legislation to eliminate the disparity—without, however, acknowledging his role as a leading drug warrior back in the 1980s, when he sponsored the bill that set it in stone in the first place. At a recent forum at Howard University, Hillary Clinton promised to "deal" with the disparity as well, although it would have been nice if she had done so back in the '90s, when, during the first Clinton Administration, the prison population was soaring by some 50 percent. Although he is not running this time around, Jesse Jackson recently castigated Dems for their hesitancy in addressing "failed, wasteful, and unfair drug policies" that have sent "so many young African-Americans" to jail. Yet Jackson forgot to mention his own drug-war past when, as a leading hardliner, he specifically called for "stiffer prison sentences" for black drug users and "wartime consequences" for smugglers. "Since the flow of drugs into the US is an act of terrorism, anti-terrorist policies must be applied," he declared in a 1989 interview, a textbook example of how the antidrug rhetoric of the late twentieth century helped pave the way for the "global war on terror" of the early twenty-first.

In other words, cowardice and hypocrisy abound. Fortunately, a small number of academics and at least one journalist have begun training an eye on America's growing prison crisis. Since there is more than enough injustice to go around, each has zeroed in on different aspects of the phenomenon—on the political and economic consequences of stigmatizing so many young people for life, on the racial consequences of disproportionately punishing young black males and on the sheer moral horror of needlessly locking away real, live human beings in supermax prisons that are little more than high-tech dungeons. Their findings, to make a long story short, are that the damage cannot be reduced to a simple matter of so many person-years of lost time. To the contrary, the effects promise to multiply for years to come. In *American Furies* Sasha Abramsky, a Sacramento-based journalist and longtime *Nation* contributor, convincingly argues that the best way to understand US prison policies is to think of them as a GI Bill in reverse. Just as the original GI Bill laid the basis for a major social advance by making college available to millions of veterans, mass incarceration is laying the basis for an enormous social regression by stigmatizing and brutalizing millions of young people and "de-skilling" them by removing them from the workforce. America will be feeling the effects for generations.

Bruce Western, a Princeton sociologist, offers the best overview. He notes in his new study, *Punishment and Inequality in America*, that mass imprisonment is actually a novel development. For much of the twentieth century, the US incarceration rate held steady at around 100 per 100,000, which would put it in the same ballpark as Western Europe today. But after a slight dip following the liberal reforms of the 1960s, the curve reversed direction in the mid-'70s and then rose more steeply in the '80s and '90s. Considering that Germany, Sweden, Denmark and Austria succeeded in reducing or holding their incarceration rates steady during this period, the US pattern was highly exceptional. But so are US crime rates. Between 1980 and 1991, US homicides hovered at between 7.9

and 10.2 per 100,000, as much as ten times the European average. (The rate has since fallen to around 5.7.) Combined with the crack wave that also exploded in the 1980s, the result was a deepening sense of panic that peaked in mid-1986 with the death of basketball star Len Bias from a cocaine overdose. Although there was no evidence that crack had anything to do with Bias's death—police found only powdered cocaine in his car—the incident somehow confirmed crack as the new devil substance, "the most addictive drug known to man," in the words of *Newsweek*, and a threat comparable to the "medieval plagues," in the considered opinion of *U.S. News and World Report* (which would have meant that the country was facing an imminent population loss of up to 33 percent). Within a matter of months, Joe Biden had helped shepherd through to victory the Anti-Drug Abuse Act of 1986, an unusually horrendous piece of legislation that etched in stone the 100-to-1 penalty ratio for crack.

Still, it is always interesting to consider which deaths fill people with horror and which ones don't. The year before Bias's death not only saw 19,000 homicides in the United States but nearly 46,000 highway fatalities too, and yet Congress somehow refrained from criminalizing motor vehicles. Crack's status as the drug du jour of a certain class of inner-city blacks should have been the giveaway. What had Congress in a tizzy was not cocaine consumption so much as black cocaine consumption, which is why the subsequent repression was bound to be far harder on African-Americans than on whites. Although there is no evidence that blacks use drugs more than whites and indeed some evidence that they use them less, Western notes that black users are now twice as likely to be arrested for drugs and, once arrested, more likely to go to prison or jail. None of this is necessarily racist, at least not in the crudely explicit way we associate with men in white sheets. The reason the police concentrate their efforts in black inner-city neighborhoods, Western notes, is that users congregate there

PART 14

in large numbers, and buying, selling and using tend to take place in public. (It's harder to make arrests behind the closed doors of some suburban McMansion.) If a judge is more inclined to send a poor black defendant to prison, similarly, it is not necessarily because he or she enjoys punishing someone with dark skin but because the judge, according to Western, may "see poor defendants as having fewer prospects and social supports, thus as having less potential for rehabilitation." If your weeping parents can afford to send you to private rehab, you're excused. If not, it's off to the state pen.

Racial and class biases are thus built into the very structure of the drug war. Western is particularly effective on the economic consequences of such grossly disproportionate policies. The standard account of American economic development since the 1970s, told and retold in countless undergraduate classrooms, is that economic deregulation and growth have done much to narrow the once-yawning wage gap between white and black workers. To quote the *New York Times:* "Unemployment rates among blacks and Hispanic people … are at or near record lows. Joblessness among high school dropouts has fallen to about half the rate in 1992. And wages for the lowest paid are rising faster than inflation for the first time in decades." A rising tide lifts all boats, whereas all that labor-market rigidity has done for "Old Europe" is to saddle it with persistently high levels of unemployment, an alienated underclass and riots in the banlieues. But as *Punishment and Inequality in America* points out, if US economic policies look good, it is only because the country's enormous prison population is not factored into the equation. If workers behind bars are counted, then it quickly becomes apparent "that young black men have experienced virtually no real economic gains on young whites" and that the real black unemployment rate is up to 20 percent greater than official statistics indicate. Rather than freeing up the markets, Western writes, the United States has "adopted policies that massively and coercively

regulated the poor." Where the Danes provide their unemployed with up to 80 percent of their previous salary and the Germans provide them with 60 percent, America has deregulated the rich while throwing a growing portion of its working class in jail.

In *Marked*, Devah Pager, who also teaches sociology at Princeton, uses a simple technique to show how mass incarceration has undone the small amount of racial progress achieved in the 1960s and '70s. Working with two pairs of male college students in Milwaukee, one white and the other black, she drilled them on how to present themselves and answer questions. Then, arming them with phony résumés, she sent them out to apply for entry-level jobs. The résumés were identical in all respects but one. Where one member of each team had nothing indicating a criminal record, the other's résumé showed an eighteen-month sentence for drugs. To help insure that the results were uniform, the résumés were then rotated back and forth among the testers.

The results? The white applicant with a prison record was half as likely to be called back for a second interview as the white applicant without. But the black applicant without a criminal record was no more likely to be called back than the white applicant with a record, while the black applicant with a record was two-thirds less likely to be called back than the black applicant without. The black applicant with a record therefore wound up doubly penalized—as a black man and as an ex-con. With the chances of a call-back reduced to just 5 percent, the overall effect, Pager writes, was "almost total exclusion from this labor market." Considering that there are as many as 12 million ex-felons in the United States, a major portion of them black, the result has been to create a huge pool of the semipermanently unemployed where one might otherwise not exist. This is not to disprove sociologist William Julius Wilson, whose study *The Declining Significance of Race* caused an uproar when it was published in 1978. Wilson may have been right: The significance of race may well have been declining by the late '70s. But thanks to a government policy of mass stigmatization, it has come roaring back.

This is not only bad news for those arrested but bad news for those who have to foot the bill for their incarceration and for dealing with the social problems that labor-market exclusion on this scale helps generate. But there are other costs too. In *Locked Out*, Jeff Manza and Christopher Uggen, professors of sociology at Northwestern and the University of Minnesota, respectively, point out that only two states, Maine and Vermont, permit felons to vote while incarcerated, that most limit felons' voting rights after they complete their terms and that, even if not legally disenfranchised, some 600,000 jail inmates and pretrial detainees are effectively prevented from voting as well. All told, this means that 6 million Americans were unable to vote on election day in 2004. This is not peanuts. Nationwide, one black man in seven has been disenfranchised as a consequence, while in Florida, the state with the most sweeping disenfranchisement laws, the number of those prevented from voting now exceeds 1.1 million.

From a right-wing perspective, this is nothing short of brilliant. After all, what could be better than disenfranchising an unfriendly racial group while persuading the rest of the nation that the group deserves it because its ranks are filled with violent criminals? Since felons and ex-felons tend to be poor and members of oppressed racial minorities, they tend to vote Democratic. Even though the poor are less likely to vote than those higher up on the socioeconomic ladder, Manza and Uggen say there is little doubt that, had the disenfranchisement laws not existed in Florida in November 2000, the extra votes would have provided Al Gore with a margin of victory so comfortable that not even the Republican state legislature could have taken it away. If the ranks of prison inmates and hence of disenfranchised ex-inmates had not multiplied since the '70s, much of the wind would also have been taken out of the sails of the great GOP offensive. Americans have not gone right, in other words. Rather, by taking control of the criminal-justice issue, the right wing has winnowed down the electorate so as to artificially boost the power of the conservative minority.

But how did the right gain control of this all-important issue in the first place? This is the problem that Marie Gottschalk, a professor of political science at the University of Pennsylvania, wrestles with in *The Prison and the Gallows*, an eccentric but compelling study of mass incarceration's ideological origins. While taking aim at the usual right-wing villains, *The Prison and the Gallows* also goes after various liberals and radicals who, inadvertently or not, also contributed to the construction of "the carceral state." Bill Clinton, for example, not only embraced the drug war and capital punishment—he interrupted his 1992 presidential campaign to fly back to Arkansas and sign the death warrant for a mentally disabled prisoner named Rickey Ray Rector—but also endorsed what Gottschalk calls "a virulently punitive victims' rights movement," going so far as to call for a constitutional amendment in 1996 as "the only way to give victims equal and due consideration."

This was important because the victims' rights movement represented an effort to inject a dose of vengeance into the judicial process and thereby blur the distinction between the private interest of the victim and the public's interest in maintaining order and justice. In Europe, reformers were also concerned with victims' rights. But "extending a hand to victims was seen from the start as primarily an extension of the welfare state," Gottschalk observes, whereas in America, where welfare is a dirty word, it was seen as a way of steering criminal justice in a more punitive direction....

Sasha Abramsky is less interested in the ideological currents that helped pave the way for mass incarceration, although in *American Furies* he does spotlight the fascinating role played by a Berkeley-educated sociologist named Robert

Martinson, who, after several years investigating the cornucopia of rehabilitation programs offered at the time by the New York State prison system, summed up his findings in a sensational 1974 article titled "What Works?" His answer: nothing. Martinson's frustration is understandable to anyone who has ever suffered through an encounter group. Yet his conclusions, published in the neoconservative journal *Public Interest*, were grossly one-sided: While many programs do not work, some clearly have a positive effect.

In short order, Martinson's article became the bible of the vengeance-and-punishment set, which seized on it as proof that rehabilitation was a lost cause and that the only purpose of prison was to penalize wrongdoers. Once this ideological impediment was removed, the criminal-justice system slid downhill with remarkable speed. If punishment was good, then more punishment was better. In short order, Massachusetts Governor William Weld was declaring that life in prison should be "akin to a walk through hell," while right-wing Senator Phil Gramm was promising "to string barbed wire on every military base in America" to contain all the criminals he wanted to round up. In Maricopa County, Arizona, which includes Phoenix, a colorful local character named Joe Arpaio got himself re-elected sheriff time and again by parading his inmates about on chain gangs, dressing the men among them in fluorescent pink underwear and serving prisoners food that, as he cheerfully admits, costs less than what he gives to his cats and dogs. "Voters like it everywhere," Abramsky quotes Arpaio as saying of such policies. "I'm on thousands of talk shows. I never get a negative. I get letters from all over the world—and I answer every one. They say, 'Come up here and be our sheriff.'" What makes this all the more repellent is that the people subjected to such humiliation and abuse are rarely killers or rapists but alcoholics, vagrants and other small fry doing time for such misdemeanors as possession and shoplifting.

Amazing how much damage a single article can do, eh? Yet when a conscience-stricken

Martinson published a *mea culpa* in the *Hofstra Law Review* five years later ("contrary to my previous position, some treatment programs do have an appreciable effect on recidivism"), the media yawned. No big shots interviewed him on TV, and no politicians called to solicit his views. No one wanted to hear that rehabilitation programs work, only that they don't. Beset by personal troubles, professional setbacks and perhaps the realization of how grievously he had allowed himself to be misused, Martinson committed suicide by throwing himself out of a ninth-floor Manhattan apartment in 1980. *American Furies* provides us with a vivid account of the horrors that have followed—the low-level pot dealers and shoplifters sentenced to life in prison in California, Oklahoma, Alabama and other states where various "three strikes" or other habitual-offender laws pertain; the supermax prisoners condemned to spend twenty-three hours a day in barren concrete cells the size of walk-in closets; the epidemics of suicide and self-mutilation; and the stubbornly high levels of violence between and among prisoners and guards—which law-and-order advocates seize upon as reason to build yet more supermax facilities. US prison policy is like a computer program that is designed to spit out the same answers no matter what data are fed into it: Arrest more people, put more of them in prison, build more cells to accommodate them.

Where will it end? As Martinson's story shows, American mass incarceration is not what social scientists call "evidence based." It is not a policy designed to achieve certain practical, utilitarian ends that can then be weighed and evaluated from time to time to determine if it is performing as intended. Rather, it is a moral policy whose purpose is to satisfy certain passions that have grown more and more brutal over the years. The important thing about moralism of this sort is that it is its own justification. For true believers, it is something that everyone should endorse regardless of the consequences. As right-wing political scientist James Q. Wilson once remarked, "Drug use is wrong because it is immoral," a comment that not only sums up the tautological nature of US drug policies but also shows how they are structured to render irrelevant questions about wasted dollars and blighted lives. Moralism of this sort is neither rational nor democratic, and the fact that it has triumphed so completely is an indication of how deeply the United States has sunk into authoritarianism since the 1980s. With the prison population continuing to rise at a 2.7 percent annual clip, there is no reason to think there will be a turnaround soon. Indeed, Gottschalk writes that mass incarceration is so taken for granted now a days that "it seems almost unimaginable that the country will veer off in a new direction and begin to empty and board up its prisons." Still, she ends on a quasi-optimistic note by quoting Norwegian sociologist Thomas Mathiesen to the effect that "major repressive systems have succeeded in looking extremely stable almost until the day they have collapsed." Indeed, repression is itself often a sign of instability bubbling up from below. This is not much to pin one's hopes on, but it will have to do.

Critical Thinking Questions

1. Some argue the consequences of mass incarceration replicate and reproduce discrimination? Where do you suppose this argument comes from?
2. Is the justice system in the U.S. an example of structural/institutional inequality?
3. How can we hold our social institutions, such as the justice system, to be responsible and function objectively for all citizens?

PART 14

Chapter 38

Population Change and Public Policy in Canada

RODERIC BEAUJOT AND DON KERR

Why study populations? The answer, as Rod Beaujot and Don Kerr make clear, is that when populations grow, or when some groups expand and others shrink in relation to one another, the repercussions in the political or social arena can be considerable. In this selection, the authors present a number of different examples that show how this can occur. As you consider each example, ask, just as Ellen Gee asked in Chapter 21, if there are factors besides the overarching shapes and changes of populations that may also explain the patterns being discussed? As well, in the debates over public policy, often empirical data is required to justify the need for certain policy development. The changes to the 2011 Canadian Census eliminated the collection of data that is often utilized to inform policy. As you read through this article, try to imagine what some of the consequences of a lack of strong empirical data may be for making changes to our public policies.

1. What are the crucial elements implicit in population change?

THE REASON FOR STUDYING POPULATION

One of the most important features of any society is the number of people and the relative size of the various subgroups. When populations grow or shrink and when subgroups change in relative size, various repercussions may follow.

Consider English–French relations in Canada. For a long time, the French constituted about a third of the population. In response to heavy English immigration, French-Canadian society emphasized the importance of births for maintaining the relative power of the French element in the country. A Catholic priest called for 'la revanche du becreau'—that is, for maintaining a high French birth rate as a means of securing the status of the French in the country.

When Quebec fertility fell in the 1960s and the French-speaking population of Canada dropped to nearly a quarter of the total, the long-term relationship between the country's two charter groups was threatened.

Particularly problematic for Quebec was the eagerness of various immigrant groups to associate themselves with the English minority of the province. In the early 1970s, it was even feared that French would no longer be the working language in the province of Quebec. Various measures have been taken in response to this demographic change, such as the Official Languages Act, the policy on multiculturalism, the granting to Quebec the right to have a voice in the selection of immigrants, and the Quebec Charter of the French Language (Bill 101). The constitutional crises of the 1990s, particularly

Source: Excerpts from Beaujot, Roderic, and Kerr, Don, *Population Change in Canada 2nd ed.* © Oxford University Press Canada 2004. Reprinted by permission of the publisher.

as they pertain to the concept of Quebec as a distinct society, show that Canada is still looking for ways to accommodate its changing demographics.

Aging is another crucial feature of the changing relative size of various subgroups of the population. Although aging is a long-term phenomenon that has been taking place for more than a century, different stages have different consequences. At first, population aging took place because there were fewer children. For instance, between 1966 and 1981 the population grew by 22 per cent but the number of people under the age of 15 declined by 17 per cent. These early stages of aging were relatively easy to accommodate. Although changes in the sizes of different age groups caused difficulties in the school system, in a broad sense, adults were freer because they had fewer children to care for. These changes both enlarged the proportion of the population that was at an employable age and freed women from family responsibilities, thereby encouraging them to join the labour force. These trends permitted an expansion of the social programs that depend on revenues from the taxation of employed persons (particularly health, education, social security, and pension programs).

However, at later stages of aging, it is no longer the relative size of the population of labour-force age that is growing, but rather the numbers of seniors. Even in the period from 1986 to 2001, whereas the population grew by 19 per cent, the number of people aged 65 and over grew by 45 per cent. In 1986, the population aged 65 and over constituted 10.7 per cent of the total, compared to 13.0 per cent in 2001. By 2036 when the baby boomers are all retired, it [the over-65 group] will probably make up a quarter of the population. In effect, our social programs were set up when the demographic and economic circumstances were very different. When the population of labour-force age is growing and real incomes are increasing, it is not hard to enrich our social programs, including those, such as health and pensions, that benefit the elderly. Some observers have come to question whether we will be able to afford all our social programs. Others call for different forms of accommodation, such as greater individual responsibility for personal health, greater repayment for the economic benefits of government-subsidized education, a longer work life, lower pension benefits, and even the promotion of higher birth rates and increased immigration.

Another phenomenon that can be studied from the point of view of population change is health. The comparison of the relative health of various sectors of the population permits an analysis of the differences across groups, and this points to the dynamics of well-being. For instance, men have a lower life expectancy, but women's advantage has shrunk from seven to five years. Besides the purely biological factors in this difference, there are important differences between men and women in the risk factors, including smoking, drinking, and driving. Although the gender differences in smoking for young people have largely disappeared, the mortality of older persons is still affected by past differences in their behaviour. Similarly, the higher life expectancy of married persons can partly be attributed to the 'protective role of marriage.' That is, married people benefit from having someone to help them when they are ill, and married men, in particular, benefit from having better diets than single men and not engaging in such risky activities (Trovato, 1998).

POPULATION AND POLICY

All societies attempt to shape the decisions made by individuals in such a way as to promote common benefit. Behaviour that promotes reproduction will sometimes be encouraged and sometimes discouraged. Behaviour that will prolong a person's life in the society will be encouraged, and the society will often take some responsibility for the health and safety of its citizens. And with respect to immigration,

PART 14

the society as a whole will establish structures, policies, and rules through which entry (and sometimes exit) are controlled in order to produce a social benefit.

There are a number of questions that interest the society as a whole. How many new members are to be added and by what means (through births or immigration)? How are the costs of these additions to be paid, and who receives the benefits? How should the costs and benefits of children be absorbed by the families into which they are born, the extended family, the community, and society as a whole? How are the costs and benefits of immigration to be distributed between, on the one hand, the immigrants themselves and their sponsoring families and, on the other hand, the receiving country, province, city, and community? To what extent are health and safety the responsibility of the individual or the surrounding society? How does society accommodate an aging population in terms of pensions, health care, and regenerating the labour force while ensuring that the young are not disadvantaged? These are among the policy questions that all societies must address.

Public policy on the changing demographics can take two forms: it can attempt to influence the course of demographic events, or it can ensure that society makes the adjustments necessary to accommodate the population change. That is, one can consider how policy may change the population, or one can consider that population changes themselves have implications for public policy. Some policies are aimed directly at influencing population processes, while others have unintended effects on population. Demographic trends also need to be considered in the analysis of such policy issues as support services for the aged, health, education, the labour force, and social security. Especially in a welfare state, that is, where the state takes some responsibility for the welfare of individuals, detailed knowledge about the population is important for those who make policy.

Such policy considerations underline the importance of gathering accurate information. Censuses were first taken to enable rulers to tax their citizens and to determine the number of men available for military service. With the advent of the welfare state, it is particularly important for governments to have accurate and up-to-date information on the population whose welfare they are trying to enhance. It is crucial to know how various groups would benefit or suffer from a given policy.

REFERENCE

Trovato, Frank, ed. 2002. *Population and Society: Essential Readings*. Toronto: Oxford University Press. This collection contains 25 well-chosen articles on the ways in which population and society are related. The readings include a wide array of research and theorizing in population studies.

Critical Thinking Questions

1. In the last paragraph of the article, the authors write, "it is particularly important for governments to have accurate and up-to-date information on the population whose welfare they are trying to enhance." The federal government has decided to discontinue the Long-Form Census, which will reduce the social data available to researchers. What do you suppose some of the consequences of this are from a population change and public policy perspective?

2. According to the Statistics Canada article, single people in Canada are now a majority over those married or in common-law relationships. What kinds of policy implications may follow from this change?

Chapter 39

Be Thin: Contradictions Within the Social Constructions of Beauty and Happiness

SHARON E. ROBERTS

Many of us can identify with unreal expectations placed upon how our bodies look. To many, our bodies are to express our ascribed statuses. Men are expected to be masculine and, through their bodies, they are expected to be strong and physical. Women, on the other hand, are expected to be feminine and more subordinate, so, while many women are expected to be fit and thin, they are not to be too strong (i.e., masculine). This article looks not only at the expectations placed upon our bodies according to our ascribed genders, but at the complex processes that reproduce and replicate those expectations. This happens in ways that can be difficult to pinpoint.

Note: If you are struggling with any issues related to body image, please visit the National Eating Disorder Information Centre (http://www.nedic.ca), the Eating Disorder Foundation of Canada (http://www.edfofcanada.com), or talk to your doctor. As well, there are numerous treatment programs available in Canada (http://www.canadadrugrehab.ca/Eating-Disorder-Treatment.html).

1. What social expectations are placed upon women regarding their appearances? What expectations are placed upon men? What are the differences and similarities between the two?
2. How are these expectations articulated or expressed? Where do they come from?

"Thin" is a ubiquitous message in Western culture as a social construction of beauty and success. Phrases such as never being "too rich or too thin," a saying credited to Wallis Simpson, Duchess of Windsor, have laid the foundation for much of popular culture in the 20th and 21st centuries. The constructions of feminine and masculine ideals in our society mandate strong compliance to certain modes of physique. Women and men are overtly and covertly guided on how to become feminine and masculine beings: women are expected to be youthful, thin, and attractive (e.g., Stice et al. 2000), and males are expected to be muscular (e.g., Frederick et al. 2007). Adherence to these ideals has become an important part of the gendered identity, and the consequences for internalizing these gendered ideals can result in negative **body image** and the potential for eating disorders (e.g., Lawler & Nixon 2011; Stice et al. 2002).

Source: Roberts, Sharon. "Be Thin: Contradictions Within the Social Construction of Beauty and Happiness." Unpublished Manuscript, 2011. Reproduced with permission of the author.

PART 15

BODY DISSATISFACTION AND EATING DISORDERS: MYTHS, FACTS, AND FIGURES

It should be no surprise that the rates of eating disorders (anorexia, bulimia, binge eating, and binge-eating related obesity) are increasing steadily in Canada. Berg et al. (2002) estimate the lifetime prevalence for women as 3.7 percent for anorexia and 4.2 percent for bulimia. Moreover, rates of young Canadians who are obese have doubled from 8.5 percent in 1978/79 to 20.5 percent in 2004 (Statistics Canada 2005), and binge eating disorder is present in a small but significant number of obesity cases—estimates range from 2–25 percent depending on the population studied (Yanovski 1999; 2003). Additionally, body image problems are rampant in our culture.

For example, Schur et al. (2000) examined young girls and boys' beliefs about their bodies, dieting, and dissatisfaction in a sample of children in grades three through six. They found that 50 percent of the 62 participants wanted to be thinner, 70 percent of the children knew about dieting from their families, and 16 percent of the children had already attempted dieting for weight loss. Clearly, our issues with food and dieting begin at an early age.

The common belief that eating disorders and poor body image are problems associated only with white, teenage girls is misguided. Gross and Rosen's (1988) study found evidence of bulimia in girls across all of the racial categories (Asian, Caucasian, Black, and Latina) in their sample (Asian and Caucasians had the highest percentages). Warren et al. (2010) studied Latina youth in the U.S. and found that Latina girls engaged in social comparison and were affected by the internalization of athletic appearance. They felt pressured by the thin ideal and, in some cases, possessed eating pathology. Hesse-Biber et al. (2010) studied African American women and found that those who subscribed more to the "white mainstream culture" were more dissatisfied with their bodies than other African American women who identified with other body types (e.g., fuller figure), and Harris (2006) concludes that "race/ethnic heritage and a high body mass index or heavy body do not necessarily shield African American college women from body dissatisfaction or prevent the development of eating disturbances. African American college women, similar to their European American peers, report dissatisfaction with their bodies and unfavourable appearance evaluations when body mass, preferred weight and weight discrepancy levels are perceived as high" (p. 46).

As such, eating disorders and negative body image are not necessarily restricted by race, nor do they have boundaries in age. Eating disorders commonly develop in the teen years; however, there are numerous cases of people who are in their 30s, 40s, 50s and older who develop eating disorders (e.g., Tolbin et al. 1995). Furthermore, Harriger et al. (2010) report that girls as young as three years old display evidence of internalizing the thin ideal, and children, both female and male, who are as young as seven years old have been diagnosed with anorexia and/or bulimia and required hospitalization (e.g., Bryant-Waugh et al. 1996).

Males, too, are susceptible to eating disorders, body dissatisfaction, and negative body image problems. The male body has come under more media scrutiny in the past 20 years (Grogan, 2010), and there are implications for internalizing the "ideal" body type (thin with a muscular build) for men, too. With regard to body image, Peat et al. (2011) found that, compared to older men, younger adult men exhibit greater body dissatisfaction. Peplau et al. (2009) explored body image dissatisfaction in gay/straight men and women. Although few differences were found between lesbian and straight women, the researchers found that gay men were at an increased risk of experiencing body dissatisfaction than were heterosexual males. Blouin and Goldfield (1995) compared the self-reports of body image, steroid use, and eating attitudes of male runners, martial artists, and body builders. Body builders reported more desire to bulk up, internalized the thin ideal, had more bulimic tendencies, reported more perfectionism, and used more steroids than the other two categories of male athletes. They also found that steroid use was associated with bulimic tendencies. The authors conclude that male body builders are at a greater risk for body image disturbances and exhibit many of the pathologies associated with eating disordered patients. Overall, Hudson et al. (2007) report that, at the national level, life-time prevalence estimates of anorexia, bulimia, and binge eating disorder for men are .3 percent, .5 percent, and 2.0 percent. Clearly, men and women of all ages and races need to be considered as we move forward with research on eating disorders, body dissatisfaction, and body image.

THE ROLE OF MEDIA IN THE CONSTRUCTION OF GENDER AND BEAUTY

One of the main contributions to the construction of gender and physical expectation is media (Lawler & Nixon 2011). Brower and Leon (1999) cite estimates that people in America are exposed to 3000 advertisements daily. Thus, the influence of media, to some extent, is unavoidable. Individuals are inundated with images of the physically "ideal" person—models not only make the merchandise seem appealing, but they also provide an idealized image of what is seemingly a lifestyle choice. The good-looking woman who stands beside a sports car in an advertisement is selling to males a particular image of success—a sense of masculinity derived from wealth, consumerism, and heterosexuality. She is also portraying an "ideally attractive" construction for women, which is a pervasive image in Western culture. Fashion magazines boast thousands of pages containing pictures of thin women and toned men selling products and

services, and movies showcase thin and beautiful actors and actresses who make millions of dollars based on their looks. In essence, images teach us that to be thin is to be happy and wealthy. However, these messages of physical "perfection" and thinness are mixed with other media messages related to food, which is a consumer-based industry, too. Food companies market successfully to consumers by attaching their food products to emotions; advertisements have fused food with notions of family cohesion, rewards, financial success, status, celebration, happiness, release, and escape (see Helmer 1992, for a discussion of how McDonald's achieved this through advertising).

A review of late night television provides a good example of this cultural contradiction. Standard late night television hosts a plethora of fast-food commercials that entice the viewer to purchase "supersized" foods. Infomercials often showcase products that feature ways to consume more food, more quickly, and at a lower cost. Better, cheaper, and faster underlie the main sales pitch for products such as the "George Foreman" grill or the "Magic Bullet Blender," which claims to do "any job in 10 seconds … or less!" Often in the same timeslot on a different channel, other infomercials are focused on how to make consumers lose weight. These infomercials showcase products that are "guaranteed" to make the customer tone up, slim down, and hide "fat." Suzanne Somers' 1980s "ThighMaster," with the sales pitch "squeeze, squeeze your way to shapely thighs" netted a reported six million sales in Canada alone. Other products provide the consumer with "thin" by selling them an alternative to exercise. For example, "Spanx" provides a variety of "comfortable, slimming garments that minimize *figure flaws*" (emphasis added). It is worth noting that young, thin people regularly model these products.

The simultaneously contrasting messages in late night television are intense: eat more, be thin. This is symptomatic of a society where, for most people, food is a consumer choice; the economic

PART 15

and technological advances in Western culture have provided the environment that makes food readily available in mass quantities, and the competitive nature of the food industry results in companies vying for consumers' attention by making their products attractive. On the one hand, Westerners are encouraged to be indulgent in every way, including the consumption of food. Food is socially constructed as a symbol of success and wealth, a treat, a celebration, a release, and the advertisements offer justification and reason for indulgence (e.g., Xu & Schwarz 2009; Miao 2011). And thin, in Western culture, is constructed as attractive, sexually appealing, and morally good. These are seemingly incompatible messages. As such, advertising contributes to the problem of over consumption—a problem that is rectified by diet products—while reinforcing the "ideal image" of thin. It should be no surprise that the inherent contradictions in these messages can leave people feeling dissonant and conflicted—the result being the internal conflict that many experience as they consume food and then feel guilty about their food consumption (e.g., Miao 2011). These conditions can contribute to negative body image, body dissatisfaction, or purging behaviours (e.g., Lawler & Nixon 2011), and they can lead to feelings of being out of control (e.g., Berg et al. 2002). This may be exacerbated by individual circumstances, such as age, personal history, or genetic vulnerability.

BODY DISSATISFACTION AND EATING DISORDERS: BEYOND MEDIA

It would be simplistic and naive to assess these complicated conditions—eating disorders—as being the result of media alone. There are numerous etiological factors to consider. For example, we know that trauma—particularly childhood sexual abuse—can have serious consequences for mental health, triggering over the

long-term eating disorders, depression, and other debilitating behaviour patterns (e.g., Schwartz & Cohen 1996; Berg et al. 2002; Briere & Scott 2007;); however, it is important to note that sexual abuse or assault is not a necessary condition for the onset of an eating disorder (Briere & Scott 2007). Studies have linked childhood trauma most commonly to bulimia (Ackard et al. 2001) as well as anorexia, and binge eating to the point of obesity (Gustafson & Sarwer 2004). In different studies, childhood sexual abuse has also been linked to objectified body consciousness as it relates to depression (theorized in Hyde et al. 2008) and poor body image and dieting in both girls and boys (Logio 2003).

In many cases of eating disorders, those who have experienced a loss of control in other aspects of life use the fixated, complete control over food as a (pathological) mechanism to gain control in their lives. In essence, in these cases, eating disorders are not actually about food at all but rather using food to deal with emotional turmoil. In the initial stages, people are often using power over eating to gain a sense of autonomy in their lives. Ironically, the eating disorder results in a total loss of control and autonomy over time (Berg et al. 2002).

Identity confusion (Erikson 1968) is often theorized to be another factor in eating disorders (e.g., Goodsitt 1985; Zerbe 1993; Berg et al. 2002; Wheeler et al. 2003; Algars et al. 2010), where "a defective sense of self is generally considered a hallmark of eating disorders" (Sigall & Pabst 2005, p. 96). Stein and Corte (2007) have linked disturbances in identity to eating disturbances. In the absence of autonomously acquired identity, whether it is a result of depression, trauma, or general struggles in the transition to adulthood, females are theorized to take on gender role ideologies that are present in media (e.g., Spence 1993). Mussap (2007), who studied gender role stress, concludes that for some women, "adopting the feminine gender role is akin to women internalizing the thin ideal" (p. 346). Thus, sociologists have argued that hyper-feminine ideologies can lead to increased body dissatisfaction and hence more negative self-appraisals. This is where the omnipresence of thin in media can be particularly influential and complicated by the pairing of food with emotion.

From biological and psychological perspectives, there are other etiological factors to consider. Research suggests that clinical patients who suffer with an eating disorder may also comorbidly present with an addictive personality. Davis and Claridge (1998) examined a clinical sample of individuals with anorexia and bulimia. They found that these patients scored high on an addiction scale and that excessive exercise and weight preoccupation were associated with addictive personality and obsessive compulsiveness. Other research (e.g., Brown et al. 2007) has focused on genetic (chromosomal) susceptibility to eating disorders and has found a link between genes and restrictive anorexia and bulimic anorexia. They argue that there may be a genetic susceptibility or predisposition to eating disorders. Brewerton (1995) reported that serotonin dysregulation can be a clinical feature of eating disorders, particularly with bulimia nervosa. Thus, in some cases, physicians may recommend medications, specifically serotonin reuptake inhibitors, to help treat symptoms. The evidence seems to indicate that these kinds of treatments, combined with nutritional and behavioural modification therapy, may be most useful in treating some eating disorders (e.g., Vaswani et al. 2003), although we clearly still have a long way to go in terms of successful treatment.

As such, eating disorders can be understood as the manifestation of serious social, medical, biological, and mental health problems. Research has also shown that comorbidities are common in people who have eating disorders: many people who live with eating disorders are also suffering from other concerning issues such as alcoholism and drug abuse (Piran & Gadella 2007), mental health comorbidities (Salbach-Andrae et al. 2008), depression (e.g., Rodgers et al. 2010), and/or self-harming behaviours such as cutting (Hintikka et al. 2009). Bradford and Petrie (2008) found a reciprocal relationship between disordered eating and depressive affect, and Tiggerman and Kuring (2004) found that depression and eating disorders were predicted by body objectification.

The seriousness of these disorders cannot be overstated, as eating disorders have high mortality rates (e.g., James et al. 2010). Feingold and Mazzella (1998) state that destructive dieting, body image issues, and sub-clinical eating disorders affect the majority of American females. It is also important to note that it is incorrect to assume that a person must look emaciated to a) have an eating disorder, and b) be at any serious health risk. Bulimia and/or binge eating may result in very different body weights than does anorexia, but all of these disorders yield serious consequences for health and survival. We should never assume that because someone who purges is at a "normal" body weight (or purges and is overweight) that he or she is not at risk for serious medical complications such as electrolyte imbalance, heart arrhythmia leading to heart failure, organ failure, tears in the esophagus, or death. Thus, from a sociological perspective, the ubiquitous nature of thin in Western culture is cause for concern, as the consequences of the omnipresence of thin can be quite severe in terms of the potential for the internalization of the thin ideal (Grogan 2010) and the resulting manifestations—particularly in vulnerable populations.

CONCLUSION

Eating disorders are extremely complicated conditions that culminate from any number of biological, psychological, and circumstantial factors that are often instigated and/or exacerbated by our social conditions. The mere existence of the "thin" and "beautiful" people in society is not the problem. The challenge relates to the lack of

PART 15

variation in this prototype and the constructed ideal physique—a challenge that most individuals will never physically be able to master. Humans come in all shapes and sizes, and the construction of feminine and masculine ideals in our society is, to some degree, at odds with most of our natural physiologies. For most people, it is a physiological impossibility to obtain the standards of beauty that are constructed as ideal, and for many who achieve them, it turns out to be grossly unhealthy. The range of healthy weights that physicians recommend does not necessarily fit in with the standards dictated by our media. The resulting focus on food is often a maladaptive attempt to deal with other personal issues. Unfortunately, a growing proportion of people are pathologically obsessed with forcing themselves to fit the media mold of "perfection." As noted, the role of culture and the resulting societal expectations and norms play a central role in the development and perpetuation of the serious problems discussed in this chapter.

REFERENCES

Ackard, D., Neumark-Sztainer, D., Hannan, P., French, S., & Story, M. (2001). Binge and purge behavior among adolescents: Associations with sexual and physical abuse in a nationally representative sample: The Commonwealth Fund survey. *Child Abuse & Neglect,* 25, 6, 771–785.

Algars, M., Santtila, P., & Sandnabba, N. K. (2010). Conflicted gender identity, body dissatisfaction, and disordered eating in adult men and women. *Sex Roles: A Journal of Research,* 63(1–2), 118–125.

Berg, K., Hurley, D., McSherry, J., & Strange, N. (2002). *Eating disorders: A patient-centered approach.* Radcliff Medical Press Ltd: Abingdon, United Kingdom.

Blouin, A. & Goldfield, G. (1995). Body image and steroid use in male bodybuilders. *International Journal of Eating Disorders,* 18, 2, 159–165.

Bradford, J. & Petrie, T. (2008). Sociocultural factors and the development of disordered eating: a longitudinal analysis of competing hypotheses. *Journal of Counseling Psychology,* 55, 246–262.

Brewerton, T. (1995). Toward a unified theory of serotonin dysregulation in eating and related disorders. *Psychoneuroendocrinology,* 20, 6, 561–590.

Briere, J. & Scott, C. (2007). Assessment of trauma symptoms in eating disordered populations. *Eating Disorders,* 15, 347–358.

Brower, M. & Leon, W. (1999). *The consumer's guide to effective environmental choices: practical advice from the Union of Concerned Scientists.* New York: Three Rivers Press.

Brown, K, Bujac, S., Mann, D., Campbell, D., Stubbins, M., & Blundell, J. (2007). Further Evidence of Association of OPRD1 & HTR1D Polymorphisms with Susceptibility to Anorexia Nervosa. *Biological Psychiatry,* 61, 3, 367–373.

Bryant-Waugh, R., Cooper, P., Taylor, C. & Lask, B. (1996). The use of the eating disorder examination with children: A pilot study. *International Journal of Eating Disorders,* 19, 4, 391–397.

Davis, C. & Claridge, G. (1998). The eating disorders as addiction: A psychobiological perspective. *Addictive Behaviors,* 23, 4, 463–475.

Erikson, E. H. (1968). *Identity: Youth and crisis.* New York: Norton.

Feingold, A. & Mazzella, R. (1998). Gender differences in body image are increasing. *Psychological Science,* 9, 190–195.

Frederick, D., Buchanan, G., Sadehgi-Azur, L., Peplau, L., Haselton, M., & Berezovskaya, A. (2007). Desiring the muscular ideal: Men's body satisfaction in the United States, Ukraine, and Ghana. *Psychology of Men and Masculinity,* 8, 103–117.

Goodsitt, A. (1985). Self-psychology and the treatment of anorexia nervosa. In Garner and PE Garfinkel (eds) *Handbook of Psychotherapy of anorexia nervosa and bulimia.* Guilford Press, New York.

Grogan, S. (2010). Promoting positive body image in males and females: Contemporary issues and future directions. *Sex Roles,* 63(9–10), 757–765.

Gross, J., & Rosen, J. (1988). Bulimia in adolescents: Prevalence and psychosocial correlates. *International Journal of Eating Disorders,* 7, 1, 51–61.

Gustafson, T. & Sarwer, D. (2004). Childhood sexual abuse and obesity. *Obesity Reviews,* 5, 129–35.

Harriger, J., Calogero, R., Witherington, D., & Smith, J. (2010). Body size stereotyping and internalization of the thin ideal in preschool girls. *Sex Roles: A Journal of Research,* 63(9–10), 609–620.

Harris, S. (2006). Body image attitudes, physical attributes and disturbed eating among African American college women. *Race, Gender & Class,* 13, 1/2, 46–57.

Helmer, J. (1992). Love on a bun: How McDonald's won the burger wars. *Journal of Popular Culture,* 26, 2, 85–97.

Hesse-Biber, S., Livingstone, S., Ramirez, D., Barko, E. B., & Johnson, A. L. (2010). Racial identity and body image among black female college students attending predominately white colleges. *Sex Roles,* 63(9–10), 697–711.

Hintikka, J., Tolmunen, T., Rissanen, M., Honkalampi, K., Kylma, J., & Laukkanen, E. (2009). Mental disorders in self-cutting adolescents. *Journal of Adolescent Health,* 44, 464–467.

Hudson, J., Hiripi, E., Pope, H., & Kessier, R. (2007). The prevalence and correlates of eating disorders in the national comorbidity survey replication. *Biological Psychiatry,* 61, 3, 348–358.

Hyde, J., Mezulis, A., & Abramson, L. (2008). The ABC's of depression: Integrating affective, biological, and cognitive models to explain the emergence of the danger differences in depression. *Psychological Review,* 115, 2, 291–313.

James, A., Clacey. J., Seagroatt, V., & Goldacre, M. (2010). Adolescent inpatient psychiatric admission rates and subsequent one-year mortality in England: 1998–2004. *Journal of Child Psychology and Psychiatry,* 51, 12, 1395–1404.

Lawler, M., & Nixon, E. (2011). Body dissatisfaction among adolescent boys and girls: The effects of body mass, peer appearance culture and internalization of appearance ideals. *Journal of Youth and Adolescence,* 40(1), 59–71.

Logio, K. (2003). Gender, race, childhood abuse, and body image among adolescents. *Violence Against Women,* 9, 8, 931–954

Miao, L. (2011). Guilty pleasure or pleasure guilt? Affective experience of impulse buying hedonic-driven consumption. *Journal of Hospitality and Tourism Research,* 35, 1, 79–101.

Mussap, A. (2007). The relationship between feminine gender role stress and disordered eating symptomatology in women. *Stress and Health: Journal of the International Society for the Investigation of Stress,* 23, 5, 343–348.

Peat, C., Peverl, N., Ferraro, F., & Butler, M. (2011). Age and body image in caucasian men. *Psychology of Men and Masculinity,* 12, 2, 195–200.

Peplau, L., Frederick, D., Yee, C., Maisel, N., Lever, J., & Ghavami, N. (2009). Body image satisfaction in heterosexual, gay, and lesbian adults. *Archives of Sexual Behavior,* 38(5), 713–725.

Piran, N. & Gadalla, T. (2007). Eating disorders and substance abuse in Canadian women: a national study. *Addiction,* 102, 1, 105–113.

Rodgers, R., Paxton, S., & Chabrol, H. (2010). Depression as a moderator of sociocultural influences on eating disorder symptoms in adolescent females and males. *Journal of Youth and Adolescence,* 39(4), 393–402.

Salbach-Andrae, H., Lenz, K., Simmendinger, N., Klinkowski, N., Lehmkuhl, U., & Pfeiffer, E. (2008). Psychiatric comorbidities among female adolescents with anorexia nervosa. *Child Psychiatry and Human Development,* 39, 261–272.

Schur, E., Sanders, M., Steiner, H. (2000). Body dissatisfaction and dieting in young children. *International Journal of Eating Disorders,* 27 1, 74–82.

Schwartz, M. & Cohen, L. (1996). *Sexual abuse and eating disorders.* Philadelphia, PA: Brunner/Mazel.

Sigall, B. & Pabst, M. (2005). Gender literacy: enhancing female self-concept and contributing to the prevention of body dissatisfaction and eating disorders. *Social Sciences Information,* 44, 1, 85–111.

Spence, J. (1993). Gender-related traits and gender ideology: Evidence for a multifactorial theory. *Journal of Personality and Social Psychology,* 64, 4, 624–635.

Statistics Canada. (2005). Adult obesity in Canada. Measured height and weight. Downloaded (www.statscan.ca/english/research/82-620-MIE/2005001/articles/adults/aobesity.htm) on September 29, 2008.

Stein, K. & Corte, C. (2007) Identity impairment and eating disorders: Context and organization of the self-concept in women with anorexia nervosa and bulimia nervosa. *European Eating Disorders Review,* 15, 58–69.

Stice, E., Hayward, C., Cameron, R., Killen, J., & Taylor, C. (2000). Body image and eating related factors predict onset of depression in female adolescents. A longitudinal study. *Journal of Abnormal Psychology,* 109, 438–444.

Stice, E., Presnell, K., & Spangler, D. (2002). Risk factors for binge eating onset: A prospective investigation. *Health Psychology,* 21, 131–138.

Tiggerman, M. & Kuring, J. (2004). The role of body objectification in disordered eating and depressed mood. *British Journal of Clinical Psychology,* 43, 299–311.

Tolbin, D., Molteni, A., & Elin, E. (1995). Early trauma, dissociation, and late onset in the eating disorders. *International Journal of Eating Disorders,* 17, 3, 305–308.

Vaswani, M., Linda, F., Ramesh, S. (2003). Role of selective serotonin reuptake inhibitors in psychiatric disorders: A comprehensive review. *Progress in Neuro-Psychopharmacology and Biological Psychiatry,* 27, 1, 85–102.

PART 15

Warren, C., Schoen, A., & Schafer, K. (2010). Media Internalization and social comparison of eating pathology among Latino adolescents: The moderating effect of gender and generational status. *Sex Roles: A Journal of Research,* 63(9–10), 712–724.

Wheeler, H., Wintre, M., & Polivy, J. (2003). The association of low parent-adolescent reciprocity, a sense of incompetence, and identity confusion with disordered eating. *Journal of Adolescent Research,* 18, 4, 405–429.

Xu, J. & Schwarz, N. (2009). Do we really need to indulge? *Journal of Marketing Research,* 46, 25–36.

Yanovski, S.Z. (1999). Diagnosis and prevalence of eating disorders in obesity. In B. Guy-Grand & G. Ailhaud (Eds.), *Progress in obesity research* (pp. 229–236). London: Libby.

Yanovski, S. (2003). Binge eating disorder and obesity in 2003: Could treating an eating disorder have a positive effect on the obesity epidemic? *International Journal of Eating Disorders,* 34, S117–S120.

Zerbe, K. (1993). The body betrayed: women, eating disorders and treatment. *American Psychiatric Press,* Washington DC.

Critical Thinking Questions

1. Our "culture of thin" is a relatively new phenomenon. Why do you think such a norm developed? What have been the consequences of this norm, besides the emergence of eating disorders?

2. Do men experience this type of pressure as well?

Chapter 40

A Tale of Two Technologies: HPV Vaccination, Male Circumcision, and Sexual Health

LAURA M. CARPENTER AND MONICA J. CASPER

The Human Papillomavirus (HPV) has become controversial with the creation of a vaccine for prevention of the development of cancers that are affiliated with the virus. While some men can contract cancers from HPV, it is more common for women to suffer cancers from HPV uptake. Researchers have created this intervention, an HPV vaccination, and for many reasons outlined in the article have determined that it is most effective when administered to young girls. While this intervention has achieved the most notoriety, primarily from public concern of young girls being sexualized through this process, similar interventions that are implemented toward men have been more ignored. This article looks at the social implications of disease interventions that have gendered dimensions. By examining interventions related to sexually linked disease, they take a look at how the research and interventions have been influenced by gender norms and social expectations.

1. How has HPV vaccination, in comparison to circumcision, been portrayed to the public?

In 2006, two technologies designed to protect sexual health—one very old and one very new—sparked headlines globally: male circumcision and the human papillomavirus (HPV) vaccine. Arguably more efficacious if administered to young children, both show considerable promise in reducing the risk of potentially fatal diseases—AIDS and cervical cancer (CC), respectively—by reducing sexually transmitted infections (STIs). Yet while proposals to promote circumcision as HIV preventive among boys and men in the United States have gone largely uncontested outside "intactivist" activist circles, efforts to implement the HPV vaccine raised an outcry among parents, politicians, and policy makers (Casper and Carpenter 2008). Much contention focused

on the possibility that intervention—that is, use of the vaccine—would lead to promiscuity among preteen and teenage girls.

Why did reactions to two technologies with ostensibly similar goals—and similarly low reported complication rates—differ so dramatically?

Here we examine two different technologies: circumcision, originating thousands of years ago and newly innovated in the context of HIV/AIDS, and the HPV vaccine, fresh from the corporate laboratory. Analyzing these divergent tools, one surgical and the other pharmaceutical, as preventive health care technologies lets us see gender and sexuality in new ways, especially as they relate to children's bodies.

PART 15

We ask, how have cultural understandings of sexuality, gender, age, race, and nationality—and their interrelations—shaped responses to the two technologies? Why have attempts to mandate HPV vaccination activated concerns about female promiscuity, whereas talk of promoting circumcision as HIV preventive for boys has not (at least regarding U.S. boys)? How, in turn, might uptake of the HPV vaccine and the reframing of circumcision against HIV alter social constructions not only of gender and sexuality but also of age and race? Our focus is on the United States, but these deeply stratified processes have transnational implications (Carpenter and Casper 2009), insofar as American responses to the technologies also influence practices in the developing world.

(RE)INTRODUCING THE TECHNOLOGIES

In 2006, with much fanfare, Merck & Co. announced U.S. Food and Drug Administration (FDA) approval of Gardasil, the first vaccine for HPV. Another similar HPV vaccine, Cervarix by GlaxoSmithKline, is currently undergoing FDA review. Composed of over 100 strains, including 30 transmissible by sex, HPV is the most common STI in the world. It is also the key agent of infection in CC (Cervical Cancer), now viewed as an STI rather than a typical cancer; however, not all HPV leads to CC (Koushik and Franco 2006). Globally, approximately 493,000 new cases of CC are diagnosed each year, representing 10 percent of all cancers in women (Koushik and Franco 2006). Over 80 percent of new cases occur in developing countries (Dailard 2006). In the United States, where screening is routine for most women, CC is rare, yet morbidity and mortality from CC are higher among women of color and women from lower socioeconomic strata (Singh et al. 2004).

Gardasil prevents infections from HPV-16 and HPV-18, two strains that cause about 70 percent of CCs, as well as HPV-6 and HPV-11, which produce 90 percent of genital warts (Harper 2004; Harper et al. 2006). Although publicly framed by their manufacturers as vaccines against CC, Gardasil and Cervarix can also protect women *and men* against anal, penile, and throat cancers caused by HPV (and transmitted through sex with male or female partners; Kubba 2008; Nack 2008). Complication rates are low, under 2 percent in most studies, and side effects are generally minor, although more than 7,000 "adverse events" have been reported and safety remains a concern of many who oppose mandating widespread vaccination (CNN 2008; Wheeler 2007).

Drugs can instigate political struggles, and potentially social change, over time; for example, the birth control pill (Watkins 1998), Viagra (Loe 2004), and now the HPV vaccine (Casper and Carpenter 2008) embody social conflicts and shifting cultural values. As a containment technology targeting disease circulation among human beings, the vaccine evokes acute and longstanding politics of risk, danger, and bodily vulnerability.

Circumcision has recently been positioned as a potentially effective intervention against HIV/AIDS following clinical trials conducted in sub-Saharan Africa, where HIV is contracted primarily via heterosexual vaginal intercourse. Trials there found that circumcision of adult men reduces female-to-male HIV transmission rates by 30 percent to 50 percent (Auvert et al. 2005; Talbott 2007). Male circumcision has not proven effective in protecting women from heterosexually transmitted HIV infection, however (Altman 2008). About 62 percent of adult men in Africa are circumcised, with rates varying widely by region and ethnic group (e.g., nearly universal among African Muslims but anathema among ethnic groups that view intact foreskins as a sign of cultural distinction). In southern Africa, where rates of HIV are highest, fewer than 20 percent of men are circumcised (see http://www3.niaid.nih.gov/news/QA/AMC12_QA.htm). Across Africa, complication rates of circumcision are high—ranging from 18 percent in public clinics to 35 percent among traditional practitioners—because of poor training and inadequate and/or unsanitary equipment (MacInnis 2008).

The HIV/AIDS epidemic is less severe in the United States but still of great concern, given an infection rate of 13.7 per 100,000 population, with the highest rates among Blacks and Hispanics (54.1 and 18.0, respectively; Centers for Disease Control and Prevention [CDC] 2007).

Although not a pharmaceutical, circumcision works like a relatively inefficient vaccine with respect to HIV. Virtually every vaccine fails to protect some of the people who receive it. Both HPV vaccination and circumcision then, are preventive technologies inscribed in the body, with delayed benefits presumed to accrue long after the procedures themselves. Both operate according to principles of herd immunity; that is, performing the procedure on a certain proportion of people—typically about 70 percent—greatly reduces a disease's chances of spreading (Colgrove 2006). The HPV vaccine and male circumcision are also similar in that they require individuals to assume embodied risks for later, perhaps invisible personal and collective benefits, something people in general dislike doing—although parents are more apt to consent to risks on behalf of their children for the sake of prevention (Colgrove 2006) and may even choose procedures for their children that they would not choose for themselves.

RESPONSES TO THE HPV VACCINE

Clinical trials indicate that Merck's Gardasil may prevent up to 70 percent of CCs and that GlaxoSmithKline's Cervarix may also protect against HPV-45 and HPV-31, the third and fourth most common strains (Harper et al. 2006). Although these strains of HPV also cause anal, penile, and throat cancers—in men as well as women—Merck focused on CC, thereby deflecting attention away from the *sexual* nature

of HPV and from same-sex transmission vectors and reinforcing the widespread tendency to treat sexual health as a women's issue (Berer 2008; Kubba 2008; Nack 2008). Despite the herd immunity rationale behind vaccination, clinical trials in boys (approximately half the population) did not occur at first. By September 2009, when the FDA Advisory Panel approved Gardasil for use in boys and men ages 9 to 26 (see http://www.webmd.com/sexual-conditions/hpv-genital-warts/news/20090909/fda-panel-oks-gardasil-for-boys), the HPV vaccine had already been "feminized" in the scientific literature and news media.

Shortly after FDA approved Gardasil in 2006, ACIP provisionally recommended the vaccine for all girls 11 to 12, and the CDC added it to the Child and Adolescent Vaccination Schedule (http://www.cdc.gov/nip/acip/). Leading medical associations such as the American College of Obstetricians and Gynecologists endorsed the recommendations—although some practitioners oppose widespread vaccination until long-term safety and efficacy are more definitively demonstrated.

Merck accompanied Gardasil's 2006 release with a massive public relations campaign including highly visible television and print ads. News of the vaccine spread like wildfire, its arrival announced with exultant headlines such as, "First-ever cancer vaccine approved."

Yet almost immediately, and in contrast to the circumcision stories analyzed below, media coverage of the HPV vaccine began to focus on the putative dangers to (and from) young women's sexuality. The vaccine is aimed at preadolescent and adolescent girls, with a recommended target age of 10 to 12, because Merck's trials found a stronger immunological response in girls 10 to 15 than in women 16 to 23 and because few girls begin sexual activity, and thus exposure to HPV, before those ages (Ault and Future II Study Group 2007). Numerous media sources, extrapolating from comments issued by the conservative organization Focus on the Family

PART 15

in 2005, began labeling the new technology the "promiscuity vaccine," in reference to its imagined capacity to encourage young women to engage in sexual activity. To those who fear that the HPV vaccine will contaminate "innocent" young people by exposing them to sexual knowledge, the technology backfires, containing HPV and CC only at the price of activating the more frightening scourge of adolescent sexual activity.

Cultural assumptions about youth and gender suggest that (some) young women (white, middle-class, heterosexual, without disabilities) are to be protected, while young men are largely expected, if not outright encouraged, to exercise their sexuality. As feminist scholars have long argued, prophylactic interventions related to sex—and sexual health—disproportionately target young women, in part because women's potential for pregnancy makes their role in reproduction more obvious and more salient (Berer 2008; Nack 2008). Although U.S. moral conservatives decry adolescent sexual activity in general, their efforts more frequently target girls. Calls to extend HPV vaccination efforts to boys have been rare in the United States (though they have been common in Canada and, to a lesser extent, Great Britain; Kubba 2008). Targeting girls not only amplifies extant concerns about their burgeoning and putatively dangerous sexuality but also brings parents and physicians into the mix.

RESPONSES TO CIRCUMCISION AS HIV PREVENTIVE

Despite initially "refus[ing] to endorse [circumcision] as a prevention tool until more evidence is produced" (*BMJ* 2006, vol. 333), by March 2007, WHO and UNAIDS were urging countries with high heterosexually transmitted HIV rates and low circumcision rates to recognize adult male circumcision as "an additional important intervention [in a comprehensive package] to reduce the risk of heterosexually acquired HIV infection in men," provided adequate medical safeguards were available (e.g., availability of sterilized instruments; WHO/UNAIDS 2007). Some experts welcomed circumcision as a sexual health intervention that, by targeting men, shifts some of the burden of sexual health from women, even as they continued to worry that, because circumcision is not 100 percent protective, women remain exposed to risk (Berer 2007; Sawires et al. 2007).

Some HIV/AIDS activists "doubted that encouraging circumcisions would significantly decrease infection rates" (*USA Today*, April 7, 2007). By August 2009, CDC had not taken an official position but was "considering promoting routine circumcision for all baby boys born in the United States" as well as "whether the surgery should be offered to adult heterosexual men whose sexual practices put them at high risk of infection" (Rabin 2009).

Anticircumcision activists responded to these developments by emphasizing that circumcision offers limited protection, causes complications, and is not cost effective. Activists have also stressed disinhibition—"Promoting circumcision to protect against HIV could provide a false sense of safety, putting sexually active males and their partners at increased risk"—and human rights grounds for opposing circumcision: "There is a very real risk that . . . encouraging adults into circumcision will . . . lead to forcible circumcision of infants and children, who are unable to consent to surgery" (NOCIRC 2005).

Most major papers published editorials and letters to the editor calling for the expansion of circumcision to combat HIV. Some of these items specified the African context, but many were vague about location—and age of the targeted males—leaving readers to interpret. One *New York Times* editorial implied the widest possible scope of intervention:

> For years, the holy grail of AIDS prevention has been a vaccine, even one that is only 50 to 60 percent effective. A real vaccine is years away. But as of yesterday, we know its near equivalent exists.

International donors and governments should join together to spread the good news about circumcision and *make the procedure available everywhere.* (December 14, 2006, emphasis added)

This item reflects the tendency of U.S. news coverage of circumcision: using HIV links to compare circumcision favorably to vaccination.

DISCUSSION AND CONCLUSION

The sexually transmitted nature of HPV/CC and HIV/AIDS affects responses to the vaccine and circumcision in two ways. First, although HIV can be contracted through injection drug use and other nonsexual means (although chief infection vectors in the United States are sexual), strains of HPV that cause CC are contracted *only* sexually (unlike strains that cause nongenital warts). Thus, the effectiveness of containment metaphors and actual containment strategies may depend on how deeply they are shaped by gender, race, sexual politics, and notions of bodily transmission. Comparing the "feminized" HPV vaccine to male circumcision brings men's bodies and health into the **intersectional** mix.

Of course, sexual transmission of disease raises the specter of sexual activity, especially among teenagers and/or outside of marriage, which is generally interpreted quite differently for men and women in most cultural contexts. Our comparative analysis demonstrates how responses to these two technologies have been powerfully shaped by intersections among gender, sexuality, age, race, and nationality. Attempts to market and mandate the HPV vaccine activated concerns about female promiscuity, whereas talk of promoting circumcision as HIV preventive has not spurred similar concerns about males in the United States (while men in Africa are treated as suspect). Cultural constructions of gendered sexuality—casting girls and women as either innocent or fallen and boys and men as sexually driven (Nathanson 1991)—helped proposals

to promote circumcision as HIV preventive to escape the association with promiscuity that has dogged HPV vaccine mandates. Proposals that boys should receive the HPV vaccine to prevent CC in their (ostensibly) female partners—a claim far more common in public discourse than claims about preventing penile and anal cancers in men—invoke (implicitly) feminist notions of "equal opportunity" (for risk *and* protection) as well as traditional understandings of men as women's protectors. Conversely, risks and responsibility for circumcision are borne by men alone, and hoped-for benefits to women have not materialized (at least regarding HIV). In fact, men who believe themselves protected by circumcision may be less amenable to partners' requests for safer sex practices. These phenomena reveal and sustain obdurate gender hierarchies.

Understandings of gender and sexuality also intersect with notions about age, race, and nationality. Although U.S. boys have historically been circumcised as infants, well before sexual maturity and activity, girls would be vaccinated as preteens on the verge of sexual maturity—a situation that many parents appear to deem far more threatening. Pervasive stereotypes of women and men of color—especially of African descent—as promiscuous not only may inhibit stakeholders' ability to see them as deserving of, or able to benefit from, containment but also may prompt calls for containing them, as in proposals to target circumcision campaigns at "high-risk" men. Both HPV/CC and HIV/AIDS are more widespread and have considerably worse prognosis in the developing world than in the West. Ironically, circumcision is a routine U.S. practice that is now being exported to the developing world, whereas the HPV vaccine is desperately needed in the developing world but (potentially) being stalled by conservative opposition in the United States. By heeding feminist theorists' call for attention to **intersectionality**, we offer a nuanced analysis of gendered technologies—for women *and* men—in transnational context.

PART 15

Finally, our analysis reveals that the introduction and/or reframing of these containment technologies is changing cultural understandings of gender, sexuality, race, age, and nationality. Most obviously, the HPV vaccine retrenches gender politics that position young girls simultaneously as sexually innocent (yet likely to fall) and sexually available. The vaccine's use is, in fact, predicated on the eventual fact of girls' sexual activity; conservative resistance to the vaccine rests on fears of adolescent female sexuality unleashed. Conversations about circumcision in the United States show no similar dynamics; indeed, in many instances boys and men are represented as somewhat inert but with the capability of infecting girls and women via heterosexual activity. On the other hand, African men, like gay men and men of African descent in the United States, are routinely framed as dangerously subject to disinhibition. Our analysis highlights the importance of considering how technologies like HPV vaccination and circumcision contribute to the ongoing construction of gender (including "good" and "bad" men and women), race, and sexuality. It is precisely at these intersections of bodies with technologies that the "double standard" is reproduced.

We began by asking why one of these technologies should be embroiled in controversy while the other is relatively free from public debate. We have shown how the politics of sexual health and use of new preventive technologies unfold in a specific cultural context in which containment—of bodies, practices, and identities—matters. Intersections of gender (meaning women *and* men), sexuality, age, race, and nation are critical here. The double standard embodied in and achieved by juxtapositions of HPV vaccination and circumcision has a distinctly American feel while relying on stereotypes about African bodies, sexuality, and transmission. We suggest that technologies are caught up in, and indeed constitute, transnational circuits of power, risk, and prevention as these are enacted on human bodies. Meanings of gender and sexuality shift and change along with bodies and practices while *simultaneously grounding* the ways in which individuals and societies consider, use, and respond to technologies.

REFERENCES

Anderson, Warwick. 2003. *The cultivation of whiteness: Science, health, and racial destiny in Australia.* New York: Basic Books.

Associated Press. 2007. Texas governor backs down on HPV vaccine bill. May 9.

Ault, K. A., and Future II Study Group. 2007. Effect of prophylactic human papillomavirus L1 virus-like-particle vaccine on risk of cervical intraepithelial neoplasia grade 2, grade 3, and adenocarcinoma in situ: A combined analysis of four randomised clinical trials. *Lancet* 369:1861–68.

Auvert, Bertran, Dirk Taljaard, Emmanuel Lagarde, Joëlle Sobngwi-Tambekou, Rémi Sitta, and Adrian Puren. 2005. Randomized, controlled intervention trial of male circumcision for reduction of HIV infection risk: The ANRS 1265 trial. *PLoS Medicine* 2 (11): e298.

Bashford, A., and C. Hooker. 2001. *Contagion: Historical and cultural studies.* London: Routledge.

Berer, Marge. 2007. Male circumcision for HIV prevention: Perspectives on gender and sexuality. *Reproductive Health Matters* 15 (29): 45–48.

Berer, Marge. 2008. Reproductive cancers: High burden of disease, low level of priority. *Reproductive Health Matters* 16 (32): 4–8.

Brandt, Allan M. 1987. *No magic bullet: A social history of venereal disease in the United States since 1880.* New York: Oxford University Press.

Carpenter, Laura M., and Monica J. Casper. 2009. Global intimacies: The HPV vaccine and transnational women's health. *Women's Studies Quarterly* 37 (1–2): 80–100.

Casper, Monica J., and Laura M. Carpenter. 2008. Sex, drugs, and politics: The HPV vaccine for cervical cancer. *Sociology of Health and Illness* 30 (6): 886–99.

Centers for Disease Control and Prevention. 2007. Table 3. *HIV/AIDS surveillance report 17.* Atlanta, GA: Centers for Disease Control and Prevention.

CNN. 2008. Should parents worry about HPV vaccine? July 7. http://www.cnn.com/2008/HEALTH/conditions/07/07/cervical.cancer.vaccine/index.html.

Colgrove, James. 2006. *State of immunity: The politics of vaccination in twentieth-century America.* Berkeley: University of California Press.

Dailard, C. 2006. The public health promise and potential pitfalls of the world's first cervical cancer vaccine. *Guttmacher Policy Review* 9 (1): 6–9.

Harper, Diane M. 2004. Efficacy of a bivalent L1 virus-like particle vaccine in prevention of infection with human papillomavirus types 16 and 18 in young women: A randomised controlled trial. *Lancet* 364:1757–65.

Harper, Diane M., Eduardo L. Franco, Cosette M. Wheeler, Anna-Barbara Moscicki, Barbara Romanowski, Cecilia M. Roteli-Martins, David Jenkins, Anne Schuind, Sue Ann Costa Clemens, and Gary Dubin. 2006. Sustained efficacy up to 4·5 years of a bivalent L1 virus-1 like particle vaccine against human papillomavirus types 16 and 18: Follow-up from a randomised control trial. *Lancet* 367:1247–55.

Koushik, A., and E. L. F. Franco. 2006. Epidemiology and the role of human papillomaviruses. In *The Cervix,* edited by J. A. Jordan and A. Singer. Oxford, UK: Blackwell.

Kubba, Tamara. 2008, Human papillomavirus vaccination in the United Kingdom: What about boys? *Reproductive Health Matters* 16 (32): 97–103.

Levine, Judith. 2002. *Harmful to minors: The perils of protecting children from sex.* Minneapolis: University of Minnesota Press.

Loe, Meika. 2004. *The rise of Viagra: How the little blue pill changed sex in America.* New York: New York University Press.

MacInnis, Laura. 2008. Circumcision problems impair HIV prevention. *Reuters Online,* September 1. http://africa.reuters.com/top/news/usnBAN155719.html.

Marx, J. L. 1989. Circumcision may protect against the AIDS virus. *Science* 245 (4917): 470–71.

Nack, Adina. 2008. *Damaged goods: Women living with incurable sexually transmitted diseases.* Philadelphia: Temple University Press.

Nathanson, Constance A. 1991. *Dangerous passage: The social control of sexuality in women's adolescence.* Philadelphia: Temple University Press.

Rabin, Roni. 2009. Officials weigh circumcision to fight HIV risk. *New York Times,* August 24. http://www.nytimes.com/2009/08/24/health/policy/24circumcision.html.

Roberts, Dorothy. 1997. *Killing the Black body: Race, reproduction, and the meaning of liberty.* New York: Pantheon.

Sawires, Sharif R., Shari L. Dworkin, Agnes Fiamma, Dean Peacock, Greg Szekeres, and Thomas J. Coates. 2007. Male circumcision and HIV/AIDS: Challenges and opportunities. *Lancet* 369: 708–13.

Seidman, Steven. 2002. *Beyond the closet: The transformation of gay and lesbian life.* New York: Routledge.

Singh, G. K., B. A. Miller, B. F. Hankey, and B. K. Edwards. 2004. Persistent area socioeconomic disparities in U.S. incidence of cervical cancer, mortality, stage, and survival, 1975–2000. *Cancer* 101 (5): 1051–57.

Talbott, John R. 2007. Size matters: The number of prostitutes and the global HIV/AIDS pandemic. *PLoS ONE* 2 (6): e543.

Tolman, Deborah L. 1996. Adolescent girls' sexuality: Debunking the myth of the urban girl. In *Urban girls: Resisting stereotypes, creating identities,* edited by B. J. R. Leadbeater and N. Way. New York: New York University Press.

Watkins, Elizabeth Siegel. 1998. *On the pill: A social history of oral contraceptives, 1950–1970.* Baltimore: Johns Hopkins University Press.

Wheeler, Cosette M. 2007. Advances in primary and secondary interventions for cervical cancer: Prophylactic human papillomavirus vaccines and testing. *Nature Clinical Practice Oncology* 4 (4): 224–35.

WHO/UNAIDS. 2007. *WHO and UNAIDS announce recommendations from expert consultation on male circumcision for HIV prevention.* Geneva: UNAIDS.

Critical Thinking Questions

1. Do you think we still expect science to be impartial and objective? How does the article address this? Are there any connections between this article and Tuskegee (Chapter 6) or Eugenics in Alberta (Chapter 7)?

2. Is it reasonable to treat female sexual health and male sexual health in different ways?

3. Should society be more worried about the sexual activity of young women than young men?

PART 15

Glossary

Aboriginal   In Canada, an all-encompassing group that includes the First Nations, Inuit, and Métis, regardless of an individual's location or status as "registered" or not under the Indian Act. (p. 194)

Assembly of First Nations/AFN   National representative organization of First Nations in Canada. (p. 207)

Body image   One's mental picture of their physical body, and the thoughts and feelings produced from that picture. (p. 227)

Census   In Canada, the systematic and detailed collection of data from Canadian citizens, which takes place every five years. (p. 71)

Cognitive abilities   Brain-based skills required to complete tasks. (p. 57)

Coitus reservatus   The deliberate delay or avoidance of male orgasm during intercourse. (p. 78)

Colloquial language   Informal, everyday, relaxed language. (p. 17)

Colonialism   Where one nation expands into and dominates another nation. Typically, the rules, regulations, and cultural practices of the dominating nation are forced onto the occupied nation. Often, this process invokes feelings that are ethnocentric as well as eurocentric. (p. 200)

Consent   Informed, granted permission, free of coercion or threat of harm. (p. 95)

Credential inflation   The devaluation of academic degrees and certificates over time, thus a decrease in the opportunities available in the job market. (p. 174)

De-skilling of workers/job de-skilling   The process by which skill levels of either jobs or individuals are reduced. This can be done through the introduction of technologies or the subdivision of complex tasks into simpler ones. (p. 164)

Disaster research   Primary research conducted on social preparation, response, and recovery from man-made and natural disasters. (p. 19)

Discrimination   Prejudicial treatment toward an individual, based upon their inclusion in a particular group or category. (p. 188)

Disneyization   Alteration of society to simulate Walt Disney theme parks. (p. 155)

Empirical   Information provided by experience or observation, rather than by theoretical means. (p. 3)

Enumerated   The counting of each citizen and/or household during a census. (p. 71)

Ethnographer   An individual who utilizes anthropological/scientific study and systematic recording of human cultures. (p. 85)

Eugenics   The concept that Darwin's "survival of the fittest" can be applied to human beings, where selective breeding can improve the genetics of a population. (p. 29, 78)

Feeble-minded   A term used during the Eugenics Movement to refer to those who were "mentally deficient," which coincidentally enough targeted those facing social and educational inequalities. (p. 29)

First-generation student   Those who are the first in their families to pursue post-secondary education through a college, university, or apprenticeship program. (p. 175)

Gender gap in earnings   The gap in incomes between men and women in the same jobs. In Canada, on average, women make 79 cents for every dollar men make in the same jobs. (p. 180)

Group marriage   Members of the group are all considered to be married to one another, and share responsibility in caring for any children that are borne into the marriage. (p. 75)

Gustafsen Lake crisis   A land dispute and standoff that took place in 1995, where members of the Secwepemc nations and other Indigenous groups in British Columbia took control of sacred lands of their peoples. (p. 207)

Institutionalized racism   Where privilege and rights are systematically denied to minorities by the structures of the society. (p. 217)

Internal colonialism Political and economic inequalities that occur between and within specific areas, ethnicities, or groups within a nation. (p. 217)

Intersectional/ity How socially constructed identities of gender, sexuality, ethnicity, age, disability, and so on, interact with one another to create complex social inequalities. (p. 239)

Ipperwash crisis A land claim crisis in 1995 that involved the Kettle and Stoney Point Ojibway nation and resulted in the death of Dudley George, a protestor, by the Ontario Provincial Police. (p. 207)

Islamophobia An irrational fear of those who are Islamic. (p. 150)

Jockocracy A coined term referring to the rule by hyper-masculine athletic men (jocks). (p. 92)

Labelling (theory) According to Becker, deviance is something that is not based on the content of a behaviour but rather created by the majority groups in society to attribute characteristics to minority groups in that society. Deviance is not inherent but socially constructed. (p. 121)

Language acquisition The set of actions or process by which human beings learn to interact verbally. (p. 53)

Male supremacy Belief that men are superior to women. (p. 64)

McDonaldization Where society takes on the attributes of production as in the fast food industry. (p. 163)

McJob A term for a low-paying job that requires little to few skills, and little chance of advancement. A job that can be easily done by others therefore the worker can be replaced. (p. 163)

Methodology/ies In sociology, the methods you choose and utilize to perform social research. (p. 11, 14)

Menses Another term for menstrual cycle. (p. 88)

Milieux (cultural) Everything happening in one's environment at a specific time that is of social and cultural significance. (p. 6)

Neo-conservative ideology A political return to what are argued to be traditional policies of individual responsibility. In the realm of aging, a return of social responsibility to the individual and personal responsibility, and a dependence upon the economic market to care not the state. (p. 109)

Object permanence According to Piaget, knowing that an object is still present, despite its being hidden. (p. 60)

Obviousness Notions that are taken for granted, accepted at face value without necessarily proper study or research to ground them in. Rather, ideas that are merely accepted by shared knowledge with others. (p. 12)

Oka crisis In 1990, the mayor of Oka approved land development for a golf course on sacred land of the Mohawk. The Mohawk peoples opposed this development and conflict escalated into a crisis because the government of Quebec and local town's officials refused to recognize the Aboriginal rights. (p. 207)

Paradigm A theoretical worldview used to explain social phenomena. (p. 2)

Patriarchy/ial A social system that is male dominated. (p. 88)

Pornography Explicit visual portrayal of sexual acts. (p. 100)

Probability sampling Population sampling that is done completely randomly, so that each member of that population has the same chance (or probability), of being sampled. (p. 14)

Production (means of) The non-human inputs such as equity, tools, and equipment that are required to produce wealth. (p. 168)

Production (mode of) According to Marx, a combination of "productive forces," which is the human power and knowledge required to perform a task, and "relations of production," which are the power and controls that dictate the roles of the social classes within production. (p. 168)

Psycholinguist A psychologist or linguist who researches the human language from a psychological standpoint. (p. 52)

Public policy Actions and programs developed by a particular government usually brought into being through legislation and/or regulation. (p. 226)

Rape Forced, unwanted sexual act, carried out without consent. (p. 94)

Rationalization Social and physical reorganizations that create increasing efficiency within an organization to improve productivity. Considerations for employees are often put aside for this. (p. 166)

Relative deprivation   Where one group seems unable to access resources other groups seem to easily acquire. (p. 208)

Residential schools   The Residential School system in Canada attended by Aboriginal students, including industrial schools, boarding schools, homes for students, hostels, billets, residential schools, residential schools with a majority of day students, or a combination of any of the above. (p. 194)

Sampling error   Statistical error accrued by using a sample of a population rather than the entire population itself. Any sample used is only one of many samples that could have been selected from a population. Consequently, a researcher may not get the same results with each sample. This error is measured and reported. The error becomes smaller when the size of the sample gets larger. (p. 15)

Secularization   A departure from the influence or domination by religion. (p. 142)

Selfless collectivism   The interests of the group were put ahead of individual interests, a group altruism. (p. 76)

Sexual assault   Any unwanted sexual act, carried out without consent. (p. 94)

Sexual violence   Violence and harm committed against a person, through a coerced sexual act. (p. 101)

Sex roles   The expected behaviours and actions of an individual according to their gender. Sociologists believe that these roles are socially, not biologically, prescribed. (p. 86)

Social capital   A group-level resource where individuals, through networks and social relationships, may have additional access to benefits and resources not available to those outside of the group. (p. 176)

Social networking   Formation of individuals into particular groups, where they may easily communicate with one another, for example, communication online through chat rooms, Skype, Facebook, etc. (p. 137)

Social structure   Social organization that shapes society as a whole and that impacts the lives of the individuals who make up that society. Examples of social structure include institutions, norms, and social networking between individuals or groups. (p. 9)

Sociocentrism   Using the social group you belong to as the ideal to which all other groups are compared. (p. 62)

Spiritual equality   According to Noyes, a lifestyle where all members of the group were to love and share amongst each other evenly, a lifestyle reflective of expectations of the "Kingdom of God." (p. 74)

Stirpiculture   According to Noyes, the employment of eugenics where particular members of the group were chosen to mate with one another to produce children. (p. 78)

Storytelling (function)   The sharing of lived experiences from elders in a group to younger members. (p. 114)

Taboo/ed   An action, activity, or belief that is strongly forbidden or sanctioned by a particular society. (p. 47, 88)

Type 2 error   Also known as a false negative: where the null hypothesis is not rejected when it should have been. By example, if a null hypothesis states that a person is guilty of a crime, and the person is actually innocent, when the test fails to reject the null it falsely implies that the person is guilty. (p. 120)

White supremacy   Belief that white people are superior to non-white people. (p. 65)

Index